Perspectives on Males and Singing

Landscapes: the Arts, Aesthetics, and Education

VOLUME 10

SERIES EDITOR

Liora Bresler, *University of Illinois at Urbana-Champaign, U.S.A.*

EDITORIAL BOARD

Eeva Antilla, *Theatre Academy, Helsinki, Finland*
Magne Espeland, *Stord University, Norway*
Rita Irwin, *The University of British Columbia, Canada*
Samuel Leong, *Hong Kong Institute of Education, Hong Kong*
Minette Mans, *International Consultant, Windhoek, Namibia*
Jonathan Neelands, *University of Warwick, UK*
Mike Parsons, *The Ohio State University, U.S.A.*
Shifra Schonmann, *University of Haifa, Israel*
Julian Sefton-Green, *University of Nottingham, UK*
Susan W. Stinson, *University of North Carolina at Greensboro, U.S.A.*
Christine Thompson, *Pennsylvania State University, U.S.A.*

SCOPE

This series aims to provide conceptual and empirical research in arts education, (including music, visual arts, drama, dance, media, and poetry), in a variety of areas related to the post-modern paradigm shift. The changing cultural, historical, and political contexts of arts education are recognized to be central to learning, experience, and knowledge. The books in this series present theories and methodological approaches used in arts education research as well as related disciplines – including philosophy, sociology, anthropology and psychology of arts education.

For further volumes:
http://www.springer.com/series/6199

Scott D. Harrison · Graham F. Welch · Adam Adler
Editors

Perspectives on Males and Singing

Springer

Editors
Dr. Scott D. Harrison
Griffith University
PO Box 3428
4101 South Brisbane Queensland
Australia
scott.harrison@griffith.edu.au

Dr. Adam Adler
Nipissing University
100 College Drive
P1B 8L7 North Bay Ontario
Canada
adama@nipissingu.ca

Dr. Graham F. Welch
University of London
Inst. Education
20 Bedford Way
WC1H 0AL London
United Kingdom
g.welch@ioe.ac.uk

ISBN 978-94-007-2659-8   e-ISBN 978-94-007-2660-4
DOI 10.1007/978-94-007-2660-4
Springer Dordrecht Heidelberg London New York

Library of Congress Control Number: 2011943564

© Springer Science+Business Media B.V. 2012
No part of this work may be reproduced, stored in a retrieval system, or transmitted in any form or by any means, electronic, mechanical, photocopying, microfilming, recording or otherwise, without written permission from the Publisher, with the exception of any material supplied specifically for the purpose of being entered and executed on a computer system, for exclusive use by the purchaser of the work.

Printed on acid-free paper

Springer is part of Springer Science+Business Media (www.springer.com)

*For men and boys who sing
and for those who don't . . . yet*

Preface

The editors identified a need for this volume after the Boys and Voices Conference in Melbourne, Australia in 2005 at which the various issues associated with boys and singing were raised. At the time, there was very little documented scholarship and practitionor reflection evident in this field. The presentations from that event formed the initial foundation for the collection: Harrison, Adler, Welch, Collins and Bayliss were key participants and gave papers and workshops. Of these, Harrison, Adler and Welch were established scholars; Bayliss and Collins were soon to publish research and practice on boys and singing. Further meetings at the International Male Voice Festival in Cornwall in 2007 and the Australian National Male Voice Festivals in 2008 and 2011 drew together practitioners and scholars with interests in this area. Together with the 2005 collaborators, participants at these events (including Davies, Young, Taberner and Allen) identified an urgent need for the documentation and dissemination of research and practice in this growing field. Throughout this period, and in the few years leading up to the Melbourne event, scholars with an interest in males and music had begun to emerge. In addition to the contributors already identified, the work of Freer, Abrahams, Russell, Mook was gaining increasing prominence. Barrett's extensive work in early childhood had clear resonances with the existing scholarship while collaborations on other projects led the editors to the work of Durrant, Faulkner and Clift. Though Jarman-Evens (2007) has recently dealt with masculinities and popular music, the editors were aware of the absence of specifically singing-focused literature in rock music and sought to engage with the work of Eastman, Bannister and perhaps most significantly, Bennett, in this area.

The volume is therefore designed to appeal to a broad cross-section: choral directors will find much material to sustain, develop and support their work. There is also information for those working with solo singers across the lifespan, and in divergent forms of music in diverse stylistic and geographical settings. A wide array of philosophical standpoints is represented; and a variety of approaches presented. Underpinning all the contributions, however, is an intention to make music accessible to all, irrespective of gender by acknowledging existing shortcomings in males' engagement with singing and to posit ways in which this can be addressed as well as to celebrate the exemplary practice in the belief that our readers can enhance their activities in the knowledge that scholars and practitioners support their work.

Scott D. Harrison
Graham F. Welch
Adam Adler

Acknowledgements

In addition to those acknowledged by each contributor within the individual chapters, the editors would like to the following people for their encouragement and assistance in the preparation of this volume: their institutions: Griffith University (School of Education and Professional Studies and Queensland Conservatorium Research Centre), Institute of Education, University of London, Nippissing University. To Melissa Cain and Jessica O'Bryan for their assistance in the final stages of editing the volume. Most importantly – the men who told their stories for this volume – for this we are most thankful.

Contents

Part I   Overview

1. **Men, Boys and Singing** 3
   Scott D. Harrison, Graham F. Welch, and Adam Adler

2. **From Boys to Men: Male Choral Singing
   in the United States** 13
   Patrick K. Freer

3. **Sex, Gender and Singing Development: Making
   a Positive Difference to Boys' Singing Through a National
   Programme in England** 27
   Graham F. Welch, Jo Saunders, Ioulia Papageorgi,
   and Evangelos Himonides

4. **Male Choral Singing in Canada: A Waning Culture** 45
   Adam Adler

5. **Singing, Men and Australian Culture** 65
   Scott D. Harrison

Part II   Singing in Formal Contexts

6. **Changing Voices—Voices of Change: Young Men in Middle
   School Choirs** 79
   Frank Abrahams

7. **Creating a Culture for Teenagers to Sing in High School** ... 95
   Anita Collins

8. **Male Singing in the University Choir Context** 109
   Colin Durrant

9. **Cathedral Choirs in the United Kingdom: The Professional
   Boy Chorister** 123
   Jenevora Williams

10	**Singing in Church: The Role of Men in Contemporary Worship Singing** Scott D. Harrison and Daniel K. Robinson	149

Part III   Singing in Informal and Community Contexts

11	**Mutuality, Belonging, and Meaning-Making** Margaret S. Barrett	167
12	**Communities of Singing Practice in the Fiji Islands** Joan Russell	189
13	**The Sounds of Gender: Textualizing Barbershop Performance** Richard Mook	201
14	**Icelandic Men, Male Voice Choirs and Masculine Identity** Robert Faulkner	215
15	**Singing, Wellbeing and Gender** Stephen Clift, Grenville Hancox, and Ian Morrison	233

Part IV   Singing in Popular Music Contexts

16	**"But I Can Write Songs Okay": Male Voices in New Zealand Alternative Rock** Matthew Bannister	259
17	**Southern Masculinity in American Rock Music** Jason T. Eastman	271
18	**"Let Me Know You're Out There!" Male Rock Vocal and Audience Participation** Andy Bennett	287

Part V   Practioner Reflections

19	**Male Singing in Early Years of School** Miriam Allan	299
20	**The Courage to Sing: Reflections on Secondary School Singing** Anthony Young	311
21	**The Male Voice Choir in the United Kingdom** Peter Davies	325
22	**Giving Voices to Gifted Antipodean Unicorns** Curtis Bayliss and Robert Stewart	337

23	**The Foolishness Came Later: The Foundation and Development of the Spooky Men's Chorale** . . . . Stephen Taberner	347

About the Editors 353

About the Authors 355

Index 363

Contributors

Frank Abrahams Westminster Choir College of Rider University, Princeton, NJ, USA, abrahams@rider.edu

Adam Adler Nipissing University, North Bay, ON P1B 8L7, Canada, adama@nipissingu.ca

Miriam Allan Westminster Abbey and Bloxham School, Oxfordshire, UK, miriam.allan@mac.com

Matthew Bannister Waikato Institute of Technology, Hamilton, Waikato, New Zealand, Matthew.Bannister@wintec.ac.nz

Margaret S. Barrett University of Queensland, Brisbane, QLD, Australia, m.barrett@uq.edu.au

Curtis Bayliss Melbourne High School, Albert Park, VIC, Australia, bayliss.curtis.w@edumail.vic.gov.au

Andy Bennett Griffith University, Brisbane, QLD, Australia, a.bennett@griffith.edu.au

Stephen Clift Sidney De Haan Research Centre for Arts and Health, Canterbury Christ Church University, Canterbury, Kent, UK, s.clift@btinternet.com

Anita Collins University of Canberra, Bruce, ACT, Australia, Anita.Collins@canberra.edu.au

Peter Davies Cornwall International Male Voice Choral Festival, London, UK, peter.davies@abcd.org.uk

Colin Durrant Institute of Education, London, UK, C.Durrant@ioe.ac.uk

Jason T. Eastman Coastal Carolina University, Conway, SC, USA, jeastman@coastal.edu

Robert Faulkner University of Western Australia, Crawley, WA, Australia, robert.faulkner@uwa.edu.au

Patrick K. Freer Georgia State University, Atlanta, GA, USA, pfreer@gsu.edu

Grenville Hancox Sidney De Haan Research Centre for Arts and Health, Canterbury Christ Church University, Canterbury, Kent, UK, Grenville.hancox@canterbury.ac.uk

Scott D. Harrison Griffith University, Brisbane, QLD 4101, Australia, scott.harrison@griffith.edu.au

Evangelos Himonides Institute of Education, University of London, London, UK, e.himonides@ioe.ac.uk

Richard Mook Arizona State University, Tempe, AZ, USA, richard.mook@gmail.com

Ian Morrison Sidney De Haan Research Centre for Arts and Health, Canterbury Christ Church University, Canterbury, Kent, UK, ian-.morrison@virgin.net

Ioulia Papageorgi Institute of Education, University of London, London, UK, i.papageorgi@ioe.ac.uk

Daniel K. Robinson Griffith University, Brisbane, QLD, Australia, daniel@djarts.com.au

Joan Russell McGill University, Montreal, QC, Canada, joan.russell@mcgill.ca

Jo Saunders Institute of Education, University of London, London, UK, j.saunders@ioe.ac.uk

Robert Stewart Melbourne High School, Albert Park, VIC, Australia, robertstewart.au@gmail.com

Stephen Taberner Spooky Men's Chorale, Blue Mountains, NSW, Australia, taberner@tpg.com.au

Graham F. Welch Institute of Education, University of London, London WC1H 0AL, UK, g.welch@ioe.ac.uk

Jenevora Williams Institute of Education, London, UK, jw@jenevorawilliams.com

Anthony Young St Laurence's College, Brisbane, QLD, Australia; Griffith University, Brisbane, QLD, Australia, AYoung@slc.qld.edu.au

List of Figures

Fig. 3.1	Longitudinal sex differences in infant children's singing ratings	30
Fig. 3.2	Longitudinal sex differences in young children's singing ratings	32
Fig. 3.3	Graph to illustrate children's singing development by chronological age 1	35
Fig. 3.4	Graph to illustrate children's singing development by chronological age 2	36
Fig. 3.5	Longitudinal singing development mean data for $n = 438$ children	37
Fig. 3.6	Overall mean attitudinal questionnaire responses by sex and age group	39
Fig. 7.1	Original boys' music ecosystem	97
Fig. 7.2	Developed boys' music ecosystem	102
Fig. 9.1	Schematic diagram of the cyclical relationship between vocal activity and vocal health	125
Fig. 9.2	Revised voice profile assessment form for use with children	129
Fig. 9.3	Non-choristers: a comparison between the perceived dysphonia of boys who are boarding and non-boarding	130
Fig. 9.4	Boarders: a comparison between the perceived dysphonia of boys who are choristers and non-choristers	131
Fig. 9.5	The distribution of perceived vocal dysfunction of all four groups	131
Fig. 9.6	The median ratings (50th percentile) and standard deviation for the four different activity groups	132
Fig. 9.7	LTAS of two examples of creaky voice 1	135
Fig. 9.8	LTAS of two examples of creaky voice 2	135
Fig. 9.9	LTAS of two examples of breathy voice 1	136
Fig. 9.10	LTAS of two examples of breathy voice 2	136
Fig. 9.11	LTAS of an example of harsh voice 1	137
Fig. 9.12	LTAS of an example of harsh voice 2	137
Fig. 9.13	The Lx waveform of boy H aged 12 years	138
Fig. 9.14	Selected portion of the Lx waveform of boy H	138
Fig. 9.15	Selected portion of the Lx waveform of boy H	139
Fig. 9.16	Selected portion of the Lx waveform of boy H aged 12 years	139

Fig. 9.17	Selected portion of the Lx waveform of boy H aged 12 years	140
Fig. 9.18	The laryngographic waveform of a two-octave slide showing the two passaggio points marked	140
Fig. 9.19	The Lx waveform of boy H aged 13 years 10 months	141
Fig. 9.20	Selected portion of the Lx waveform of boy H aged 13 years 10 months 1	141
Fig. 9.21	Selected portion of the Lx waveform of boy H aged 13 years, 10 months 1	142
Fig. 9.22	Selected portion of the Lx waveform of boy H aged 13 years, 10 months 1	142
Fig. 9.23	Selected portion of the Lx waveform of boy H aged 13 years 10 months 1	143
Fig. 9.24	Efficiency of vocal fold closure in boy C at C5, aged 10 years 9 months 1	143
Fig. 9.25	Efficiency of vocal fold closure in boy C at C5, aged 13 years 7 months 1	144
Fig. 9.26	LTAS of /i/ vowel on C5, Boy C aged 10 years 9 months	144
Fig. 9.27	LTAS of /i/ vowel on C5, Boy C aged 13 years 10 months	144
Fig. 10.1	Age and gender of contemporary worship singers	155
Fig. 10.2	Worship styles	156
Fig. 10.3	Participation in worship by gender	157
Fig. 10.4	Reasons men may not attend church	158
Fig. 10.5	Music styles appealing to male worshippers	159
Fig. 11.1	In the kitchen	174
Fig. 11.2	Baby crying now	177
Fig. 11.3	Telephone ringing	178
Fig. 11.4	Chair song	178
Fig. 11.5	No no yes yes	183
Fig. 13.1	Tag of "Running Wild" as arranged by Freddie King	208
Fig. 13.2	Tag of "Running Wild" as arranged by "Mark" and "Jane" (2002)	211
Fig. 15.1	Members of *The Silver Singers*, The Sage, Gateshead, UK	247
Fig. 15.2	Comparative histograms of the distributions of scores on the singing scale for the total sample of men and women	250
Fig. 22.1	Melbourne High School speech night	340

List of Tables

Table 7.1	Stages of boyhood (Biddulph, 2008, p. 11)	100
Table 9.1	Comparisons of perceived levels of dysphonia between the four different activity groups	132
Table 15.1	Studies considering the effects of amateur group singing on well-being	235
Table 15.2	First principal component for six countries by sex groups	248
Table 15.3	Singing scale descriptive statistics for country by sex subgroups	249
Table 15.4	Gender differences in response to singing items	251

Part I
Overview

Chapter 1
Men, Boys and Singing

Scott D. Harrison, Graham F. Welch, and Adam Adler

1.1 The State of Play

The engagement of men with singing has a long and varied history. In Western art music, some of the earliest references to males and singing come from William Byrd in 1588: "Since singing is so good a thing, I wish all men would learne to sing.[1]" Whether Byrd was referring to men or to humankind remains a point of conjecture, although his significant involvement in the (traditionally male-only) English Cathedral choral tradition would suggest that it was the former.

Three hundred years later, Brower (1894) examined the relationship of composition and gender in the paper "Is the musical idea masculine?" in the Atlantic Monthly concluding, in part, that musical composition was the domain of the male. Koza (1993) undertook a retrospective of "missing males" in music education, and more specifically in choral participation. While there is a gap in quantitative research in this area, by examining multiple, small-scale reports of choral imbalance in specific ensembles and venues over time, a picture of the decline of male choral singing begins to emerge. For example, Giddings (1915, in Koza, 1993) observed a choir with sixty sopranos, ten altos, two basses and no tenors. More recently, Harrison (2007) and Freer (2008) scanned the literature on the interrelationship of men with music. Freer located over 400 papers including articles such as "Music and Manliness, (1902)," "Is Music an Effeminate Art? (1923)" and "Why Do Not More Men Take Up Music? (1923)."[2] Harrison's search found an historical trend reflecting a paucity of males in singing: Grace (1916, p. 368) noted "a shortage of men, boys and money in choirs" Damon (1936, p. 41) described a class of eighth grade boys who "never sing." The reasons for non-involvement in choral singing were explored as far back as the 1940s: Viggiano (1941) commented, "too large a percentage of boys are banded together in their aversion to singing, and not without reason." He attempted to find ways of "reaching the adolescent who thinks it's sissy

S.D. Harrison (✉)
Griffith University, Brisbane, QLD 4101, Australia
e-mail: scott.harrison@griffith.edu.au

to sing" while Winslow (1946, p. 58) explained that "probably nothing perplexes the secondary school teacher more than the vocal education of boys... most boys enter high school with negative attitudes towards vocal music and music education in general." One of the reasons for this, Winslow noted, is that "vocal music suggests femininity" (ibid.). Adler (2002) posited that the femininity ascribed to males as the result of singing was not the same as "femaleness"; rather, the male femininity associated with their engagement in the gender-incongruent activity of singing was perceived as an indicator of homosexuality. Castelli (1986, p. 18) scanned the years between 1946 and 1986 in one particular high school, reporting that the ratio of boys to girls had never risen above one in four, and had been as low as one in eight.

References to such terms as "femininity" and "sissy" suggest that some definition of concepts surrounding males' involvement with singing is required. Three terms are frequently used interchangeably and erroneously: sex, gender and sexuality. These categories are independent, yet related, but there is no intention that definitions or labels are fixed across time and place. Drawing on the earlier work of Harrison (2010) and Adler (2002) the following definitions will be employed throughout this volume: *Sex* is described as a biologically determined entity, related to male and female anatomy, while *gender* refers to the societal expectations associated with being male or female, typically described in terms of masculinity and femininity. While sex remains a biological constant over time, the societal expectations associated with gender change over time and can differ between societies and cultures. *Sexuality* is the preference for male and/or female partners and the performance of the acts associated with those preferences. While sexuality is in essence a behavioural construction, there are societal values associated with (somewhat limited) static delineations of heterosexual, homosexual, bisexual, etc. identities. *Gender congruence* is described as the extent to which an individual's described personal attributes and behavior conform to societal expectations for the gender which is traditionally prescribed for their biological sex within that society. In Western society, subordinate sexualities (i.e. all sexualities other than heterosexual) and behaviours and choices which are perceived to be gender incongruent are in some circumstances met with negative social implications.

The biological sex of individuals and the relationship of sex with musical activity has been connected to musical participation in a number of studies undertaken from the late 1970s to the mid 1990s (Abeles & Porter, 1978; Delzell & Leppla, 1992; Griswold & Chroback, 1981; Fortney, Boyle, & DeCarbo, 1993; O'Neill & Boulton, 1995). These works, largely focused on the sex stereotyping of instruments, found flute to be the instrument played most by girls and lower brass and percussion to be dominated by boys. The seminal work (Abeles & Porter, 1978, p. 65) focused on the problem stereotyping of instruments can cause:

> The association of gender with musical instruments can, as can stereotyping of any kind, serve to constrict the behaviour and thus the opportunities of individuals. Stereotyping is particularly irrelevant when applied to a group of objects such as the association of maleness with playing the drums and femaleness with playing the violin. The sex-stereotyping of musical instruments therefore tends to limit the range of musical experiences available

to male and female musicians in several ways, including participation in instrumental ensembles and selection of vocations in instrumental music.

Harrison (2001, 2004) confirmed the findings of Abeles and Porter and those of the studies in subsequent years. More recently, the work of Sheldon and Price (2005) with over 8 000 wind and percussion students revealed more females in the upper woodwinds (with flute dominating) with males still strongly represented in the lower brass. It is no surprise that Hallam, Rogers, and Creech (2008, p. 10) found that "Girls predominated in harp, flute, voice, fife/piccolo, clarinet, oboe and violin, and boys in electric guitar, bass guitar, tuba, kit drums, tabla and trombone." They noted that there were three contributors to the choice of instrument: the instrument itself, individual factors and social factors. In relation to individual factors, they observed a correlation between boys and instruments that are struck or require high levels of physical exertion. Harrison (2007) also found that instruments that have wider dynamic ranges, are larger and lower in pitch are more likely to be played by boys. Hallam et al. (2008) also commented that stereotyping "may be an inhibitory factor for boys, who may come under great pressure from peers if they engage in any activity that is seen as 'feminine'" (p. 15). Abeles (2009) revisited his earlier work, noting that boys and girls are mostly choosing the same types of instruments they played in the 1970s and 1990s.

1.2 Mind the Gaps

There are four significant and interrelated issues to emerge from this literature: Firstly, as discussed previously, there is a slippage in the use of terms between sex and sex stereotyping; gender and gender stereotyping, as well as inconsistent use of the terms sexuality and gender; secondly, singing is frequently omitted from studies on stereotpying and gendered attributes; third, there is an almost exclusive focus on school-based choral music, particularly in the middle years; and fourthly, there exists a lack of research into popular music or music outside the Western art music tradition. These gaps will be explored in more detail here, and throughout the volume.

Adler and Harrison (2004) found that the term *gender* was used by some authors to refer to girls and women, and consequently *gender issues* referred to the societal limitations on girls' and womens' freedoms and power. This made invisible many aspects of femininity and things socially ascribed as "feminine" as well as any positive aspects of male identity or masculinity (or even male femininity) that should also fall under the definition of "gender". They proposed that in order to discuss the phenomenon of males in music, the term *gender* must be reclaimed to refer to "issues of gender across the entire gender spectrum" (p. 274).

With the exception of Abeles, studies frequently interchange the terms "sex stereotyping" and "gender stereotyping." From the earlier definition, sex-stereotpying studies simply count the number of students of each sex playing particular instruments. Gender-stereotyping would involve considering whether the instruments have masculine or feminine attributes, regardless of whether they are played by males or females. Harrison's work (2005a, 2007) however, found a correlation between sex stereotyping and perceptions of masculine and feminine attributes of instruments: flute, and to a lesser extent clarinet and violin, were considered feminine; brass and percussion were considered masculine. While the differential involvement of each sex has been demonstrated, "masculine-feminine perceptions of musical participation continue to exist in the minds of both musicians and the broader population" (Harrison, 2008, p. 278). The underlying reasons for the link between gender associations and sex-stereotyping appear to be related to pitch, size and dynamic level. As with the stereotyping described in the studies above, the "masculine" instruments seem to be lower in pitch, larger in size and capable of wider dynamic ranges.

The second issue associated with the sex-stereotyping of instruments is at the core of the problem examined in this volume. In the hundreds of studies undertaken, very few measures were made of the exact numbers of males and females undertaking singing and whether singing was deemed to be masculine or feminine. As Ashley (2007, p. 7) points out, it is difficult to avoid biological elements in discussing the voice "because of the physiological differences between child and adult male voices and the protracted period of vocal metamorphosis which all boys undergo." There are obvious physical differences in the voice as reported by Welch (2001), Gackle (2000) and others. Three of these are of particular significance to this volume:

1. At puberty, the male vocal folds change by 4 mm up to 11 mm in length, while female change is much smaller (1.5–4 mm);
2. The male voice, once changed, usually sounds a sixth to an octave lower than the female voice;
3. Voice change is most active between 12.5 and 14 years. The male voice also changes again at around age 70 when it becomes higher;

The changing voice is a critical factor in males' engagement with singing as noted by the large body of work in this domain (Cooper & Kuersteiner, 1965; Swanson, 1977; Collins, 1981; Groom, 1984; Phillips, 1992; Cooksey, 1977a, 1977b, 1977c, 1992, 2000). Of these, Phillips emphasizes the difficulty of register transition as a major deterrent to singing while Cooksey's development of a six-stage "eclectic theory of adolescent male voice change" (Cooksey, 1977b, p. 17) offers a helpful way in which choral directors and studios can manage the transition. The male voice, because of this physiology, is one place in which the sex stereotyping and the gendered attributes collide. Harrison (2008) and Ashley (2007) both point to this as unavoidable in the study of boys, men and singing.

It is striking to observe the absence in the literature of hard evidence of the lack of males' involvement in vocal activity. No singing studies have come close to the more the 8 000 plus instrumental participants of Sheldon and Price (2005). Bell (2004), in profiling the amateur adult singer, makes the following generalizations:

All studies to date show that women singers significantly outnumber the men singers, some by as much as a 2:1 ratio in community-based choirs. This finding is consistent with Gates' (1989) suggestion of the gradual shift from predominately male singers to predominately female participation during the 250 years of choral singing activity.

What is unclear, however, is whether this is because singing deemed to be feminine. There have been a small number of studies in recent years centred on the work of four or five researchers (Koza, 1993; Adler, 1999, 2000; Harrison, 2002, 2005b, 2007, 2008; Freer, 2006, 2008, 2010; Ashley, 2007). The findings from these studies would seem to indicate that is singing is socially perceived and valued as feminine, but only in certain socio-cultural and geographical contexts. Of these, Adler (2000) suggests that because "singing does not construct or defend masculinity it therefore embodies gender incongruence and attracts homophobic labels." Adler's point raises a further issue in relation to the interplay of sex, gender and sexuality: The use of homophobia as a controlling mechanism brings a discussion of sexuality to the debate. For example, Adler and Harrison (2004) described a gendered hierarchy of school ensembles, with choirs near the (devalued) bottom, and concert and marching/military bands at the (more highly valued) top – again, an illustration of the gendered associations of dynamic range and perceived physical exertion. This hierarchy opens up potential discussions of not only singing, but the social devaluing of any activities that are gendered as "feminine", and the implications of this hierarchy for both males and females.

For many scholars in this field, sexuality does not have a part to play: the preference for particular sexual partners should have no bearing on musical participation. However, arguably it does become important when musical choices, based on sex stereotyping, become gender incongruent. The lack of alignment between biological sex, gendered attributes and sexuality confronts normality: for the biological male who takes on a so-called feminine activity such as singing, questions about sexuality may emerge depending on the genre (Harrison, 2001; Adler & Harrison, 2004). Adler (2002) and Harrison (2003, 2004) take up the notion of homophobia and singing extensively, with their participants commenting on name-calling using terms such as "gay, sissy, faggot and poofter" being applied to male singers as a social punishment for engaging in a gender incongruent activity.

Thirdly, it is fair to note that singing is only considered feminine in certain contexts, and that these labels are almost exclusively applied in school choral contexts. Given the rate and type of vocal mutation taking place at this stage, and the importance of this period in overall as well as musical and vocal identity development, it is difficult to argue with the large body of work that has been devoted to the study of singing in schools, particularly in the middle years and specifically focusing on choir. While these studies have significance for music education, males sing in a wide variety of other contexts, many of which remain unexplored. Furthermore, as Kenway and Fitzclarence (1997, p. 119) state, "masculine identities are not static, but historically and spatially situated and evolving." This is certainly the case of masculine identities in music, and this volume seeks to explore these identities in contexts outside mainstream music education.

Singing in male-dominated popular music domains, for example, is a rich source of counter-commentary on the gendered attributes of singing. Similarly, male voices in adult and community settings, particularly barbershop, have a long and rich history, largely under-researched. Furthermore, studies into male singing in cultures outside the Western art music tradition are scant. Russell's (1991, 2001, 2002) work on the singing of Fijian men is one notable exception, as is the extensive work of Faulkner (2008) on Icelandic Men. Faulkner's work (op. cit.) explores the notion of vocal patriarchy in some detail, emphasizing the concept of role model. In addition to Russell's work on Fijian men, male singing in other Pacific Island cultures and in the male voice choirs of Cornwall and Wales are testament to environments in which this activity is valued. While Cornish and Welsh male voice singing has high status in society it is not, as Harrison (2007) notes, attracting younger men and is literally dying out.

In the popular music domain, Jarman-Ivens (2007) in *Oh Boy, Masculinities and Popular Music* has interrogated the interface of men with popular music, though not specifically from the perspective of singing. In a refreshing diversion from the art-music focused texts, Jarmen-Ivens et al. examine how both male and female artists have engaged masculinity in popular music. This is significant in that it troubles the accepted sex/gender correlation. Walser (1993, p. 109) also examines rock music and masculinity:

> Notions of gender circulate in the texts, sounds, images and practices of heavy metal, and fans experience confirmation and alteration of their gendered identities through their involvement with it.

The experience of fans will be discussed later in this volume (see Bennett, Chapter 18) but at this point it is important to acknowledge the absence in the literature of male as audience member and consumer of music. Bennett's chapter goes some way to alleviating this however the overwhelming emphasis on studies into participation could be balanced somewhat by an expansion into this domain. The alteration of gendered identities to which Walser refers is a recurring theme in rock music. In addition, the feminization of mainstream performers, the effeminate sounds of falsetto singing and the marginalization of gay men through this process has been the topic of research by Eastman and Schrock (2008) and others.

1.3 Addressing the Gaps

Several key themes emerge from the existing literature, along with several gaps to be explored in this volume. The interaction of men with singing clearly has a long history. In the last 100 years, the apparent lack of male involvement in mainstream vocal activity has been researched, evaluated and documented. The literature to date has largely focused on choral music, with school music as a subset. The current volume seeks to add to that mainstream literature. In addition, it will explore music of other cultures, solo singing and popular music. Notions of masculinities, sex stereotyping and sexuality will be interrogated in a variety of contexts, with additional attention to the physical aspects of voice changes across the lifecycle. This volume therefore presents a range of perspectives on males and singing. By no means exhaustive, it represents a broad sweep of genres, styles, experiences and geographical locations. The opening chapters describe the scope of activity and research in Australia, United Kingdom, Canada and the United States. There is commentary on choral singing, informal singing, school and community singing in each of these locales.

The second part of the volume centres on singing in formal settings – the school, the university and the church, an examination of the latter in both traditional and contemporary settings. Colin Durrant explores music making at the tertiary level for both auditioned and un-auditioned groups, with a particular emphasis on participants' motivation to sing in choirs. Jenevora Williams invites us into the world of the cathedral chorister, with data about the vocal loading and daily life of this young yet highly specialised group of vocal musicians.

The third part of the volume examines musical experiences in less formal, community and popular music contexts including Margaret Barrett's telling case study of Jay's experiences inventing songs and the work of Clift et al. who examine data from both sexes, drawing conclusions about the well-being benefits of singing. In the Pacific, Joan Russell talks of Fijian music, with several examples provided of village life, school and church singing. On the other side of the world, Robert Faulkner tells of Iceland Men's music making in choirs. The community of Barbershop is examined through the stories of men who were interviewed by Richard Mook in Arizona. Jason Eastman, who has spent almost a decade examining Southern Rock, gives an historical and sociological rendition of the role of the male voice in this location. In Matthew Bannister's take on alternative guitar rock in New Zealand, a diversity of engagements is evident. The third part of the volume closes with a contribution from Andy Bennett on the role of the male voice in the audience of rock performances.

A feature of the collection is an emphasis on materials for the practitioner. This is particularly apparent in the final section of the volume that gives voice to a singing teacher, a festival director, a school teacher and a conductor, all of whom work exclusively with boys and men. Miriam Allen breaks down the door of Westminster Abbey to provide an insight into choral training there, while Peter Davies gives an overview of the extensive but reportedly waning network of male voice choirs in the United Kingdom. Anthony Young tells of creating a culture for singing in a boys' school, as does the chapter on Melbourne High School, and the volume concludes with a challenging and sometimes irreverent account of the Spooky Men's Chorale. In this final chapter, academia is replaced by pragmatic advice, born of substantial success of middle-aged men singing in the Blue Mountains of Australia, and beyond.

1.4 Moving Forward

It is our intention that this collection encourages and supports thought, dialogue and debate about males and singing. One consideration for this text was that, in music as in many areas of scholarly research, the time has come to give positive voice to the experiences and voices of males in what are sometimes disadvantaged or disadvantaging contexts, and also in some culturally valued contexts which are quickly disappearing. Another consideration was that issues raised herein might serve to launch further inquiry, so that gaps in the literature might begin to be filled.

Notes

1. Byrd, W. (1588). *Introduction to Psalmes*. Sonnets & Songs.
2. "Music and Manliness" *Theh'atioi* 75 (July 24, 1902) p. 66; "Is Music an Effeminate Art?" *Current Opinion, 75* (November 1923) pp. 586–587; Harold Randolph, "Why Do Not More Men Take Up Music?" *Etude, 41* (May 1923) pp. 299–300.

References

Abeles, H. (2009). Are instrument gender associations changing? *Journal of Research in Music Education, 57*(2), 127–139.

Abeles, H. F., & Porter, S. Y. (1978). The sex-stereotyping of musical instruments. *Journal of Research in Music Education, 26*, 65–75.

Adler, A. (1999). A survey of teacher practices in working with male singers before and during the voice change. *Canadian Journal of Research in Music Education, 40*, 4.

Adler, A. (2000). *Male gender issues in music education: A three dimensional perspective*. Paper presented at Research in Music Education Conference, 6–8 April in Exeter England.

Adler, A. (2002). *A case study of boys' experiences of singing in school*. Doctoral dissertation, University of Toronto, Toronto, ON, Canada.

Adler A., & Harrison, S. (2004). Swinging back the gender pendulum: Addressing boys' needs in music education research and practice. In L. Bartel (Ed.), *Research to practice: A biennial series: Questioning the music education paradigm* (pp. 270–289). Toronto: Canadian Music Educators Association.

Ashley, M. (2007). *Exploring young masculinity through voice*. Arts Based Education Research Conference, Graduate School of Education, University of Bristol, 5–7 July. Retrieved July 6, 2011 from http://ocs.ilrt.org/papers.php?cf=8

Bell, C. (2004). Update on community choirs and singing in the United States. *International Journal of Research in Choral Singing, 2*(1), 39–52.

Brower, E. (1894). Is the musical idea masculine? *Atlantic Monthly, 73*(437), 323–339.

Castelli, P. (1986). *Attitudes of vocal music educators and public secondary school students on selected factors which influence decline in male enrolment occurring between elementary and secondary public school vocal programs*. Unpublished doctoral dissertation, University of Maryland, College Park, MD.

Collins, D. L. (1981). *The Cambiata concept*. Conway, AK: Cambiata Press.

Cooksey, J. M. (1977a). The development of a contemporary, eclectic theory for the training and cultivation of the junior high school male changing voice: Part 1, existing theories. *The Choral Journal, 18*(2), 5–14.

Cooksey, J. M. (1977b). The development of a contemporary, eclectic theory for the training and cultivation of the junior high school male changing voice: Part II, scientific and empirical findings: Some tentative solutions. *The Choral Journal, 18*(3), 5–16.

Cooksey, J. M. (1977c). The development of a contemporary, eclectic theory for the training and cultivation of the junior high school male changing voice: Part III, developing an integrated approach to the care and training of the junior high school male changing voice. *The Choral Journal, 18*(4), 5–15.

Cooksey, J. M. (1992). *Working with the adolescent voice*. St. Louis, MO: Concordia Publishing House.

Cooksey, J. M. (2000). Voice transformation in male adolescents. In L. Thurman & G. Welch (Eds.), *Bodymind and voice – Foundations of voice education* (pp. 718–738, 821–841). Collegeville, MN: The VoiceCare Network.

Cooper, I., & Kuersteiner, K. O. (1965). *Teaching junior high school music*. Boston: Allyn and Bacon.

Delzell, J., & Leppla, D. A. (1992). Gender association of musical instruments and preferences of fourth-grade students for selected musical instruments. *Journal of Research in Music Education, 40*(2), 93–103.

Eastman, J. T., & Schrock, D. P. (2008). Southern rock musicians' construction of white trash. *Race, Gender & Class, 15*(1–2), 205–219.

Faulkner, R. (2008). Men's ways of singing. In K. Adams, A. Rose, & L. Chisholm (Eds.), *Sharing the voices: The phenomenon of singing IV: Proceedings of the international symposium*, St. John's, Newfoundland, Canada, 26–29 June, 2003. St. John's, NL: Memorial University of Newfoundland.

Fortney, P. J., Boyle, J. D., & DeCarbo, N. J. (1993). A study of middle school band students instrument choices. *Journal of Research in Music Education, 41*, 28–39.

Freer, P. K. (2006). Hearing the voices of adolescent boys in choral music: A self-story. *Research Studies in Music Education, 27*, 69–81.

Freer, P. K. (2008). Teacher instructional language and student experience in middle school choral rehearsals. *Music Education Research, 10*(1), 107–124.

Freer, P. K. (2010). Two decades of research on possible selves and the "missing males" problem in choral music. *International Journal of Music Education: Research, 28*(1), 17–30.

Gackle, L. (2000). Understanding voice transformation in female adolescents. In L. Thurman & G. Welch (Eds.), *Bodymind & voice: Foundations of voice education* (pp. 739–744.). St. John's University, Collegeville, MN: VoiceCare Network Publication

Gates, J. T. (1989). A historical comparison of public singing by American men and women. *Journal of Research in Music Education, 37*(1), 37.

Giddings, T. P. (1915). The high school chorus'. *Music Supervisors Journal, 1*(3), 8.

Grace, H. (1916). A choir problem of today. *The Musical Times, 57*(882), 367–369.

Griswold, P. A., & Chroback, D. A. (1981). Sex-role associations of musical instruments and occupations by gender and major. *Journal of Research in Music Education, 26*, 57–62.

Groom, M. D. (1984). A descriptive analysis of development in adolescent male voices during the summer time period. In E. M. Runfola (Ed.), *Proceedings: Research symposium on the male adolescent voice* (pp. 80–85). Buffalo, NY: State University of New York at Buffalo Press.

Hallam, S., Rogers, L., & Creech, A. (2008). Gender differences in musical instrument choice. *International Journal of Music Education, 26*(1), 7–19.

Harrison, S. D. (2001). Real men don't sing. *Australian Voice, 1*, 31–36.

Harrison, S. D. (2002). *Devaluing femininity: Its role in determining musical participation by boys*. Paper presented at International Society for Music Education Conference, 13 August, Bergen, Norway.

Harrison, S. D. (2003). *A male flautist, female drummer: The persistence of stereotypes in musical participation*. Paper presented at Research in Music Education Conference, 10 April 10, Exeter, England.

Harrison, S. D. (2004). Engaging boys, overcoming stereotypes: Another look at the missing males in vocal programs. *The Choral Journal, 45*(2), 21–25.

Harrison, S. D. (2005a). Let's ear it for the boys: The place of boys' music in a feminist world. In E. Mackinlay, S. Owens, & D. Collins (Eds.), *Aesthetics and experience in music performance* (pp. 115–122). Newcastle upon Tyne: Cambridge Scholars.

Harrison, S. D. (2005b). Music versus sport: A new approach to scoring. *Australian Journal of Music Education, 1*, 56–61.

Harrison, S. D. (2007). Where have the boys gone? The perennial problem of gendered participation in music. *British Journal of Music Education, 24*(3), 267–280.

Harrison, S. D. (2008). *Masculinities and music*. Newcastle upon Tyne: Cambridge Scholars.

Harrison, S. D. (2010). The global positioning of gender in music education. In J. Ballantyne & B. Bartleet (Eds.), *Navigating music and sound education* (p. 11). Newcastle: Cambridge Scholars.

Inez Field Damon. (1936). The boys who did not sing. *Music Educators Journal, 21*(1), 41.

Jarman-Ivens, F. (2007). *Oh boy! Masculinities and popular music*. London: Routledge.

Kenway, J., & Fitzclarence, L. (1997). Masculinity, violence and schooling: Challenging poisonous pedagogies. *Gender and Education, 9*(1), 117–133.

Koza, J. E. (1993). The "missing males" and other gender issues in music education: Evidence from the *Music Supervisors' Journal*, 1914–1924. *Journal of Research in Music Education, 41*(3), 212–232.

O'Neill, S. A., & Boulton, M. J. (1995). Is there a gender bias towards musical instruments? *Music Journal, 60*, 358–359.

Phillips, K. (1992). *Teaching kids to sing*. New York: Schirmer.

Russell, J. (1991). *Music in Fiji*. Research paper presented at the Annual Conference of the Canadian Music Educators Association, Vancouver.

Russell, J. (2001). Born to sing: Fiji's 'singing culture' and implications for music education in Canada. *McGill Journal of Education, 36*(3), 197–218.

Russell, J. (2002). Sites *of learning: Communities of musical practice in the Fiji Islands*. Bergen: International Society for Music Education.

Sheldon, D. A., & Price, H. E. (2005). Gender and instrumentation distribution in an international cross-section of wind and percussion ensembles. *Bulletin of the Council for Research in Music Education, 163*, 43–51.

Swanson, F. J. (1977). *The male changing voice ages eight to eighteen*. Cedar Rapids, IA: Lawrence Press.

Viggiano, A. (1941). Reaching the adolescent who thinks its sissy to sing. *Music Educators Journal, 27*(5), 62.

Walser, R. (1993). *Running with the devil: Power, gender and madness in heavy metal music*. Hanover: University Press of New England.

Welch, G. (2001). *Singing voice development in childhood and adolescence*. Paper presented at Young Voice in Focus Symposium, September 21, Sydney, Australia.

Winslow, R. W. (1946). Male vocal problems in the secondary school. *Music Educators Journal, 34*(4), 58–61.

Chapter 2
From Boys to Men: Male Choral Singing in the United States

Patrick K. Freer

2.1 Background

The development of the a cappella choral tradition in the United States laid a foundation for decades of performances by choirs that are recognized worldwide. Choral scholars representing many nationalities regularly seek to study these traditions of choral performance. However lauded, these performance traditions often represent the pinnacle of choral work, but there is an underlying concern about the participation rate of men and boys in the nation's vocal ensembles at large. This concern, often noted with the appellation "the missing males of choral music," is the subject of an increasing body of research that seeks to identify reasons males participate in, withdraw from, or never engage in choral singing. This chapter will present an overview of male choral singing in the United States, with emphasis on the historical development of philosophical and pedagogical responses to changes in curricular goals, attrition patterns, and research-based knowledge about the changing male adolescent voice. The purpose of this chapter is to provide a context for comparison with the historical and current states of male singing in other countries. To that end, the following topics will be briefly explored as they relate to the United States: The history and organization of boys' choral singing in schools, churches, and community ensembles; current issues, research trends and emerging themes; current concerns related to vocal/choral pedagogy for boys and men; and reform initiatives related to choral music education. The chapter will close by noting trends and offering implications for educators, researchers, and conductors.

P.K. Freer (✉)
Georgia State University, Atlanta, GA, USA
e-mail: pfreer@gsu.edu

2.2 Boys' Choral Singing in Schools, Churches, and Community Ensembles

Vocal music education began to take its place in public schools in 1838 under the leadership of Lowell Mason in Boston, Massachusetts. The goal of music education has since been to provide quality music instruction to all students. The earliest efforts were prompted by a perceived decline in the public singing of congregations and community groups. As music education became widespread throughout American schools in the early 1900s, students could expect to receive music instruction in classes that were sometimes taught by specialized music teachers, but instead were often taught by their regular classroom teachers who relied on vocal music and singing as the primary modes of lesson content. Until the early part of the 1900s, instruction in these "general music" settings lacked coordination or uniformity between schools – even those in the same town or city. The lack of specific music training for teachers led to the prominence of "music supervisors" who were responsible for training teachers with regard to their personal musicianship, sequential music instruction, and the musical development of children and adolescent youth.

The founding in 1907 of the Music Supervisors National Conference (later to be known as the Music Educators National Conference) spurred conversations about the teaching of singing to America's youth. Since the goal was to involve all children in music education, questions arose about how to handle the developing adolescent male voice. The philosophical and pedagogical debates around this issue paralleled the emergence in Europe of research about the boys' changing voice. In Great Britain, for instance, the time-honored tradition of removing boys from choirs at the onset of voice change was questioned as researchers began to codify stages of voice change and the parameters wherein boys could sing successfully. That research extended across the Atlantic to the United States at mid-century, most importantly with the work of the British emigrant Duncan McKenzie.

McKenzie's primary influence was to provide a set of specifications for the inclusion of boys with changing voices within the singing activities of general music classes. Though his resulting "alto-tenor" plan was applicable to choral ensembles, McKenzie wrote extensive resources for teachers about how they could include all boys in the singing instruction of general music classes. McKenzie was the first in a succession of researcher-pedagogues that was to greatly influence the teaching of singing in United States schools. These contributions will be discussed a bit later in this chapter.

McKenzie's work corresponded with the development of the a cappella choral movement in the United States. In the period following World War I, ensemble music began to take a place of prominence in high schools. This can be traced to the success of military bands during the war years, and many of the bands' highly trained musicians were subsequently sought to develop similar ensembles in high schools. Succeeding decades saw the development of high school ensembles displaying high levels of musical virtuosity and skill. Though choral ensembles did not receive the same amount of scholastic attention during the post-World War I years, there was no lack of choral activity in the United States. During these years, immigrant groups representing the rich choral backgrounds of northern Europe re-established these traditions within the churches and choral societies of their communities. Several of these became formalized in the ensembles and instruction of local colleges. These ensembles became known specifically for their vocal timbres, stylistic flexibility, and intonation when singing without instrumental accompaniment. Two of these ensembles, the St. Olaf Choir and the Westminster Choir, achieved national and worldwide prominence. The St. Olaf Choir's 1920 performance in Carnegie Hall is considered the beginning of the "a cappella choral movement" in the United States that raised the standards of choral singing in all types of American choruses, specifically those in high schools. A singular event crystallized these standards and set a direction for generations of high school choirs: the 1928 performance of the Flint (Michigan) Central High School A Cappella Choir at the convention of the Music Supervisors National Conference in Chicago. The Westminster Choir later contributed to the prominence of the a cappella tradition as it served ambassadorial functions for the United States government during World War II.

Through a coincidence of timing, the emergence of research about the male adolescent changing voice was closely linked to the development of the a cappella choral tradition. High school choral teachers looked to junior high schools to provide a well-educated and musically literate population of singers who would eventually become members of their choirs. There was considerable debate, reflected in the profession's academic journals, about whether young adolescent boys were capable of learning and performing refined skills of singing during the period of vocal change. Some teachers felt strongly that all students should sing in unison, regardless of the voice change, while others advocated for the development of multi-part repertoire to accommodate variations in the voice change process among boys of the same age.

A 1930 article by a music supervisor in Minneapolis highlighted the necessity for vocal music instruction that reflected the needs of the changing boys' voice:

> In many junior highschool singing classes nothing but unison singing is done.... It is a wonder that any good voices ever grow up when they are mistreated like this. The junior high age is the changing period, and all agree that the changing period is the tenderest vocal age ... The instrumentalist plays in tune as a matter of course, and he brings out good tone quality from his instrument or he is promptly called to account by the leader. In the vocal field it is just the opposite; if the tone is anywhere near the right pitch, it passes. Let us strike a good blow for music and eliminate the unison song from the junior high school, and set our vocal house in order that it may function as it should! (Giddings, 1930, pp. 19, 23)

The years that followed saw the gradual development of a research base that served as a foundation for the eventual growth of choral opportunities for boys with changing voices.

2.3 The Emerging Research Base

A succession of vocal/choral pedagogues, all researchers in their own ways, progressively redefined knowledge of adolescent male vocal development, appropriate vocal pedagogy, and implications for ensemble singing: Duncan McKenzie, Irvin Cooper, Frederick Swanson, and John Cooksey (see Friddle, 2005). Their work collectively spanned six decades from about 1940 to 2000, a period in which choral music in United States schools expanded beyond the high school a cappella choir movement of the early to mid-1900s to include the highest levels of musicianship for children and young adolescent singers of today.

McKenzie identified the changing male voice as an "alto-tenor" with an approximate octave range of g below middle C to G above. While some seventh and eighth grade boys might be able to sing lower pitches, McKenzie regarded the bass voice as a rarity. McKenzie's focus on downward vocalizations to aid in the smooth transition between head and chest registers found favour with many music teachers who saw similarities between his approach and traditional Bel Canto vocal technique. In a 1987 survey, teachers identified as producing "performance successful" choirs indicated that they employed McKenzie's techniques and approach toward vocal classification (Funderburk-Galvan, 1987). One influence of McKenzie's work was the identification of a specific vocal range that composers and arrangers of choral literature could use as a guide toward accommodating the majority of boys with changing voices.

McKenzie, though, noted that his alto-tenor plan was intended to address the singing of students in general music classes and that other approaches might be "more suitable for choirs" (1956, p. 136). Irvin Cooper's work was also primarily intended to assist general music teachers working with young adolescent singers, not "special performing groups such as choirs or ensembles" (Cooper & Kuersteiner, 1965, p. 12). His concern, at the outset, was to improve the quality of instruction in music reading by providing guidelines for the ranges of sight-reading and other singing exercises so that all students could be successful. It was within this context that he indicated a composite unison range of a fifth – in octaves – for all students, male and female, in a typical junior high general music classroom. Cooper did advocate the application of his suggestions to junior high choral ensembles, but it is important to remember that these would have involved students in grades seven-nine, not the typical grouping of grades six-eight found in present-day middle schools. Cooper's ranges for boys at varying stages of change included a designation of "cambiata" (changing voice) and his approach has become widely associated with the term "Cambiata Concept." Cooper advised, however, that "the range criteria under discussion apply to singing activity in the general music class" (1965, p. 25), and the fewer, selected students in choral ensembles would likely possess wider ranges with more individual variety. This point was echoed by many current leaders in the field of adolescent vocal pedagogy in a recent special focus issue of the *Choral Journal* (American Choral Directors Association, 2006). These leaders included Don L. Collins, who has applied Cooper's work to the current conception of choral ensembles within schools and churches.

Fredrick Swanson's (1977) research with adolescent male singers was most influential because of its resulting vocal pedagogy techniques, many of which have proven to be highly effective in choral settings. Swanson's focus was the timbral effects of the changing voice as it descended in pitch and, consequently, forced boys to make decisions about whether and how to sing in different vocal registers. Swanson specifically disagreed with Coopers' assertion that the voice change process was gradual and that bass voices were rare in adolescent choirs. These disagreements were publicly argued in the pages of the *Music Educators Journal* during the early 1960s (see Freer, 2008a). In retrospect, these fascinating discussions heralded a shift from observational research techniques to the gathering of empirical data about the male changing voice.

In the mid-1970s, John Cooksey began to collect and conduct research in an effort to determine what actually happened physiologically and acoustically to the boy's voice throughout the change process. Cooksey built on previous research in Czechoslovakia and Austria and theorized that there are several distinct vocal development stages through which young men all progress (see Cooksey, 1989). First published in 1977, Cooksey's five stages of adolescent male voice change have been substantiated by numerous studies involving thousands of young men from several continents (see Cooksey, 2000). Main findings of Cooksey's research indicate that each boy progresses through the stages (identified by range, tessitura and timbre) at different rates, lingering in some stages and passing rapidly through others. Some young men will experience smooth transitions between stages, while others will encounter more abrupt transitions. This research indicates that each boy will move sequentially through each stage before eventually settling into a more mature vocal range and timbre during his late teens and early 20s.

The philosophical decision to keep boys singing during the voice change process was nowhere more evident than in boy choirs. The European boy choir models were among those emulated in the United States as the a cappella choral movement took hold in the first half of the twentieth century. When these followed a strict British cathedral choir model, boys were removed from the choral ensemble either at a certain age or at the onset of vocal change. One of the boldest moves came from the conductor of the American Boychoir, James Litton, at the height of the choir's popularity in the early 1990s. The choir had numerous recording contracts for commercial work and was making regular appearances in the nation's premiere concert halls. Upon becoming aware of the research of Cooksey and others, Litton removed the requirement that boys leave the American Boychoir at the onset of vocal change. Instead, he developed a flexible system of repertoire selection that matched the boys in the choir rather than matching the boys to the repertoire (Freer, 1992).

Any account of the singing of boys in the United States would be incomplete without mention of a group of women who greatly influenced teachers and choral directors in the years surrounding the close of the twentieth century. The development of research and instructional techniques for boys with changing voices allowed for the refinement of amateur singing in many facets of American life as championed most visibly in children's church choirs by Helen Kemp, treble choirs of children and youth by Doreen Rao, junior high school choirs by Sally Herman, and amateur adult choirs by Frauke Haasemann. These leaders and others like them created a framework within which males, assisted by the advances in research and pedagogy described above, could engage in choral artistry of the highest level at any point in their lifetimes.

The expansion of the choral art in late twentieth century United States was therefore made possible by the intersection of three complementary and simultaneous efforts: knowledge about the male changing voice, the development of the North American children's choir movement, and a focus on teaching vocal technique to amateur singers of any age.

2.4 The Current Situation: Status, Issues, and Themes

2.4.1 Status

Despite advances in research and pedagogy, concern remains about the participation of males in choral music. This well-documented concern has persisted for over a century (Freer, 2008a; Gates, 1989; Koza, 1993), with an ever-widening ratio of male to female participation rates. Current research (Chorus America, 2009) indicates that regardless of gender, choral singing is the most popular form of participation in the arts. This survey reports that 22.9% of American households have a choral singer and that 32 million adults regularly sing in choruses – a figure that rises to 42.6 million singers when children are included. This survey also reports that there are nearly 270,000 choruses in America, including 12,000 professional and community choral organizations, 41,000 school choruses, and 216,000 religious choirs. At the same time, however, the adult survey participants report a decline in choral singing opportunities for children and youth between the years of 2005 and 2009. At present, 25% of educators report that there is no choral program in their school, and 20% of parents say there is no choral opportunity for children in their communities. Twenty percent of parents say their child involuntarily stopped singing because their school choir was eliminated in the past 5 years. Most pertinent to the discussion of choral music's missing males, however, is the finding that one in eight parents report their child involuntarily stopped singing because they were no longer eligible for their particular chorus due to their changing voice. It is reasonable to suggest that this lack of choral opportunity disproportionately affects young adolescent male singers.

Music education in the United States is considered a core academic subject – at least in theory and policy as outlined in the major educational legislation and school reform efforts that define public schooling in America. These theoretical and political positions lack the funding and assessment requirements that might ensure the place of music education in schools. School funding and curricular issues are decentralized from the federal government to states, from states to local school districts and, ultimately, from districts to individual school administrators. Decisions about music education curriculum and implementation are effectively made at the local level of school districts and, often, the particular level of the school itself.

The strength of school music programs, consequently, fluctuates in response to budgetary conditions and how academic priorities are tied to school accountability measures. Much of this impacts the participation of youngsters in choral music and their eventual participation as adults. It does not, however, explain the disparity in male and female choral participation rates in America's school and community ensembles.

2.4.2 Issues

Some of the factors contributing to choral music's problem of missing males can be identified as structural, developmental, and motivational. Teachers of young adolescents in general, and of young adolescent boys in particular, are often caught between knowledge of appropriate practices for working with youngsters and tradition-bound practices of choral music instruction and performance. The stereotypical yet dominant authoritarian model of conductor conflicts with the cognitive, psychological and physical functioning of young adolescents (Freer, 2007). Likewise, the most celebrated models of American choral performance are of high school and college choirs, with children's choirs serving as more recent models for choral teachers. Exemplary performances of choirs with young adolescent boys are uncommon, raising the perception that these boys are incapable of the highest levels of choral singing. And, that is true – but only if the measures are repertoire and tone quality appropriate for ensembles of younger or older singers. In the United States, many publishers and composers attempt to incorporate the results of research about the changing adolescent voice (see Crocker, 2000), but these efforts are recent enough that the music publishing industry has not yet effectively developed time-honoured standards of quality literature.

These structural issues concerning appropriate pedagogy, lack of conductor-teacher models, and lack of exemplary performance and repertoire models become overtly problematic when adolescent choirs are evaluated at festivals and contests. In the United States, participation in annual contests is often required. Contests serve functions similar to standardized testing, as teachers are evaluated by how their students perform. When these contests lack adjudicators who are well-versed on the subject of young adolescent choirs and male changing voices, teachers risk receiving lowered scores because of a lack of males (choral balance), developing voices (choral blend and tone), and the weak quality of selected repertoire. These are structural problems within the choral profession that need to be addressed, for the result is that many choral teachers hesitate to actively seek boys with changing voices for inclusion within their choirs.

The complexities of adolescent cognitive and physical development also contribute to the missing males problem in choral music. The onset of puberty sets in motion a developmental sequence that involves physical growth, strength and coordination; the ability to hypothesize and reflect; the acquisition of varied potential affective responses; and an awareness of social interactions and perceptions. While the research discussed earlier has provided clarity for choral teachers about the vocal (physical) development of adolescent boys, the profession has been less responsive to the other developmental issues associated with adolescence. For instance, medical research indicates that: (1) there are significant differences in the cognitive development of girls and boys of the same chronological age, (2) emotion and motivational development parallels pubertal development rather than chronological age or experience, (3) adolescence is often characterized by periods of low self-esteem for both girls and boys, and (4) the physical growth of adolescent boys includes the auditory system, potentially accounting for the problems of pitch-matching often seen in these boys (Demorest & Clements, 2007; Freer, 2008a).

It is important to reiterate that membership in most choral music ensembles is voluntary, whether the ensembles are associated with schools, churches, or are community-based. Boys will choose membership in activities wherein they experience success and enjoyment, and their motivation to sing chorally may be related to how music educators adjust their instruction to meet the needs of adolescent males. Research with adolescent boys in the United States suggests that they seek: musical experiences where their skills match the challenges (Freer, 2009a); in-class competitions and learning-based games (Stamer, 2009); physical knowledge of their own voice change process (Freer, 2009c); the acquisition of skills rather than the perfection of a particular repertoire selection; skill-based feedback from peers and/or teachers; and challenging, highly-rhythmic, multi-voiced repertoire (Freer, 2009b).

2.4.3 Themes: Alignments and Misalignments

These and other research findings point to structural, developmental and motivational impediments to boys' participation in choral music. Several themes emerge when these issues are considered collectively. First, there is a set of misalignments between how choral music is practiced and how it might be optimized for adolescent boys. These have been alluded to in previous sections as misalignments between idealized choral performance models and the realities of appropriate performance, repertoire and instruction for adolescent youth. These misalignments may occur when a teacher's goal of choral performance does not match a boys' goal of acquiring musical skills that can be transferred to other musical activities that also appeal to him. And, research indicates that some choral teachers experience tensions between professional, artistic expectations and their understandings of how adolescent boys learn, think, and grow (Freer, 2008b).

A way forward may be found in areas where alignments occur among performance, pedagogy and practice. For example, young adolescent males express the desire for peer support and recognition of their achievements – they may find a collaborative choral experience to be an optimal platform for this support. Adolescent boys of diverse backgrounds have a nearly universal interest in acquiring the skills to create music and engage in musical activities with peers. Finally, research indicates that the reciprocal nature of the teacher-student relationship is particularly motivating to boys when they function as "co-musicians" with their teachers in the process of learning and refining music (Freer, 2010).

2.5 What Boys Suggest

The recent growth of narrative research in music education has afforded researchers the opportunity to ask boys why they participate in choirs, why they may have once participated yet withdrew, or why they never considered joining in the first place (Barrett & Stauffer, 2009; Freer, 2006, 2010). Narrative research conducted in the United States has produced a wealth of information about what boys suggest choral teachers might do to attract and retain adolescent males.

First, boys suggest that teachers shift away from an emphasis on continuous participation in choral music, instead focusing on the musical skills that will enable choral singers to return to the ensemble experience whenever and wherever they wish as they mature into adulthood (Freer, 2009c). Boys report feeling a sense of pressure from their conductors to never withdraw from choral music, especially from school-based choirs. But, most boys would like to explore the many opportunities open to them, and this experimentation may lead to schedule conflicts requiring the withdrawal from choral music. This is particularly problematic in the United States when school-based choirs are judged competitively with a balance among voice parts listed as one category for evaluation. And, if the existence of choral programs is dependent upon enrolment, the attrition of any boy is of great concern – no matter the teacher's empathy for the boy's rationale. Whether this withdrawal is temporary or permanent largely depends upon the response of the teacher at the moment the boy announces his intention. Boys would like their teachers to be supportive of their entire development, not just their musical development.

Boys report that they enjoy variety in rehearsal instruction (e.g. Freer, 2009b). Adolescent boys like to move, to interact with one another, to work in groups in various locations of the room, and with changes of activity every 12 min or so. These suggestions are supported by other research about the pacing of choral rehearsals for young adolescents (Freer, 2008b, 2007). In these activities, boys want to focus on the development of vocal skills, vocal technique, and music reading skills rather than repeatedly drilling the pitches and rhythms of a small number of repertoire selections (Freer, 2009a). Although most boys enjoy the goal of singing choral music accurately and well, they want to learn skills that can transfer to other musical situations – often beyond choral music.

A good deal of related research in the United States involves how teachers use instructional language during rehearsals. In one study, adolescents reported frequent confusion about whether a teacher's criticism was intended for specific individuals or for the entire group (Taylor, 1997). This may be related to brain function: although a hallmark of adolescence is the development of abilities to interpret social situations in multiple ways, not all adolescents develop these abilities in tandem. Other research in choral rehearsals with young adolescents suggests that teachers give specific feedback about skills students exhibit or how they have accomplished a learning goal (e.g. Freer, 2008b; Stamer, 2009). When generalized praise is given instead of specific feedback, boys especially may interpret the praise somewhat differently than the teacher intended. They may instead experience embarrassment, particularly if girls are nearby (Freer, 2009b).

Because choral music is not often a required subject in United States schools, students must be recruited to join, hopefully as they transition from elementary school to junior high or middle school. One frequent recruitment strategy is to have older boys perform for younger boys as role models. Adolescent boys do indicate that this strategy is effective, but they repeatedly suggest that the greater benefit occurs when a "generation" is skipped . . . when high school boys visit elementary boys, or college-age boys visit middle school boys (Freer, 2009a, 2009b, 2009c). It may be that young boys seek ideas of who they can become if they pursue the right strategies and school activities. This conception is similar to the "possible selves" construct beginning to be explored within motivational research in music education (Freer, 2010). This research indicates that adolescent boys and girls begin to hypothesize about their future selves, including those they wish to become or fear becoming. They can then plan strategies to achieve or avoid the realization of those possible selves (Freer, 2009c). It appears that boys seek role models of these possible selves, but it is most effective for those models to be at least 4 or 5 years older.

Boys do need their teachers to be role models in many ways, however, and one of the most important is as a vocal model. Adolescent boys in the studies reviewed for this chapter did not indicate a preference for male or female choral music teachers, but they did ask for the teacher to provide vocal models of males who could sing the notes they would be expected to sing. When female teachers sing in their lower register in well-intentioned efforts to model the pitch for boys with changing voices, the result is that boys will often either sing an octave lower – imitating the vocal technique rather than the pitch – or not want to sing at all. In these instances, boys report feeling as though female teachers emasculate the pitches young men are so proud of finally being able to sing with their newly changing voices (Freer, 2009b). Boys also state that they are willing to experiment with their upper pitches or falsetto voices, but only once they gain confidence singing the lower pitches (Freer, 2009a).

These points are all suggestions from boys about how conductors can utilize what research indicates about how adolescents think, grow, learn, and mature. One unifying link unites each of these suggestions: boys want to be treated as the young men they are becoming.

2.6 The Problem of Masculinity (or Masculinities)

Whenever issues of masculinity are discussed there is the possibility that femininity is presented as an opposite, in opposition, or in confrontation. That is not the intent of this discussion. This discussion of masculinity in no way assumes that there should be minimization of what is currently tremendously effective for the vast majority of adolescents and young adults currently involved in choral music in the United States. Rather, the suggestion here is that choral conductors and teachers consider how males might interpret choral music as being oriented toward or away from them, no matter what stereotypical, gender-based terminology is used. A set of terminologies must be employed, and for that reason the term "masculinity" will refer to those ideas that are most commonly identified with adolescent boys. It is acknowledged that even this term is limited, since male and female are demarcations on a broad continuum of behaviors, orientations, and viewpoints. The goal here is to highlight ways in which boys might come to know choral music as "their own music."

Choral repertoire that is appropriate for changing male voices is a rarity, and the United States publishing industry has attempted to fill this void during the past two decades. Many of the texts utilized in this repertoire lack masculine appeal, and those that do are frequently arrangements of sea chanteys (which brings to mind a recently popular choral arrangement for male choirs titled "[I'm] Sick of the Songs of the Sea"). Choral music conductors and teachers need to reflect current research about literature and texts that appeal to young adolescent boys and other texts intriguing for older adolescent males (Brozo & Gaskins, 2009; Freer, 2009b).

Related to the textual element of choral literature is the level of musical difficulty presented by compositions. Choral conductors often assume that the vocal limitations that are experienced by some boys during voice change indicate a concurrent limitation in musicianship. That is not the case. While the voice change may temporarily render a boy unable to fully express his musical skills, those skills are still very much part of his musical identity and capability. Teachers attempt to assist these boys by selecting simple literature with unappealing melodic lines and static rhythmic figures. This only adds to the frustration of boys who were likely singing far more complex repertoire before the onset of vocal change. These boys come to view choral music as emasculated or feminine. Research indicates that adolescents want to be challenged to increase their skills by singing difficult yet attainable repertoire (Stamer, 2009).

Many rehearsal strategies common in choral rehearsals for young adolescents emulate those of older choirs without regard for how boys think and learn. One result is that many boys are perceived as having behavior problems when they either don't respond to instructional activities or engage in physical activity as a form of self-stimulation to prevent boredom. In these instances, aren't the choral teachers the folks with behavior problems because they behave in a manner unresponsive to these boys?

Adolescence is an extended period of increasing growth, strength and physical coordination. This involves the vocal mechanism just as it involves the rest of the boys' body. Yet, choral teachers don't often provide the detailed physiological descriptions of the voice change process that fascinate boys (Freer, 2009c). Boys experiencing frustration in choral music tend to be drawn away, attracted to where their developing growth and strength is celebrated – sports. It is within these activities that boys learn about sport-specific anatomy and physiology from their coaches. Choral music teachers need to be "coaches" of singing and musicianship, leading boys to understand the physical changes within their vocal mechanisms, what will happen next in the change process, and what outcome can be expected.

2.7 Conclusion

From the earliest days, researchers and teachers have endeavoured to improve the choral experience of males so that they know about their changing voices, are able to realize their skills as musicians, and can engage in music making at all stages of their lives. This tightly woven relationship between research, pedagogy and philosophy has been evident throughout the history of American choral music.

Public school music began as a result of a need in community choral singing. The a cappella choral movement created a need and desire for choral music ensembles in schools, and those ensembles gradually increased in musical stature to become among the finest in the world. These high expectations required a well-trained set of youngsters to replace those who graduated from the ensembles. Research about the changing voice and appropriate vocal practice followed, aided by an interest in how pedagogy could address the needs of young adolescent boys. Changes in philosophy were made as boys with changing voices became viewed as maturing musicians.

But, the question remains, "why do so many boys drop out of choral music?" That is an externally-focused question, with implication that a solution is beyond the control of choral conductors and teachers. Perhaps the question should be completed with the phrase, "…and what can we do to ensure that they stay?" Asking that question would shift the focus to issues teachers can control: repertoire, rehearsal techniques, assessment methods, goals, and philosophies. As these boys become men, they will then experience a smooth pathway on a lifelong journey of music making, singing, and camaraderie.

References

American Choral Directors Association. (2006). *Choral Journal, 47*(5).
Barrett, M. S., & Stauffer, S. L. (Eds.). (2009). *Narrative inquiry in music education: Troubling certainty*. New York: Springer.
Brozo, W. G., & Gaskins, C. (2009). Engaging texts and literacy practices for adolescent boys. In K. D. Wood & W. E. Blanton (Eds.), *Literacy instruction for adolescents: Research-based practice* (pp. 170–186). New York: The Guilford Press.
Chorus America. (2009). *The chorus impact study: How children, adults, and communities benefit from choruses*. Washington, DC: Author. Retrieved August 14, 2011, from http://www.chorusamerica.org/about_choralsinging.cfm
Cooksey, J. (1989). Understanding male-adolescent voice maturation: Some significant contributions by European and American researchers. In G. Paine (Ed.), *Five centuries of choral music: Essays in honor of Howard Swan* (pp. 75–92). Hillsdale, NY: Pendragon Press.
Cooksey, J. (2000). Male adolescent transforming voices: Voice classification, voice skill development, and music literature selection. In L. Thurman & G. Welch (Eds.), *Bodymind & voice: Foundations of voice education* (pp. 821–841). Iowa City, IA: National Center for Voice and Speech.
Cooper, I., & Kuersteiner, K. O. (1965). *Teaching junior high school music*. Boston: Allyn and Bacon.
Crocker, E. (2000). Choosing music for middle school chorus. *Music Educators Journal, 86*(4), 33–37.
Demorest, S. M., & Clements, A. (2007). Factors influencing the pitch-matching of Junior high boys. *Journal of Research in Music Education, 55*(3), 190–203.

Freer, P. K. (1992). The changing voice as an artistic instrument: Interview with James Litton, American Boychoir. New Jersey Music Educators Association. *Tempo, 46*(3).

Freer, P. K. (2006). Hearing the voices of adolescent boys in choral music: A self-story. *Research Studies in Music Education, 27*, 69–81.

Freer, P. K. (2007). Between research and practice: How choral music loses boys in the "middle." *Music Educators Journal, 94*(2), 28–34.

Freer, P. K. (2008a). Boys' changing voices in the first century of MENC journals. *Music Educators Journal, 95*(1), 41–47.

Freer, P. K. (2008b). Teacher instructional language and student experience in middle school choral rehearsals. *Music Education Research, 10*(1), 107–124.

Freer, P. K. (2009a). Boys' descriptions of their experiences in choral music. *Research Studies in Music Education, 31*, 142–160.

Freer, P. K. (2009b). Boys' voices: Inside and outside choral music. In J. L. Kerchner & C. Abril (Eds.), *Music experience throughout our lives: Things we learn and meanings we make* (pp. 217–236). Lanham, MD: Rowman & Littlefield Education.

Freer, P. K. (2009c). "I'll sing with my buddies" – fostering the possible selves of male choral singers. *International Journal of Music Education: Practice, 27*(4), 341–355.

Freer, P. K. (2010). Two decades of research on possible selves and the "missing males" problem in choral music. *International Journal of Music Education: Research, 28*(1), 17–30.

Friddle, D. (2005). Changing bodies, changing voices: A brief survey of the literature and methods of working with adolescent changing voices. *Choral Journal, 46*(6), 32–43, 46–47.

Funderburk-Galvan, J. (1987). *Junior high school choral music teachers' philosophies of vocal mutation, choices of music, and teaching situations*. Doctoral dissertation, University of North Carolina at Greensboro.

Gates, J. T. (1989). A historical comparison of public singing by American men and women. *Journal of Research in Music Education, 37*(1), 32–47.

Giddings, T. P. (1930). Unison songs in the junior high school. *Music Supervisors' Journal, 16*(4), 19, 21, 23.

Koza, J. (1993). The "missing males" and other gender-related issues in music education: Evidence from the *Music Supervisors' Journal* (1912–1924). *Journal of Research in Music Education, 41*(3), 212–232.

McKenzie, D. (1956). *Training the boy's changing voice*. New Brunswick, NJ: Rutgers University Press.

Stamer, R. A. (2009). Choral student perceptions of effective motivation strategies. *Update: Applications of Research in Music Education, 28*(1), 25–32.

Swanson, F. J. (1977). *The male changing voice ages eight to eighteen*. Cedar Rapids, IA: Lawrence Press.

Taylor, O. (1997). Student interpretations of teacher verbal praise in selected seventh- and eighth-grade choral classes. *Journal of Research in Music Education, 45*, 536–546.

Chapter 3
Sex, Gender and Singing Development: Making a Positive Difference to Boys' Singing Through a National Programme in England

Graham F. Welch, Jo Saunders, Ioulia Papageorgi, and Evangelos Himonides

3.1 Introduction

One of the enduring paradoxes within the literature on children's singing development is that boys are generally reported as less developed in their singing skills compared to girls, but that in many Western cultures, particularly in the English-speaking part of the world, there are longstanding historical gender-biased traditions of musical performance by highly skilled male cathedral choristers. One possible explanation for this paradox might be that singing is a form of musical behaviour that is naturally more polarised in the young male of the species, with boys tending to be found towards the two extremes of a singing capability spectrum, whereas girls tend to be more homogenous as a group. Another explanation is that boys are genetically less capable of singing than girls. However, at least in the UK context, such explanations are challenged by the ongoing outcomes of two recent cultural initiatives, namely a shift towards the establishment of girls' choirs in the majority of cathedrals since 1990 (i.e., in addition to the established male choristers, Welch, 2011) and the impact of a new, four-year National Singing Programme *Sing Up* in England for children of Primary school age (cf., Himonides, Saunders, Papageorgi, Vraka, Preti, & Stephens, 2009; Welch et al., in press).[1] These twin initiatives have had the effect of confirming that children's singing is subject to both sex and gender differences, i.e., although *sex* differences are evidenced in the relative size of the vocal anatomy and physiology – the physical source of the singing voice (e.g., Titze, 1994), *gender* differences are found in the ways that such sex differences are reflected in the socio-cultural shaping of developing vocal behaviours.

G.F. Welch (✉)
Institute of Education, University of London, London WC1H 0AL, UK
e-mail: g.welch@ioe.ac.uk

3.2 Gendered Similarities and Differences in *Trained* Children's Singing Voices

The first of these two cultural initiatives – a shift towards the establishment of girls' choirs in the majority of cathedrals since 1990 – has its roots in sacred music performance. From the end of the sixth century, when the first Benedictine abbey was founded by St Augustine in Canterbury to the present day, there has been a tradition of young children being inducted into religious establishments in England to participate in the musical performances associated with daily religious life. For almost the first thousand years until the time of the split with the Church of Rome by King Henry VIII in 1534, boys and girls had opportunities to sing as members of religious communities in monasteries or nunneries (respectively), notwithstanding the establishment of a growing number of city-based cathedrals and chapels that were more likely to be all male in their musical personnel (Mould, 2007).

With the dissolution of the monasteries, there was a relative absence of opportunities for girls to sing in cathedral and chapel choirs in England for over 400 years until the end of the twentieth century. In the late 1980s, however, twin pressures emerged that challenged the existing overarching bias towards an all-male choral tradition. Firstly, there was a general political consensus and associated legislation to promote demonstrable equal opportunities in many different aspects of UK society, notably related to race and gender in the workplace. Secondly, around that time there had been a relative decline in the recruitment of boy choristers that was causing concern to cathedral organists and Cathedral Choir Schools. A combination of these cultural and pragmatic forces led to Salisbury Cathedral to introduce girl choristers in 1990. Although this was not the first cathedral to do so (Leicester, Bradford and Manchester had already challenged the status quo, each for their own, local reasons, including recruitment needs), the resultant media interest had a seismic effect on the dominant cathedral music culture. The hegemony of the all-male cathedral tradition was severely weakened, such that, in the space of two decades, by 2009 cathedrals where the choristers were solely male were in the minority (31%, $n=15$), whereas approximately two-thirds of English cathedrals and major chapels (65%, $n=31$) now employed both girls and boys of similar ages, even though they often continued (and continue) to sing daily services separately in rotation across a week and only occasionally performed together for particular major festivals or concerts (see Welch, 2011 for more detail).

For some, this musical and cultural initiative was controversial, particularly within the more traditionally minded membership of the cathedral music community.[2] Amongst the concerns expressed was whether or not girls could sing to the same high standard as boys and with the same vocal quality (a somewhat paradoxical position, given the focus for this chapter and underlying concern that has underpinned the rationale for this book). Nevertheless, subsequent empirical studies indicate that, at least in terms of the standard of performance, there is no observable difference between the two sexes. In addition, it is often difficult (if not always impossible) for the listener accurately to perceive the sex of the choristers from listening to their voices in performance (e.g., see Howard, Barlow,

Szymanski, & Welch, 2001; Howard, Szymanski, & Welch, 2002; Howard & Welch, 2002; Sergeant & Welch, 1997). This suggests that the argument concerning the unique male vocal quality (the perceived timbre of the singing voice) in sacred music performance may be overstated, at least for the naïve listener.

In contrast, there are usually perceivable differences between the sung products of *untrained* girls' and boys' voices. These derive from stereotypically characteristic differences in their sung spectra that originate from slight physical variances between the sexes in the size of the vocal instrument, especially as the children get older. These differences become more notable and significant acoustically (e.g., Sergeant, Sjölander, & Welch, 2005; Sergeant & Welch, 2008, 2009) as children grow up in particular socio-cultural soundworlds that shape their vocal behaviours. For example, the gendered vocal products of young boys' singing pre-school at aged four is reported to be perceived as feminine in quality – probably because their prime carers in infancy will be female – but becomes characteristically more masculine as they get older, such that by the age of eight years the gender assignment of their singing tends accurately to match their sex (Sergeant et al., 2005; Welch, 2006).

Whereas normal enculturated experiences shape children's singing towards a clear differentiation perceptually between the sexes, the socio-cultural context for choristers' singing is biased towards the generation of more similar vocal acoustic products. The typical 'chorister' sound derives from the established organisational practices of the English choral tradition that embodies an induction as a novice into a sustained and systematic socio-cultural voice education that is sustained by practice routines on a daily basis (e.g., see Chapter 11). The impact of the cathedral music culture is to create much closer acoustic correspondences between the sexes in their singing, evidenced in the choristers' vocal behaviours throughout childhood and into early adolescence (Welch & Howard, 2002; Welch, 2006, 2007, 2011).

3.3 Sex and Gender Similarities and Differences in *Untrained* Children's Singing Voices

There is a consistent finding across the twentieth century research literature on (untrained) children's singing development that girls as a group tend to be more advanced, in the sense of more accomplished at an earlier age, than boys. This is evidenced, for example, in the relative proportions of boys to girls reported in the research as 'out-of-tune' singers in Western cultures, being 2 or 3:1 for any given age group across childhood (e.g., Welch, 1979, 2009; Mang, 2006). Nevertheless, as demonstrated by the cathedral choral tradition, some boys are extremely accomplished in their singing and capable of performing at the highest levels professionally, whether in the sacred music environment of the cathedral, or on the more secular opera stage.

The underlying reasons for this reported bias in general singing development between the sexes across childhood is believed to relate more to cultural effects than any underlying genetic differences. In part, this is because singing is recognised to be culturally located, i.e., what counts as singing – and singing accomplishment – is defined in terms of local cultural values and practices, as well as in the individual's 'singer identity' (Welch, 2005). This is exampled by educational research evidence that boys can become significantly more accomplished in their singing in an appropriately nurturing environment. For example, an Australian study of five-year-old boys found that same sex older-peer modelling of singing had a measureable positive impact on the younger male participants' singing development (Hall, 2005).

Similar evidence of environmental impact is demonstrated in a longitudinal Italian study that followed children's singing development from birth across their pre-school years (Tafuri, 2008). Mothers and their children ($n = 37$) experienced weekly collective music classes over several years from early infancy onwards, with the musical activities being sustained by the mothers at home between classes. Analyses of previously unpublished data for the purposes of this chapter challenge the concept of girls' singing development always being more advanced than boys'. Although there were observable differences between the sexes at the age of two years in their rated singing abilities, it was the boys that were slightly more competent in singing complete songs in-tune. In contrast, girls were at an earlier developmental stage that was more focused on the development of accurate singing of constituent song phrases (Fig. 3.1).

Longitudinal data comparison reveals that, although the girls subsequently made more marked improvement in their complete song singing, such that any earlier sex differences had virtually disappeared eighteen months later when the children were

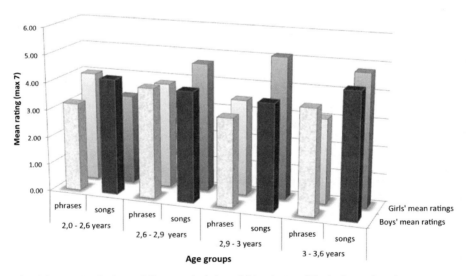

Fig. 3.1 Longitudinal sex differences in infant children's ($n = 37$) singing ratings by age group and mean rating of vocalisation elements (song phrases or complete songs) (Tafuri, with Welch, unpublished data, using a singing development scale of 1–7, where 7 represents accurate singing in-tune with no errors or shifts in tonality)

aged three and a half years, participant boys were at least as skilled in their song singing as their female peers (Fig. 3.1).

This complex mix of gendered singing behaviours related to age and vocal task is echoed in other longitudinal research previously published in the 1990s in one of the first major studies of children's singing behaviour. This research focused on the singing development of young children ($n = 184$) from their first term in Primary school, at age five, onwards (Welch, 1998; Welch et al., 1996; Welch, Sergeant, & White, 1997). The young children were drawn from ten London schools and assessed annually as individuals across three successive school years until the age of seven. The main research foci were twofold, namely on the children's current abilities to sing two songs (different each year), as well as their ability to sing musical material that was 'deconstructed' from the songs as a test battery and that required performance without words. This embraced the vocal pitch matching of individual pitches, groups of three and five pitches (termed 'melodic fragments'), and simple and complex pitch contours that were based on the original song melodies. This methodological design allowed a comparison to be made of the effects of adding words (i.e., lyrics) to musical material (as in the selected songs). All sung responses were recorded onto digital tape for subsequent analysis and rating by of panel of six experienced judges using a seven-point scale.

The longitudinal data reveal an explicit hierarchy in children's developing singing competences. At each age, children were much more accurate in their vocal pitch matching when asked to copy simple glides (uni- or bi-directional, being equivalent to simple melodic contours), single pitches and (from age six) melodic fragments. In contrast, more complex pitch glides (multi-directional contours) and songs were less accurate. There was also clear evidence of a general, systematic and statistically significant improvement in vocal pitch matching skills across school years, but with the notable exception of pitch matching in song singing, which was consistently judged as being much poorer by comparison (Welch et al., 1996).

With regard to the sex of the subjects, evidence of gendered singing behaviours also emerged. Although there were no statistically significant sex differences in ratings for vocal pitch accuracy at ages five and six, girls generally had greater mean ratings for song performance compared to boys, who had greater means for responses on simpler test items. However, there were clear sex differences between responses to the songs and the test battery items. Both boys and girls demonstrated identical year-on-year improvements in the vocal pitch accuracy on the non-song musical materials from ages five to seven (see Fig. 3.2). In contrast, for both sexes, song singing was significantly less skilled developmentally. The clear inference is that the addition of lyrics to musical material – as in a cultural artifact conventionally termed as a 'song' – the same children's musical competency was observed to be less skilled. Moreover, the mean ratings for the participant boys' ($n = 87$) song singing actually declined linearly across all three years, whilst the means for the girls ($n = 97$) remained relatively constant – but still significantly less developed than their singing of non-song items (Fig. 3.2).

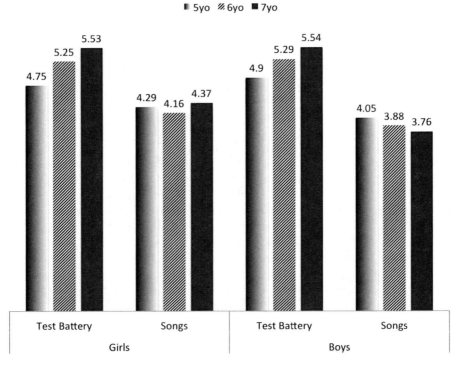

Fig. 3.2 Longitudinal sex differences in young children's ($n = 184$) singing ratings by age group (5–7 years) and mean rating of vocalisation tasks (test battery items or complete songs) (data from Welch et al., 1996); rated on a singing development scale of 1–7, where 7 represents accurate singing in-tune with no errors or shifts in tonality

As reported at the time (Welch et al., 1996, 1997), the reasons for this developmental disparity between songs and other forms of musical vocal pitch matching appear to be closely related the generic nature of song design. A song can be seen as a complex perceptual structure that utilises basic musical elements that are organised within a conventional musical 'grammar' concurrent with text (an equivalent of spoken language). In the face of such task complexity – which is also reflected neurologically in the multi-sited processing of lyrics and music (cf. Brown, Martinez, Hodges, Fox, & Parsons, 2004; Brown, Martinez, & Parsons, 2006) – it is normal for some children's vocal pitch matching to be less accurate in the early phases of singing development (cf. Rutkowski, 1997; Welch, 1986; Welch et al., 2009). However, simpler, more purely *musical* structures – in the sense that there are no words attached that are required to be learned at the same time, such as in the singing of single pitches and patterns of pitches (e.g. melodic fragments) – are reproduced vocally more accurately because they are perceptually less complex and, consequently, effective 'error labelling' (Welch, 1985) is enhanced to support corrective vocal pitch adjustment in singing schemata.

Relatively musically inexperienced young children, when faced with a novel song task that requires them to learn and reproduce an example of a musical grammar combined with elements of their spoken language (i.e. to learn and sing a new song), are likely to focus on those features that have the greatest perceptual (and socio-cognitive) significance for them, namely the words (lyrics). Indeed, when the ratings for word (text) accuracy are compared to the accuracy ratings for melodies in the London study, there is a significant and persistent difference between the two (Welch et al., 1997). In each of the three years of testing, the children's ability to reproduce the words of the chosen songs was rated extremely highly by the judges. Moreover, in each year, these ratings for lyrics accuracy were significantly higher than the ratings for the same songs' constituent pitches. This finding has resonances with the research data from investigations of preschoolers' invented notations of songs, in which lyric content is reported to be perceptually dominant compared to the same songs' musical features (Barrett, 1997, 2001).

The differences between song performance and the singing of deconstructed musical features of the songs in this London-based study were evidenced for both sexes across all three years. However, the unexpected longitudinal finding of a relative *decline* in vocal competence in boys' song singing compared to girls suggests that there might be something about the *combination* of words and music that creates a particular task difficulty for a significant proportion of young male developing singers. Although, in general, the research literature suggests that the incidence of 'out-of-tune' singing declines as children get older (cf. Welch, 1979, 2006), for a small minority of children – particularly boys – song singing continues to be a challenge, i.e., unless they are able to experience an appropriate singing pedagogy that is matched to their developmental needs (see below).

The significance of the learning environment in children's singing development provides an important caveat in the juxtaposition of these two studies from Italy and England. The Italian infants had sustained musical input from the final stages of foetal life onwards because their mothers had attended collective singing lessons within the antenatal and postnatal phases of the longitudinal research study. Indeed, the study was designed so that the mothers and toddlers participated in weekly music workshops across several years in the local Conservatoire (see Tafuri, 2008 for details). When the singing competency data for these Italian children are compared to that reported elsewhere in the literature for children of similar ages (such as Davidson, McKernon, & Gardner, 1981), these children demonstrate precocious development. It can be hypothesised that sustained, active experience in a rich musical environment is more likely to ensure that children's singing potential is realised. In contrast, the children from the UK study were older and had not experienced any special musical intervention. School selection (and by inference, participant selection) was primarily based on ensuring a wide diversity of socio-economic research contexts across urban and suburban locations, as well as a willingness to participate in a three-year longitudinal study. The question arises, therefore, of what might have happened if the London study children had experienced a similarly rich and sustained music programme with lots of opportunity to develop their singing skills.

Although it is not possible to go back in time to initiate such an intervention study for those children, inferences can be drawn from new data emerging within an impact research evaluation into a novel, national programme of singing education in England.

3.4 The National Singing Programme *Sing Up* and Its Impact on Children's Gendered Singing Development and Attitudes to Singing

In 2004, the UK Government initiated a 'Music Manifesto', sponsored by the Ministries for Education (DCSF) and Culture, Media and Sport (DCMS) to campaign 'to ensure that all children and young people have access to high quality music education'.[3] Under the umbrella of the 'Music Manifesto' in England, one major initiative focused on Primary school-aged children's singing. A four-year, £40m National Singing Programme *Sing Up* was officially launched in November 2007 with the intention of ensuring that singing became part of Early Years and Primary education for all children in England by 2012,[4] a cultural programme initiative that was designed to link, in part, to wider preparations for the London-based Olympic Games in 2012.

3.4.1 Gendered Singing Development

Across the opening three school years of *Sing Up* (2007–2010), a research team from the Institute of Education, London[5] visited 177 schools nationally and collected individual data from 9,979 children (Welch, Himonides, Saunders, & Papageorgi, 2010). Some of the children were seen more than once as part of a longitudinal focus, resulting in a total of 11,388 assessments of individual children's singing being made. Data were collected from approximately equal numbers of girls (51.8%) and boys (48.2%), with 1:4 children coming from ethnic minority groups (i.e., in line with the proportions in official DfE/DCSF statistics data for the demographics of English Primary schools). Overall, as an intended part of the research design, 95% of the assessed children were aged from 7+ to 10+ years.

Children were drawn from two main umbrella constituencies as the programme rolled out across the country: (i) children with experience of *Sing Up* initiatives (69% of the dataset) – with experience being related to (a) their teachers participating in the national *Sing Up* 'workforce development' programme to improve the teaching of singing in schools and community settings; and/or (b) using a new on-line resource to support singing teaching and learning – the *Song Bank*; and/or having sustained specialist singing teaching in their school – such as provided by the Choir School Association's *Chorister Outreach Programme* or Ex Cathedra's *Singing Playgrounds* initiative. Data from the children exposed to *Sing Up* in one or more of these ways were compared to that from (ii) children without any *Sing Up* experience at the time of their assessment (31% of the dataset).

Across the opening three years of the *Sing Up* research, children's singing behaviour and development were assessed by the application of a specially designed protocol. This included noting each individual child's performance of two well-known songs against two established rating scales of singing development (Rutkowski, 1997; Welch, 1998 – after Mang, 2006 – see Welch et al., 2009 for more detail) and combining the resultant data into a 'normalised singing score' to facilitate easy comparison between children. In addition, participant children's attitudes to singing and self were assessed by a specially designed questionnaire that embraced six themes.

Subsequent data analyses revealed sex differences related both to developmental singing behaviours and also in children's attitudes to singing (Welch et al., 2010). In general, based on an analysis of $n = 11,388$ individual singing assessments, girls were rated as significantly more developed in their singing competency compared to boys for each participant age group (Fig. 3.3[6]). This developmental difference between the sexes appears to be relatively stable across age groups, with girls approximately three years in advance developmentally. Nevertheless, both sexes demonstrate an improving trend in singing competency with age.

However, notwithstanding this general trend for untrained girls to be more developed in their singing, both boys and girls that had experience of *Sing Up* tended to have higher mean singing development ratings compared to their non-*Sing Up* peers (Fig. 3.4). Closer inspection of this sub-division in the dataset provides interesting evidence of other trends:

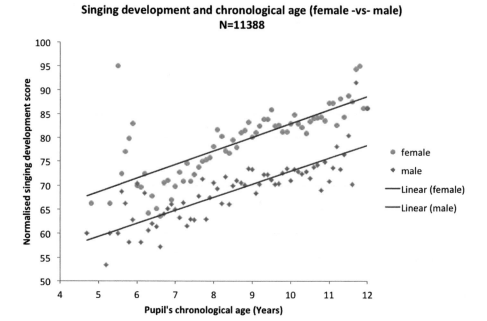

Fig. 3.3 Graph to illustrate children's singing development by chronological age, separated by children's sex ($n=11,388$ *Sing Up* assessments from 2007 to 2010)

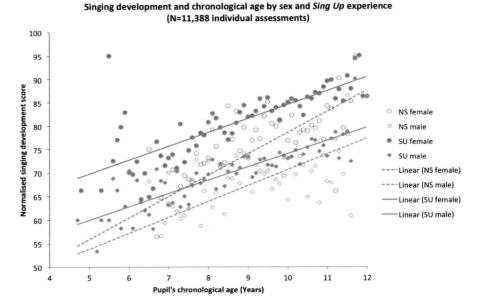

Fig. 3.4 Graph to illustrate children's singing development by chronological age, separated by children's sex and whether or not they have experience of *Sing Up* (based on $n = 11{,}388$ *Sing Up* assessments from 2007 to 2010)

- Within the non-*Sing Up* age-related mean development data (the dotted lines in Fig. 3.4), the two sexes appear to be much closer in their singing competence at the beginning of Primary schooling where girls have an advantage of approximately six months at age five (a finding not dissimilar to the earlier London study data reported above);
- The non-*Sing Up* difference between the sexes becomes larger with successive age groups, with girls approximately two years in advance by the age of nine years. This suggests that, for whatever reasons, normal singing development is subject to gendered socio-cultural effects that can exert a growing influence with age;
- In contrast, the difference between the sexes is larger and more consistent for *Sing Up* participants, with at least three years difference developmentally across age groups between girls and boys in favour of the former;
- Furthermore, a comparison of *Sing Up* and non-*Sing Up* data indicates that girls within the non-*Sing Up* grouping, although less skilled at age five years, begin developmentally to overtake *Sing Up* boys around the age of eight. This is again suggestive of a powerful gendering influence in development by which singing competency appears to be accelerated particularly for girls with experience, but less so for boys;
- Nevertheless, boys with experience of *Sing Up* are on average two years in advance from the age of five onwards compared to boys *without* such experience, a difference that reduces slightly to around one year developmentally by the age of eleven;

- In contrast, *Sing Up* girls are over three years in advance developmentally compared to their non-*Sing Up* peers at age five; this reduces to around a year and a half's advantage by the age of ten plus.

Additional evidence of the beneficial impact of *Sing Up* on participants' singing of both sexes is provided by longitudinal data analyses of $n = 438$ children. Boys with experience of *Sing Up* had a developmental advantage over their non-*Sing Up* peers and maintained this across two school years (2008–2010) (Fig. 3.5). The girls' data analyses demonstrate a similar trend.

Data analyses focused on determining the relative proportions of children who achieved the highest singing development rankings provides another way of exploring possible gender effects. This analysis indicates that the 34% of children had their singing development rated within 10% of the scale maximum (i.e. with individual singing development ratings between 90 and 100 out of a developmental maximum score of 100). Within this grouping, there was a sex ratio of 2:1 in favour of girls, i.e., $n = 2,677$ girls' assessments compared to $n = 1,225$ for boys. Moreover, this 2:1 sex ratio bias was identical for singing development ratings between 80 and 100, i.e., within 20% of the maximum. Overall, in line with the age-related trend data reported earlier in Fig. 3.4, fewer boys have their singing rated at the highest developmental levels compared to girls.

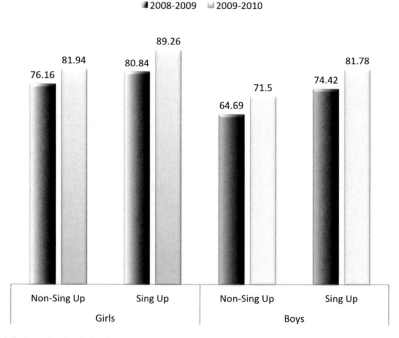

Fig. 3.5 Longitudinal singing development mean data for $n = 438$ children across two school years (2008–2009/2009–2010), characterised by *Sing Up* experience x sex (maximum singing development score = 100)

One exception to this gender-based trend concerned participant cathedral choristers. Their singing development ratings were statistically very similar – as might be expected, given the daily requirement across much of each year for highly skilled performance of an extensive sacred music vocal repertoire.

Within the dataset, there is also evidence of how participation in an extended programme of singing education can have a powerful impact on the untrained children's singing competency development. Although the cathedral choristers (not unsurprisingly) achieved the highest ratings, these ratings were statistically similar to those for non-chorister children who had participated in the *Chorister Outreach Programme*. This was a special intervention programme offered under the *Sing Up* organisational umbrella where experienced choral leaders and a small number of their choristers from a Cathedral Choir Schools visited a selection of local Primary schools to provide a series of singing workshops. These were usually offered across one school term (and sometimes longer) and customarily led to a large end-of-term concert of the combined music forces in the local cathedral (school children and choristers) and at which parents attended.

3.4.2 Gendered Attitudes to Singing

All the children in the *Sing Up* impact research study also completed a 60-question survey that sought to gather information about their attitudes to singing, clustered under six themes,[7] e.g., in school, at home and elsewhere, as well as their views of themselves, both as singers and in general. They were required to circle a series of Smiley Faces on the basis of their agreement with each of the 60 statements, using a seven-point scale where circled agreement was scored as seven and circled disagreement as one. Inferential statistical analyses on the resultant data sets ($n = 10,425$) revealed a complex interaction between sex, age and singing experience (Fig. 3.6). Overall:

- Girls were more positive than boys on all six themes;
- Younger children tended to be more positive about singing than older children; and
- *Sing Up* experienced children tended to be slightly more positive than non-*Sing Up* children overall, but particularly so concerning singing in school and singing in the home.

The attitudinal data findings are somewhat paradoxical for both sexes in that there is a general tendency for children to be less satisfied with singing as they get older, but this finding is in a context where, developmentally, they are becoming more skilful (cf. Fig. 3.3), i.e., they are getting better at singing, but appear to like it less. The exception to this general trend is for *Sing Up* experienced children who are on average more positive than their non-*Sing Up* peers about particular aspects of singing, such as in school.

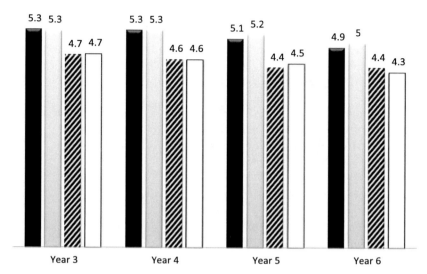

Fig. 3.6 Overall mean attitudinal questionnaire responses by sex and age group (children aged 7+ [Year 3] to 10+ [Year 6]; for $n = 10{,}425$ sets of data) across all six survey themes combined; this demonstrates a relative overall decline in positivity towards singing with increasing age (scale: min = 1; max = 7)

3.5 Successful Singing Pedagogy Can Address Gendered Tendencies in Children's Singing Development

The reasons for attitudinal differences in the *Sing Up* research findings between the two main constituencies towards school-based singing are likely to derive from the marked advances in singing competency demonstrated by the *Sing Up* participants, both boys and girls. This appears to be a direct outcome of a richer musical experience within a comprehensive, specially designed, singing development programme.

In order to understand the features of successful *Sing Up*-based teaching and learning in more detail, over twenty hours of systematic detailed observation were undertaken across twenty schools throughout 2010 (Saunders, Papageorgi, Himonides, Rinta, & Welch, 2011). Schools were selected on the basis of their children's previously assessed success in singing competency as part of the main research data collection. Detailed minute-by-minute observations were made of example singing lessons, noting the teacher/song leader's actions and the children's responses. Drawing on published literature on generic features of effective teaching and learning,[8] as well as OfSTED's (2009) recent inspection report on music making in primary schools, clear features of successful singing teaching emerged. For example:

- Pupils were *actively engaged* for a high percentage of time across the observed session;
- The *pupils' voice was dominant* within the session, either being expressed in song or used to question, reflect and review their own progress;
- The *criteria for success* were made *explicit and reinforced* throughout the session;
- Pupil performance was *monitored and assessed* and musically informed feedback instantly provided, with *clear indications of how to improve*;
- Achievement was *celebrated and valued* and related to the criteria for success.
- A *suitably paced session* was evidenced – such as a fast paced session that built to a crescendo, or a more intermittent pace that allowed space for discussion;
- Learning was placed within a *wider context of pupils' lives* (Saunders et al., 2011).

The application of these pedagogical principles will be of benefit to both boys and girls in their singing development. This is further exampled when participant schools across the *Sing Up* research impact dataset are ranked in terms of children's observed singing competences. School classes in the upper quartile of assessed singing competencies include those where boys are in the majority (Welch et al., 2009). Notwithstanding the overall trends in favour of girls' singing reported elsewhere in this chapter (cf. Figs. 3.3 and 3.4), across the country there are individual Primary schools where boys are at least as successful as their female peers.

3.6 Conclusions

Data from three major, longitudinal studies of children's singing development have been set alongside evidence from research into cathedral choristers. Collectively, it is argued that these provide a comprehensive perspective of how boys and girls singing becomes gendered through exposure to particular biases in their musical enculturation. The Italian pre-school data (Tafuri, 2008) suggests that boys are capable of singing as well as girls from infancy onwards if they experience an appropriately nurturing environment. This finding is reinforced by an earlier London-based study of the first three years of schooling (Welch et al., 1996). This research indicates that, on entry to school, boys continue to be at least as competent as girls in their vocal pitch matching skills in musical tasks where lyrics are absent. However, as soon as lyrics and musical material are combined in song singing, the same boys' vocal competency is compromised. Building on these earlier studies, previously unpublished data analyses from a national study of slightly older children in England suggest a trend for boys to continue to lag behind girls developmentally in their song singing, but that they are capable of becoming significantly more skilled if provided with appropriate, sustained music education experiences. There is nothing immutable about the gendered differences that are commonly reported in studies of children's singing. Many more boys, as well as girls, will fulfil their singing potential – arguably, their singing birthright – if those responsible for music education policy and practice in our schools and community settings ensure that a nurturing singing development pedagogy is in place.

Notes

1. These conceptions of a major difference between the singing of girls and boys is also challenged by observed cultural practices in sung music in other parts of the world, such as Afghanistan and South Africa, where there are strong traditions of boys' singing (e.g., see the research reported by Doubleday & Baily, 1995; Blacking, 1967).
2. See, for example, the 'Campaign for the Traditional Cathedral Choir' (CTCC, formerly labelled the 'Campaign for the Defence of the Traditional Cathedral Choir') with its aim 'To champion the ancient tradition of the all-male choir in Cathedrals, Chapels Royal, Collegiate Churches, University Chapels and similar ecclesiastical choral foundations'.
3. See http://www.musicmanifesto.co.uk/about-the-manifesto retrieved 21 August 2009.
4. See http://www.singup.org/ retrieved 2 September 2009.
5. The core members of the team were the authors of this chapter.
6. The 2007–2010 *Sing Up* research dataset has been mined for the purposes of this chapter to identify particular features of boys' singing that are reported here for the first time.
7. The six themes in the survey instrument were:
    1. Identity as a singer (emotional connection with singing)
    2. Identity as a singer (self-efficacy)
    3. Singing at home
    4. Singing at school
    5. Singing in informal settings
    6. Self concept and sense of social inclusion
8. See the UK Economic and Social Research (ESRC) Teaching and Learning Programme (TLRP) website for more details of its 'TLRP's evidence-informed pedagogic principles' at www.tlrp.org

References

Barrett, M. (1997). Invented notations: A view of young children's musical thinking. *Research Studies in Music Education, 8*(1), 2–14.

Barrett, M. (2001). Constructing a view of children's meaning-making as notators: A case-study of a five-year-old's descriptions and explanations of invented notations. *Research Studies in Music Education, 16*(1), 33–45.

Blacking, J. (1967). *Venda children's songs*. Johannesburg: University of Witwatersrand Press.

Brown, S., Martinez, M. J., Hodges, D., Fox, P. T., & Parsons, L. M. (2004). The song system of the human brain. *Cognitive Brain Research, 20*, 363–375.

Brown, S., Martinez, M. J., & Parsons, L. M. (2006). Music and language side by side in the brain: A PET study of generating melodies and sentences. *European Journal of Neuroscience, 23*, 2791–2803.

Davidson, L., McKernon, P., & Gardner, H. (1981). *The acquisition of song: A developmental approach*. Documentary Report of the Ann Arbor Symposium, Reston, VA: MENC.

Doubleday, V., & Baily, J. (1995). Patterns of musical development among children in Afghanistan. In E. J. Fernea (Ed.), *Children in the Muslim Middle East* (pp. 431–444). Austin, TX: University of Texas Press.

Hall, C. (2005). Gender and boys' singing in early childhood. *British Journal of Music Education, 22*(1), 5–20.

Howard, D. M., Barlow, C., Szymanski, J., & Welch, G. F. (2001). Vocal production and listener perception of trained English cathedral girl and boy choristers. *Bulletin of the Council for Research in Music Education, 147,* 81–86.

Howard, D. M., Szymanski, J., & Welch, G. F. (2002). Listener's perception of English cathedral girl and boy choristers. *Music Perception, 20*(1), 35–49.

Howard, D. M., & Welch, G. F. (2002). Female chorister development: A longitudinal study at Wells, UK. *Bulletin of the Council for Research in Music Education, 153/4,* 63–70.

Mang, E. (2006). The effects of age, gender and language on children's singing competency. *British Journal of Music Education, 23*(2), 161–174.

Mould, A. (2007). *The English chorister: A history.* London: Hambledon Continuum.

OfSTED [Office for Standards in Education]. (2009). *Making more of music: Improving the quality of music teaching (primary).* London: Author.

Rutkowski, J. (1997). The nature of children's singing voices: Characteristics and assessment. In B. A. Roberts (Ed.), *The phenomenon of singing* (pp. 201–209). St. John's, NF: Memorial University Press.

Saunders, J., Papageorgi, I., Himonides, E., Rinta, T., & Welch, G. F. (2011). *Researching the impact of the National Singing Programme 'Sing Up' in England. Diverse approaches to successful singing in primary settings: Evidence from the Chorister Outreach Programme and other Sing Up schools (2009–2010).* London: International Music Education Research Centre, Institute of Education. Retrieved from http://imerc.org

Sergeant, D. C., Sjölander, P. J., & Welch, G. F. (2005). Listeners' identification of gender differences in children's singing. *Research Studies in Music Education, 24,* 28–39.

Sergeant, D. C., & Welch, G. F. (1997). Perceived similarities and differences in the singing of trained children's choirs. *Choir Schools Today, 11,* 9–10.

Sergeant, D. C., & Welch, G. F. (2008). Age-related changes in long-term average spectra of children's voices. *Journal of Voice, 22*(6), 658–670.

Sergeant, D. C., & Welch, G. F. (2009). Gender differences in long-term-average spectra of children's singing voices. *Journal of Voice, 23*(3), 319–336.

Tafuri, J. (2008). *Infant musicality: New research for educators and parents.* Surrey: Ashgate Publishing.

Titze, I. (1994). *Principles of voice production.* Englewood Cliffs, NJ: Prentice-Hall.

Welch, G. F. (1979). Poor pitch singing: A review of the literature. *Psychology of Music, 7*(1), 50–58.

Welch, G. F. (1985). A schema theory of how children learn to sing in-tune. *Psychology of Music, 13*(1), 3–18.

Welch, G. F. (1986). A developmental view of children's singing. *British Journal of Music Education, 3*(3), 295–303.

Welch, G. F. (1998). Early childhood musical development. *Research Studies in Music Education, 11*(1), 27–41.

Welch, G. F. (2005). Singing as communication. In D. Miell, R. MacDonald, & D. J. Hargreaves (Eds.), *Musical communication.* (pp. 239–259). New York: Oxford University Press.

Welch, G. F. (2006). Singing and vocal development. In G. McPherson (Ed.), *The child as musician: A handbook of musical development* (pp. 311–329). New York: Oxford University Press.

Welch, G. F. (2007). Om Sångutveckling [Singing as a developmental behaviour]. In G. Fagius (Ed.), *Barn Och Sång. Hur, Vad Och Varför Sjunger Vi Med Barn?* [Children and singing. How, what and why are we singing with children?] (pp. 55–66). Lund: Studentlitteratur AB. [13:978-91-44-01935-2]

Welch, G. F. (2009). Evidence of the development of vocal pitch matching ability in children. *Japanese Journal of Music Education Research, 39*(1), 38–47.

Welch, G. F. (2011). Culture and gender in a cathedral music context: An activity theory exploration. In M. Barrett (Ed.), *A cultural psychology of music education* (pp. 225–258). New York: Oxford University Press.

Welch, G. F., Himonides, E., Saunders, J., & Papageorgi, I. (2010). *Researching the impact of the National Singing Programme 'Sing Up' in England. Main findings from the first three years (2007–2010): Children's singing development, self-concept and sense of social inclusion.* London: International Music Education Research Centre, Institute of Education, London. Retrieved from http://imerc.org

Welch, G. F., Himonides, E., Saunders, J., Papageorgi, I., Rinta, T., Preti, C., et al. (in press). Researching the first year of the National Singing Programme *Sing Up* in England: An initial impact evaluation. *Psychomusicology: Music Mind and Brain.*

Welch, G. F., Himonides, E., Saunders, J., Papageorgi, I., Vraka, M., Preti, C., et al. (2009). *Researching the second year of the National Singing Programme in England: An ongoing impact evaluation of children's singing behaviour and identity.* Institute of Education, University of London, pp 95. ISBN 978-1-905351-10-7

Welch, G. F., & Howard, D. (2002). Gendered voice in the cathedral choir. *Psychology of Music, 30*(1), 102–120.

Welch, G. F., Sergeant, D. C., & White, P. (1996). The singing competences of five-year-old developing singers. *Bulletin of the Council for Research in Music Education, 127*, 155–162.

Welch, G. F., Sergeant, D. C., & White, P. (1997). Age, sex and vocal task as factors in singing 'in-tune' during the first years of schooling. *Bulletin of the Council for Research in Music Education, 133*, 153–160.

Chapter 4
Male Choral Singing in Canada: A Waning Culture

Adam Adler

As social trends such as secularization, population mobilization and diversification changed Canada's social landscape, our educational landscape was also being drastically reshaped. Since the end of World War II, vocal music education has become increasingly rare, pushed out by the middle-class popularity of instrumental music education. Under the auspices of neo-conservative governments in the 1990s and early 2000s, curricular reform and restructuring combined with "crisis education" and its ensuing focus on literacy and numeracy have rapidly removed options for students, and drastically limited their access to arts education. Private-sector endeavors such as community children's choirs have thrived as parents seek to maintain singing in their children's lives, but such opportunities are not always open to all, and in many cases males are left out.

Fewer Canadian children are singing, and as a corollary, even fewer males are singing. A glimpse of the Canadian choral landscape now shows community and church choirs struggling to find male singers. These aging bastions of choral music making are the last vestiges of the liberal "baby boom" years, and as their singers age and retire and are not replaced by a new generation, we stand to lose choral singing as a component of Canadian musical culture. It may be that we have less than a generation to address this trend; it may also be that it is already too late. However, particular successes in the re-establishment of vocal music in the private sector by organizations which are focused on the recruitment and retention of male singers show that a turnaround may be possible with appropriate will and goodwill. Strategies for the regeneration of choral singing for males in Canada are discussed.

A. Adler (✉)
Nipissing University, North Bay, ON P1B 8L7, Canada
e-mail: adama@nipissingu.ca

4.1 Prelude

When I was going through elementary school in the 1970s and 1980s in the new suburbs north of Toronto, everyone sang – boys as well as girls, at least in elementary school. We sang in class, urged on by enthusiastic classroom teachers playing autoharps and ukuleles, and we produced musical shows in which everyone participated, and then some that were auditioned for the extra-keen singers. At Christmas, we gathered in the gymnasium to sing carols and Christmas songs read off the wall from badly scrawled overhead transparencies. As one of the few Jewish students in my school, I missed the significance of a lot of the lyrics of those carols, but certainly singing with hundreds of other people was a great thrill, a feeling of unquestioned community, a sharing of massed musical expression and fun. In middle school singing became extra-curricular and self-selective as curricular classroom music became entirely instrumental (I learned to play the saxophone), and singing was relegated to the spring musical show – Joseph and the Amazing Technicolour Dreamcoat. I was Benjamin AND Potiphar, and I had a terrible crush on the grade eight boy who played Joseph. Thinking back, I can't imagine that Potiphar's line "Joseph I'll see you rot in jail..." carried much authority or rage sung in my declining treble, but it was certainly my perception that I was outstanding. Then in high school, a complete absence of singing for several years as our only choice was continued instrumental music, until the school had the vision to employ a vocal/choral teacher in my grade 11 year. In our founding vocal/choral class and school choir the girls outnumbered the boys two to one, but we never had a shortage of boys and our recruiting performances at our feeder elementary schools were always very well received.

What I didn't know at the time was that we were singing in the waning days of school choral culture in Canada – the final days signalling the decline of singing in schools, and with it opportunities for males to engage in singing as children, as adolescents, an onwards for life.

4.2 Male Choral Singing in Canada: The Years Following Confederation

By the second half of the nineteenth century, choral music had become a popular form of music making in Canada; this popularity continued following the first World War (Kallmann et al., 2010, p. 1). The influence of the Protestant churches was significant in this movement. Singing formed a part of church citizenship, its function being both to facilitate worship and to bind together denominational communities through music, performing the function of replicating culture within those communities, a practice which Dunsmore (1998, p. 5) describes as "denominational utilitarianism". Photographs of church choirs of the time show thriving, gender- and age-balanced membership, singing for congregations that were similarly balanced and full.

From these church choirs emerged larger community choral groups or "singing societies" in the tradition of the British "choral society" that could perform large-scale oratorios and other large Baroque, Classical and Romantic choral works, as well as the generous body of new British and Canadian choral repertoire that facilitated the rise of large choirs in the productive period following World War I. Frequently named after well known composers such as Elgar, Bach, Handel, and Mendelssohn, many of these choirs remain in operation to the present day. Just as men's choirs in late nineteenth century and early twentieth century Iceland, Finland and Sweden provided a venue for the establishment and transmission of a national and cultural identity in the face of the move to independence from occupying powers (Faulkner & Davidson, 2006; Durrant, 2005), in the still new Dominion of Canada, these choral societies facilitated the establishment of a new, distinctly Canadian "creative class" (Bartel, 2004) within the British-Canadian choral tradition. As venues for the establishment and replication of dominant cultural norms, choral societies carried significant social capital.

During these early days of choral singing in Canada, a tradition of male voice, "homo-social" (Faulkner & Davidson, 2006) choral singing groups emerged. Several of these groups have received entries in the Encyclopedia of Music in Canada.[1] The Arion Male Voice Choir was founded in 1893 in Victoria, British Columbia as a male voice choir "devoted to the singing of secular music" (Reid Lower & Bowman, 2010, p. 1). While the group's membership has fluctuated over the years since its founding, it has continued to operate without interruption to the present day.[2] The Winnipeg Male Chorus is a similar example: Founded in 1916 as a male quartet by members of the "Men's Music Club" in Winnipeg, Manitoba, its membership grew to 46 by 1918 (Gibson, 2010, p. 1). Membership declined to 30 by 1960 when, having broken ties with the Men's Music Club, it was renamed the "Metro Male Chorus"; this was changed to its present name in 1974.[3] A more specifically culturally- and ethnically-oriented choir, The St. David's Welsh Male Voice Choir was first organized in 1908 by new Welsh immigrants to Edmonton, Alberta. Since its founding, this group has undergone a number of reorganizations and amalgamations with other, smaller Welsh male choirs, but it has retained its cultural focus on the performance of Welsh equal-voice music (McIntosh, 2010, p. 1).

Singing in harmony is described as "not only a metaphor for human relationships, but an essential and enriching way of relating to others, fulfilling basic needs for vocal and social connectedness" (Faulkner & Davidson, 2006, abstract) and as way to "derive satisfaction from social approval and acceptance" (Durrant, 2005, p. 92). It is also described as a multi-dimensional experience with both aural/physical and social components (Dolloff, 1999, p. 19). These early male voice choirs provided a socially acceptable and culturally valued way for men to share a form of communication and connection that was more subtle and intimate than their regular lives may have afforded.

Like their men's choir counterparts in nineteenth and early twentieth century Scandinavia, these ensembles provided a venue of common interest for their members; specifically, making music and socializing with other men, within a shared activity that reinforced cultural values and, in the case of the St. David's Welsh Male Voice Choir, also facilitated the maintaining of minority cultural, linguistic and national/ethnic identity within a country of multi-national immigrants dominated by (English and Scottish) British culture. Faulkner and Davidson (2006) state, "When singing in harmony in a large collective, singers appear to make sense of themselves and their place in the world by recognizing their own voices and the different voices of those around them and by collaborating to find an ideal vocal and social state" (p. 235). During the tumultuous years of World War I, Canada first asserted its nationhood through violent sacrifice of many of our young men on the battlefields of Europe. In the years that followed, male voice choirs became a peaceful venue for Canadian men to continue to define domestically their individual, masculine and class-oriented identities.

4.3 Choral Growth During and After World War II

> [F]or most of the twentieth century, choral music education programs were provided by the school for those interested in taking the course, by the church for those with a connection to that faith, or by ethnic communities for immigrants to Canada who chose to stay connected to their culture (Beynon, 2003, p. 29).

In the years following World War II, a growing economy combined with waves of immigration fuelled the growth of cities and suburbs and the building of new schools. From the post-war "baby boom" years through to the period of liberal cultural expansion 1960s and 1970s, music was seen as an integral part of schooling. To support its delivery, music training was an essential part of elementary school teacher preparation, and new teaching methods using recorders and ukeleles, Orff and Kodály became popular. New degree programs in music education at the larger universities provided specialist teachers for growing secondary school music programs that diversified to include new band and orchestral programs as well as vocal music. At the same time, in the absence of soldiering, curricular and extra-curricular sports resumed a role as a masculine proving ground in school (Adler & Harrison, 2004, p. 276) and became a dominant focus for the efforts and engagements of male students. However, while music was offered as a subject for credit, there remained an extrinsic value to the subject and motivation to enrol. Since students sang as part of general music education in elementary school, and since it was common for students to be able to pursue multiple option subjects in every year of secondary school, the "continuous vocal music student" was a reality.

Waves of immigration which had begun in the late nineteenth century increased following the conflicts of the First and Second World Wars, redefining the cultural makeup of Canada – particularly in the large urban areas of Toronto, Montreal, and Vancouver. Amidst increased geographic mobility, rapid urbanization and refocus on the nuclear family, the idea of "the community for life" – an individual's participation and engagement as investment and citizenship in one's larger familial and local geographic community – came into decline. In a more diverse, secular, mobile and nuclear family-centred Canadian society, not only were there fewer people attending church, but also an increasing percentage of the population who, not being Christian, wouldn't attend anyways. This meant fewer people learning to sing, or having opportunities to sing chorally through worship.

The continued public drive to sing communally found its resolution through secular community choirs that developed to meet the need for group singing as recreation as well as continued musical and social engagement. It is during this period that many of our urban community choirs were founded. At the peak of this choral growth was the formation of Canada's first professional choirs. The Festival Singers of Toronto were formed in 1954 by conductor Elmer Iseler; they assumed professional status in 1968 as the Festival Singers of Canada (Kallmann, Riddell, & Bowman, 2010), and disbanded in 1979 – 1 year after declining to renew Iseler's contract.[4] Iseler went on to found the Elmer Iseler Singers in 1979 (Norman & Nygaard King, 2010). The Vancouver Chamber Choir was founded by conductor Jon Washburn in 1971.[5] The Elora Festival Singers was founded in 1980 by conductor Noel Edison as the "principal choral ensemble of the Elora Festival" and was incorporated in 1992 as a separate organization.[6] While no doubt these new community and professional choirs all had to do their share of recruiting, the fact that they were able to form demonstrates two things: First, that there were enough individuals who wanted to sing together in the community to form viable choirs, and that there were enough trained male choral singers to sustain the founding of these groups.

During the post-World War II "baby boom" years a new growth of male voice choirs occurred, associated with employment in male-dominated sectors such as industry and public service. Like their counterparts of the early twentieth century, the men who formed these groups shared socio-economic status, but in this case as primarily "working class" collectives whose common links were the industries and professions for which they worked. These men came together amidst a growing movement of unionization and collective bargaining, and a need to foster unity and fellowship. Their founding of musical ensembles as the public face of their workers' collectives might be compared to the nationalist male choral movements in nineteenth century Finland and Iceland.

The Schneider Male Chorus (as presently named) was founded as the Schneider Men's Chorus 1938 by employees of the J. M. Schneider Meat Packing Company in Kitchener-Waterloo, Ontario (Countryman & Bowman, 2010). A more profession-oriented industrial chorus, The Toronto Men Teacher's Choir formed in 1941 and had a successful run of national and international performances until it disbanded in 1976.[7] The Dofasco Male Chorus was formed in Hamilton in 1945[8] by a group of steel workers who enjoyed singing. Some police associations also developed male voice choirs, early examples of which include the Toronto Police Association Male Chorus (1966[9]) and the Winnipeg Police Male Voice Choir (1973). This latter male-voice police choir became a mixed-voiced choir in 1992 "to greatly enhance its overall appearance and sound".[10] While the move of this group to a mixed-voice format certainly brought greater recognition to the gender diversity of the Winnipeg police force, it could also be evidence of an effort to bolster a declining membership of male singers.

Best known of all of Canada's "working man's" choirs is Men of the Deeps, an organization of singing Cape Breton coal miners and retirees that was formed in 1966. This choir has achieved widespread popularity with "ordinary" Canadians with whom their "just-plain-folks" authenticity resonates (Norman & King, 2010), and with substantial media support from the Canadian Broadcasting Corporation and other television and radio networks they have been able to share their music across the country. With the later decline of the mining industry on which the economy of Cape Breton was dependent, Men of the Deeps remains as a symbol of times past, their musical efforts now largely serving to preserve and memorialize a rapidly disappearing way of life.

Barbershop singing made its way from the United States during the "barbership revival" years during World War II, with the first Canadian Chapter of the Barbershop Harmony Society (BHS) chartered in Windsor, Ontario in 1944 (Poole, 2010). As the popularity of this a cappella choral art form spread through recordings and radio, new Barbershop choruses spread across the country; the BHS is now represented in Canada by four large regional districts. Part of the success of this type of singing may be attributed to the element of competition which differentiates it from its less competitive community choir counterparts. In the absence of a national competitive choral culture, "inter-choral competitive structures" such as those built into the Barbershop movement serve as motivators for participation and as a source of "peak experience" (Faulkner & Davidson, 2006, p. 231) which can enhance the appeal for some participants. Since it is common for Barbershop repertoire to be learned by rote, this genre also enables individuals to learn to sing chorally to very high levels of performance without the need for formal musical training.

4.4 Changing Social Capital and the Decline of Choral Education in the 1980s and 1990s

While today very little remains of vocal music education in Canadian schools, particularly at the middle and secondary school level, evidence remains of the years when vocal music was delivered consistently as a curricular subject. In Ontario, music teachers are certified at the intermediate (grades seven–ten) and senior (grades eleven and twelve) levels to teach either "instrumental" or "vocal" music. From the late 1970s through the 1990s, a shift occurred towards instrumental (band) music as the dominant paradigm in middle years schooling. This was the culmination of a trend of program growth that began following World War II, supported by the greater availability instrumental music educators and the increased prosperity that supported the purchasing of instruments and the building of purpose-built facilities. Instrumental music became a popular paradigm with parents as it facilitated pubic performance and competition, and because its first emergence in urban, middle-class schools served as a symbol for middle class education and social status, regardless of whether it contributed to students' post-secondary education plans. Instrumental music education is/was also popular among male students because of its perceived implementality (tool usage) that symbolically reinforces masculinity in a way that vocal music does not (Adler & Harrison, 2004, p. 279). Since the perceived social capital for participation in instrumental music surpassed that of vocal music, it was easy to allow vocal music to be supplanted.

Beatty (2001a, p. 40) found that while 77.2% of Ontario elementary schools had choirs, less than 39.9% of students at those schools were participating in them. According to Vince (2005, p. 198), by 2005 vocal music was not occurring in many elementary schools. However, even today at the middle school level, music classes which are not band-centred may still remain labelled as "vocal music" even if no singing occurs in the method of delivery. The term "vocal" has come to mean the absence of band instruments, rather than a focus on singing as the primary vehicle to the development of musicianship. This was the case in the last school in which this author taught in the late 1990s and early 2000s; a suburban middle school built in 1969 with both "instrumental" and "vocal" music "on the books" but with the vocal music delivered in recent history as "general" music, or rather as a more passive "music appreciation". Long-serving teachers in that school could recall that in the 1970s and early 1980s, vocal music there was still singing-based, and that students produced a high level of choral music which involved boys and girls to similar levels of participation. This paradigm had become eroded over time as the hiring focus had been placed on the instrumental classes,[11] leaving the vocal music to be taught by non-singers who, while possibly well-trained instrumental musicians, were not "comfortable" trying to get middle school students to sing. This phenomenon occurs commonly in jurisdictions such as the province of British Columbia that require elementary music to be delivered by generalist teachers (Hanley, 1998, 2005), a group for whom singing often poses great risk and anxiety. Further, given that the majority of teachers in elementary schools across Canada are female[12] (Gosse, 2009, p. 1), even for boys who are fortunate enough to be taught music by a specialist, there remains an absence of competent, confident male singing role models.

As instrumental music education came to dominate in middle schools, it also became the dominant paradigm in secondary schools. Students who have only ever been exposed to instrumental music, and who have not had positive crystallizing experiences in singing are not going to be as likely to choose vocal music as their arts credit option at the secondary level. In Ontario, this was further impacted by curricular reform (Beatty, 2001c) that lead to the introduction in 1998 of a more utilitarian, "no-frills" provincial curriculum that removed prerequisites for some option subjects and allowed students to skip grades in music in a way which was not permitted in the "academic" subjects. Allowing students to skip grades meant fewer sections of music required and fewer teachers available to teach those sections, and where students numbers fell below a critical mass, schools rapidly lost their vocal sections altogether. By the late 1990s, it was not unusual to find entire districts with no curricular vocal music on offer, and to find the few remaining secondary vocal programs consisting of a single, multi-grade class in all but the strongest programs. Where vocal music did exist at the secondary level, it was more likely than instrumental music to be extra-curricular (Cooper, 1989, p. 52; Beatty, 2001b, p. 32; Beynon, 2003, p. 30), thereby losing academic credit as a remaining motivator.

Exceptions to this phenomenon occurred where there was/is cultural capital to maintaining singing in school. A prime example can be found in the schools of Newfoundland, where singing has fared better than in most other provinces. Newfoundland and Labrador joined Canada as a province in 1949; citizens born prior to that date hold both British Territorial and Canadian citizenship. The assembly and singing of a "canon" of popular cultural songs, which according to Rosenberg (1994) was later called "folk" following the Folk Revival of the 1940s, served to maintain the national unity and identity of Newfoundlanders amidst their new place in the Canadian confederation; singing "was also an activity that could enhance their social status at parties with visitors from outside Newfoundland" (Rosenberg, 1994, p. 3). Following the collapse of the cod fishery in 1992, the tradition of singing songs based in a culture of fishing has served to memorialize Newfoundland culture – to ensure that Newfoundlanders remembered who they were (Jones, 2001), much as the previously mentioned role of Men of the Deeps has served for the lost mining culture of Cape Breton, Nova Scotia. Over the past several decades this body of songs has been taken up by a number of popular, all-male Newfoundland folk music groups such as Great Big Sea and The Irish Descendents, who have provided positive and popular role models and social capital to male singing in Newfoundland, particularly in all-male vocal groups.

Until 1998, a tradition of denominational schooling existed in Newfoundland in which singing formed part of regular school life and served to replicate denominational culture (Barresi & Olson, 1994, cited in Dunsmore, 1998, p. 5); this normalized singing as a part of school, community and denominational citizenship for students within those schools. A provincial K-12 music curriculum has supported the singing of Newfoundland folk songs at all levels (Adams, 1999). The creation of an undergraduate degree in music education at Memorial University of Newfoundland has supported the delivery of this curriculum by specialist music teachers (Dunsmore, 1998, p. 7). This author's observations of school choirs in Newfoundland indicates that there is a healthy population of boys singing through secondary school in both mixed and male-voice choirs.

Beatty (2001b, p. 37) identified a decline in enrolment in secondary school music, which Vince (2005, p. 215) described as the loss of an early training ground for band musicians,[13] with students increasingly dependent upon private studio study as a route to music study at the university level. Vince (2005, p. 203) also found a decreasing percentage of male participants in secondary school and tertiary music. Since private studio study requires from parents both financial support and a value system in which it is important for children to be studying a particular instrument, and since vocal study is perceived as a feminine endeavour (Adler & Harrison, 2004, p. 282) this route has limited such preparatory opportunities in singing for males.

In a culture where often the only models of male singing are provided by popular culture and the cult of reality television shows such as American Idol and Canadian Idol, the inclination to study privately is more likely to be motivated by a desire to become the country's next "pop" music star than to develop the sort of technique and musicianship needed to pursue study at the post-secondary level. While the "idol" goal certainly carries social capital, it is realistically achievable by a very limited number of males who are graced by high tenor voices, natural musicality, charisma and good looks – certainly not the profile of the average Canadian male singer.

Certainly in our university music degree programs, where for several decades female singers have outnumbered male singers, the decline of male singers comes as no surprise. It is common in Canadian university music programs to have a women's choir that houses the extra female singers in order to maintain an effective balance in their mixed choirs. Unlike our university counterparts in the USA, where men's "glee clubs" are common and well subscribed, men's choirs as stand-alone credit ensembles are rare in Canadian universities. This phenomenon may be due to the fact that, unlike in the American universities, participation in Canadian university choirs for degree credit is often limited to students in music degree programs; in essence, a distillation of the chorally privileged from urban and suburban centres where our few secondary vocal programs have managed to sustain. Instead, most non-music majors who wish to sing must do so in recreational campus community choirs, which appear to be more effective in maintaining a gender balance – particularly as these groups are able to draw in the male singers who have chosen more traditionally "masculine" academic routes such as engineering and sciences. A few smaller universities have united these two endeavours, and offer only a campus community choir for both recreation and for credit – perhaps out of necessity in order to be able to offer any mixed for-credit choir at all, but certainly to the advantage of their non-music students of both sexes.

4.5 Into the Twenty-First Century: A Shift in Youth Choral Culture

As music provision and particularly singing education has declined in elementary schools, and as fewer children are seeking opportunities to learn to sing through faith-based choirs, children's choral singing has increasingly moved into the private sphere with "an unprecedented increase in the development of community-based programs, especially choral programs for children and youth" (Beynon, 2003, p. 29). Beynon explains that these community children's choirs are often directed by school music teachers, who, like many of their students, seek to achieve musically in the community what they are not able to achieve in schools. While the development of community children's choirs has provided both students and teachers with otherwise unavailable musical opportunities, this movement also brings with it problems of cultural, fiscal and musical accessibility that can leave males out.

Since children's enrolment in community children's choirs is a parental decision, participation is influenced by multiple familial factors. Guèvremont, Findlay, and Kohen (2006, p. 65) state, "The likelihood that children will take part in organized extracurricular activities varies by factors such as their age and gender, family income, and family structure (one- or two-parent family)." Participation is first limited to children of parents who can afford to enrol their children in pay-for-service activities, and also to those whose parents have the time and means to transport their children to rehearsals and performances; children in single parent families with lower incomes are particularly disadvantaged in this regard. Since parental motivation to enroll their children in community choirs is influenced by their own experiences and values, it is logical that parents who themselves had positive crystallizing experiences in choirs may value this as a personal and cultural growth activity for their own children, while conversely other parents' lack of exposure may mean that choir participation is not a consideration for their children.

Recent Statistics Canada data shows that from ages 6 through 17, boys are less likely than girls to be enrolled in non-sports activities such as those involving the arts (Guèvremont et al., 2006, p. 66); this gender gap grows from 8.9% at ages 6–9, to 14.8% at ages 10–13, to 20.4% at ages 14–17 (Guèvremont et al., 2006, p. 67). The same statistics show that boys are more likely than girls to be enrolled in sport s activities. Eder and Kinney (1995) found that middle school males experience greater status gains through extracurricular participation, while Parker (1996) discussed sports as a proving ground for masculine identities. Adler and Harrison (2004) explain that, since choral singing does not reinforce aspects of identity which are socially constructed as masculine, it is less likely to be viewed as a worthy investment for boys; rather, parents are more likely to enrol their sons in sports activities which afford opportunities for competition, implementality, physical athleticism and aggression.

While community children's choirs provide venues for learning and growth through choral singing, greater priority is sometimes given to the level of musical polish they can achieve than to the experience of the participants. One way to support this priority is to audition for entry, which Beynon (2003) explains is within the purview of ensembles in the private sector. Auditioning can disadvantage boys in several ways: First, because boys typically find their "singing voices" later than girls, and are often less adept at singing because they have not been encouraged to sing through play in the way that girls are from a young age. Given the disappearance of music and singing education in Canadian elementary schools, many boys lack the support to develop their singing voices, as well as opportunities for positive crystallizing experiences which could incline them to pursue singing as an extracurricular activity. As a result, boys enter auditions as generally less experienced singers than girls. Further, since the perceived *identity liability* (Adler, 2002, p. 54) presented by auditions via the risk of admission failure and subsequent loss of self- and social-esteem (Adler & Harrison, 2004, p. 286) may outweigh the perceived *identity capital* (Coté, 1990; Evans & Eder, 1992) associated with membership in that activity, boys may be disinclined to even consider an audition.

In an effort to create ensembles with a well-balanced and blended sound, and to facilitate repertoire choices, some Canadian community children's choirs operate solely as treble voice ensembles. This format disadvantages boys when their changing voices no longer contribute to the ensembles' blended treble sound. Examples can be seen in some of our highest profile children's choir organizations – The Toronto Children's Chorus (Toronto, Ontario) and Shalloway[14] (St. John's, Newfoundland). In the Toronto Children's Chorus the boys have traditionally been dismissed when their voices change, while the girls are allowed to continue their membership through secondary school. In Shalloway, changing- and changed-voice boys are permitted to remain in the organization and move up to the senior group, but they must sing in their falsetto because the ensemble's repertoire is in multiple treble parts. The Winnipeg Boys' Choir successfully operates as a treble boys' choir, but does not offer opportunities for boys to continue singing after their voices change.

Because of the high profiles these groups enjoy, their retention practices can send problematic messages to their members and to potential singers in the broader community: First, that singing is an activity appropriate only for children and women, and is to be avoided by males once they reach adolescence and adulthood. Second, that the changed male voice is in some way damaged or inferior, not worthy of sharing, and in some cases needing to be suppressed and denied. This latter case is tantamount to assigning or conditioning boys into beliefs that are akin to the psychological pathology of puberphonia – a treatable condition in which some boys maintain their treble voices into adolescence through the use of falsetto, in response to their denial of the physical and/or psycho-social aspects of puberty and maturation (Edwards, 2007).

The practice of running a children's or "youth" choir as an exclusive treble choir creates a cyclical, self-fulfilling pattern: Where there are too few boys with changed voices, it is difficult to program repertoire, challenging for small sections of changed-voice boys to learn and hold their parts, and virtually impossible to achieve a good choral balance. Additionally, the learning needs of boys during the voice change can set them back developmentally while girls continue to improve their vocal technique and skill level, creating a gap in musical learning needs within the ensemble. Choral directors may therefore need to decide whether to address the needs of the many over the needs of the few[15] in order to facilitate a musically successful and aesthetically superior outcome that will support retention, recruitment and concert attendance. However, by organizing as a treble-only ensemble, the opportunity to develop the voices of male choristers is lost, and potential male singers may be dissuaded from joining a choir in which they do not see themselves reflected and valued. This may certainly be the case for Shalloway, given evidence of successful male-voice ensembles in secondary schools within their catchment. By denying adolescent boys a continuing and authentic singing space, they are doubly robbed of voice – actual as well as personal/metaphorical, and as some go on to pursue other endeavors that present greater identity capital, they may never return to singing.

Happily, a number of successful boys' choir organizations[16] have been established across the country: The British Columbia Boys' Choir (Vancouver and Burnaby), the Calgary Boys' Choir (Alberta), the Grand Prairie Boys' Choir (Alberta), and the Amabile Choirs of London (Ontario). These ensembles are helping to renew male singing in Canada by offering welcoming environments which nurture male singing throughout their development; specifically, by offering ensembles for unchanged, changing, and changed-voice males. These groups succeed because they recognize singing as a gendered and socially constructed phenomenon, wherein boys' singing in mixed-sex contexts can carry problematic meanings and personal-social implications that can negatively influence recruitment and retention. By operating as boys-only ensembles, they create a unique sense of belonging and ownership for their members in the same way that sports teams can, while providing a cooperative and non-competitive atmosphere which is desired by many boys (Adler, 2002). By offering separate ensembles appropriate to each stage of boys' vocal development, these organizations support boys' unique vocal/developmental and music literacy-based pedagogical needs.

> The history of the Amabile Choirs of London offers a particularly unique demonstration of how choral organizations can meet the needs of male singers. This organization began in 1985 as the Amabile Youth Singers, a choir for girls and young women aged 12–23 under the direction of John Barron and Brenda Zadorsky. A treble boys' choir was added in 1990 under the direction of Carol Beynon and Bevan Keating (Nygaard King, 2010). As the boys' entered adolescence, their positive experience and ownership of their ensemble lead them to demand a continued singing space; the Amabile Young Men's Ensemble was formed to meet this need. Similarly, as a choir for male alumni of the Amabile Young Men's Ensemble, Primus: The Amabile Men's Choir,[17] has furthered the goal of male-singing-for-life in the London community.

4.6 The Changing Canadian Choral Scene

At the beginning of the twenty-first century, many of the traditional bastions of male choral singing in Canada are in decline. Increased globalization and consequent movement of jobs to cheaper, "offshore" sites has resulted in a steady decline in the primary and secondary industries around which our industrial choruses were centred. The increased instability in industry and mobility of industrial labour has presented challenges to renewing and sustaining a critical membership in these groups, leaving them with an aging and declining membership who perform a static repertoire of songs sung by memory.

While many of our choral societies remain, some are failing to renew. Their aging membership and a classical repertoire that fails to connect with younger singers and the limited, "popular" music being learned by rote in schools, and in the absence of a culture of inter-ensemble competition, these large groups offer decreasing cultural and social capital. Some exceptions to this trend have occurred, however. In large, urban centres, ensembles such as the Toronto Mendelssohn Choir have maintained long-established relationships with the middle-class arts communities for whom their work continues to hold social and artistic capital that facilitates recruitment as well as financial support.

Similarly, community and church choirs are aging and retiring – the waning musical bounty of singers who were chorally educated in churches and schools during the artistically generous "baby boom" years. Given the best hoped for ratio of two female singers to each male singer in these groups, as memberships decline, the bass and tenor sections will fall below critical mass before the soprano and alto sections do. With a lack of critical mass in the tenor and bass sections, it becomes more challenging for amateur, non-reading male singers to learn and maintain their parts, while the prospect of performing in more exposed sections also makes singing less "safe" and socially desirable. For choral conductors, trying to program repertoire that can be successfully performed by the remaining balance of their choirs becomes a challenge. Their repertoire may be thinner in texture and less musically challenging, with condensed "baritone" parts that suit neither tenors nor basses. While greater musical success might be achieved by moving to an all-female membership, the general participatory tenets of community choral music making would not usually permit such a move; nor would it be desirable, as the likelihood of restoring a treble community choir to mixed format through future recruitment is slim.

Some community and church choirs attract younger male singers by offering choral scholarships or paid section lead positions, but in any discussion of sustainable choral communities these individuals cannot be considered among the numbers of the permanent voluntary membership. In any case, the total availability of male singers in any population centre is limited, and competition for their services is great; choirs must be creative in their recruitment efforts. In 2009, the Jubilate Chamber Choir of Vancouver found themselves in the common situation of being down to their last two tenors. They embarked on a recruiting campaign in which the remaining male singers took to the streets in tuxedos and waived recruiting signs at passing motorists, carrying the message "Free: the Tenors!" along with their choir website address. Interested tenors were able to join the choir with their membership fee waived (Bellett, 2009). This campaign gained the ensemble considerable attention in the local and national media, which further aided their recruiting efforts while also providing positive promotion of the organization.

In contrast to the decline of mixed-voice community and church choirs, Barbershop choirs have held on with some degree of success. Since Barbershop choirs have traditionally recruited members from an older demographic, they may have become better at renewing their membership by focusing their recruiting efforts on this specific group. The rote-learning nature of this choral paradigm which makes it possible for members with no previous musical experience to participate, and a focus on regional, provincial, national and international competition have further facilitated recruitment.

A more recent emergence on the Canadian choral scene over the past decade, the College A Cappella movement has made late inroads to university campuses in Toronto and Montreal. First emerging in the early 1990s in the USA, small, student-directed vocal ensembles perform arrangements of primarily "pop" music, often with a solo line and the remainder of the ensemble singing instrumental lines, alternating with tight, close-harmony singing and often performed with a hint of comedy. Music is arranged for equal-voice as well as mixed-voice groups, with equal-voice groups appearing to be the most popular, possibly owing to the closer harmonic interactions of the voices. By contrast, the primary growth of these ensembles in Canada appears to be of the mixed-voice sort. This paradigm might be viewed as a more contemporary relation to Barbershop or Jazz ensembles, in which the repertoire and arrangement styles are less appealing to many young people. It is common for American university campuses to have one or more groups, often extra-curricular but comprised of both music- and non-music majors – an excellent opportunity for males to sing in a highly socially valued venue. Whereas a well developed network that encourages state- and national-level competition provides further energy to this paradigm in the USA, in Canada a more cooperative scene appears to be developing. Lacking the well-established inter-collegiate network that exists in the USA, our a cappella groups have become effective self-promoters at the local level, with an annual Acappellooza concert featuring multiple ensembles drawing large audiences (Terauds, 2008).

Beginning in the early 1990s, a new wave of equal-voice community choirs emerged across the country. The Victoria Scholars was formed in 1993 by graduates of Toronto's St. Michael's Choir School.[18] Under the direction of Dr. Jerzy Cichocki, the Victoria Scholars began as a male-voice ensemble devoted to music of the Renaissance, but has since expanded its repertoire to include the entire "classical" canon as well as newly composed art music.[19] Originally a choir of 24 voices, the Victoria Scholars' membership has persevered with an entirely volunteer membership despite the effects of the "missing men" phenomenon that has resulted in periodic decline.[20] One reason for this trend in Toronto may be that the large number of community choirs there has placed a significant strain on the limited number of available male singers.

Chor Leoni Men's Choir formed in Vancouver, British Columbia in 1992 under the direction of Diane Loomer.[21] Originally founded as a choir of 20 voices, they have since grown to 54 voices (Church, 2010) and achieved national and international renown as both a touring and recording ensemble. Newman Sound Men's Choir[22] formed in St. John's, Newfoundland in 2005 under the direction of Kellie Walsh. With a membership incorporating male singers from across St. John's society, this ensemble has in a very short time achieved huge success at the provincial level through its performance of a broad and appealing repertoire. Both Chor Leoni and Newman Sound are also unique in having female-voiced choral counterparts under the same conductors (Elektra Women's Choir[23] and Ladycove Women's Choir[24] respectively). These choral pairs are in essence split choral organizations based on the highly desirable aesthetic of equal-voice close harmony, and as "homo-social" (Faulkner & Davidson, 2006) singing organizations they provide constructive venues for men (in the case of Newman Sound) to work with each other in a shared activity that is qualitatively different from their day-to-day lives and interactions.

Several other attributes have set these men's choirs apart from their equal-voice predecessors: First, their dedication to the performance of a more diverse and challenging repertoire than traditional Barbershop or community men's choirs have sung; Second, their striving for exceptional music-making at an otherwise semi-professional level. These attributes have made them attractive to singers of all ages, and in particular to young adults who wish to hone their singing skills despite pursuing non-musical careers, and have thus supported recruitment and retention and a generally younger membership than is typically found in traditional Barbershop or community men's choirs. Additionally, these groups appear to draw their membership from a broader socio-economic spectrum than did their historical predecessors.

Perhaps Canada's most successful and well sustaining male choral community exists in the GLBT (gay, lesbian, bisexual and transgender and allies) choruses that have formed in virtually every major Canadian city, linked to others in North America and around the globe by the international organization GALA Choruses. These unique choirs provide opportunities for members of the GLBT community to come together in a shared activity that is musical, social, and political in a constructive, non-sexualized environment, that provides an expressive voice to their members. As social/political entities, GLBT choirs positively increase the visibility of their communities by advocating while entertaining. A unique body of GLBT-centred repertoire that includes art music as well as comic and novelty music allows choirs to express themselves beyond the traditional, heteronormative choral literature.

These groups are as diverse as the GLBT community itself, with opportunities for singing in mixed and/or equal-voice choirs, as well as in groups with varying degrees of musical/artistic or social/political focus. The most prolific GLBT groups in Canada are the male-voice choirs in which, unlike their community choir counterparts, there does not appear to be a shortage of singing men; this may be facilitated by their recruiting from groups that are underserved by traditional community choirs. Like their Barbershop counterparts, GLBT choirs in Canada commonly allow for a broad range of musical expertise, while providing their members opportunities to learn from skilled conductors. As music education and the teaching of musical literacy have declined in our schools, this open membership aspect is increasingly important in facilitating participation in our community ensembles.

4.7 Choral Singing for Males, Choral Singing for All

Looking forward, prospects for a sustainable Canadian choral culture are bleak. With the decline of music education provision, the disappearance of singing and a focus on instrumental music in our schools, few opportunities exist for children to experience crystallizing experiences with singing that could motivate them to pursue singing opportunities in higher education and as recreation as adults. Private children's choirs offer excellent musical opportunities for their participants, but many do not welcome or support boys' membership or development. For the average adult Canadian male with little to no music education and few if any positive experiences in singing, neither the inclination nor opportunities to engage in singing are likely. While Barbershop and GLBT choirs continue to recruit successfully, these paradigms serve very specific musical and social communities that may not be attractive to the broader population. Musical success is becoming increasingly elusive for our aging mixed community choirs as they fail to replenish their membership and struggle to compete for male singers. Within one or two generations, our mixed community choirs could fail, and a generation of primarily female engagement in youth singing among a socio-economically distilled population will leave us with only a few, privileged women's choirs in the community and post-secondary institutions. Canada will no longer be a choral country.

Some organizations, however, are succeeding in slowing this trend. A small new wave of male-voice community choirs is striving to engage Canadian men in singing diverse repertoire at a high standard of performance, becoming popular with audiences and listeners and providing positive modeling for young males. Similarly, a new wave of community boys' choir organizations is providing fun and engaging music learning experiences to the next generation of Canadian male singers. Taking their lead, it may be possible to reverse the decline of choral singing in Canada, to ensure continued engagement by Canadian males in this uniquely personal form of artistic expression. The solution lies in public education. Since public schools provide opportunities and experiences regardless of socio-economic status, familial culture and gender, that can be mandated and guided by public policy, this is our best hope for reviving singing in Canada.

This endeavour would begin with educational policy that recognizes the importance of music education in elementary schools by mandating curricular music time with music education specialists. Music teachers who are comprehensively prepared in instrumental, vocal and elementary/general music would be better able to provide positive and crystallizing singing experiences as part of a comprehensive music education that includes singing and music literacy. Policies and programs that encourage the recruitment and retention of more male elementary music teachers would facilitate much needed male role modelling for boys' musical and singing engagement. The creation of single-sex learning environments – either entire schools, or single-sex classes within mixed schools – would create safe singing spaces for boys that recognize boys' unique personal/social and vocal/developmental needs (Adler, 2002, pp. 279/280). This would increase both engagement in classroom singing as well as in voluntary extra-curricular singing, supporting a positive cycle of musical success and engagement.

At the secondary school level, addressing restrictive educational reforms that have limited students' choices in the arts and discouraged prerequisite coursework, and greater flexibility with class sizes would facilitate opportunities for students who wish to pursue vocal music. Hybrid timetables that allow for non-semestered programs in semestered schools would recognize and support the pedagogical and developmental paths to developing vocal musicianship,[25] and would facilitate continued involvement in choral performance activities. Better preparation of school administrators that includes an understanding of arts curriculum and pedagogy would further support the implementation of these measures.

At the post-secondary level, faculty/school of music ensembles could be made available to all students as an arts credit, regardless of their academic degree stream. Even where this credit is not usable towards a degree, it would provide a concrete incentive and institutional support for university and college students' continued participation in performance activities. Having at least one for-credit choral ensemble with open entry at each university would give all post-secondary students the opportunity to continue to develop their musicianship regardless of their present ability. Where possible, male voice and a cappella groups should be encouraged on university and college campuses to motivate a culture of male singing and to draw attention to performance opportunities for male students.

Finally, in our community children's choirs, which – for the most part, are already providing an exemplary music education to their participants: The maintenance of at least one open-entry ensemble in each organization would provide encouragement for more young people to engage in community singing by reducing the risk of failure and rejection at the outset. While all-female ensembles might be maintained to provide an outlet for girls to continue to develop at their own best level, it remains crucial that opportunities are maintained for boys' continued participation during and after their voice change so that they will see themselves reflected and valued in these organizations and within the activity of choral singing. Government funding might be directed in such a way as to encourage more gender-equitable service by children's choir organizations. The example provided by the Amabile Choirs of London demonstrates the tremendous success that is possible for both boys and girls as well as young adults in nurturing singing-for-life.

With a concerted effort in both private and public domains, it may be possible to sustain choral singing in Canada, and along with it to nurture a culture of male singing across the lifespan.

Notes

1. www.canadianencyclopedia.ca
2. http://www.arionchoir.ca/arionchoir/default.asp
3. http://winnipegmalechorus.org/history.html
4. http://www.thecanadianencyclopedia.com/index.cfm?PgNm=TCE&Params=U1ARTU0001202. No author.
5. http://www.vancouverchamberchoir.com/vancouver_choir.htm
6. http://www.singers.com/choral/elorasingers.html
7. http://www.canadianencyclopedia.ca/index.cfm?PgNm=TCE&Params=U1ARTU0003441. It should be noted that no author is specified for this short entry, however the information appears to be derived from a single primary source, listed as McIver, Murdoch. *A Musical History: The Story of the Toronto Men Teachers' Choir*, priv published (Toronto no date). Another source confirms information regarding the name and dates of one of the ensemble's conductors, Harvey Perrin (1958–1969) (Laughton & Nygaard King, 2010).
8. http://www.dofasco.ca/bins/content_page.asp?cid=315910-410-415
9. http://www.tpa.ca/TPA/TPAMaleChorus.aspx
10. http://www.winnipeg.ca/police/Choir/history.stm
11. It should be noted that in the school board in which this particular school was located, instrumental music was only available to students who could afford to rent or purchase instruments. Since this school was in a largely working- and welfare-class catchment area, only one class in each of grades seven and eight were "instrumental", while the remaining seven or so classes in each grade had received "vocal" music as music appreciation prior to this author's arrival. This socio-economic inequity in terms of the quality of instruction and potential for students' development of musicianship was and remains problematic from a social justice perspective.
12. Gosse states that, according to Statistics Canada data from 2008, there were 108,267 male and 267,788 female teachers in Canada, with only one in ten elementary teachers being male.
13. The focus of Vince's concern on the loss of a preparatory ground for band musicians may be further evidence of the predominance of this paradigm in Canadian music education.

14. Formerly the Newfoundland Symphony Youth Choir.
15. Paraphrased gratuitously from the Paramount Pictures film Star Trek: The Wrath of Khan (1982), Nicholas Meyer, director.
16. http://www.bcboyschoir.org/; http://www.calgaryboyschoir.ab.ca/; http://gpboyschoir.org/; http://www.amabile.com/
17. http://www.amabile.com/
18. St. Michael's Choir School was established as a private Catholic boys' school in Toronto in 1937 "to facilitate the training of a boys' choir for St. Michael's Cathedral" and was later incorporated into the Toronto Catholic District School Board as a choral-specialized public Catholic school. http://www.tcdsb.org/schools/stmichaelchoir.asp.
19. http://www.victoriascholars.ca
20. From a professional correspondence with a member of the Board of Directors of the Victoria Scholars, June 29, 2010.
21. http://chorleoni.org/
22. http://newmansound.ca/
23. http://www.elektra.ca/
24. http://www.ladycove.ca/
25. Semestering – the practice of block scheduling of classes in a single semester, can have devastating impact on music learning and participation. Secondary school students who take a music course in the fall semester may not have music again until spring semester of the following year, leaving an entire year gap between periods of study during which they may unlearn much of what they learned in the first semester. Additionally, students are less likely to continue to participate in co-curricular ensembles during the semesters in which they are not registered for the matching curricular course; this makes it difficult to sustain a co-curricular performance program over the entire academic year.

References

Adams, K. (1999). Like a bridge over troubled waters: The use of folk song in the intermediate music curriculum. *The Canadian Music Educator, 40*(3), 5.

Adler, A. (2002). *A case study of boys' experiences of singing in school*. Doctoral dissertation, University of Toronto, Toronto, Canada

Adler, A., & Harrison, S. (2004). Swinging back the gender pendulum: Addressing boys' needs in music education research and practice. In L. Bartel (Ed.), *Questioning the music education paradigm*. Volume 2 of the biennial series *Research to Practice* (pp. 270–289). Toronto: Canadian Music Educators Association.

Bartel, L. (2004). Another way to justify music education? A look at the rise of the creative class by Richard Florida. *Canadian Music Educator, 46*, 34–35.

Beatty, R. (2001a). The status of music education in Ontario elementary schools. *The Recorder, 43*(4), 38–42.

Beatty, R. (2001b). The status of music education in Ontario Secondary Schools. *The Recorder, 44*(1), 30–34.

Beatty, R. (2001c). Through the looking glass: A reflection of our profession. *The Recorder, 44*(1), 35–39.

Bellett, G. (2009, March 25). Vancouver choir hits streets in search of tenors. *Vancouver Sun*. Retrieved August 13, 2011, from http://www.vancouversun.com

Beynon, C. (2003). The rise and fall and rise... of choral music education in Canada. *Canadian Music Educator, 45*(3), 23–31.

Church, S. (2010). Chor Leoni Men's Choir. *The Encyclopedia of Music in Canada* (Online). Retrieved August 13, 2011, from www.canadianencyclopedia.ca

Cooper, T. (1989). School music teaching in Canada. *Canadian Journal of Research in Music Education, 31*(1), 47–80.

Coté, J. E. (1990). Sociological perspectives on identity formation: The culture-identity link and identity capital. *Journal of Adolescence, 19*, 417–428.

Countryman, J., & Bowman, D. (2010). Kitchener and waterloo. *The Encyclopedia of Music in Canada* (Online). Retrieved August 13, 2011, from www.canadianencyclopedia.ca

Dolloff, L. (1999). The singing classroom: A community of musicians. *Canadian Music Educator, 40*(3), 19–22.

Dunsmore, D. (1998). The effect of government policy on choral music education in Newfoundland and Labrador. *Dialogue in Instrumental Music Education, 22*, 1–15.

Durrant, C. (2005). Shaping identity through choral activity: Singers' and conductors' perceptions. *Research Studies in Music Education, 24*(88), 88–98.

Eder, D., & Kinney, D. A. (1995). The effect of middle school extracurricular activities on adolescents' popularity and peer status. *Youth and Society, 26*(3), 298–324.

Edwards, D. (2007). Puberphonia. *The Canadian Music Educator, 48*(4), 54.

Evans, C., & Eder, D. (1992). No exit: Processes of social isolation in the middle school. *Journal of Contemporary Ethnography, 22*(2), 130–170.

Faulkner, R., & Davidson, J. W. (2006). Men in chorus: Collaboration and competition in homosocial vocal behaviour. *Psychology of Music, 34*(2), 219–237.

Gibson, R. (2010). Winnipeg male voice choir. *The Encyclopedia of Music in Canada* (Online). Retrieved August 13, 2011, from www.canadianencyclopedia.ca

Gosse, D. (2009). *Will any teacher do as long as they are good? Male teacher role models and the interplay of race, sexual orientation, and culture.* Conference proceedings: EDGE conference, St. John's, NL, October 16.

Guèvremont, A., Findlay, L., & Kohen, D. (2006). Organized extracurricular activities of Canadian children and youth. Statistics Canada, Catalogue no. 82-003-XPE. *Health Reports 19*(3), September 2008.

Hanley, B. (1998). Music in elementary teacher education in British Columbia. *Canadian Music Educator, 39*(3), 36.

Hanley, B. (2005). Lifelong learning and music in elementary teacher education. *International Journal of Community Music, Volume B-2005*. Retrieved August 13, 2011, from http://www.intljcm.com/archive.html

Jones, G. (2001). Airs from the rock. *Performing Arts & Entertainment in Canada, 33*(3), 36–39.

Kallmann, H., Riddell, W., & Bowman, D. (2010). Choral singing; Choirs. *The Encyclopedia of Music in Canada* (Online). Retrieved August 13, 2011, from www.canadianencyclopedia.ca

Laughton, W., & Nygaard King, B. (2010). Harvey Perrin. *The Encyclopedia of Music in Canada* (Online). Retrieved August 13, 2011, from www.canadianencyclopedia.ca

McIntosh, R. (2010). One hundred years of singing. Arion male voice choir of Victoria, BC.

Norman, B., & Nygaard King, B. (2010). Men of the deeps. *The Encyclopedia of Music in Canada* (Online). Retrieved August 13, 2011, from www.canadianencyclopedia.ca

Nygaard King, B. (2010). The Amabile choirs of London. *The Encyclopedia of Music in Canada* (Online). Retrieved August 13, 2011, from www.canadianencyclopedia.ca

Parker, A. (1996). The construction of masculinity within boys' physical education. *Gender and Education, 8*(2), 141–157.

Poole, C. (2010). Barbershop. *The Encyclopedia of Music in Canada* (Online). Retrieved August 13, 2011, from www.canadianencyclopedia.ca

Reid Lower, T., & Bowman, D. (2010). Arion male voice choir. *The Encyclopedia of Music in Canada* (Online). Retrieved August 13, 2011, from www.canadianencyclopedia.ca

Rosenberg, N. (1994). The Canadianization of Newfoundland folksong; or the Newfoundlandization of Canadian folksong. *Journal of Canadian Studies, 29*(1), 55.

Terauds, J. (2008, January 27). Acappellooza shows a cappella singing on the rise. *The Toronto Star*. Retrieved August 13, 2011, from www.thestar.com

Vince, N. (2005). *A decade of change: Music education enrolment in Ontario secondary schools from 1993–2002 and the Don Wright Faculty of Music from 1994–2003.* Doctoral dissertation, The University of Western Ontario, London, ON.

Chapter 5
Singing, Men and Australian Culture

Scott D. Harrison

5.1 Australians Can't Sing ... They Chant, They Don't Chime

So said George Megalogenis in the national newspaper *The Australian* in 2004. Under the headline "Anthems are useless in a nation of tone-deaf chanters" this article purports to give some of the reasons as to why Australians don't sing. Chief among them are cultural diversity and an inability to recall the lyrics of the national anthem. Evans (2009) concurs that Australians "can't sing to save themselves." In contrast to this assertion, Saatchi & Saatchi (2000, p. 84) found that people in Australia who

> ... feel most positive about the arts are also most likely to directly participate in them in various ways... people will be more likely to support an activity and appreciate the efforts of others in that activity if they also participate in it, or at least have personally tried it, or believe that the option is available to them.

The extent to which these contrasting statements have any foundation will be explored throughout this chapter. Megalongenis' contention regarding the Australian anthem may have some merit. The song has five verses, of which verses two, four and five are almost never sung. Of the remaining two verses, lyrics such as "we've golden soil and wealth for toil, our home is girt by sea" are not conducive to memorization and communal singing. Megalongenis' other assertion that cultural diversity is at the heart of Australian's reluctance to sing is worthy of further investigation. Letts (2003, p. 3) noted that Australians do not embrace one homogenous style of music:

> Australians perform and listen to a plethora of musical styles. Participation is numerically greatest in styles promoted by the international popular music industry – e.g. rock music, hip-hop, dance/electronica. Other styles include country music, including a stream identified with indigenous musicians; classical music in all its forms; jazz; Australian folk and bush music derived from Anglo-Celtic folk styles; ethnic styles, especially but not

---

S.D. Harrison (✉)
Griffith University, Brisbane, QLD 4101, Australia
e-mail: scott.harrison@griffith.edu.au

exclusively those associated with the cultures of immigrants; including "world music"; traditional indigenous musics; fusion musics that experiment with couplings of any of the above; experimental music/computer-generated music/multimedia.

From this, it is not possible to discern one distinctive attribute that quantifies a Australian musical identity. Harrison commented in 2005a (p. 227) that

> Through the processes of cultural appropriation or cultural indigenization, musicians appropriate various qualities of musical forms from diverse cultures and societies, contributing to the difficulties in trying to determine national identity through music.

Hayes (1995) contends that, in spite of this variety, there is a recognizably Australian music, because of the country's history, location and geography. Australian music is not therefore beholden to European or American music history. Saatchi and Saatchi (2000, p. 88) found that 68% of people thought: "... the arts reflect who we are as Australians." Australian identity, at least as perceived by those beyond the Pacific, is largely associated with geographical features: the land, the beach, the weather and the outback. Alongside this, distinctly Australian music reflects historical events: indigenous-owned, convict-settled and, more recently, heading towards cultural diversity.

In relation to diversity of music, Schippers (2004) claims that there are three identifiable layers: immigrants from various European cultures, immigrants from within the Asia-Pacific region and the cultural background of Aboriginal people and Torres Strait Islanders. Each of these presents major cultural and musical challenges in addition to political protocols. As far as music education is concerned, what occurs inside classrooms is somewhat at odds with this culturally diverse reality. Dunbar-Hall (in Volk 1998, p.135) comments that until the 1970s when the first multicultural policies were implemented (after 60 years of the "White Australia Policy"), there was almost no non-Western music in education programs. Dunbar-Hall further notes that approaches used in Australia "encouraged musical plurality, but promulgated it through a contravening universalist teaching paradigm" (Dunbar-Hall, 2000, p. 133). While curriculum documents call for "ensembles from a range of cultural and historical contexts" practical music making activities are not defined. This lack of practical application is not uncommon. Campbell, writing in 1994 (p. 73) mentions that "professional policy statements that refrain from recommending specific musical repertoire may prove meaningless in the long run." In reality, therefore, the culture is diverse, but the education system is not. More recent research (Cain, 2010; Schippers & Cain, 2009) has focused on this phenomenon, noting that formal engagement in music comes through the education processes. This presents significant dilemmas for males' participation in music, and forms of singing. Saatchi & Saatchi (2000, p. 86) reported that 85% of Australians agreed "the Arts should be an important part of the education of every Australian kid" and that this should involve all types of education, not just that available through the formal school system. Trends in co-curricular engagement with music is therefore of interest.

In relation to involvement in the arts during non-school hours, the Australian Bureau of Statistics Survey of Children's Participation in Cultural and Leisure

Activities (2006) revealed that an estimated 869,600 children were involved in at least one of four selected cultural activities (playing a musical instrument, singing, dancing and drama) in their non-school hours. Furthermore, in the year to April 2006, 20% of 5–14 year olds played a musical instrument outside of school. The survey also indicated that these activities were more popular with girls than boys: 572,400 of the figure above were girls and approximately half that number (297,200) was male. Research by this author over the last 10 years has indicated that 80% of the singing in primary schools is done be girls, increasing to 90% in secondary schools (Harrison, 2003). Similarly, Pickering and Rapcholi (2001), noted that:

> The perceived risk associated with playing ... a gender-inappropriate instrument [on a survey] was probably much greater for the boys than for the girls. Boys in particular could benefit from exposure to multiple examples of a counter-stereotyped behaviour (p. 642).

This is not a recent trend. Over 40 years ago Bartle (1968, p. 188) commented, "a cause of some concern is the frequency in co-educational Australian schools of choirs of girls only". Over the 474 schools in his sample, half was not using the voices of the senior boys to any significant extent.

Given this context, the central question in this chapter is "What is the interaction of men with singing in Australian culture?" There has been a resurgence of interest in this field in the last decade in Australia as evidenced in studies by this author (Harrison, 2001, 2004, 2007, 2008, 2009a) and related studies by Hall (2007, 2010), Young (2009), Holley (2009) and Bayliss, Lierse and Ludowycke (2009). In these studies, mate-ship is considered central to the discussion of men in Australian society. McLean (1995, p. 85) describes mate-ship as being

> ... founded on sharing the rituals of masculine identity. The exclusion of women is an integral aspect, and many of these rituals turn out to be destructive or oppressive. Binge drinking, gambling and violent sports are obvious examples.

The emphasis on binge-drinking, gambling and violent sports creates a two dimensional, stereotypical image of the Australian male and the promotion of this image results in the restriction of gender role development and expression. In contemporary Australia, the media continues to present these two-dimensional roles thereby reinforcing the stereotypes by promoting actors, sports stars and businessmen. The majority of men may not consciously subscribe to this singular form of masculinity, but it asserts its influence through cultural and institutional practices. Pollack (1999) notes that this results in "gender straight-jacketing" in which boys are ashamed to express signs of neediness, dependence, sadness or vulnerability. Harrison (2009b, p. 220) comments on the key elements that contribute to the construction of the hegemonic Australian male citing

> ... the role of feminism since its rise in the 1960s; the prevalence of patriarchy ... avoiding and devaluing femininity through gender straight-jacketing and complying with the expectations of compulsory heterosexuality and homophobia.

An emphasis on sport, risk-taking, and drinking leaves little room to pursue the arts. Men who do participate in certain art-forms can be perceived as living outside the expected models of Australian masculinity and risk ridicule, bullying and social rejection. Whether it is harassment by physical, verbal or other means, engagement in music is affected by these behaviours.

Recent research in this field (Collins, 2009; Hall, 2005, 2007; Harrison, 2007; Holley, 2009; Young, 2009) has indicated that men do sing in certain circumstances. In 2001 Harrison noted, "boys will engage in singing in musicals, rock and jazz. In some schools, boys sing in choirs. Anecdotal evidence suggests that this is particularly the case in some single sex schools". Furthermore, Hall (2005) contends

> ... that concerns about the "missing male" trend in school singing need to consider the ways boys learn to be masculine in early childhood, given the evidence of alarming negative attitudes toward singing in boys in their first year of school.

However, familiar trends are still apparent: almost no boys are singing in a co-educational environment. The price of engagement in this setting can be high. Harrison (2001) found that males are subjected to bullying and suspicion about their sexuality at school when they are involved in certain musical activities. Epstein, Elwwod, Hey, and Maw (1998) commented that homophobic abuse is leveled at boys who "dislike rough and tumble games... preferring gentler pursuits" (p. 103). Gentler pursuits may include the arts. Lehne (1995) describes jobs such as singer, dancer, musician, artist, actor with the term "sissy" work. Plummer (1999) takes this further, suggesting that an Australian boy who doesn't play or avoids sports is considered a "poofter". This trend persists through the middle years of schooling, but towards the senior years a noticeable reversal becomes apparent. As one of Harrison's (2009b) participants noted "In Year 11 and 12 with school productions, suddenly music, acting and singing were accepted by the majority of students."

The apparent contrast between a culturally diverse society, and a hegemonic view of masculinity throughout most of the schooling years presents some challenges for researchers and practitioners attempting to bring about the maximization of engagement in singing for males. The cases below therefore provide examples of ways in which this can be managed in school and out-of-school settings.

5.2 Singing in School: Melbourne High School and Plums Mountain State School

> At Melbourne High School every student sings. At first it is very tentative, but eventually most boys make more than a token effort. By Year 12, the enthusiastic involvement, expertise and sheer volume of the singing are astonishing. Most boys eventually take the risk of letting go of their fears and begin to contribute their energy wholeheartedly into learning to make controlled beautiful singing (Cropley, 2005).

The phenomenon of singing at Melbourne High School extends beyond the classrooms, choirs, orchestras, bands and other ensembles to the broader school community. At this school, everyone is involved in music making. This is typically driven by the school leadership: successive principals have promoted and maintained full school singing, with the incumbent declaring "The soul of Melbourne

High School is expressed through its singing" Ludowyke (in Bayliss, et al., 2009). His predecessor thought similarly:

> Central to music at Melbourne High School is the whole School singing program, which holds a unique place in the ethos and culture of the School and is founded on the love of music and the commitment to make excellent music education accessible to all (Willis in Bell, 2004)

Singing is therefore firmly entrenched in the ethos and traditions of Melbourne High School and has been regarded as a valued activity for the students and staff since the School began in 1905. An academically selective school (the school ranks in the top five schools in the country on numeracy and literacy measures), music staff and the principal are keenly aware that real educational and institutional benefits must be gained by the inclusion of Massed Singing in a demanding and crowded curriculum. Current music teachers note that

> A massed singing program is a simple and cost effective means of generating a strong collective sense of community, pride, respect and self and group expression. In an era where there are few rituals and ceremonies for young people, massed singing imparts a sense of cultural occasion and purpose. Few students have encountered any equivalent experience previously, yet no prerequisite expertise or talent is necessary except for a willingness to participate and intelligently explore the music (Bayliss, et al., 2009, p. 187)

The aims of massed singing are clearly articulated in this school. They include: participation and community; limited but valuable music-making for non-musical students and opportunities for students to take on the role of performing/presenting roles. Specifically in relation to music, objectives include exposure to diverse vocal-choral literature; language skills; confident healthy vocal expression; rhythmic accuracy and pitch accuracy incorporating capacity to sing in harmony.

Ultimately, the purpose is for

> Beautiful music to be made but not at the expense of inclusion of as many students as possible... Singing as a whole-school activity strives for unity and enjoyable competition to co-exist (Bayliss et al., 2009, p. 185).

At Plum's Mountain, there is a critical mass of children who sing. While it is not a whole school activity, it is an activity in which many children in the school participate. There are two choirs of approximately 100 choristers each, and the profile of music in the school is equal to, if not greater than sport and academic achievement. Much of this is due to strong leadership from the principal, but also a long serving (and long suffering) music teacher.

Students at the school are champions for Australian choral music: they sing it, they commission it and their teacher presents workshops on it. The standard of music is very high: students have to negotiate difficult melodic and harmonic challenges and movement is an expectation in performance. The maintenance of high standards is one of the key findings from this author's earlier work (Harrison, 2001).

5.3 Singing in Communities: Birralee Blokes and the Kelly Gang

It is not always possible for boys to find a school environment that supports their desire to sing after the voice change. The Birralee Blokes was formed as a community group designed to keep school-aged boys singing when their voice changed. The three pillars of the organisation are to provide a *relaxed, rewarding* and *empowering* environment in which singing can take place unimpeded by school strictures. As one of its members noted in Connolly (2006) "In school choirs it can be embarrassing singing in front of people who see choirs as "gay" or "lame". The Blokes gets rid of that stupid stereotype." Connolly (2006) also found that the conductor Paul Holley

> encourages a relaxed mood and emphasises there must be an element of trust that they will sing the best they can, this gives them a sense of freedom to have little fear of singing confidently. He encourages an energised and relatively homogenous sound without losing the individuality of the performers.

Holley (2009) identifies two issues as critical to the maintenance and development of male singing. Like the teachers at Melbourne High School, he found repertoire selection to be of paramount importance, including the commissioning of new works if required. The second issue is the professional development of music teachers in managing the male voice change:

> This training would be about helping them encourage every kid to sing. I am not saying primary teachers are failing, they mostly don't know what to do with boys when their voices change. But to get a teenage boy back who has been told that he can't sing is nigh on impossible (Holley in Connolly, 2006)

Connelly's commentary on the Birralee Blokes concludes with:

> It is apparent that [the Birralee Blokes] is a place where adolescent boys can grow in safety emotionally, musically, psychologically and spiritually. What more could any parent want for their son, what more could a boy who enjoys singing ask for?

Similarly, the Kelly Gang is a training group associated with the Australian Boys Choral Institute. The Institute consists of different levels for boys in vocal training for boys and men. Using the Kodály method and starting out at around the age of seven or eight are the "Probationers", who spend around one or two school terms of basic understanding of musical methods and singing. Following this training stage, the "Tyros" spend up to 9–12 months working on more musicality. "Junior Singers" follow the "Tyros", with an introduction to performance, and further vocal training. Finally, after months of training, boys will reach the Performing Choir. The Performing Choir is the group who perform professionally across the Australia and, on occasion, internationally.

The Kelly Gang is a group of boys whose voices have begun to change and who have chosen to continue their vocal and choral interest and learn to cope with their "new instrument". Most members of the Gang are therefore former senior members of the Australian Boys Choir. They are named after the founder of the Australian Boys Choir, Vincent J Kelly. The happy co-incidence is that the Kelly Gang is also the name of a notorious band of nineteenth century bushrangers, led by the infamous Ned Kelly. Ned Kelly epitomises the contempt for authority apparent in hegemonic Australian masculinities. This is evident in this extract from his *Jerilderie Letter* (1879)

> ... big ugly fat-necked wombat headed big bellied magpie legged narrow hipped splay footed sons of Irish Bailiffs or English landlords which is better known as officers of Justice or Victoria Police

Like the Birralee Blokes, individual development is promoted in an *enjoyable, stress-free environment*. Emphasis is on vocal control, development of the changing voice and consolidation of reading and other musical skills, together with the opportunity to maintain social contact with others of similar interests and skills. This approach has strong associations with the direction of boys at St Laurence's. Given the Kodaly influence in both settings, it is unsurprising that there is a strong emphasis on a sequential development of vocal technique and musicianship.

5.4 Singing for Adult Men: Menwotsing and The Spooky Men's Chorale

Menwotsing and the Spooky Men's Chorale provide avenues for adult men to sing. Unlike traditional male voice choirs (see Peter Davies' practitioner reflection, Chapter 21, this volume), these vocal ensembles rely on smaller numbers of middle-aged men singing a variety of works arranged specifically for their combination of voices.

The founder of Menwotsing, Brian Martin, recognized that in "most choirs and singing workshops the women outnumber the men by a large majority" (menwotsing.com.au). Like the founders of the Kelly Gang and Birralee Blokes, Brian believed that more men would become involved by creating a *safe, friendly and supportive* singing environment: an environment where men could sing without having to live up to the sometimes overwhelming presence of female choristers. The ensemble's core value is to assist men wanting to find their voice whilst building self-confidence.

Menwotsing had some initial challenges. In the early stages, numbers were small and music literacy standards less than ideal. Five years after their formation, the group had grown to around 25 in number, though few of these had any singing experience other than this ensemble. The opportunity was provided for men to learn to sing together for the first time.

Beyond the ensemble itself, the organization facilitates singing workshops. These sessions were originally part of men's support networks and have evolved into popular events at festivals and competitions. The foundation for this work as "support for men" has continued with appearances at men's health conferences and events promoting well-being for men, particularly in mid-life.

The current musical director employs a dynamic teaching style that involves "movement, rhythm and lots of laughter. His sense of fun provides a host of inspirational and wacky ideas which take us on an emotional and spiritual journey" (ensemble member, personal communication). The humour is also evident in the choice of name. The original name in 1998 was Ancestral Tones and, after one performance as "Thundershed" the current name was chosen.

Repertoire is also a key issue. Menwotsing's material focuses on "the things we love, hence all our songs are about beer, sex and goats!" One of their mainstays is Monty Python's "Philosophers' Song." This is described by the group as "A challenging sing ... both physically and mentally, the Philosophers' Song is the glorious conclusion to a trilogy of European drinking songs".

The Spooky Men's Chorale was established as a novelty act in 2001. Their material is based on traditional Gregorian music, but has expanded to encompass songs by Queen, ABBA and other popular artists. Repertoire also includes the original tunes such as *Spooky Theme; Don't Stand Between Man and his Tool* and *Vote the Bastards Out*. In relation to their repertoire, Brown (2007) commented that

> ... while superficially a comedy act, the Spooky Men are also fine close harmony singers, their tuning, timing and dynamics impeccable. Alongside other examples of Georgian table singing – similar in parts to Russian orthodox music but more robust – there are straight a capella ballads (Paul McCartney; a moving rendition of Joni Mitchell's "The Fiddle and the Drum") and celebrations of "boys' things" like sheds, tools and stamp collections.

Their website (www.spookymen.com) also gives an indication of the humour inherent in their music making "The repertoire is largely inspired by the pointless grandeur of everyday maleness, in the shower, in the shed and after breakfast."

The appearance of the group is also a significant feature. They are essentially a bunch of amateur singers from the Blue Mountains in New South Wales. There is a sound engineer and a few casual singer-songwriters among them, but ostensibly this is just a regular collection of dads and teachers, carpenters and architects. As Shand (2006) noted there is:

> no chintz, no bling and no kitsch in their routine. Instead this rugby team-size choir of boofy blokes settles for a healthy blend of eccentricity, scariness and laughs.

Like Menwotsing, workshopping is a strong feature of the Spooky Men's agenda. They have two streams: *Workshops for Kids* and their *Sing Like a Bloke* workshop, which is for "blokes of all genders." Reviewing their workshop processes in 2004 Noonan observed:

> You are standing at the tent door listening to what sounds like archangels singing ethereal harmonies. But it's a bunch of 40 boofy men from the Blue Mountains with a wise guy out the front wearing a furry deerstalker hat ... If you have preconceived ideas about choirs leave them at the tent flap. This sound is sexy, powerful, at times impossibly gentle and sad, unmistakably male.

Noonan (2004) also observed "School choir was never like this".

5.4.1 Emergent Themes

As a result of rigid forms of masculinity, Australian men have expressed reluctance to sing in certain settings. There are several opportunities in educational and community settings that create environments that promote participation. While each of these settings has unique features, some common themes are apparent in the cases described above.

In each ensemble, leadership was a key issue. In the school setting, the leadership of the school principal was significant. In all the contexts, the ensemble facilitator was described as dynamic, energetic, enthusiastic and interesting in the education of their members, and the community beyond their membership. Almost all leaders were providers of professional development for teachers and/or leaders of community workshops. Of these, perhaps the most interesting is the work of Menwotsing in actively promoting health and wellbeing for men.

Repertoire was also a central concern. In many cases, the works performed were composed or arranged by the facilitator or ensemble members. Diversity in repertoire, along with an almost total avoidance of traditional male voice choir material is a feature. Vocal health was paramount in groups comprising changing voices, while humour played a large part in the material for adult ensembles. The adult groups also incorporated strong political messages, with tunes such as "Farewell Johnny Howard" (former Australian Prime Minister) and "Vote the Bastards Out!" Schools made the most of community singing to promote themes of tolerance, diversity and acceptance.

Directors of groups in this chapter report on the importance of getting the name right to attract men to singing: Birralee Blokes took its name after much consultation with the membership, and the Spooky Men are, well, exactly that! The term "choir" is almost unanimously avoided.

Related to this theme, in all cases the appearance was significant. Traditional black and white attire was shunned in favour of themed outfits incorporating hats, monochromatic uniforms, or the absence of uniforms altogether. Presentation tended to focus on less formal staging, including casual stances and movement that still employed correct body alignment.

Perhaps the most significant theme is the creation of a safe, supportive environment for singing. The above themes contribute to this but the conscious maintenance of a relaxed, enjoyable setting was consistently noted as the most significant contributor to the successful engagement of men in singing in Australian contexts.

References

Australian Bureau of Statistics. (2006). *Survey of children's participation in cultural and leisure activities*. Canberra: Australian Bureau of Statistics.
Bartle, G. (1968). *Music in Australian schools*. Australian Council for Education, Melbourne: Wilke.

Bayliss, C., Lierse, A., & Ludowycke, J. (2009). Singing throughout life at Melbourne High School. In S. Harrison (Ed.), *Male voices: Stories of boys learning through making music* (pp. 135–155). Melbourne: ACER.
Bell, S. (2004). Melbourne High School Speech Night Program.
Brown, F. (2007). The spooky men's chorale. *The Independent*, 27 October 2007.
Cain, M. (2010). Singapore International Schools: Best practice in culturally diverse music education. *British Journal of Music Education, 27*(2), 111–125.
Campbell, P. S. (1994). Musica exotica, multiculturalism, and school music. *Quarterly Journal of Music Teaching and Learning, 5*(2), 65–75.
Collins, A. (2009). A boy's music ecosystem. In S. Harrison (Ed.), *Male voices: Stories of boys learning through making music* (pp. 33–47). Melbourne: ACER.
Connolly, J. (2006). Changing voices. *Music Forum, 12*(4). Retrieved August 19, 2008, from http://www.mca.org.au/web/content/view/65/6
Cropley, R. (2005). Rituals, assemblies and singing. In J. Prideaux (Ed.), *More than just marks* (pp. 174–175). Melbourne: Pennon Publishing.
Dunbar-Hall, P. (2000). Concept or context? Teaching and learning Balinese gamelan and the universalist-pluralist debate. *Music Education Research, 2*(2), 127–139.
Epstein, D. J., Elwwod, J., Hey, V., & Maw, J. (Eds.). (1998). *Failing boys: Issues in gender and achievement*. Buckingham: Open University Press.
Evans, R. (2009). Welsh rarebit. *Griffith review: Participation society No 24*. ABC Books.
Hall, C. (2005). Gender and boys' singing in early childhood. *British Journal of Music Education, 22*(1), 5–20.
Hall, C. (2007). Singing spaces: Boys getting vocal about singing in and out of school. *Redress, Association of Women Educators, 15*(3), 23–27.
Hall, C. (2010). *Voices of distinction: Choirboys' narratives of music and masculinity*. Doctoral dissertation – in progress, Monash University, Melbourne.
Harrison, S. D. (2001). Real men don't sing. *Australian Voice, 7*, 31–36.
Harrison, S. D. (2003). Music versus sport: What's the score. *Australian Journal for Music Education, 1*(1), 10–15.
Harrison S. D. (2004). Engaging boys, overcoming stereotypes: Another look at the missing males in vocal programs. *Choral Journal, 45*(2):25–28.
Harrison, S. D. (2005a). Who'll come a Waltzing Matilda: the search for identity in Australian Music Education. In H. Schippers et al. (Eds.), *Cultural diversity in music education: Directions and challenges for the 21st century* (pp. 113–124). Brisbane: Australian Academic Press.
Harrison, S. D. (2005b). Music versus sport: A new approach to scoring. *Australian Journal of Music Education, 1*, 10–15.
Harrison, S. D. (2007). Where have the boys gone? The perennial problem of gendered participation in music. *British Journal of Music Education, 24*(3), 267–280.
Harrison, S. D. (2008). *Masculinities and music: Engaging men and boys in making music*: Newcastle-upon-Tyne: Cambridge Scholars.
Harrison, S. D. (2009a). The challenge of music making in adolescence. In S. D. Harrison (Ed.), *Male voices: Stories of boys learning and loving music in Australia* (pp. 48–61). ACER: Melbourne.
Harrison, S. D. (2009b). Aussie blokes and music. In S. D. Harrison (Ed.), *Male Voices: Stories of boys learning and loving music in Australia* (pp. 4–15). Melbourne: ACER.
Hayes, D. (1995). *Australian music and the contemporary world*. Paper presented at 1995 ASANA Conference, Orlando, FL, 16–18 March, 1995.
Holley, P. (2009). The Birralee blokes. In S. Harrison (Ed.), *Music and men down under: Stories of boys learning and loving music in Australia* (pp. 156–172). Melbourne: ACER.
Kelly, N. (1879). *Jerilderie Letter*. State Library of Victoria. Retrieved May 22, 2010, from http://www.slv.vic.gov.au/collections/treasures/jerilderieletter1.html

Lehne, G. (1995). Homophobia among men: Supporting and defining the male role. In M. Kimmel & M. Messner (Eds.), *Men's lives* (pp. 416–429). Needham Heights, MA: Allyn and Bacon.

Letts, R. (2003, October). The effects of globalization on music in five contrasting countries: Report of a research project for the Many Musics program of the International Music Council, Music Council of Australia.

McLean, C. (1995). Homophobia among men: Supporting and defining the male role. In M. Kimmel & M. Messner (Eds.), *Men's lives* (pp. 291–301). Needham Heights, MA: Allyn and Bacon.

Menwotsing. (2010). Retrieved May 22, 2010, from http://www.menwotsing.com/

Noonan, K. (2004). Thug, wimp and romp. *Courier Mail*. 30 December, 2004.

Pickering, S., & Rapcholi, B. (2001). Modifying children's gender-typed musical instrument preferences: The effects of gender and age. *Sex Roles, 45*(9/10), 623–642.

Plummer, D. (1999). *One of the boys: Masculinity, homophobia and modern manhood*. New York: Harrington.

Pollack, W. (1999). *Real boys*. New York: Holt.

Saatchi & Saatchi. (2000). *Australians and the arts. A report to the Australia council from Saatchi & Saatchi Australia*. Sydney: Australia Council.

Schippers, H. (2004). *Blame it on the Germans! A cross-cultural invitation to revisit the foundations of training professional musicians*. Paper presented at ISME Conference, Spain, August, 2004.

Schippers, H., & Cain, M. (2009). A tale of three cities. Dreams and realities of cultural diversity in music education. In J. Ballantyne & B. L. Bartleet (Eds.), *Navigating music and sound education* (pp. 161–174). Newcastle: Cambridge Scholars.

Shand, J. (2006). A cappella gets creepy at the Blue Mountains Music Festival. *Sydney Morning Herald*, 10 March 2006.

Spooky Men's Chorale. (2010). Retrieved May 22, 2010, from http://www.spookymen.com.au/reviews.htm

Volk, T. M. (1998). *Music, education, and multiculturalism. Foundations and principles*. New York: Oxford University Press.

Young, A. (2009). The singing classroom: Singing in classroom music and its potential to transform school culture. In S. Harrison (Ed.), *Male voices: Stories of boys learning through making music* (pp. 62–78). Melbourne: ACER.

Part II
Singing in Formal Contexts

Chapter 6
Changing Voices—Voices of Change: Young Men in Middle School Choirs

Frank Abrahams

6.1 Background

When I first conceived this chapter, it was to be about boys' changing voices. It would have informed middle school music teachers, as if they did not already know, that at puberty and during adolescence changes in hormones affect the pitch and timbre of the male speaking and singing voice. It would have described the physiology of the change and suggested that choral teachers encourage boys to continue singing throughout the middle school years. In addition, it would have recommended that choir directors consider both the text and the range carefully when choosing music for boys. But this is not news or new information. Everyone knows that boys' voices change.

However, after seeing research that shows music has different meanings to boys and girls in middle school and that those meanings are significant in constructing students' social identity (North & Hargreaves, 1999), I decided to focus on the factors that boys consider both consciously and unconsciously when deciding whether or not to affiliate themselves with a choral ensemble in middle school. I will also explore ways that choir directors can help young men in middle school positively construct their self-identity and pursue music in the context of choir.

The chapter uses social identity theory as well as the concept of performatives as a framework to understand young men during adolescence and suggests that the principles of critical pedagogy for music education (CPME) may be helpful to middle school choral teachers working with these students.

6.2 Music and Gender

Even in ancient Greece, Plato recognized the study of music as "analogous to moral order—music could better the soul" (Harrison, 2006, para. 8). Swanwick (1988) writes, "the special function of the arts is to illuminate, to transform and ultimately

---

F. Abrahams (✉)
Westminster Choir College of Rider University, Princeton, NJ, USA
e-mail: abrahams@rider.edu

to make life worth living" (p. 50). In spite of this almost universal acknowledgement of the value of music, studies show there is a steady decline in participation by boys in school music activities between elementary and middle school (Austin, 1990; National Center for Education Statistics, 1999; Pogonowski, 1985).

Issues of identity as they impact music education have focused almost exclusively on women and come from feminist literature on gender, sexuality, and social justice. Green (1997) studied choices boys and girls make relative to participation in the musical offerings at school. Her research suggested that students and their music teachers, both male and female, consider singing to be a feminine activity and playing in band to be more suited to boys. Svengalis (1978), agrees.

Koza (1994) investigated the issue of gender in choir when she examined the textbooks college students use in choral-methods classes. Her research confirmed that these texts suggest that boys, especially adolescents, avoid singing in choir because it threatens their self-image as men. The methods texts also explain that teachers who acknowledge this are more successful in attracting boys to the choir than those who do not. But, acknowledging the issue as one of homophobia and misogyny is difficult for most middle school choral directors and speaking about it openly almost impossible.

Harrison (2003) noted that verbal bullying in the form of homophobic name-calling and sexual harassment by peers coupled with complacency on the part of music teachers reinforce fears young men face when electing to sing in middle school choir. He found that "almost all the existing literature ... indicated that a gender stereotypical bias exists in music: participation in activities that are soft, gentle, small, and high-pitched are not considered the domain of males" (p. 224). This implies singing. Harrison writes that, "according to the dominant code of masculinity anything that could be in any way construed as being un-masculine is suspect" (pp. 224–225).

Green (1997) found that boys call their peers who participate in music sissies. As a result, the boys thus harassed often chose to participate in sports instead. She concludes that for a boy to join a choir involves taking a risk with his symbolic masculinity. Hanley (1998) agrees that "boys don't sing because they are hung up on the image that boys don't sing, and those who do are gay or sissies or weak or whatever" (p. 51).

6.3 Theories of Identity

Self-identity would seem to be an "inescapable issue" (Gauntlett, 2002, para. 1). While earlier cultures had more clearly defined roles, in today's society everyone has to invent their own. Even people who say they have given no thought to their self-identity are constantly making decisions about clothes, employment, and friends that shape that identity. Giddens (1991) concurs and adds that what to do, how to act, and who to be are questions everyone has to answer, and they do so in their day-to-day social behavior.

Franzoi (1996) suggests that using multiple theories of self-identity can increase understanding more than a single perspective (p. 156). In this chapter, I combined the theory of social identity and the concept of performativity to provide a theoretical framework.

Social identity theory, which asserts that belonging to particular groups impacts individuals' construction of their social identity, comes from social psychology, particularly the research of Tajfel and Turner (1979). Performativity, relating to expressions that constitute an act, is a term from speech act theory (Austin, 1962, 1970) and is now prominent in literature on gender (Butler, 1990, 2000). Together, social identity theory and performativity provide a lens to help teachers understand issues relative to preteen young men and their experiences singing in middle school. And for these young men in middle school, their conception of who they are is a very high priority.

6.3.1 Social Identity Theory

Social identity theory (Tajfel, 1978; Tajfel & Turner, 1979) is based on the idea that belonging to particular groups, called in-groups and out-groups, impacts a person's construction of his or her social identity. Clearly, the in-group consists of those who conform to the normative values assigned to young men by media, their peers and the constructs of social capital. Those young men that resist those archetypes constitute the out-group.

Tajfel and Turner (1986) suggest that the mere act of individuals categorizing themselves as members of either the in-group or out-group is a mark of in-group favouritism. Students believe that identifying themselves with in-groups enhances their status by differentiating them from a comparison out-group on some valued dimension. That is, if the sports team is the in-group and the middle school choir is the out-group, students perceive that they will feel better and be happier on the sports team than they will be singing in the choir. Research by Tarrant, North, and Hargreaves (2002) confirms this. Their research found that young men preferred the in-group, describing it as "more fun, more masculine, more sporty, less boring, less snobbish, and less weird" (p. 134) when compared with the out-group.

6.3.2 Performativity

A performative is when saying something makes it so. For example, at the end of the wedding ceremony when the couple is pronounced husband and wife, the very words "I now pronounce you" make it so. Or, in the confessional, when the priest absolves and forgives, the words are the action. When a parent says, "I promise" that also constitutes a performative act.

Roberts (2006) points out that because "identity is a socially constructed action" (p. 3), it is therefore, a performative. Butler (1990) writes, "identity is performatively constituted by the very 'expressions' that are said to be its results" (p. 25).

In other words, "our identities are the dramatic effect (rather than the cause) of our performances" (Gauntlett, 2002, para. 10).

I contend that young men in middle school are fearful that if their peers pronounce them "gay" they will indeed be gay. This is profoundly significant. Butler (1990) develops this idea in depth. She posits that what we believe influences how we act. If adolescent boys believe that singing in choir will make them gay, they will be less likely to participate. Adler's (2005) research confirms that homophobic harassment is the most frequent contributor to boys choosing not to sing in choir. One young man Harrison (2003) interviewed said, "People heard that I sang opera and they immediately assumed that I was gay ... it goes to show how narrow-minded our culture is in Australia that we can't accept 'real men' to be artists" (p. 182).

Thus, those teachers who ignore the inner struggles of young men in middle school to develop their self-identity and dismiss how those struggles impact decisions students make regarding their participation in choir give legitimacy to the peer pressures outside the choir that influence young men in negative ways and may unknowingly reinforce these beliefs based in performativity theory. This reinforces the idea that the construction of a young man's identity is influenced by teachers and the policies and practices enacted repeatedly in the institutions where learning takes place. Acknowledging the power of performatives and the profound ability performatives have to influence how students view themselves in the world, teachers must choose their words carefully and be sure their meanings are precise. Abramo (2006) has researched the issue of identity with his middle school ensembles, but is optimistic when he writes, "We, music educators, have the power to help students shape themselves" (p. 18).

6.4 Critical Pedagogy for Music Education

Critical pedagogy for music education (CPME) provides an approach to the middle school choral program that acknowledges and embraces the theories of social identity and performativity. CPME uses dialogue between students and their teachers to uncover problems and solve them together, effecting a change in the way that both students and their teachers perceive the world. CPME could be considered a pedagogy of resistance or a radical pedagogy because advocates of critical pedagogy for music education break down barriers between in-groups and out-groups by honouring the world of each individual student. Teachers who embrace critical pedagogy for music education foster a teaching environment that encourages dialogue between teacher and student so that students take ownership of their learning. It is a perspective that abhors marginalized groups and silenced voices and instead seeks to create open space for true democracy.

CPME traces its roots to the work of Paulo Freire in Brazil. Freire (1970) developed a method for teaching the oppressed poor to read by finding texts for study that came from his students' daily lives. Students learned to read using labels on food cans, newspapers, road signs, and the like—all things that were familiar to them. Freire's teaching methods were the opposite of direct instruction, or what he termed "banking," where teachers assume students know nothing. In that scenario, teachers deposit information into the learner's memory (or bank account) where it is stored until the teacher asks the student to recall or withdraw it on a test. Freire found such teaching to be ineffective. Instead, he posed problems for his students to solve, and in the process of problem-posing and problem-solving, students entered into conversations or dialogues with him and with each other. One positive result was a shift of power inside the classroom where all, including Freire, were teaching each other and learning together. Freire's goal was to create space inside the classroom where all had an equal and valued voice and where it was acknowledged that all brought something to the experience. Freire's classes were called cultural circles, where students were empowered to learn. The cultural circles were fertile ground for constructing knowledge and attaining what Freire called conscientization, which he defined as that state when pupils know that they know (Freire, 1970).

A primary goal of CPME is for the teacher and students to engage in experiences that are transformational. Teachers who embrace this ideology believe that the results of teaching and learning should add value to the lives of those who participate by changing the perceptions that learners have as they interact in and with the world. CPME refers to how teaching and learning can be a catalyst for students and their teachers to see themselves in the world and to change or transform how they act and interact with the world.

What singing in a choir based on CPME can do is to provide a safe and comfortable place where young men feel valued and appreciated for who they are and the musical gifts they bring to the ensemble. In the language of critical pedagogy, it "honors their world" (Abrahams, 2005d) by giving them "voice" (O'Toole, 2005). That is to say, their issues and concerns, fears, and doubts are acknowledged and considered with empathy and acted on directly by their conductors. Conductors set the tone for that by defining the space and place where music making happens.

6.5 Four Essential Questions

Middle school choral directors might consider four questions (Abrahams, 2004, 2005a, 2005b, 2005c; Abrahams & Head, 2005) from the literature on curriculum and critical pedagogy that to further their understanding of the ways boys in middle school choir construct their identities: Who am I? Who are my students? What might they become? What might we become together? Asking and answering these questions will inform such issues as repertoire choice, where boys with unchanged voices sit (e.g., with tenors rather than sopranos and altos), voice-part labels (e.g., high, and low instead of soprano and alto), and so forth. Such issues connect to the roles gender and identity play in the decisions boys make as they consider singing in the middle school choir.

6.5.1 Who Am I?

Perhaps this question can best be answered with additional questions. Do you unconsciously influence young men away from choir? As stated earlier, Green (1997) found that teachers considered singing in school choirs to be a feminine activity. Clearly, such an attitude is detrimental to the desire young men have to sing. It does not take long for these boys to decode the hidden and subtle messages such teachers send. And the media does not help either. It often includes images of "real men" that are both narrow and stereotypical. The idea that a "real man" can be defined in one way causes confusion. "Real men" look a certain way, wear clothing of a particular brand, don't shave every day and on and on. Those messages are influential to boys searching for an identity as a young man and teachers are cautioned to use language carefully. "Real men may play contact sports; but they also dance, cook, babysit, take pride in their physical appearance, and yes, they sing in choir" (N. R. McBride, personal communication, January 19, 2010).

Are you more concerned with how many boys are in your program than with the quality of the experience those boys have? Middle school choir directors are often concerned with the number of boys in their choirs. Many teachers believe that the ability to boast a large contingent of young men in their choirs is a testament to their ability as choral directors. Teachers are proud when they can say that they have a large number of young men participating. Parents and administrators are impressed as well.

Do you create an atmosphere where young men feel safe and supported? Middle school choir directors who acknowledge not only the physical changes that occur in their male students, but the developmental, psychological, and emotional baggage they carry into the choral rehearsal connect to who their male students are. Roberts (2006) reminds us that education is socially constructed. That means that schools build their own cultures. Urban schools, suburban schools, rural schools, public schools, private schools, charter schools, parochial schools and more, provide the parameters upon which decisions about repertoire, activities, and experiences are determined. There are no uniform approaches that will work for every middle school choir in every school. However, advocates of critical pedagogy acknowledge that students come to school with considerable knowledge that they have gleaned from the world they experience outside schooling. A goal of critical pedagogy then is to use that knowledge as a bridge to new learning. Beginning with experiences suggested by students themselves is one way that students feel valued and validated. It fosters self worth and self-esteem and contributes to their emerging identities as adolescents. Do you provide good role models for your students? Kohlberg (1966, 1969) suggests that children's attitudes and beliefs about gender roles are shaped by the behaviours of same-sex role models. The male choral director may be that person. If that isn't the case, try including male singers who work in the school or from the high school choir or a local college in your program.

6.5.2 Who Are My Students?

Belonging to a group is important to middle school students. Belonging to the in-group fosters their self-esteem and helps construct their identity. Many students perceive the middle school choir as the out-group. The popular American TV series Glee is based on the discrimination students face from their peers and other adults in the school when they choose to be members of the choir. Can they be in the glee club and on the football team? What will their friends think about them? These are important questions to young men in early adolescence.

Working to make your choral ensembles more like the in-group may increase participation. For example, the choir could be run more like a sports team or include other males, from inside or outside the school building.

6.5.2.1 Real-Life Interview: "Phillipe"

To prepare this chapter, I interviewed two young men who were singing in middle school choirs. "Phillipe" attends a suburban middle school in the Northeast that serves a diverse population. The school principal reports that 52 different languages are spoken in students' homes. A display of flags from the different nations represented hangs in the vestibule outside the school auditorium. Choir, orchestra, and band are the only options for students who wish to include music in their middle school experience. There are no classes in general music.

Phillipe (the pseudonym he chose for me to use in this chapter) is 13 years old. In addition to singing, he likes to write fan fiction, compose his own music, edit photos on the computer, and create his own art. On his Web site, Phillipe notes that he has heard people at school call him "that manga freak; that Broadway freak; that fire-emblem freak; that awesome singer dude" and he is "proud to be the first sixth grader to win best male vocalist in a musical" but hates "the cute little boy of the grade." On the Web, his fiction depicts superheroes, those über-macho men who save the weak and innocent from evil.

Phillipe's voice has not yet changed. He has been soloist in Bernstein's Chichester Psalms many times. One can easily imagine him in the white surplice of a choirboy rather than as the creator of the characters that abound in his fiction. That writing is rich in images of masculine sexuality, of men and the women who love them. Philippe sings in the middle school choir and also with the choir in a community music school at the local college. He performs professionally as a singing actor. He is often cast as Amahl in Amahl and the Night Visitors during the Christmas season. On his MP3 player he listens to "a lot of rock and also soundtracks and Broadway shows." "Last year," he tells me, "there were more girls in choir than boys. But, this year, they have them separated," and so many more boys are singing. Interestingly, last year there was a woman director, and this year there is a man. "I don't feel comfortable in the school choir," he confesses, "because in the school choir they force us to sing as low as we can and it's really annoying. [Then] most of the kids are really shy and so I have to pack in most of the sound [and] it's really difficult." Phillipe hopes that when his voice changes, it will change to tenor because on Broadway, he tells me, "Most of the singers I like are tenors." When I asked why Phillipe thinks boys join the choir he said, "Most of them do it because they actually like to sing and stuff. They like the teacher, but honestly, actually about half do it because they want to get out of culture and the arts." Apparently there is a choice: choir or a course dealing with culture and the arts. Phillipe offered that the choir is not very good because the pieces the director picks are "way too low. We have only two people in the entire school with changed voices that are really low." When asked what advice Phillipe would have for middle school choir directors, he said "You can't try to make the young men go all the way low, and you can't make them try to sing high soprano. Most of the time, they [the directors] just choose the music, and you have to sing it no matter what your voice is."

Clearly Phillipe feels some discomfort when speaking about the middle school choir and its director. He loves to sing and is loyal to the school ensemble; however, he is uncomfortable being forced to sing in a range that is not suited to his voice. Often, with the intention of making the young men feel "manly," directors push them to sing lower before their voices are ready. As we see from the comments above, Phillipe does not like it.

6.5.2.2 Real-life interview: "Gus"

Gus attended a traditional elementary school until grade 5, when he transferred to an all boys private boarding school that students attend specifically to sing in the choir. Choir is central to the curriculum, and students in choir tour and perform with major orchestras in the Northeast. Gus (also a pseudonym chosen by the boy) recalls that his interest in singing began in elementary school when he was 11 where "everyone's doing it." But, "whenever all the boys are out there playing football, and I'm in there singing, sometimes you get made fun of." At 13, he is still a soprano with no evidence of his voice beginning to change. I asked him why, with the football players poking fun at him, he continued to sing. He answered, "I didn't really care what they said about me when I was singing, because singing is for other people. People can walk into an audience," he explains, "and they hear beautiful music, you know that you are helping someone. They are in a different place for maybe an hour and a half or two hours. They won't think about all the terrible things that have happened. And that's why I joined. I've always wanted to help people so I thought that if I joined the choir I could give it a try."

Like Phillipe, Gus enjoys drawing. But, where Phillipe's identity is connected to his fantasy life, Gus enjoys fencing and martial arts. On his MP3 player are soundtracks such as film scores by John Williams, but he also listens to Mahler's 8th symphony, which is subtitled the Symphony of a Thousand. This is clearly a strong masculine selection. "I'm not into rap," he confesses. Instead, he prefers Sting. "Whenever I sing," he explains, "it brings out a side of me that I don't show a lot. And sometimes I think about things that I give, and it helps me a lot." He goes on, "It's kind of like a healing medicine. Say, if someone hurt my feelings, then that's all gone when I sing. It brings energy like a healer."

What is consistent is that both boys may have ideas of how men behave and have conjured their own images of "real" men. While Phillipe's is a fantasy, the interest Gus has in fencing and martial arts is outwardly physical. Fencing and martial arts may be one way he prepares himself to confront the football bullies if he is called upon to do so. Both boys like action-film soundtracks and identify with action heroes like Indiana Jones. Nonetheless, both boys are confronting their identities in different ways. And, both have positive things to say about being in choir.

6.5.3 What Might They Become?

Markus and Nurius (1986, 1987) developed a theory they call possible selves to explain how young men think about who and what they may become. This view of the future can be defined as the "cognitive manifestation of enduring goals, aspirations, motives, fears, and threats" (Markus & Nurius, 1986, p. 954). The notion of possible selves provides a bridge to join the concept of self in the present to a vision of self in the future (Markus & Nurius, 1987). Adler (2005) concludes that when boys choose not to sing in choir they "are deprived of potential growth experiences that contribute to the construction of identity and self-esteem, and are therefore limited in their life possibilities" (p. 1). When studying boys in particular, Knox (2006) found that young men completely avoid possible selves in domains they perceive as feminine.

Both Adler (2002) and Harrison (2003, 2006) have addressed the issue of boys singing in middle school choirs. Adler (2002) suggests that "by denying themselves the full range of activities that could be available to them, boys are deprived of potential growth experiences that contribute to the construction of identity and self-esteem and are therefore limited in their life possibilities" (sec. 4.1). While such choices are clearly in flux during middle school, many young men are looking to their future. The power of music to change lives, however, is a power teachers need to embrace. Being a member of a choral community and participating in the re-creation of wonderful literature, regardless of genre and style, is empowering and life-changing. And for young men in particular, it is about constructing their own identity. The life skills used in learning to make and enact musical decisions with their teacher and to explore multiple solutions to musical problems posed in the repertoire and solved in the rehearsal are the same life skills seen in great leaders regardless of profession

6.5.4 What Might We Become Together?

Brazilian educator Paulo Freire (1970) believed that a goal of education was the attainment of conscientization, a deep understanding that comes when students and their teachers "know that they know." However, Freire (1970) writes that learning is conditioned on the teacher learning as well as the student. In critical pedagogy, learning occurs when students and their teachers are changed and when the content and context of the learning adds value to the lives of both students and their teachers. However, while change in the student may be obvious and immediate, change for the teacher does not always happen in the moment.

By happenstance, as I was writing this section of the chapter, I received an e-mail from Jessica (not her real name), a former high school student I had taught from 1982 to 1986. She writes,

> You are one of the few teachers that I remember fondly. That may come as a surprise to you. After graduation I never really participated in our church choirs. I didn't find them challenging enough. I would get easily bored. Then I was called as the choir director in the ward that we currently live in. I love it! We've had two practices and I'm already using some of your famous quotes. I've always wondered where you went and what you've been up to. I guess you could say that you are a person I really look up to. I'd love to be able to just sit and take classes from you. You were such a magnificent teacher. I'm sure you still are. Please write (personal correspondence, January 29, 2010).

The point here is that we don't always know the impact or the influence we have with our students or the impact of various experiences students have while in our charge when they are happening. While I remember Jessica clearly, she was not a "superstar" in the choir. Instead, she was a quiet young lady who was there when she was supposed to be. I never would have predicted that the choir experience would have been so profoundly influential for her. Nor would I ever have predicted that she would remember things I said in rehearsal or strategies I used to prepare the music and incorporate them into her own teaching nearly 25 years later. This e-mail made me feel as though all the time I had spent working on critical pedagogy was worth it and encouraged me to continue thinking and writing about the power of performativity and the importance of thoughtful discourse when interacting with adolescent students.

6.6 Strategies for Change

Young men in middle school choir want to be valued and want an opportunity for their voices to be heard (O'Toole, 2005). When teacher and students work collaboratively toward a common goal, the young men in choir create meaning on their own. Once singers take ownership of the music, they are empowered. It is appropriate for young men in middle school choir to contribute ideas about style and interpretation and to assess how well the choir is progressing. They can take ownership for tuning, diction, and learning notes outside the rehearsal. In many ways they can teach each other. Such democratic practices create an in-group and contribute to building and reinforcing esteem and loyalty to the ensemble. These democratic practices also transform the students and add value to their lives. They are consistent with the tenets and principles of critical pedagogy for music education.

There are some specific rehearsal strategies that can be used in a CPME-based ensemble. These may be helpful to middle school choral directors when working with adolescent male singers in choir. While the strategies are not specific to young men, they do nurture positive self-identity for all students and particularly for young men.

One strategy I call "Circle All Around" is a variation on a language-literacy strategy called think-pair-share (Billmeyer, 2003). For each voice part, chairs in the room are arranged in two circles, one inner and one outer, so that singers can face each other. The conductor instructs the singers to scan the music and predict the places where they think they might find a musical challenge. Such challenges may be ones of rhythm, intervallic leaps, foreign language texts, dynamic contrasts, inner harmonies, and the like. Once individual singers have identified their own issue, they share it with the person they are facing. Together, the two singers brainstorm a strategy to conquer the challenge. For example, if one singer identifies an issue of rhythm, then he and his partner figure out the rhythm together. The conductor then asks representatives of each voice part to share their challenges and solutions. In this example, students identify and solve the musical challenges on their own. The conductor acts as a facilitator. Students feel valued and empowered when they are able to do this and proud when the conductor acknowledges students' ability to pose and solve problems together. Problem posing and problem solving are components of the critical pedagogy for music education approach.

Another strategy I call "Maestro, If You Please." In this instance the choral teacher chooses a student to be the conductor. Being a student conductor is an empowering and transformational experience for a young person. Accepting the responsibility of leading the choir contributes to a young man's self-identity in positive ways. When the teacher tells a student he may conduct the choir, that pronouncement makes the student a conductor. It is therefore a performative. Such experiences for young men are positive ones that mirror the leadership opportunities afforded to athletes who are the captains of their teams.

"Catch Me Being Good" is another strategy that connects to the principles of critical pedagogy. In this strategy, the conductor recognizes a particular singer who is contributing in positive ways to the execution of a particular piece. Each conductor may determine the criteria for "being good" in a particular musical selection. Offering praise to that student in front of his peers nurtures a positive and healthy self-identity.

Working to make choral ensembles more like the in-group may increase participation. When he taught middle school, Nicholas McBride an experienced and successful middle school choral director, formed a boy's choir called Pitch Black. As he describes it, the ensemble was run like a sports team. They met after school, and he was called only by his last name just as students do with their athletic coaches. McBride often played basketball or touch football with his singers after rehearsal. In addition, "coach" McBride conducted a faculty chorus that included many prominent male faculty members and administrators in the building. These men served as positive role models for the boys in the school. The building principal, as well as several athletic coaches and male guidance counsellors sang. At concerts, the male faculty members stood alongside the male students as a powerful exhibit of solidarity. This helped the young men in Pitch Black feel safe and comfortable (N. R. McBride, personal communication, January 19, 2010). Cristine Bass, in

Cherry Hill, New Jersey, conducts a high school male ensemble she calls Men of Note. In addition, she has an ensemble called Dads of Note. The fathers of the choir members come weekly to rehearsal and then perform with their sons in concert. Both groups wear athletic jackets for uniforms, and the repertoire includes oldies as well as some new repertoire. The joint performance is always a highlight of the spring concert. As a consequence, there are many young men singing in the choral program at her school. This strategy would work well in middle school.

King and Gurian (2007) suggest "boy-friendly" strategies that they use in their own classrooms to engage young men in meaningful learning experiences. They recommend single-gender learning environments. For the middle school choral director, that means a separate boys chorus. They advocate including boys in choosing topics to include in the classroom. In a middle school choir, that could mean including boys in decisions about what to sing. Perhaps offering several pieces to the boys and listening to their comments and input would make them feel ownership in the choir. Finding repertoire beyond the sea shanties sung by male glee clubs a generation ago is a good idea (see, for example, Abrahams & Head, 2011).

Considering the hidden and often coded messages embedded in the texts of songs young men sing is another. One example of a questionable text is Aaron Copland's choral arrangement "Stomp Your Foot" from his opera The Tender Land. Arranged for mixed or men's chorus, the verse reads, "Men must labor to be happy, plowing fields and planting rows. But ladies love a life that's easy, churning butter, milking cows." Later in the song is the text, "Ladies love their fine amusement, putting patches in a quilt, but men prefer to bend their shoulder to something that will stand when built." Clearly, these images conjure a picture of men's roles that is suspect. Although it is taken out of the context of the opera, I wonder how many choral directors actually address the hegemonic implications of how men and women are portrayed in Horace Everett's text?

In the American minstrel song (circa 1843), "The Boatmen's Dance," we learn that the boatmen squander their money on whiskey and women with the goal to "go home with the gals in the mornin'." Again, this promotes a hegemonic stereotypical view of what men do. In the American folk song, "I Bought Me a Cat' the text says, "I bought me a wife, My wife pleased me." While on the surface, some may argue that these texts are innocent; to an impressionable young man they include hidden messages.

According to Tarrant (1999) and Van Wel (1994), adolescents prefer music that is also preferred by their peers. Such preferences "may be a valued and important dimension of adolescents' social identity" (Tarrant, North, & Hargreaves, 2002, p. 568). Directors who select music that supports the preoccupation of their young students with action figures and movie soundtracks may notice a bond developing between teacher and student that is powerful and healthy.

In that same vein, conductors who choose music for young men that is in ranges that are comfortable and encourage their young singers to move among and between voice parts as appropriate will find a happier constituency within the choir. Choral scores that include a part for the cambiata voice are very appropriate as are choral scores where the voicing is flexible and labeled parts I, II, and III instead of tenor, tenor, bass or soprano, alto, and baritone.

Nicholas McBride, whose group Pitch Black was described above, suggests that engaging with students in activities they love outside the choral rehearsal is beneficial. But, he cautions us to ensure that these activities do not foster a hidden message that promotes normative masculine behaviour as the only desired behaviour for all adolescent male students (N. R. McBride, personal communication, January 19, 2010).

King and Gurian (2007) also recommend finding male role models. A faculty choir, such as the one McBride had, which includes men who work in the school building, is a wonderful strategy here. Finding male singers from a local college or the high school choir is another helpful suggestion. Outfitting the choir in uniforms that are urban chic instead of choir robes helps with the concern boys have for their identity.

Then, remembering the power of performatives, middle school choral directors should choose their words carefully and thoughtfully when addressing young men both inside and outside the choral rehearsal. In an interview with Osborne and Segal (1993), Butler explains that discourse works in part to stabilize and destabilize those speaking and those spoken to. She reiterates how powerful discourse is in shaping a person. Specifically, she suggests that performative speech acts, when repeated with consistency, bring into being that which they name. Thus, middle school choral directors who repeatedly tell young men to "stop singing like girls" or demand "some muscle" unknowingly replicate the performatives those young men seek to avoid from their peers. Such acts of performativity on the part of the choral director may cause adolescent young men to avoid singing in the middle school choir all together.

6.7 Conclusions

Young men such as Phillipe and Gus like to sing but confess that they sing in choirs at some risk to their socialization as members of their peer group. When they feel safe and supported in environments where their emerging self-identities are nurtured in thoughtful ways, they derive great pleasure from participating. Middle school choral directors are most successful when they are sensitive to the developmental socialization of their male students in addition to accommodating the physical changes in their voices. There are a number of strategies directors can employ to encourage middle school boys to participate in chorus, such as selecting music that is in line with their students' interests as well as fitting their vocal ranges and separating the young men into their own ensemble.

Then, remembering the power of performatives, choosing words carefully and thoughtfully when addressing these young men can contribute to positive feelings between and among young male students and their teachers.

Finally, critical pedagogy for music education offers a framework to help middle school choral directors shape musical experiences that break down barriers between out-groups and in-groups. The approach shifts power inside the rehearsal and empowers musicianship in the young men who sing. Such practices create dialogue among singers when they, with their teacher, pose and solve problems together. All these ideals foster a democratic atmosphere in the middle school choir and provide the place and space where young men can read the world and better understand who they are and their places in that world.

References

Abrahams, F. (2004, January). The application of critical theory to a sixth-grade general music class. *Visions of Research in Music Education, 4*, 43–53. Retrieved August 13, 2011, from http://www.rider.edu/~vrme

Abrahams, F. (2005a, September). *Critical pedagogy for music education: A best practice to prepare future music educators.* Paper presented at the meeting of the Society for Music Teacher Education, Greensboro, NC.

Abrahams, F. (2005b). The application of critical pedagogy to music teaching and learning: A literature review. *Update: Applications of Research in Music Education, 12*, 12–22.

Abrahams, F. (2005c, January). The application of critical pedagogy to music teaching and learning. *Visions of Research in Music Education.* Retrieved August 13, 2011, from http://www.rider.edu/~vrme

Abrahams, F. (2005d, September). Transforming classroom music instruction with ideas from critical pedagogy. *Music Educators Journal, 29*(1), 62–67.

Abrahams, F., & Head, P. D. (2005). *Case studies in music education* (2nd ed.). Chicago: GIA.

Abrahams, F., & Head, P. D. (2011). *Teaching music through performance in middle school choir.* Chicago: GIA.

Abramo, J. (2006, October). *Yea, I'm fat, who the hell cares: Performativity, agency and school rock bands."* Paper presented at the International Conference on Music Education, Equity, and Social Justice, Teachers College Columbia University, New York.

Adler, A. (2005, September). *Let the boys sing and speak: Masculinities and boys' stories of singing in school.* Paper presented at the Boys and Voices Symposium, Melbourne, Australia.

Adler, A. H. W. (2002). *Case study of boys' experiences of singing in school.* Unpublished doctoral dissertation, University of Toronto. Abstract retrieved August 13, 2011, from http://post.queensu.ca/~grime/v11n1.html#4.1

Austin, J. L. (1962). *How to do things with words.* Cambridge, MA: Harvard University Press.

Austin, J. L. (1970). *Philosophical papers.* Oxford: Clarendon Press.

Austin, J. R. (1990). The relationship of music self-esteem to degree of participation in school and out-of-school music activities among upper-elementary students. *Contributions to Music Education, 17*, 20–31.

Billmeyer, R. (2003). *Strategies to engage the mind of the learner.* Omaha, NE: Dayspring Printing.

Butler, J. (1990). *Gender trouble: Feminism and the subversion of identity.* London: Routledge.

Butler, J. (2000). Critically queer. In P. du Gay, J. Evans, & P. Redman (Eds.), *Identity: A reader* (pp. 108–118). London: Sage.

Franzoi, S. L. (1996). *Social psychology.* Dubuque: Brown & Benchmark.

Freire, P. (1970). Pedagogy of the oppressed. New York: Continuum Press.

Gauntlett, D. (2002). *Media, gender and identity* (2nd ed.). New York: Routledge. Retrieved August 13, 2011, from http://www.theory.org.uk/giddens4.htm

Giddens, A. (1991). *Modernity and self-identity: Self and society in the late modern age.* Palo Alto, CA: Stanford University Press.

Green, L. (1997). *Music, gender, education.* London: Routledge.

Hanley, B. (1998). Gender in secondary music education in British Columbia. *British Journal of Music Education, 15*(1), 51–69.

Harrison, S. D. (2003). *Musical participation by boys: The role of gender in the choice of musical activities by males in Australian schools*. Doctoral dissertation, Griffith University, Queensland, Australia.

Harrison, S. D. (2006). Why boys limit musical choices. *Gender Research in Music Education, 10*(1). Retrieved August 13, 2011, from http://post.queensu.ca/~grime/v10n1.html

King, K., & Gurian, M. (2007). With boys in mind: Teaching to the minds of boys. *Educational Leadership, 64*(1), 56–61.

Knox, M. (2006). Gender and possible selves. In C. Dunkel & J. Kerpelman (Eds.), *Possible selves: Theory, research, and applications* (pp. 61–77). New York: Nova Science Publishers.

Kohlberg, L. (1966). A cognitive-developmental analysis of children's sex-role concepts and attitudes. In E. E. MacCoby (Ed.), *The development of sex differences* (pp. 82–173). Stanford, CA: Stanford University Press.

Kohlberg, L. (1969). Stages and sequences: The cognitive-developmental approach to socialization. In D. A. Goslin (Ed.), *Handbook of socialization theory and research* (pp. 347–380). Chicago: Rand McNally.

Koza, J. E. (1994). Big boys don't cry (or sing): Gender, misogyny, and homophobia in college choral methods texts. *The Quarterly Journal of Music Teaching and Learning, 4/5*(4/1), 48–64.

Markus, H., & Nurius, P. (1986). Possible selves. *American Psychologist, 41*(9), 954–969.

Markus, H., & Nurius, P. (1987). Possible selves: The interface between motivation and the self concept. In K. Yardley & T. Honess (Eds.), *Self and identity: Psychosocial perspectives* (pp. 157–172). Great Britain: Wiley.

National Center for Education Statistics. (1999, June). *NAEP 1997 Arts Summary Data Tables*. Retrieved August 13, 2011 from http://nces.ed.gov/nationsreportcard/tables/art1997/

North, A. C., & Hargreaves, D. J. (1999). Music and adolescent identities. *Music Education Research, 1*, 75–92.

Osborne, P., & Segal, L. (1993). *Gender as performance: An interview with Judith Butler*. Retrieved August 13, 2011, from http://www.theory.org.uk/but-int1.htm

O'Toole, P. (2005). I sing in a choir but I have no voice! *Visions of Research in Music Education, 6*. Retrieved August 13, 2011, from http://www-usr.rider.edu/~vrme/v6n1/vision/otoole_2005.htm

Pogonowski, L. M. (1985). Attitude assessment of upper elementary students in a process-oriented music curriculum. *Journal of Research in Music Education, 33*(4), 247–257.

Roberts, B. A. (2006). *A sociological deviation*. Ecclectica: The Future of University Music Study in Canada. Retrieved August 13, 2011, from http://www.ecclectica.ca/issues/2206/2/

Svengalis, J. (1978). Music attitude and the preadolescent male. *Dissertation Abstracts International, 39*, 4800A (University Microfilms No. 79-02953).

Swanwick, K. (1988). *Music, mind, and education*. London: Routledge.

Tajfel, H. (1978). *Differentiation between social groups*. London: Academic.

Tajfel, H., & Turner, J. C. (1979). An integrative theory of intergroup conflict. In W. G. Austin & S. Worchel (Eds.), *The social psychology of intergroup relations* (pp. 33–47). Monterey, CA: Brooks-Cole.

Tajfel, H., & Turner, J. C. (1986). The social identity theory of inter-group behavior. In S. Worchel & L. W. Austin (Eds.), *Psychology of intergroup relations* (pp. 2–24). Chicago: Nelson-Hall.

Tarrant, M. (1999). *Musical and social development in adolescence*. Unpublished doctoral dissertation, University of Leicester, Leicester, UK.

Tarrant, M., North, A. C., & Hargreaves, D. J. (2002). Youth identity and music. In R. A. R. MacDonald, D. J. Hargreaves, & D. Miell (Eds.), *Musical identities* (pp. 134–150). Oxford: Oxford University Press.

Van Wel, F. (1994). A culture gap between the generations? Social influences on youth cultural style. *International Journal of Adolescence and Youth, 4*, 211–228.

Chapter 7
Creating a Culture for Teenagers to Sing in High School

Anita Collins

7.1 Introduction

As a practicing music educator in an all boys secondary school I was frustrated. As each new cohort of Year Seven boys entered the school at the start of the school year the music staff were buoyed; so many aspiring musicians who bought new life and enthusiasm to the program. Yet somehow, slowly but steadily, a significant number of these boys would lose their initial enthusiasm, show greater interest in activities outside of the music program and finally, predictable, give up their musical activities entirely by half way through Year Eight. A small percentage would not give up their music activities but would shift their interest to another instrument and musical genre. This was also predictable; boys who had learnt clarinet for 4 years now favoured electric guitar, boys who loved to sing in primary school now refused to utter a note and any boy who listened to Classical music on his iPod was ridiculed by his peers.

Each year the staff and myself would ask what we could do stem this phenomenon, how should we change our teaching and structures to keep more of the boys involved in their musical activities. Or was this the natural way of things, did boys' musical interests evolve during their early secondary school years and our role was to cater for their shifting foci. I continued to feel as if we were groping in the dark for answers and consequently I needed to look outside our sphere of experience for solutions.

The literature did not offer the plethora of instant solutions that I had hoped for. The focus area, boys music education, needed to bridge two established research areas; Music Education and Gender Education and also needed to be culturally relevant, incorporating the current trends and historical influences in Australian culture and education.

A. Collins (✉)
University of Canberra, Bruce, ACT, Australia
e-mail: Anita.Collins@canberra.edu.au

Two important studies stood out as being particularly significant in the research. Trollinger's (1993/4) "Sex/Gender Research in Music Education: A Review" is an exceptionally comprehensive evaluation of research to date on the subject. The second was a study by Green (1993), based primarily around the anecdotal evidence of teachers concerning the differences between boys and girls in music over a wide range of topics. Their findings are reiterated in the research work of Koza (1993), West (2001), O'Neill and Boulton (1996) and Abeles and Porter (1978) who effectively examine historical issues, teaching strategies, parental influence and instrumental choice of boys' in music education. These studies informed the most recent and comprehensive volume specific to boys music education in Australia, *Male Voices: Stories of boys learning through making music* (Harrison, 2009).

Throwing a broader net across the literature, the current trends in Music Education are incredibly varied, as one might expect for such a broad field of knowledge and practice. Stevens and McPherson (2004) aimed to map the present state of music education research in Australia, and concluded that Australian research had "come of age" in terms of both the quantity and the quality. Researchers are adopting and exploring a variety of social research techniques including practice-oriented and socio-cultural approaches as well as inductive theory construction (Saarikallio & Erkkilä, 2004; Weaver-Hightower, 2003; Mills, Martino, & Lingard, 2007; Keddie, 2005). Interestingly, the field of Music Psychology, outlined by Hodges (2003) as the study of the phenomenon of music, is evolving rapidly and will have significant effects on music education and research in the future. This field of research has recently entering the more populist sphere with the book "This is Your Brain on Music" by Levitin (2006). All of these developments enhance our understanding of music education, but it is this last field that may, along with further research on adolescent development in boys, shed new light on this area.

The focus on specific educational needs of boys' has truly come to the fore in the last decade. Marcus Weaver-Hightower (2003) eloquently highlights the need for the "boy's turn" in gender education research, and indeed, Australian academics and government in particular has made significant forays into this area. In 2002 the Australian Federal Government released a report on their inquiry into the education of boys, *Boys: Getting it Right*, which has placed the spotlight squarely on the specific needs of boys in education. This report has been used as a springboard for discussions on a practice-oriented versus theoretical-oriented approach for effective boys' education, curriculum development and teacher education (Mills et al., 2007). Amanda Keddie (2005), from the University of Queensland, has developed the *Productive Pedagogies Framework* by using socio-cultural research to move from the current skills focus towards a pedagogy based on an understanding of gender inequities as a product of social practice.

While there was a plethora of information and papers, few useful solutions arose from my review; indeed the most useful findings came from the anecdotal evidence provided by practicing music educators in the same position as myself. This lead to the design of a research project to gather the collective wisdom of music educators who had maintained the participation levels and consistently higher standard of achievement in the area of boys music education in Australia. The findings resulted

7 Creating a Culture for Teenagers to Sing in High School

in a model, the *Boys Music Ecosystem* (Collins, 2009a) model, which music educators could use to conceptualise the multiple facets of their music programs and practices.

The model begins with the boy at the centre. Each boy is surrounded by an ecosystem, a complex and delicate balance of messages and experiences that influence each boy's attitude towards their musical activities. To maintain the boys interest in their musical activities, three Essences' need to be positively balanced – Essence 1 – *Interest* and *Positive Attitude*, Essence 2 – *Success* and *Accomplishment* and Essence 3 – *Acceptance* and *Praise*. If one of these Essences is contaminated by negative messages or experiences then the entire ecosystem could be in danger, leading to a rapid loss of interest by the boy in his musical activities. The seven Elements that can contribute to both positive and negative messages and experiences for boys are *School Culture, Relationships, Peers, Parents, Role Models, Student Character, and Teaching Strategies* (Fig. 7.1).

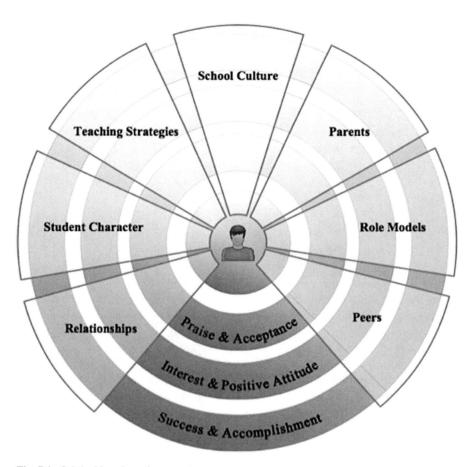

Fig. 7.1 Original boys' music ecosystem

In this form the model provides two important perspectives. The first perspective, the Essences, is a set of key principles upon which to base teaching and structural decisions in any music program. The second perspective, the Elements, is a list of significant areas and stakeholders that need to be considered in light of the key principles. The test of this model is when it is applied to a given musical activity. Singing is a particularly good test of this model as Australian music educators have had varied success with the participation and retention of boys in singing activities.

7.2 Developing the Model

The source of the *Boys Music Ecosystem* model was the collective wisdom of a select group of music educators and Year 11 boy musicians. The music educators were selected because of their successes in motivating and retaining boys in their music programs in large numbers beyond Year 9. These music educators came from three separate all-boy schools in three different Australian states. A thematic analysis was conducted on the data that was collected in semi-structured interviews and compared with the existing literature on boys music education.

Within the scope of the original research project it was not possible to delve extensively into the area of boys educational psychology. However the model that developed out of the research highlighted the importance of constructive relationships between boys and their teachers, parents and peers in terms of their musical activities. Furthermore to motivate boys to remain engaged in their musical activities required a firm understanding of boys educational psychology in the areas of school culture, teaching practice and curriculum design. It is appropriate at this point to enrich the model with the greater detail that researchers in boys' educational psychology can provide.

7.3 Psychology of Boys

While models such as the *Boys Music Ecosystem* can attempt to outline more universal truths about boys' music education, when adding a layer of boys' educational psychology to the model, it is important to consider the cultural context that the boys are involved in. In this case the work of Celia Lashlie and Steve Biddulph can contribute to the development of the *Boys Music Ecosystem* model. The work of both Lashlie and Biddulph is based within the New Zealand and Australian cultural and educational context. These two researchers provide a good of experience and knowledge with Lashlie's work with at-risk boys and men in New Zealand prisons and Biddulph's experience as a psychologist working as closely with parents as he does with boys.

Lashlie's experience in boys' educational psychology, outlined in her book *He'll Be OK* (Lashlie, 2007a), came from her career as the first women prison officer in a male prison in New Zealand and her experience as a parent. While she does not classify herself as a researcher she holds a degree in anthology and Maori and combines this training with her extensive experience with the NZ "Good Man Project" to produce insights into boys developmental, social and emotional needs. While she has worked primarily with "at-risk" boys and men she has distilled a series of important truths about the pivotal Year 9 (15 years of age) experience for boys. Consequently Lashlie has focused, among many other areas, on successful strategies to use directly before this pivotal period, between the ages of 12–14 years. As relationships with teachers, peers and parents were identified as significant areas within the Boys Music Ecosystem her insights could enhance the understanding of many areas of the model.

Lashlie, an engaging orator who undertakes a significant number of public speaking engagements each year, works primarily in a narrative style. In working with boys she speaks of relaxing into the male essence in order to understand the boy mythology. As a female working with boys Lashlie felt she needed to learn to be silent and to follow a conversation rather than direct it. Boys have an "intense wisdom if you pause long enough to pick it up" (Lashlie, 2007b) and that using humour and answering with the unexpected will strengthen the relationship and level of trust you share with them. For a boy, the world is shifting somewhat uncomfortably in Year 9, and they are trying to find a pathway through that shift. The relationship a boy establishes with his teachers can act as a stationary pillar during this shifting time. The retention of staff therefore becomes a significant issue for a school in maintaining a positive school culture and music program.

Although Lashlie is known for her work with and about boys, she began her post prison officer career with a desire to help women and mothers understand boys. Ironically it is a desire to make contact with male role models such as male teachers, men who share hobbies, family friends and extended family. As a consequence of this desire boys move further away from their mothers and female carers. This focus on role models, the type of role models and modes of contact with those role models, is a significant area of enquiry for Lashlie. Boys need a variety of role models to choose from and the best contact comes through pathways being created to those role models, rather than specifically targeted or orchestrated contact for the boys. An example Lashlie uses is that instead of organizing a fishing trip with a male role model for her son, she simply mentioned that a fishing trip was taking place without a specific invitation for her son to attend. This gave her son the pathway to make the contact as well as the choice not to make that contact. In terms of teaching strategies for boys this could mean a greater number and variety of male musical role models. The interactions may incorporate more freedom for the boys to interact with the musicians, rather than the 30-min concert with no questions or free time to connect with the musician, with pathways for future conversations with the role models.

Lashlie observes that boys are extremely visual and will form a very graphic picture in the minds. In Lashlie's experience this has been a useful tool when educating boys about prisons, and the need to make positive decisions in their teenage years to avoid entering the prison system, but could this technique be used more extensively in teaching music, in engaging boys with the art form? Imagery and metaphor have been shown to be effective in improving engagement and musicianship in student musicians and the more physical and detailed the image, the more effective the students understanding of complex musical ideas (Collins, 2009b). By the time boys have reached Year Nine Lashlie describes them as "living in 30 s moments" that has a number of consequences for teaching and understanding boys. Boys do not effectively work through the consequences of their actions if those consequences fall outside that 30 s. They may also struggle to commit to memory content or conceptual information that takes more than 30 s to follow through or understand. Working with this rule of thumb could radically change teaching practices used in Year Nine, but may also have an effect the approach in Year Seven and Eight in preparation for Year Nine. The incorporation of the use of imagery, visual stimuli, graphic detail, fast-paced lesson and including physical learning techniques as boys progress through Year Seven and Eight into Year Nine could be more effective in managing the transition from boy to young man.

In Biddulph's work in *Raising Boys* (Biddulph, 2008) he identifies the three different stages of boyhood and the varying needs of boys during those stages. Of most relevance to the *Boys Music Ecosystem*, which focuses on early secondary school years (12–14 years), are Biddulph's second stage of boyhood (6–14 years) and the third stage of boyhood (14-adult years) (Table 7.1). The fact that the age span modelled in the *Boys Music Ecosystem* bridges Biddulph's stages of boyhood is significant, and could indicate a reason for the intermittent success experienced by music educators in this area. Biddulph proposed that the boys' internal motivation and external needs also changes significantly between these two stages (Biddulph, 2008).

Biddulph stresses that these changes are not a flick of a switch but gradual and highly individual. If the rate and intensity of these changes is different for each boy it is not surprising that music educators can experience both success and challenges on a daily basis and need to be responsive to the shifting needs and interests of the boys. This can be accommodated in a classroom environment and within individual teaching practices, but when it comes to structural decisions and broader music program issues, music educators could find that what was successful last year may be unsuccessful the following year. Consequently the *Boys Music Ecosystem* needs

Table 7.1 Stages of boyhood (Biddulph, 2008, p. 11)

Second stage of boyhood (6–14 years)	Third stage of boyhood (14-adult years)
• Own internal drivers • Starts to want to learn to be a man • Looks more and more to his father for interest and activity • Purpose of this stage is to build competence and skills while developing kindness and playfulness – becoming a balanced person • This is the age when a boys becomes happy and secure about being a male	• Need input of male mentors to complete his journey • Aim is for the boy to learn skills, responsibility and self-respect by more and more with the adult community

to be flexible, adaptable and under daily review to deliver the best and most effective music experiences for boys. The question for music educators may be when is it time to alter a given teaching practice or structure to accommodate the changing needs of the boys and when is it more effective to maintain the course in order to provide limits and stability for the boy. This is a highly individual and contextual decision and can only be made by the music educator working with the boys.

Biddulph's outlines the effects of testosterone on boys' development at the ages of 13 and 14 years and this may have an impact on the Boys Music Ecosystem. At 13 boys experience rapid growth and disorientation while at 14 testosterone leads them to begin the test limits in a period that Biddulph describes as "breaking through to manhood" (p. 60). As stated in the initial research project, could the sudden change to a different (manly) instrument, rejection of singing activities which previously filled their lives or abrupt halt of musical activities all together at the age of 13 be evidence of boys moving into the third stage of boyhood. If so, considering the need for input of male mentors outlined in this boyhood stage, might this be an indication to focus musical experiences not on the needs of the second stage of boyhood but on helping the boys transition into the third stage with a different set of expectations of their musical activities. Could a remedy to the exodus of boys from musical activities at the age of 14 be in how we anticipate, or proactively plan for, the transition from the second to third boyhood stage, rather that dealing with the decline once the boys have begun testing the limits?

One of Biddulph's many suggestions to parents is entitled *praise is the antidote*, 'a male teacher or a friend sees a boy tapping on a table in a complex rhythm. "You know, you could be a drummer – that's a really hard rhythm". Such a comment boosts the boy's sense of himself. He is less dependent on peer approval and more willing to take risks.' (p. 165). Similarly the theme of authentic and deserved praise falls under the *Success and Accomplishment* principle in the Boys Music Ecosystem model. Praise has a significant impact on a boy when originating from a male role model rather than a parent. Therefore a significant element of the proactive planning for the transition between the second and third stage of boyhood could be the explicit use of male musical role models.

7.4 Developing the Boys Music Ecosystem

When re-examining the *Boys Music Ecosystem* model in light of the work of Lashlie and Biddulph there is scope to develop. A fundamental change is the re-ordering of the Elements. This re-ordering no longer has all seven Elements as seperate areas or stakeholders within the Ecosystem, but groups *Parents, Peers and Role Models* together. These three elements have an internal influence on a boy's motivation to maintain his involvement in musical activities. As music educators we need to understand these elements but we are unable to influence them directly. The remaining four elements, *Relationships and Student Character, School Culture and Teaching Strategies* are external influences on a boy. As music educators we

Fig. 7.2 Developed boys' music ecosystem

have far more control over these influences on a boy and it is here that we can enact changes which may alter the internal influences of peers, parents and role models. This development implies a sequence which music educators could use to continually evaluate their music programs, a factor that was not present in the first incarnation of the model (Fig. 7.2).

The grouping of *Parents, Peers and Role Models* arose from the focus both Lashlie and Biddulph put on the move boys make physically, socially and psychologically around the age of 14 years. The effect of testosterone, living in 30-s moments, searching for role models and learning responsibility shifts the basis of a boy's life. The relationship between each boy and his parents and peers alters and they seek pathways to a variety of male role models. In order to maintain a boy's motivation in his musical activities a music educator needs to understand the role of and changes within these three areas at all points of each boy's transition out of boyhood and into manhood. Music educators can use these three areas to design boy-focused music programs which provide a variety of male role models that boys can interact with freely, activities which involve their peers actively and equally and appropriate involvement from parents that give boys space to think, express themselves and choose their own musical pathways.

Using this developed model music educators can look to the quality of the relationships they have with the boys and ask question such as "are they providing boundaries for each boy with techniques for effective correction of behaviour without losing the basis of a respectful relationship between teacher and boy?" and "is their laughter in the classroom and a chance for boys to express their intense wisdom?" Similarly how can music educators be more effective at recognizing individual student characteristics and provide an environment for boys to explore their own strengths and vulnerability?

In the outside circle, the boys must be appropriately supported by the underpinning teaching strategies used in all music activities and the school culture that surrounds those activities. Teaching strategies in each music activity can evolve during the Year

Seven and Eight (12–14 years of age) experiences to support the significant physical, social and psychological changes that occur in Year 9 (15 years of age). The school culture of announcements, rewards and recognition can maintain boys' motivation to continue their involvement in musical activities if pitched effectively by both instrumental and classroom music teaching staff. The teaching and support staff can be made aware of their potential to be musical role models for boys, conveying how they use music in their lives and the importance it holds for them.

Each school and cultural context is different and therefore every music program is different. No model could be applied to a school without the invaluable knowledge of the music educators and school leaders who work in each context. The most important aspect of any model is how it could translate to a specific school environment. As mentioned in the introduction above the test of a model is when it is applied to a given musical activity such as singing. The following section is a suggestion of how this model could come alive in a school music program with an emphasis on the musical activity of singing.

7.5 Using the Model in Context

For a boy, the transition from one stage of development to another at the age of 14 is a significant one, and brings with it different needs and foci. The original research project identified a trend for boys to alter their musical activities in large numbers at this age, either changing from a conventional instrument such as trumpet to a pop based instrument such as electric guitar, express a distain for activities such as singing which they had been involved with for several years, or give up their musical activities entirely. Within the initial project there was explicit and extensive reference by boys and staff to singing. A significant amount of data was gathered on both successful methods for encouraging and maintaining a culture of singing in a school and, more importantly, the less successful approaches when it comes to boys and singing. Some of the useful principles are;

- Boys identify singing as a feminine pursuit so the repertoire, rehearsal and performance experience needs to reinforce the opposite attitude
- Boys love to sing but are particular about what (the repertoire) they sing
- Repertoire choice is vital, enough challenge to be interesting but within their technical grasp (especially when their voice is breaking) to guarantee success during performance
- Boys support a high quality of singing performance, whatever the genre of music
- Boys need to enjoy themselves when they are singing. Even if they are singing hymns the choice of a more modern arrangement or fuller pop accompaniment can change their attitude immediately
- Boys enjoy singing together
- If the boys have not seen men they know singing they assume it is not fit the description of a male, and therefore it is not an activity appropriate for a man
- Boys need to be allowed to smile, to enjoy themselves and be physical in their singing. The key elements to motivating boys to sing are appropriate repertoire choice, enjoying rehearsals and seeing high quality results

In order to counter the significant changes that will occur to all boys at the age of 13 and 14 years, a music program needs to implement proactive planning for musical activities when boys are 12 years of age (Year 7). These plans need to address the three areas central to the developed model (Peers, Parents and Role Models) while also intertwining new approaches to the other four Elements (Teaching Practices, Relationships, School Culture and Student Character). The planning must embody the following principles: boys need to physically, emotionally and socially enjoy the singing experience, the repertoire needs to be challenging yet within their ability to perform well, they need to perform separately and not in contest with girls, parents need to be involved and express their support for their son's achievements but in a manner appropriate for a man not a boy, and during the singing experience boys need informal and formal access to a variety of professional male musicians and role models from their own educational context such as their male teachers and leaders.

What might this look like in a school context? A music concert is the most likely focus to use as it has clearly defined process (rehearsal) and product (performance) elements. A strong theme in the original research project was the need for critical mass, for enough boys to be involved in musical activities so that it becomes an expectation for boys to enjoy and learn music, not an outlier activity for musically gifted or effeminate boys. To encourage this critical mass such an event needs to be compulsory. There may be many arguments to this approach but there is no better time in a boy's life to expose him to the many benefits of musical activities, and indeed it is vital to do so before the effects of increased testosterone overwhelm many parts of his life.

The concert could include an all-boys singing item which involves movement, costumes and theatrical staging. During the rehearsal process the boys could select from a limited field of suggestions the song they would like to sing and either collaboratively or democratically elect a choreographer or director. In a co-ed school rehearsals might be closed to the girls in the class or year group. External music professionals may collaborate with the boys in their design and rehearsal of the event, providing external role models for the boys to interact with. This allows time for the school staff to develop stronger relationships with the boys on an individual level. Male role models within the school may be asked to attend a late stage or dress rehearsal to create an opportunity for feedback and support for the boys' musical activities. Depending on the event fathers and male guardians of boys may be asked to assist in the event, ideally by both singing with the boys at home and rehearsals as well as other activities where pathways between boys and a variety of role models are created, but not manufactured. The penultimate performance could be in a public arena where boys can gain musical confidence and public recognition for their work.

Where does a supportive School Culture fit into this type of activity? There is a profound difference between a school culture that provides *opportunities* for boys to be involved in arts activities and a school culture that *supports* arts activities. Support is both providing the opportunities and positively discriminating towards musical activities. This means recognizing the negative values and misconceptions boys have about being involved in musical activities and working to lessen or counter those beliefs. One of the simplest adages that arose from the original research was "let boys be a sportsman AND a musician". A supportive school culture makes this possible by conscious planning that does not allow music rehearsals and sports training to overlap on any given school day and recognized that a Eisteddfod performance is more important than a weights training session and a semi-final game takes precedence over a music rehearsal. A supportive school culture recognized boy's achievements in music along side his sporting achievements. A school principal's conscious choice to counter the perceived hierarchy of activities by discussing a music tours before sporting results in their weekly assembly address can speak volumes to the boys in the audience.

Putting music activities out in front of the school, but not just at assemblies but the cricket dinners or school fetes. Every school context and culture is different, and more importantly, it is constantly changing. Therefore the manner in which school culture support boy's musical activities must be responsive and reactive to those changes. Boys perceive many of their own beliefs and attitudes from the male role models around them; therefore part of the positive discrimination of musical activities needs to originate from the male role models within the school.

7.6 Conclusion

The question which needs to be asked around the music staffroom table is "how can we create a unique musical experience for the boys that embodies inclusion, develops relationships, pathways to role models, high quality musical outcomes and creative input from the boys themselves?" How, in short, can we help them relax into their male essence and maintain a positive attitude towards musical activities as they travel into Year Eight? In doing so respectful and strong relationships can be build between boys and music staff where boys are valued for their own characters and journey into the shift sands of Year Eight and Nine with a positive attitude towards musical activities where they can bond with their peers on an alternate social level.

This type of program cannot be viewed in isolation and needs to be followed up by an equally appropriate Year Eight program. The design of such a program is highly dependent on the experience boys have had in Year Seven and must take into account the tricky balance of flexibility and limit setting for boys entering Biddulph's third stage of boyhood. Music teachers, with support of the wider school community and culture, have the ability to affect boys' attitudes towards musical activities. They can maintain motivation and interest in Year Eight and None by approaching Year Seven as a foundation year, a year to set the bar, and create that critical mass and expectation that boys will maintain their musical activities into their upper secondary school years. Of course there will be natural attrition within any program, boys will pare back the number of activities they put their time into or naturally gravitate away from musical activities, but this shouldn't be due of misconceptions and for non-musical reasons. As music educators we would agree that investing in a boy brings may rewards, but the more we invest in understanding boys the more that investment will pay off – the more we invest in the whole boy, the more he will invest in himself.

References

Abeles, H., & Porter, S. (1978). Sex-stereotyping of musical instruments. *Journal of Research in Music Education, 26*(2), 65–75.

Biddulph, S. (2008). *Raising boys: Why boys are different – And how to help them become happy and well-balanced men*. Australia: Finch Publishing.

Collins, A. (2009a). A boy's music ecosystem. In S. Harrison (Ed.), *Male voices: Stories of boys learning through making music* (pp. 33–47). Australia: ACER Press.

Collins, A. (2009b). *Enhancing musical understanding using imagery, metaphor and thinking styles*. In: Australian society of music educators: Proceedings of the XVII National Conference in Launceston 10–14 July 2009, pp. 14–22.

Green, Lucy. (1993). Music, gender and education, a report on some exploratory research. *British Journal of Music Education, 10*(3), 19–254.

Harrison, S., (Ed.). (2009). *Male voices: Stories of boys learning through making music*. Australia: ACER Press.

Hodges, D. A. (2003). Music psychology and music education: What's the connection? *Research Studies in Music Education, 21*(1), 31–44.

Keddie, A. (2005). A framework for 'best practice' in boys' education: Key requisite knowledges and productive pedagogies. *Pedagogy, Culture and Society, 13*(1), 59–74.

Koza, J. (1993). Missing males and other gender issues in music education: Evidence from the music supervisors' journal, 1914–1924. *The Journal of Research in Music Education, 41*(3), 212–232.

Lashlie, C. (2007a). *He'll be ok: Growing gorgeous boys into good men*. Australia: Harper Collins.

Lashlie, C. (2007b). Interview with Richard Fidler, ABC Radio, March 14, 4:00 pm. Retrieved Jan 11, 2010, from http://www.abc.net.au/queensland/conversations/stories/s1871891.htm?nsw

Levitin, D. J. (2006). *This is your brain on music: The science of a human obsession*. New York: Dutton/Penguin.

Mills, M., Martino, W., & Lingard, B. (2007). Getting boys' education 'right': The Australian Government's Parliamentary Inquiry Report as an exemplary instance of recuperative masculinity politics. *British Journal of Sociology of Education, 28*(1), 5–21.

O'Neill, S., & Boulton, M. (1996). Boys' and girls' preferences for musical instruments: A function of gender? *Psychology of Music, 24*(2), 171–183.
Saarikallio, S., & Erkkilä, J. (2004). The role of music in adolescents' mood regulation, *Research Studies in Music Education, 23*(1), 18–31.
Stevens, R. S., & McPherson, G. E. (2004). Mapping music education research in Australia. *Psychology of Music, 32*(3), 330–342.
Trollinger, L. (1993/4). Sex/gender research in music education: A review. *Quarterly Journal of Music Teaching and Learning, 4*/4–5/1 (Winter 1993–Spring 1994), 22–39.
Weaver-Hightower, M. (2003). The 'boy turn' in research on gender and education. *Review of Educational Research, 73*(4), 471–498.
West, P. (2001). Ideas schools could use to increase boys' achievement, *Recommendations from the Report on Best Practice in Boys' Education*, published by Research Group on Men and Families & Men's Health Information and Resource Centre, University of Western Sydney, Australia.

Chapter 8
Male Singing in the University Choir Context

Colin Durrant

8.1 Background

As a conductor for some years now of university choirs, it has come to my attention that the inclusion and involvement of young men in choral singing activity is variable and dependent on, or rather related to, a number of factors. My current choirs include (i) an open access large choir of some 140 voices at Imperial College, a university college that attracts high-level, mostly science-based students and, (ii) a university chamber choir of 26 singers auditioned from the various colleges, schools and institutes of the federal university of London. Although the composition of these choirs varies considerably from year to year, as compared for example to other similar sized adult choral groups, both choirs have an active, vibrant, if transient membership. In each choir there is a 50/50 male/female ratio – in the large choir luckily by default and in the chamber choir by design. (At my first rehearsal with the large choir, I found 35 male tenors singing – a luxury equivalent to wallowing in the hot springs in the mountains around Taipei on a balmy spring evening!) That may be sheer luck, but the inclusion of such a proportion of men merits more detailed investigation and research, though it should be recognised at the outset that the science-based subjects, especially Physics and Engineering still attract more men than women and this is likely to have significant impact on the membership therefore of this particular choir and other activities within this particular college. Both choirs are 'extra-curricular' and do not carry academic credit.

Research into the singers in my choirs has been carried out both informally (in conversations during committee meetings, rehearsal breaks and in the bar after rehearsals, as well as more social occasions like tours and extended weekends) and more systematically and formally through questionnaire ($n = 107$) and interview ($n = 10$). The male membership of each choir (as does the female) reflects a diverse group in terms of nationality with, in addition to the UK, singers from a number of

---

C. Durrant (✉)
Institute of Education, London, UK
e-mail: C.Durrant@ioe.ac.uk

Asian countries, particularly Hong Kong and Singapore, but also Thailand which is not noted for its choral singing tradition, most European countries, more recently including Poland and Bulgaria, as well as the more expected Germany, France, Italy and Luxembourg. While the nature of university choirs means that the age of singers will normally be within 18–22 for undergraduates, a significant number of older, postgraduate masters and doctoral students also take part, as do staff – from faculty and administration. Each choir is supported and sponsored by the college and university student unions, and consequently are organised and maintained by official student committee structures.

The other consideration for the conductor is that singers, particularly in the open access larger choir, come with a wide range of singing experiences. Some are very experienced and have already sung extensively in school, church and other youth choir contexts, while others are fairly new to singing and have made a significant leap by joining. This is often the result of attractive marketing at the beginning of the academic year, persuasion by their peers, or genuine curiosity and seeking something new. This also impacts upon the role of the conductor in rehearsal to make the singing experience both accessible to the less confident and less experienced and offer sufficient challenge to the more confident and experienced singer (Durrant, 2003).

Vocally, males by the age of 18 are usually settled (Cooksey, 1992) and experienced singers will have planted themselves in the tenor or bass sections, with the occasional male student opting for alto. Occasionally (as with females) they are not sure about their voice part and will ask for advice. This often means that they are very inexperienced in singing and maybe do not read notation, or that they may fit in a baritone range with, as yet, undeveloped lower and upper pitches. More rarely, more experienced males will volunteer to fit in with whatever part needs more voices in order to ensure choral balance.

So, questions arise: who are these male singers? What are their previous singing and musical experiences and activities? How do they perceive themselves within the choir? What does singing in the choir mean to them? There have been a number of significant research studies exploring the social dimension of choirs (Durrant & Himonides, 1998; Faulkner & Davidson, 2006) and it is evident from these that choirs are as much social as musical groups. This is certainly the case in these two university choirs, where participation in a variety of non-musical events is encouraged, centring mostly on drinking and, once in a blue moon, eating. But there is a general feeling that socialising acts as a gelling agency, enhancing a 'togetherness' appropriate for these choirs. Many students are new to university life, often coming from perhaps a more sheltered school environment and are often, for the first time, alone. The choir student committees in each case attach almost as much importance to the social dimension as to the musical side of things.

Over the years I have carried out research into choirs and conducting and various students of mine have also contributed to the body of knowledge in this area. This chapter draws on some the findings from these studies to illuminate the phenomenon of males singing, in this instance, in university choirs. To assume that these males have had extensive and formative singing experiences in their schools is misleading. Some join university choirs by accident or through persuasion, while others join because they have indeed had positive school choir experiences and want to continue to join in singing activities. As with boys singing in schools, so some of these students were teased because they sang in a choir, while others formed comfortable camaraderie groups within the choir quite quickly, depending on their personalities and skill at making friendships (Freer, 2009). It should be noted that universities (certainly in the UK) have 'freshers' fayres' [sic] at the beginning of the academic year so that societies, clubs, sports and music groups can promote themselves and encourage new members largely through emphasising the social dimension.

Where individual colleges have a Christian foundation, there will usually be well-established chapel choirs, where singers, often on scholarships, will be required to sing in regular chapel services on an almost professional basis. This is the case in Cambridge and Oxford, King's London and others. Some universities that are located in cathedral cities are likely to have connections with the cathedral choir with the provision of choral scholarships or such-like. Clearly in these situations, the singers have to remain committed to their role. The audition and selection process for these usually require a highly developed sight-singing skills as well as vocal acumen in order to perform, in some cases, regular, even daily services to a high standard. Many of these college chapel choirs are male only, thus perpetuating a long tradition of male hegemony in the church (Ashley, 2008). However, I do not intend to rehearse the issues and arguments concerning boys and men singing in the church in this chapter – that has been covered adequately in several places – notably in the research and writings of Martin Ashley from the sociological perspective and of Graham Welch from the acoustical, developmental and psychological. Rather, I wish to gain access to the narratives of male singers who are not compelled to sing by virtue of payment, but choose to join (in this case my) choirs voluntarily either through audition, or not. The intention is to provide some insight into (i) the backgrounds and previous singing experiences of these young men, (ii) the perceptions of themselves as singers, (iii) their perceived musical and social benefits and (iv) whether there are patterns of personal characteristics and traits among these males. I am indebted to one of my doctoral students, Flora Yeung, who has carried out interviews with particular singers as part of her own study looking at choirs in Hong Kong; where appropriate, I have used some of her interview material. Also, I have been very aware of the almost ethical issues surrounding interviewing singers myself who sing in the choirs I conduct. Inevitably, this methodology is open to challenge. However, I believe that I have sufficient credibility and honesty not to influence the responses. Yes, I clearly influence these men as singers and participants in the choral activity, but I think I am trusted. It is the singers themselves I am interested in – not specifically what they think of me as their conductor. I seek their narratives, perspectives and feelings of their singing lives as young men.

8.2 Previous Singing Experiences and Background

One of the most interesting aspects of conducting university choirs in the UK today is the diversity of the student body. Both choirs have a significant proportion of males and females from S.E. Asia – in particular from Hong Kong and Singapore, where there is an undoubted influence from British cultural practices. Not only do they drive on the left, but also choral singing is a widespread activity in schools, including secondary schools. Both have choral singing festivals where school choirs are expected to take part, as this contributes to their cultural standing (Yeung, 2007). I have been an adjudicator at the Singapore Youth Music Festival, where 129 secondary school and 20 junior college choirs performed. Therefore, in the region of 6,000 young people sing in school choirs. This is a significant number of young people between the ages of 11 and 18 out of a total population of four million.

Kelvin, now a postgraduate mathematics student and member of my chamber choir, sang in one of the successful highly rated school choirs in Singapore and this clearly had impact on his future participation in choral singing. Although initially he was reluctant to join a choir in London, he came upon the audition process by accident in the student union as a new 'freshman' undergraduate. He is now in his fourth and final year in the choir. Surprised by his success in the audition, he went on to become the choir librarian after a year and certainly shared his views on repertoire with me. Asked how he came to join his school choir, he said

> Okay it's a long story. In Singapore, I think for guys you don't think about to doing a choir much or it's not your first choice. So, in my secondary school all the guys have to go for an audition, it's compulsory. Apparently I did the audition so well and the teacher in charge asked me to join. And I think, why not? I did like singing but I didn't really consider singing in a choir at that time. Just she asked and I thought, arh [*in a high voice*], just join! And it has been fun.

Kelvin then went into detail about expectations and choir rehearsals and revealed that there was quite a different approach between his experience in Singapore and in London.

> ... it's enjoyable singing here, very different from singing in Singapore. We don't rehearse that much over here [London]. We don't sing as much. We rehearse once a week for two hours. In Singapore, in school choirs, we have at least twice a week, and each rehearsal lasts about three or four hours. And we meet many, many times before every concert. And over here, for this Christmas concert we just have three rehearsals, which is never ever happened in Singapore. We practise for at least half a year, at least, for a concert. And we sing so much together, so, by the time of concert, we make sure everyone memorises all the music and everything is done in a way ... sort of ... over-rehearsed ...

Hiro joined the chamber choir as a young tenor from Japan; he referred to the different expectations between the two cultures, mentioning that it was not unusual for his university choir in Japan to rehearse for 9 or 10 h per week.

> Yea, I think it's pretty natural. When I was singing in the high school choir, I don't know.... two each day. And I got five days practices, so basically I was having 10 hours when I was in high school days.

Both Kelvin and Hiro referred to the practice of learning the voice parts separately and thoroughly before the conductor put the singers together in their choirs in Singapore and Japan. This contrasted with the normal practice in the UK of singing all parts together for most of the rehearsal times. They believed this also impacted on sight-singing skills: both commented on the perceived high level of sight-singing skills in the London chamber choir as compared with their own previous experiences.

> What really struck me most was everyone did sight-singing and sing together immediately. I can sight-sing but most of the people I know [in Singapore] need several times to sing. These are the major differences.

Notably, however, neither singer had any experience of singing in church or chapel choir settings, which was found to be the case with a significant number of British male singers. In fact, Hiro pointed out that Japan, while having a strong and significant choral tradition, was not a Christian country and, therefore, most of the music was not sacred. Both referred positively to their experiences of singing Japanese and the music of contemporary Asian composers, but were eager to experience the English choral repertoire and choirs.

Aaron, an engineering undergraduate, went to a boys' selective grammar school in the Birmingham area of England where he joined the school choir at the age of 11. In Year 7 (age 11) they sang in the ordinary music classes and the teacher persuaded some of the boys to join the choir. Although he still had his unchanged treble voice in Year 8, he tailed off somewhat and did not sing in Year 9 and 'got back into it' in Year 10 with a mixed choir.

> Year 8 I had to sing alto 'cos there were new trebles there and Year 9 we were neglected – it seemed the choir was Year 7s, a few hangers-on in Year 8, then older kids. Year 13 we formed our own Barbershop kind of thing.

What to do with the male adolescent around the period of voice change is often perceived as problematic; it is a sad indictment on our lack of understanding of these issues and the negative impact it could have on boys and their attitudes to singing. It is possible to maintain motivation during this time and various studies have addressed this (Cooksey, 1992; Durrant, 2000, 2003; Freer, 2009).

Omega is a PhD student in Physics and sings in the large college choir. He is from Thailand, a country with little in the way of a choral tradition. Indeed, in an interview he mentioned that his first contact with choral singing was in Cambridge where he was an undergraduate student. He became friendly with musicians and tended to socialise with them in the small collegial context, rather than with other Physics students. He was then persuaded to join the chapel choir – more as a 'fill in substitute singer', as he puts it, and a friend taught him to read music. Brought up as a Buddhist, Omega converted to Christianity while at Cambridge, influenced by the choral singing environment, a friendly Dean and by being among a group of gay musicians where, being openly gay himself, he entered into his comfort zone. He commented: '... well it's natural in the music community...' and suggested that about 40 percent of males singing in his choirs were gay and acknowledged that musicians tended to be more open about it than the Physics student community.

Another overseas student, Ingram from Hong Kong, attended secondary school in England in a catholic independent boarding school from the age of 13. Here he joined the school choir after a patchy and not-so-positive singing experience in Hong Kong in his primary school, which he referred to as a 'mess-around choir'. Asked why he joined the school choir he said: 'I don't know, but I had nothing else to do so I said yes.'

Although he was not initially brought up a Christian, like Omega, Ingram sang regularly in chapel services at school and now, in addition to the chamber choir, sings in a church choir – clearly this being important to him. As it was a good experience, he then at 'Freshers' Fayre', found and auditioned for the chamber choir to continue and extend his singing experience.

Paul came to choral singing through music theatre and was inspired by his drama teachers at his catholic comprehensive school in the north of England. After taking the male lead in *Guys and Dolls*, he joined the school choir, having found his voice, and then went on to sing in a male quartet.

> ... there was a strong drama musical ethos in the school and the teachers were really, really good. My drama teacher was my favourite teacher throughout school – she was really passionate about it and so made me passionate.

Passionate was a word he used a lot in his interview; he was clearly inspired by the passion of his drama teacher and that remained for him a formative influence on his attitude towards music and theatre.

While the majority of males who sing in these university choirs had previous school experience of singing, there were exceptions in the large choir, as revealed in a questionnaire. Three male singers in the auditioned chamber choir had experience as boy choristers in cathedrals in England. They were therefore familiar with a great deal of the sacred repertoire, but still gained much from singing it again and meeting new challenges.

8.3 Perceptions of Themselves as Singers

One noticeable feature of these young men is the nervousness with which they approach new choirs and new singing situations, regardless of their previous experiences and levels of confidence. All commented on a perceived confidence issue, but all also did acknowledge that they had improved throughout their choir membership vocally and in their sight-singing skills. The competitive edge is still there, even if I as conductor aim to create a safe environment in which to learn and vocally develop without competing. It is easy for conductors to forget or even ignore these perceptions, particularly in a high-level chamber choir. The onus is still on these young men to prove themselves. Such covert competition was noted in a research study of an adult community choir, reported in Durrant and Himonides (1998). The older men also engaged in competitive banter. The testosterone gives a high five!

Aaron was particularly articulate about the confidence issue, stating that singing is about exposing yourself, recognising not only that others may hear your singing voice, warts and all, but that there is an emotional exposure as well.

> ... you have to be confident to sing in front of other people – kind of rips open the soul – you can't hide basically.

While he also belonged to another auditioned choir, Aaron mentioned that he thought there was a degree of 'self-auditioning' that goes on in the large un-auditioned choir; people self-select and that, while singers may perceive themselves as lacking in confidence and make little real vocal contribution, some do in fact leave, realising that they cannot find a suitable voice within the choir. (Indeed, I allow a three rehearsal 'trial' at the beginning of each academic year, before we ask people to decide to commit or not.) This also involves existing choir members and myself encouraging, particularly the men, to stay with us, to return for the next rehearsal, noting that some might find the music initially challenging given the range of singing abilities and levels of confidence among the singers. The social dimension is put on high alert, with cava, biscuits, active chatting, flirting, seducing and cajoling with new members and invitations to the pub or union bar after the rehearsal. This is to address any perceived doubt and concern in self-confidence for these new singers, to encourage them to understand that musically and vocally things will develop, if there are feelings of uncertainty. The chamber choir singers who had sung previously in cathedral choirs regarded themselves as confident singers and were, indeed in practice, very capable sight-singers.

Jörg commented that ability to sight-sing was given a similar emphasis within the German choral tradition, thus he did not feel particularly phased by the expectations within the chamber choir that he should be able to read fairly efficiently. However, he had also been a member of a choir where singers were expected to memorise rather than sight-read. He did mention that he found no problem with Latin text, but was not always familiar and at ease with older perhaps Shakespearean texts in English and often found this challenging especially if the music was in a fast tempo.

Ardi, originally from Indonesia, who had been educated at an independent school in England, was very distrustful of his singing abilities generally and stated that he often just opened his mouth in rehearsal, especially in the large choir, and went home to learn the music, playing the notes through on the piano. Although he wanted to sing and enjoyed the music he experienced in his school choirs, he perceived himself lacking in confidence both musically and socially.

8.4 Musical, Social and Emotional Benefits

When asked how he felt at the end of a rehearsal, Omega said

> Happy. After a whole stressed day I feel – this is the first hobby I have above everything else. The social aspect is important outside my research group – hard to socialise in my Physics research group.

While there are varying levels of socialising within the choir community, the social dimension of the groups are considered important, even by those who don't particularly commit to socialising themselves. Anecdotal commentary on the male gay fraternity with the university choirs is not so much a reflection on real or potential sexual activity, as on singers feeling safe to be open about their sexuality if they so wish.

Ingram, while acknowledging that being ethnically Chinese was part of his identity, wanted to use choir as a means of socialising beyond that, meeting new people from outside the Hong Kong milieu.

> ... I don't stick around too much time with them [Hong Kong students] – I try not to. Seeing I am here – I should know some non-Chinese people. That's one of the reasons why I wanted to do lots of extra-curricular activities like singing. Because then you can know a lot more people through doing activities – know people rather than going to pubs.

Getting acquainted with new people was, for him and the others, important, and choir provided that opportunity to socialise, both with other singers from Hong Kong, but also within a wider network. In fact, Ingram implied that he wanted to get to know new friends – more closely, perhaps, than as mere acquaintance. He also noted that it seemed to him that the gay guys were much more open about their sexuality within the choir context. Maybe this was to do with being in London in contrast to Hong Kong or an independent boarding school. Interestingly, both Ingram and Aaron (in different choirs and colleges) were first year undergraduates and had each put themselves up for a committee position within the choir. They clearly wanted to extend their influence and contribute to each choir beyond the singing. Aaron was particularly keen to enhance the social element of the choir by taking a more active role in organising events and tours. A number of students in each choir are eager to take on responsibilities both administrative ones like chair, treasurer, librarian and more social ones, such as social secretary, tea-break and biscuit organiser. Some see this as a useful contribution to their personal profiles and CVs as well as to the communal life of the choir.

Both Ingram and Omega saw their membership of the choirs as almost compensating for the absence, as they perceived it, of a social dimension within their main subject study areas. Interestingly also, was the fact that, both being from overseas, they perceived choir as being a means to integrate with people outside their study areas and outside their cultural backgrounds. They wanted to experience Englishness in the choral singing. This was also the case with Kelvin and Hiro. These young men had some experience and taste of English choral music and wanted more. The social and musical were intertwined. Those singers already situated within the English choral tradition, either in church or school, wanted to maintain their association with the music and also to extend their experiences with new repertoire.

Commenting on his feelings in choir, Jörg said:

> ... it's so joyful and brilliant. I mean, singing is one of the best things you can do. The best way to express your feelings, and singing together with others is even better.

When asked whether it was singing or the social side that kept him coming back for more, Ingram responded that it was a bit of both

> It feels natural singing – so probably the music side and it feels non-natural not singing. So like during the holidays I have to sing in my room.

This suggests that he misses the choir when it is not operating and that, to compensate, he still sings – even on his own. Rather, as Jörg also mentioned, they prefer to sing with others as a natural means of expression. They recognize singing as essentially a collaborative phenomenon, but it is also a physical and emotional activity that they need to do. Choral singing is a social thing – but it is the music that drives them, as a sort of means of expression and it would appear that the emotional side of it keeps them coming back for more. As Frederick Delius referred to music as an outburst of the soul, so these young men acknowledged the complex associations of singing with expression and emotions. Aaron stated that singing gave him a 'buzz' and, when asked what sort of buzz, he responded

> ... it's partly an intellectual exercise – sight reading and everything – you can listen to your part in the choir and your part might not be amazing but when combined with the choir it's part of something bigger. In the way that it's like being on a sports team – if you play with a team – it's kind of hard to....

He went on to articulate that

> It's the music that has the tingly bits – let me just think about this for a minute – and sometimes the music can sound so beautiful and takes you aback because whenever you sing to yourself – I sing to myself a lot – it kind of reminds me of what the choir sounded like when we did that...

Paul, a Physics undergraduate who sings in both choirs also referred to the buzz, remarking: 'it's that amazing feeling when you sing in a concert – that buzz you get – absolutely terrifying ....'

Such responses accord with a theory, put forward by Persson (2001), that musicians construe elaborate meaning based on 'triggers of emotional responses inherent in musical structures' (p. 285). Aaron was also able to recognise that his own attempts at singing in his room alone reminded him of the feelings encountered in the collective environment of the choir singing as a whole. We can recount those feelings; they are not necessarily specific emotions, but rather reminders of the heightened awareness of our emotional response to the music's expressiveness and the shared experience of singing and our attempts to give meaning to those experiences (Meyer, 1956; Langer, 1957; Davies, 2001). What Aaron refers to as the 'intellectual' might also be determined as the philosophical explanation of cognition, acknowledging the musical structures as being the essential element in aesthetic response. We seek for patterns, in melodies, rhythms and harmonies to gain understanding of our involvements in the expressive and the aesthetic. Here, there is also recognition of the whole being bigger than the constituent parts. And this is what gives the buzz. Some even recognised the health and well-being benefits of choral singing (Clift & Hancox, 2001).

Asked if music is an important part of his life even though he is studying engineering, Aaron responded:

> Pretty much – it's a distraction from engineering. They are so different but they are both sort of mathematical. For me maths gives me the same buzz as music does. It's the sense of accomplishment – the sense of everything fitting together. For example in music you have the harmonies, in maths when you complete a proof everything fits together.

So he sees music as structures and patterns that fit together and his role as a singer is also to fit together with other singers. Talking of accomplishment and fitting together suggests that Aaron certainly had the intellectual capacity to sort out what music and choral singing in particular meant to him. Of course, for some, taking about their responses and feeling towards music is limited by the very limitation of the vocabulary of verbal language. Paul referred to the 'release' from Physics he found in the choir:

> It's a release from Physics because it's very demanding – doing the theoretical course – I think intensively all the time and it's nice to think in a different way.

He also played a lot of chess, which, as with Physics, was mentally demanding; he takes an interesting perspective suggesting that choir made him think in a different way.

Jörg enthusiastically described his feelings before and after rehearsals:

> ...during the day you think 'oh god I don't want to go to the rehearsal' [with a tired voice] and in the afternoon you think 'oh I rather like to go home', but then once you've been there, two hours or even longer, talk to the people and just sing some music, I am always in such a right mood afterwards, I am really [em...] not really exhausted, but really like sports, after running, you turn your anxiety to hope, and singing with others and share the music with others and the feeling is right. And it's a great thing."

A previous study carried out in Finland and Sweden (Durrant, 2005) revealed that singing was almost fundamental to the shaping of identities, personally, culturally and even nationally. Singers had to sing their Finnish or Swedish folk songs – if they didn't, who would? For a number of these young people, school and university students, singing was not only a means of personal expression and satisfaction, but also testament to the creation of a national identity.

8.5 Who Are They? Personal Characteristics and Concluding Comments

But what is it to be male and sing in the choir? Are there recognisable traits in character and personality? Do those males who sing in university choirs tend to be geeky, gay, sociable, wear anoraks or simply love singing and the music? Are they technology freaks and appreciate the aesthetic potential of a mathematical equation as much as of a choral singing experience? Indeed, do you need to have a certain level of intelligence to sing in choirs like these? Do you need to be acquainted with and knowledgeable about the music in order to gain understanding, appreciation and commitment to its expressive and emotional potential? Is the joining of these groups a self-indulgence of emotional expression or an intellectual exercise and challenge? Or rather like Grimes (who 'is at his exercise', as the chorus sings in Britten's opera) – it's what they simply have to do? Kemp (1996) in his book on musical temperament suggests that singers are a particular kind of people who cannot hide behind an instrument and, although he refers largely to the solo singer, it is interesting to note that Aaron thought that singing in a choir was not always for the introverted, conservative types:

> I think being introvert prevents you from joining a choir like this anyway because what I said about being confident. Being confident socially and standing up in front of people to sing – maybe I am confusing....

Nevertheless, many of those interviewed referred to confidence – some saying that by singing in a choir they grew in confidence musically and socially – that it was actually instrumental in assisting this growth. Some, however, accepted their 'geekiness' (indeed a number ticked the geeky box in the questionnaire) and also their ostensible unsociability, making out they had to go and work after rehearsals or maybe simply did not wish to join in the drinking culture often associated with student activities.

While some male singers, revealed in a questionnaire and in interviews, were openly gay, others recognised that this was acceptable and perfectly normal in a choral singing group, while not necessarily being totally open about their own sexuality. Indeed, some male singers adopted overtly gay behaviour – or mannerisms that are associated with particular gay males (Brett et al., 2006). This was apparent both in discussions (both formal interviews and general social situations) and informal observations in and out of rehearsals. Two interviewed males readily recognised the acceptable gayness of being a singer in the choir. Another said that, being gay himself was not an issue, but that he could understand others not being at ease with their sexuality and finding choir a safe outlet. It was part of the genial social, musical and sexual ambience created in these choirs. Also of note is the acceptance from the female singers; gay males are often perceived as in tune with their feminine side (to use a rather clichéd phrase), non-threatening and fun! Koestenbaum (1991) goes further by aligning the act of singing with sexual longing: he suggests that like the 'essence' that makes gay people what they, the 'spark' that produces the singing voice is 'nature and acquired, free and expensive, speakable and unspeakable, pathogenic and curative' (p. 207). Hayes (2007) notes the rise of GLBT choirs in urban USA and Henderson and Hodges (2007) studied the characteristics of an urban gay choir and its interactions with other communities within their city. Indeed, gay and lesbian choirs are now in evidence in most major cities in the western world – though, as yet, not in places like Hong Kong and Singapore.

It is, in all probability, somewhat capricious to seek to formulate conclusions from this tiny sample of interviews and questionnaires of traits and generalised characteristics of those males singing in university choirs. A telling comment from Paul, when comparing singing with team sports activities like football or rugby, was that he felt they (the sports guys) had to conform by adopting in some cases 'loutish' and 'competitive' – or 'extremes' of behaviour, which was different to conforming behaviours in a choir context.

> ... in a sporting situation you conform more – you have people who are very insecure in choir and in whatever you do and I guess with football or rugby they go more to the extremes in order to conform – you know what I mean? I think there's always a norm in any situation where people can communicate on the same level."

Nevertheless, conforming, within whatever convention of behaviour, was what people do in collaborative activities. Maybe the evidence of a testosterone high is not so apparent in choir as it is in rugby, but males are still behaving like males, with subtle differences between ethnicities – as yet un-researched – and sexualities. These young men through their choral singing, as in everything else they do, are still finding out who they are. But does that ever stop?

I have merely cultivated a small patch of a very small back garden; no pretence here of a Chelsea Flower Show, just a few but attractive bedding plants in rich compost. The narratives of these young men in my choirs are indeed insightful, giving validity to the choral singing activity, in this case while they are at that very formative stage at university. All of these guys have been able to articulate their feelings and perceptions without the fear of embarrassment or ridicule, which may not be the case for other young boys and men engaged in choral singing. So let us take note. It therefore falls on the universities, particularly in a climate of financial restraint, to ensure that their choirs continue to be resourced; it falls on the choir conductors to take responsibility to provide effective, vibrant and meaningful choral singing opportunities for these young people.

References

Ashley, M. (2008). *How high should boys sing: Gender, authenticity and credibility in the young male voice.* Farnham, Surrey: Ashgate.

Brett, P., Wood, E., & Thomas, G. (Eds.). (2006). *Queering the pitch: The new gay and lesbian musicology* (2nd ed.). New York: Routledge.

Clift, S., & Hancox, G. (2001). The perceived benefits of choral singing: Findings from preliminary surveys of a university college choral society. *Journal of the Royal Society for the Promotion of Health, 121*(4), 248–256.

Cooksey, J. (1992). *Working with the adolescent voice.* St. Louis, MO: Concordia.

Davies, S. (2001). Philosophical perspectives on music's expressiveness. In P. Juslin & J. Sloboda (Eds.), *Music and emotion: Theory and research.* Oxford: Oxford University Press.

Durrant, C. (2000). Making choral rehearsing seductive: Implications for practice and choral education. *Research Studies in Music Education, 15*, 40–49.

Durrant, C. (2003). *Choral conducting: Philosophy and practice.* New York: Routledge.

Durrant, C. (2005). Shaping identity through choral activity: Singers and conductors' perceptions. *Research Studies in Music Education, 24*, 88–98.

Durrant, C., & Himonides, E. (1998). What makes people sing together? Socio-psychological and cross-cultural perspectives on the choral phenomenon. *International Journal of Music Education, 32*, 61–71.

Faulkner, R., & Davidson, J. (2006). Men in chorus: Collaboration and competition in homo-social vocal behaviour. *Psychology of Music, 34*(2), 219–237.

Freer, P. (2009). 'I'll sing with my buddies' – Fostering the possible selves of male choral singers. *International Journal of Music Education, 27*(4), 341–355.

Hayes, C. (2007). Community music and the GLBT chorus. *International Journal of Community Music, 1*(1), 63–69.

Henderson, S., & Hodges, S. (2007). Music, song, and the creation of community and community spirit by a gay subculture. *Sociological Spectrum, 27*(1), 57–80.

Kemp, A. (1996). *The musical temperament: Psychology and personality of musicians.* Oxford: Oxford University Press.

Koestenbaum, W. (1991). The queen's throat: (Homo)sexuality and the art of singing. In D. Fuss (Ed.), *Inside/out: Lesbian theories, gay theories* (pp. 204–234). New York: Routledge.

Langer, S. (1957). *Philosophy in a new key: A study in the symbolism of reason, rite, and art.* Cambridge: Harvard University Press.

Meyer, L. (1956). *Emotion and meaning in music.* Chicago: University of Chicago Press.

Persson, R. (2001). The subjective world of the performer. In P. Juslin & J. Sloboda (Eds.), *Music and emotion: Theory and research* (pp. 275–290). Oxford: Oxford University Press.

Yeung, F. (2007). *To compete or not to compete: A study in choral singing activities in Hong Kong with respect to the participation in the Hong Kong Schools Music Festival.* Unpublished MA dissertation, Institute of Education, University of London, UK.

Chapter 9
Cathedral Choirs in the United Kingdom: The Professional Boy Chorister

Jenevora Williams

At the outset, it should be pointed out why this chapter only concerns boy singers. It is a particular cultural artefact that the professional cathedral choirs in the UK, which require children to perform at the highest levels of performance, mostly have only male singers. The findings from the research could have wider implications for teachers and choral directors working with both boy and girl singers. If the specialist children assessed in this study were performing at their optimum in terms of vocal health, this suggests that intensive training with an emphasis on advanced vocal technique places children in an advantageous position. Voice researchers and clinicians may be interested in the findings related to assessment techniques. The question of appropriate use or otherwise of falsetto singing during voice change has implications for all boy singers, especially those attempting to sing in traditional SATB choirs.

9.1 Cultural Background to the English Cathedral Chorister

Children have sung in the daily worship of cathedrals, abbeys and collegiate churches for fourteen hundred years; the fate of singing in the daily liturgy has been subject to much upheaval with invasions, reformation, civil war and neglect (Mould, 2007). This heritage itself arose from the Jewish practice of training Levite boys to sing psalms. In Canterbury from the start of the seventh century, Augustine included boys from the age of seven in the Episcopal *familia*. These boys were essentially in training for the clergy, but they would sing in the daily worship. In 680, Bede tells of a choral workshop at Wearmouth, where an expert musician gave instruction to the cantors in the 'theory and practice of singing'. Incidentally, for the first few hundred years of Christianity in Britain, girl oblates sang in nunneries. The re-introduction of girls into singing in modern cathedral foundations from

---

J. Williams (✉)
Institute of Education, London, UK
e-mail: jw@jenevorawilliams.com

the 1990s was controversial at the time but can be seen to have ancient roots. Child oblation would have been considered the highest honour for an Anglo-Saxon family. From the twelfth century, the practice of child oblation was dropped and boys were educated in secular cathedrals and collegiate churches where they were not bound for monastic life.

Between 1350 and 1550 there was a great flowering of church music with a huge expansion of the number of churches and chapels in which choristers could be heard. Monasteries reintroduced boys into their singing as lay-members. Adult (male) singers in the choirs were employed primarily for their musical skills and were increasingly lay clerks and not ordained clergy. Collegiate churches were established at Eton; Winchester; New College, Magdalen and Christ Church, Oxford; and King's College, Cambridge. The music itself was notated and complex; polyphony for five parts or more can be seen in the Old Hall Manuscript and in the Eton Choirbook. Little music survives from this period as much was destroyed during the following reformation of religious practice in England. We know that by the close of the fifteenth century there were approaching 200 professional liturgical choirs with boys in England. During the reformation in the 1530s, many monastic foundations were re-founded as secular cathedrals. In the final years of Henry VIII's reign, composers such as Tallis, Sheppard and Tye produced some of their finest music for cathedral choirs.

Some accounts suggest that choristers could be quite unruly; in Southwell in 1503 the choristers' vestments were 'disgracefully torn' and the boys themselves were known to 'rave and swear'. There are numerous accounts of lay clerks and organists in the late sixteenth and early seventeenth century as drunkards, gamblers, blasphemers and fornicators. There were, however, centres of excellence such as the Chapel Royal, and the sacred music of composers Purcell, Byrd, Mundy, Morley, Weelkes, Gibbons and Tomkins whose works are still central to cathedral music today. A sideline of some of the choristers in places such as Westminster, St Paul's and the Chapel Royal, was participating in dramatic performances. Some of these were at court and others were in public theatres. In the 1570s the choristers of St Paul's Cathedral had their own raised stage with seating for about a hundred people.

With the Restoration of the monarchy in 1660 following Cromwell, the destiny of cathedral music and the boy chorister went into slow decline. Between 1700 and 1850 secular music in England flourished. Opera was popular, music societies were common as were choral societies. Church music was, however, almost wholly neglected by the most able composers of the time. Chorister numbers dwindled, the boys suffered neglect and maltreatment in much the same way as other children employed in the mines and factories. A report of a Sunday evensong at St Paul's Cathedral in 1871 stated that 'at no time did there appear to be more than an irregular confused hum of children's voices, trying to sing something of which the majority seemed incapable'.

Reform of the choristers' welfare was initiated by Maria Hackett in 1811 and continued by her until the 1870s. She was an educated lady with some financial means, enabling her to devote her life to improving the welfare of choristers. This was in a small way resembling the work of Elizabeth Fry in the prisons and Florence

Nightingale in nursing. By the middle of the century chorister numbers had begun to rise in many foundations.

The twentieth century has seen some changes in chorister education. Many choirs have seen the introduction, from the 1980s, of a specialist singing teacher to complement the work of the choirmaster in training the singers. From the 1990s many choral foundations have introduced girls, either to join the boys or to form a parallel choir. All but one of the designated choir schools (Westminster Abbey Choir School) have opened their classrooms to non-choristers. This means that the choristers have their daily school curriculum classes in a mixed environment of both choristers and non-choristers.

Boys are members of cathedral and collegiate choirs, of which there are a total of 38 in the UK, from the age of 8–13. UK chorister entry requirements are purely on musical and vocal aptitude, their education is often subsidised by the cathedral and choir school foundations. However, the socio-economic and cultural background of choristers is predominantly white (92%) and middle-class (95.6%) (Capon, 2009).

9.2 Vocal Loading and Voice Disorders

Vocal loading is defined as the stress inflicted on the vocal apparatus during periods of usage. This may be when speaking or singing. Factors known to increase levels of vocal loading are the proportion of time (within a given time frame) for which the voice is operating, the intensity (loudness) level at which the voice is operating and the level of psychological stress of the vocalist (Artkoski, Tommila, & Laukkanen, 2002; Sala et al., 2002; Titze, 1994).

If supranormal performance expectations are taken higher than is possible for the individual, the resulting collapse renders their performance level subnormal (Fig. 9.1).

Any increase in pressure both in terms of academic attainment and the expectations of maturity and leadership can raise the anxiety levels of the boy and increase

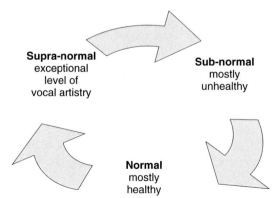

Fig. 9.1 Schematic diagram of the cyclical relationship between vocal activity and vocal health

the possibility of vocal dysfunction. It could be suggested that these UK choristers are subject to greater vocal loading than any other professional child singer.

Some recent changes have, arguably, increased the pressure on the boys involved. They are expected to attain the same rigorous academic levels as their non-chorister peers, and to achieve a high level of performance on at least one other musical instrument. The potential for performance-related stress is greater with regular live television and radio broadcasts, these are inevitably compared with edited commercially available recordings. We have seen a drop in the age of onset of puberty in both boys and girls since the middle of the twentieth century. During the early and mid-twentieth century it was not uncommon for boys to remain on the soprano line for 2 or 3 years beyond the onset of voice change. It is now considered unwise to encourage this prolongation of exclusive soprano singing. Boys of 11 or 12 years old are now expected to exhibit leadership qualities such as prompt and accurate musical entries, advanced sight-reading skills, and exemplary discipline and behaviour both in public performances and also during choir practice.

A comparison between the boys' choirs of two major German foundations (Williams, 2004) found that English choristers are potentially subject to greater vocal loading. The proportion of rehearsal to performance time in the German choirs was 10:1, whereas in the English choirs it was 3:1. The English choristers are also required to match a mature adult sound from the alto, tenor and bass sections; the German choirs have young voices (under 18 years) throughout the choir. The training of the German choral directors is as a singer, whereas, in general, the training of UK cathedral choral director is as an organist; it is not usual for the director of music to have had any formal training as a conductor or any specific training in vocal pedagogy.

A body of research exists into the health and growth of child athletes and dancers, relating the pressures of the training to the developmental outcomes. There is also research into the vocal health of adult professional singers. When considering environmental factors such as background noise, as well as performance stress on professional adult musicians, findings suggest that musicians are perhaps not as unhealthy as they should be. There may be an element of subconscious self-regulation which is reducing the impact of these factors on the health of professional musicians. This possibility of self-regulation is a key finding of this research on boy choristers.

Vocal abuse is common among children with up to 40% of children at any time suffering from some level of dysphonia (Arnoux-Sindt et al., 1993; Sederholm, 1995). Those at risk often are involved in shouting and loud activities in play, speaking over high levels of background noise, speaking on inappropriate pitch, prolonged talking, and coughing or harsh clearing of the throat. The speech habits and voice hygiene of family members and role models can play an important role. Children with allergies, asthma or chronic upper respiratory tract infections also are at risk. Additionally, abuse of the voice is common among those who demonstrate aggressive or emotionally unstable personality traits (Brandell, 1982; Green, 1989). Fortunately, because of the adaptability of the developing larynx children are more likely to recover spontaneously from voice disorders with vocal rest.

There are five characteristics that can be used to define a problem voice (Wilson, 1979):

1 Disturbed voice quality caused by laryngeal dysfunction,
2 Hypernasality or hyponasality,
3 Voice too soft to be heard or unpleasantly loud,
4 A speaking pitch too high or too low for the age, size and sex,
5 Inappropriate inflections of pitch and loudness,

9.3 Methods of Data Collection

The main participants were a cohort of choristers at a major London cathedral and aged eight to thirteen years. These boys lived on site as boarders in the choir school. They had a demanding daily schedule of rehearsals and performances as well as the usual classroom curricula, and sporting and leisure activities of schoolboys of this age. Each of the participant boys' voices was recorded at six-monthly intervals over a three-year period. A subgroup of the boys was recorded at six-monthly intervals over a period of three years. The participants followed a specially designed vocal behaviour assessment protocol that embraced speaking and singing activities. The resultant vocal behaviour was recorded digitally prior to (a) perceptual and (b) acoustic analyses. Voice source data were collected in parallel to the acoustic data via an electrolaryngograph (Lx) for subsequent analysis. The Lx data represent the activity of the opening/closing mechanism of the vocal folds in running speech or singing. Recorded data was supplemented with information from questionnaires and a junior personality profile.

In order to provide a perspective on whether the choristers were typical or untypical of boys of a similar age and background, other groups of participants were recruited to provide a comparative perspective.

There were four groups of participants:

1 Choristers (boarders) from a major UK cathedral in London;
2 Their non-chorister 'day pupil' peers in the same school;
3 Other choristers ('day pupils') who were from a provincial cathedral in South East England;
4 Groups of boys who boarded in two traditional (non-music specialist) preparatory schools in South East England.

9.4 Measurement of Voice: Perceptual and Acoustic Perspectives

There are two types of assessment which are conventionally used in both laboratory and clinical settings. The main type of assessment used in this study was perceptual. The expert listener hears any deviations from an accepted standard of 'healthy' or 'normal'; these are qualified and quantified in order to reach a conclusion (Carding, Carlson, Epstein, Mathieson, & Shewell, 2000). Acoustic measurements such as observation of the long term average spectrum, or analysis of electroglottogram data can be applied as a way of reinforcing and validating these perceptual judgements.

The perceptual analysis employed in this study was of two main types. The first was a detailed assessment of many aspects of vocal function, derived from Voice Profile Analysis Scheme (Laver, Wirz, MacKenzie, & Hiller, 1981; Shewell, 2009). This is a descriptive system that allows the listener both to describe and to analyse conversational or reading voice quality. The aspects of voice use are divided into categories and individual settings of the larynx and vocal tract. Each feature is compared with a neutral baseline setting. It is a comprehensive and detailed system of analysis and is a potentially more useful tool for analysing normal voice use. In this study, 36 parameters of voice use were evaluated.

The second type was a single-score evaluation of vocal efficiency, or perceived vocal dysfunction. Dysphonia is a general term referring to any unusual or unhealthy vocal behaviour. Hoarseness is a more common term. It has been defined as the presence of hyperfunction, breathiness or roughness and seemed to be reasonably well defined and unequivocal between judges (Sederholm, McAllister, Sundberg, & Dalkvist, 1993). The nature of the perceptual evaluation in these cases was to consider aspects of laryngeal behaviour, namely: breathiness, harshness and creak. These are all known to indicate dysfunctional voice.

Both types of perceptual assessment were carried out by a panel of expert judges. These judges were taken from various professional backgrounds: singing teaching, spoken voice teaching, voice research and clinical speech therapy. This was intended to represent the wide range of training and experience from professional practitioners involved in the assessment of children's voices in the UK.

Acoustic measures used included long-term average spectrum (LTAS) and electroglottogram analysis. The LTAS shows the distribution of sound energy at different frequencies within the signal, averaged over time. In the LTAS the spectral variation from the vowels is smoothed and the peaks and troughs show the overall characteristics of the sound. In speech the LTAS will show evidence of non-harmonic 'noise' at higher frequencies, generated by breathiness in the sound, or enhanced groups of harmonics or formants. These contribute to any 'ringing' quality in the voice (Howard & Williams, 2009). From the LTAS it was possible to infer aspects of vocal health in terms of vocal quality and implied efficiency.

The Portable Field Laryngograph uses a pair of electrodes to measure current flow across the larynx. When the vocal folds are together, the current flows between the electrodes. An increase in current flow between the electrodes is plotted as a positive change on the vertical axis; as the area of vocal fold contact becomes greater, the inter-electrode soft tissue contact increases (Abberton, Howard, & Fourcin, 1989). A display of this current against time gives an indication of the degree and duration of glottal closure with each cycle. Analysis of this signal using Speech Studio will give a quantifiable reading of cycle-by-cycle irregularity in amplitude, frequency or degree of glottal contact. This irregularity is evidence of vocal dysfunction.

9.5 Vocal Behaviour of Choristers – Perceptual Analyses

Analysis of the Voice Profile Analysis data illustrated patterns of vocal behaviour and general trends exhibited by the cohort as a whole. This analysis also clarified the relevance of the categories in the VPA using factor analysis; a revised VPA assessment form was generated (Fig. 9.2).

Analysis of the single-score evaluation of vocal efficiency gave some interesting results. Figure 9.3 shows the perceived vocal health of non-chorister boys. The x-axis is the degree of perceived dysphonia with 1 being clear and 7 being voiceless. The y-axis shows the percentage of the whole sample. This chart showed that boarders had a higher incidence of perceived dysphonia at level 4 and a lower incidence of perceived dysphonia levels 2 and 3 than non-boarders. This suggested that the boarding environment may have caused a higher level of voice disorder. This agreed with the current literature (Casper, Abramson, & Forman-Franco, 1981;

Context	Type of measure	Category	Normal/ Neutral	Sub-categories perceived as *'non-normal'* features				Comments (e.g. singing *vs* speech)
Observations in performance	Measures of muscular tension in the vocal tract	Phonation Type		Harshness				
				Whisper				
				Creak				
		Velo-pharyngeal		Nasal				
				Denasal				
Observations in rehearsal		Excess tension		Pharyngeal constriction				
				Jaw – minimised range				
		Tongue		Lisp				
				Backed				
Observations in special test	Measures of vocal skill and maturity	Vocal skill		Pitch stability				
				Wide range				
		Junior voice		High pitch mean				
				Narrow pitch range				
				Easy passaggio management				
Observations from recording of special test		Voice change		Modal-falsetto in speech				
				Pitch instability				
				Low pitch mean				
				Upper passaggio obvious				
				Lower passaggio obvious				
Other comments								
Health								
Self rating of voice								
Vocal ability/progress in choir								

Fig. 9.2 Revised voice profile assessment form for use with children and especially trained child singers

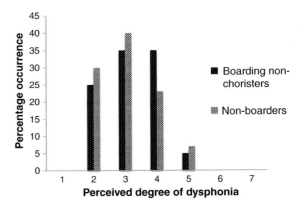

Fig. 9.3 Non-choristers: a comparison between the perceived dysphonia of boys who are boarding and non-boarding

Sederholm, 1996) referring to the increased likelihood of voice disorder in children who spend a large part of each day in noisy environments.

Anecdotally, anyone who has been into a school dining room will have observed that the level of background noise in the school environment is particularly high during mealtimes and playtimes. Individuals trying to make their voices heard above this noise will be using more vocal effort, higher intensity and a greater force of vocal fold collision. All of these factors are contributory to the development of vocal disorders. For children attending a day school, their environment changes when they leave school at the end of the day (normally between 3.30 p.m. and 4.30 p.m.). They are more likely to go to homes which are quieter than school. In a boarding school, individuals may be in noisy environments for a much greater part of the day. These data in Fig. 9.3 show a higher incidence of vocal dysphonia in the non-chorister boys attending boarding school, and suggest the possible effect of this environment on the level of perceived voice disorder.

Considering that the choristers not only boarded but also sang for many hours a week, resulting in an even greater vocal loading, we may have expected to have seen an even higher incidence of perceived vocal dysfunction. However, their underlying vocal health appeared to be significantly better than that of the non-choristers as shown in Fig. 9.4. The choristers have a lower incidence of perceived dysphonia in level 4 and a higher incidence in levels 2 and 3. This would suggest that, although they have been exposed to an environment encouraging a greater vocal loading, they have learned vocal behaviours to reduce their level of dysphonia within this environment.

The distribution of the perceived vocal dysfunction for all four groups can be seen in Fig. 9.5. Figure 9.6 shows the box plots for the perceived vocal dysfunction of each activity group. There is a greater spread of scores for the non-chorister non-boarders. There is one outlier from the non-boarding non-chorister group; he has a particularly high score for perceived vocal dysfunction. He may have been suffering from an acute respiratory tract infection on the day of recording; this is itself is a totally normal occasional occurrence in every child. It was not possible to separate the cases of perceived dysphonia as a result of illness, from that as a result

9 Cathedral Choirs in the United Kingdom: The Professional Boy Chorister

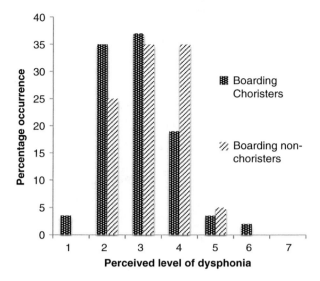

Fig. 9.4 Boarders: a comparison between the perceived dysphonia of boys who are choristers and non-choristers

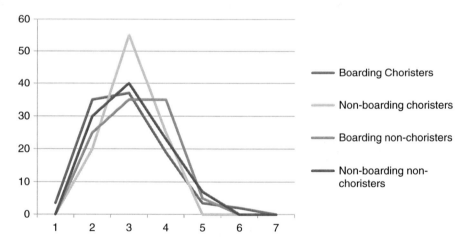

Fig. 9.5 The distribution of perceived vocal dysfunction of all four groups. The x axis is the perceived level of dysfunction with 0 as healthy and 7 as voiceless. The y axis is the percentage frequency of occurrence of each level within the group

of poor habitual voice use. It was assumed that respiratory tract infections would be occurring to some degree in all of the groups of boys.

There was a statistically significant difference between the perceived vocal health of boarding choristers and boarding non-choristers (Table 9.1).

This suggests that the chorister factor is significant for ratings of vocal health. The position of Cathedral Organist and Director of Music was subject to a new appointment one-third of the way through this longitudinal study. This fact probably rules out the possibility for the data to be significantly influenced in the long-term by

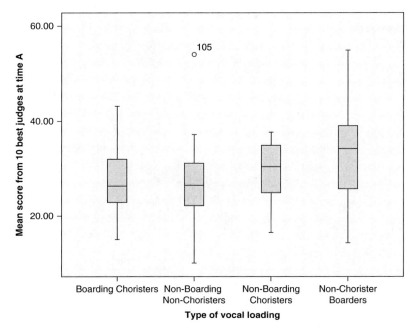

Fig. 9.6 The median ratings (50th percentile) and standard deviation for the four different activity groups

Table 9.1 Comparisons of perceived levels of dysphonia between the four different activity groups; dependent variable: mean score for ten best judges

(I) Type of vocal loading	(J) Type of vocal loading	Mean difference (I–J)	Std. error	Sig.	95% Confidence interval Lower bound	Upper bound
boarding choristers	non-boarding non-choristers	0.413	2.102	0.845	−3.751	4.577
	non-boarding choristers	−2.596	2.315	0.265	−7.182	1.991
	boarding non-choristers	−6.555(*)	1.938	0.001	−10.393	−2.717
non-boarding non-choristers	non-boarding choristers	−3.009	2.378	.208	−7.719	1.702
	boarding non-choristers	−6.968(*)	2.012	0.001	−10.953	−2.982
non-boarding choristers	boarding non-choristers	−3.959	2.234	0.079	−8.384	0.466

*The mean difference is significant at the 0.05 level

the training methods of one individual, although there may be a dominant culture in cathedral music that transcends the individual, given that the adults are often likely to be ex-choristers.

There was a significant statistical difference between the boarding non-choristers and the non-boarding non-choristers, which suggests that the boarding factor is significant for ratings of vocal health, as observed by the increase in the incidence of perceived vocal dysphonia in the boarders. There are still differences (although not statistically significant) between all of the groups except the boarding choristers and the non-boarding non-choristers. This is also illustrated in the distribution graph, Fig. 9.5.

Looking at the distribution of the scores, one can observe that the choristers in fact have a higher incidence of low-level disorders. This suggests that they were indeed vocally fatigued, but that their vocal health tended not to degenerate beyond a certain level. It suggests that they are either athletically conditioned to support these activities, and/or that they are self-regulating their voice use at all times in order to maintain a healthy vocal system. One could hypothesise the reasons for this. It is possible that this is a result of education, persistent and regular reminders, but it is more likely that the boys will only modify their behaviour if there is a tangible pay-off for them. It would only take a few occasions on which they have missed an opportunity as a result of over-use of their voice for them to learn to self-regulate. This of course applies to all of their voice use, especially in sport and social contexts. Furthermore, the collective singing voice of the choristers as a group is presumably 'healthy', so it is likely that any one individual would have their own individual sound and underlying vocal behaviour shaped by the collective, i.e., there is convergence within the group towards sounds that are more healthy and, as part of a virtuous circle, such healthy sounds tend to condition the voices to sustain this type of production.

From informal discussions with the boys, it is evident that they are consciously aware of their voice use in the choral environment and make adjustments accordingly. A senior boy may give a strong lead at the start of a musical phrase in order to give confidence to the younger boys; he may then ease off vocally once the phrase is underway. In sport and social contexts it is much less likely that the boys will be consciously regulating their voice use. Listening to them in the playground would suggest that they are free and uninhibited with their voice use. The evidence from the distribution of ratings would suggest, however, that caution is being exercised at some level, conscious or subconscious, at all times. A similar caution can be observed when one is watching young pianists and string players from a specialist music school when they are playing competitive team sports. It is much less tactile and confrontational as a result of their self-regulatory care.

It is possible that the choristers in the London cathedral had healthier voices from the outset of their training as a result of the selection procedure. It was possible to assess the baseline vocal health of the London choristers before any training, as the first set of recordings were made in the first week of term. The boys new to the choir at this time (probationers) would not have been influenced by their training or by the increased vocal loading of the boarding chorister schedule. A statistical ANOVA test was made to compare the means of the vocal health scores from the London probationers with the equivalent age of boys from both the non-boarding non-chorister environment, and the boys from the non-boarding chorister environment. The analysis shows a significance of .690. For the probationer group to have a significantly healthier voice use than the other boys, this figure would need to be less than .05. From this it can be assumed that the boys selected as choristers in the London cathedral do not have healthier or unhealthier voices than their non-selected peers. Any subsequent significant difference in vocal health is likely to be as a result of experience and learned behaviour.

The results of the tests for personality type showed that the boys with the highest score for perceived vocal dysfunction also had unusually high scores in either extroversion or neuroticism. This has been shown to be the case in previous research on Swedish non-choristers (Sederholm, 1996). One final observation was that there was a striking similarity between the boys who are both boarders and choristers, and the boys who are neither boarders nor choristers. These two groups had very different activities, but happen to go to the same school between 8.45 and 3.30, Monday to Friday. Perhaps the influence of peer group on voice use is more powerful than either that of activity or voice education (Wiltermuth & Heath, 2009).

9.6 Vocal Behaviour of Choristers – Acoustic and Voice-Source Analyses

In order to make comparisons between recordings, it was important to calibrate the sound pressure level of each recording. All LTAS plots are calculated to absolute dB SPL values.

The LTAS graphs are shown with both a linear and a logarithmic frequency scale. The logarithmic scale represents our aural perception more closely and provides more detail regarding the lower frequencies. The upper frequencies (1000–10000 Hz) show other timbral factors of the voice. These upper frequencies are more clearly observed in the linear frequency scale. The creaky, breathy and harsh voice examples were selected as samples which had been given a high score for these particular qualities on the VPA, but not high scores in other voice qualities. In most cases, however, these voice qualities occurred in various combinations.

9.6.1 Creaky Voice

Figures 9.7 and 9.8 show the LTAS for two examples of creaky voice, alongside one example of healthy voice. The creaky voices have a lower intensity from 100 to 5000 Hz; above this the intensity rises. This shows a level of higher frequency noise in the signal, possibly generated by 'noise' from air escaping through a constricted larynx.

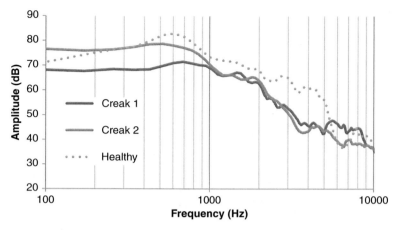

Fig. 9.7 LTAS of two examples of creaky voice and one example of healthy voice (*dotted line*), using a logarithmic frequency scale

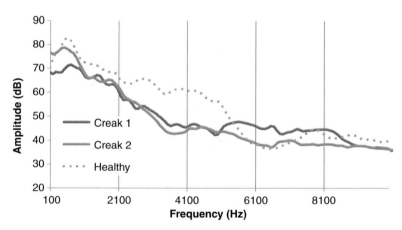

Fig. 9.8 LTAS of two examples of creaky voice and one example of healthy voice (*dotted line*), using a linear frequency scale

9.6.2 Breathy Voice

Figures 9.9 and 9.10 show examples of breathy voice in a LTAS. They show a characteristic rise in intensity of the upper frequencies (above 10000 Hz) created by 'noise' as air rushes through the glottis. The orange line is a particularly weak intensity; it is at least 10 dB lower than the healthy voice signal. This difference makes the breathy voice half as loud as the normal one (Howard & Angus, 1996, second edition 2001). This boy is unable to project his voice effectively due to the inefficiency of the breathy phonation.

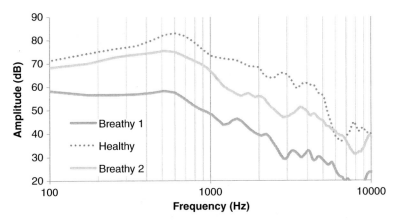

Fig. 9.9 LTAS of two examples of breathy voice and one example of healthy voice, using a logarithmic frequency scale

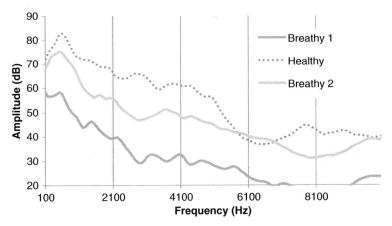

Fig. 9.10 LTAS of two examples of breathy voice and one example of healthy voice, using a linear frequency scale

9.6.3 Harsh Voice

Figures 9.11 and 9.12 show the LTAS of a harsh voice. This has a similar spectral profile to the healthy voice, but it is at a significantly lower amplitude; this voice quality is less efficient at projecting.

The observation of the elements seen in the LTAS was unsurprising. Creaky voice had evidence of irregular vocal fold vibration; creaky, breathy and harsh voice showed a reduced ability for loud phonation. The analysis of the laryngographic waveform gave more detailed results. These showed evidence of irregularity in the vocal fold vibrations in all cases. Breathy voice showed a significant proportion of the vocal fold collisions to have inefficient closure (97%). Creaky voice had a marked irregularity in the degree of vocal fold closure with a small figure for

9 Cathedral Choirs in the United Kingdom: The Professional Boy Chorister

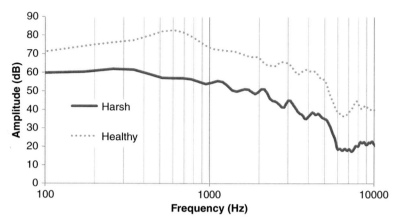

Fig. 9.11 LTAS of an example of harsh voice and an example of healthy voice (*dotted line*), using a logarithmic frequency scale

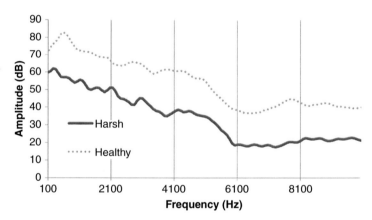

Fig. 9.12 LTAS of an example of harsh voice and an example of healthy voice (*dotted line*), using a linear frequency scale

coherence (17%). Harsh voice showed irregularity in the cycle by cycle amplitude measurement with a coherence of 23%.

9.7 Lx Waveform of a Voice in the Early Stages of Voice Change

The laryngographic (Lx) waveform gives information of the degree of vocal fold closure. This can be used to assess the efficiency of phonation (steeper closing slope, longer closed phase) and can show the changes in vocal fold closure patterns with the onset of adolescent voice change.

Figures 9.13, 9.14, 9.15, 9.16, and 9.17 show the vocal fold closure pattern over a two-octave pitch range in an unchanged voice. Each window showing a selected portion of the waveform is of 20 ms duration; there are fewer cycles at the lower pitches as the frequency is lower. This boy shows a fairly consistent pattern of closure over the pitch range. Figure 9.18 shows the whole two-octave pitch range; pitches where the larynx is functioning with a degree of instability are seen as disturbances to the overall pattern of the waveform. These are the passaggio points between vocal registers and are circled.

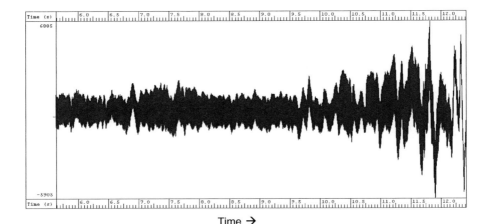

Fig. 9.13 The Lx waveform of boy H aged 12 years, 0 months (pre-puberty), singing a descending slide from G5 to G3

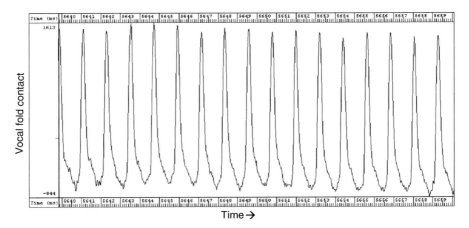

Fig. 9.14 Selected portion of the Lx waveform of boy H aged 12 years, 0 months, singing G5 from a descending slide from G5 to G3

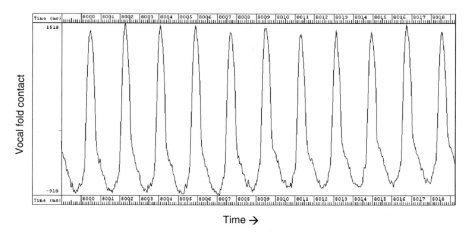

Fig. 9.15 Selected portion of the Lx waveform of boy H aged 12 years, 0 months, singing G4 from a descending slide from G5 to G3

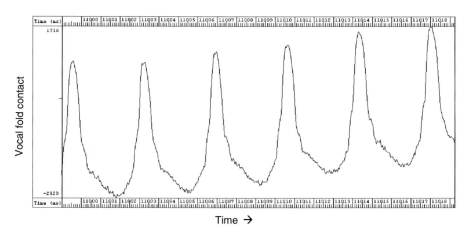

Fig. 9.16 Selected portion of the Lx waveform of boy H aged 12 years, 0 months, singing G3 from a descending slide from G5 to G3

9.8 Lx Waveform of a Voice at the Mid-Point of Voice Change

Figures 9.19, 9.20, 9.21, 9.22, and 9.23 show a noticeable difference in vocal fold contact patterns over the two-octave pitch range. At the lower pitch (G3) the closed phase is longer and the opening slope has a 'knee'. This is typical for thick-fold phonation of the adult voice; the 'peel apart' of the lower edges of the vocal folds is at a slower rate than the mid to upper edges.

The second-lowest pitch in Fig. 9.22 shows extreme instability in the waveform. There appear to be two peaks, one strong and one weak. This is caused by an irregular vibratory pattern leading to weakness in alternate vocal fold collisions. Aurally,

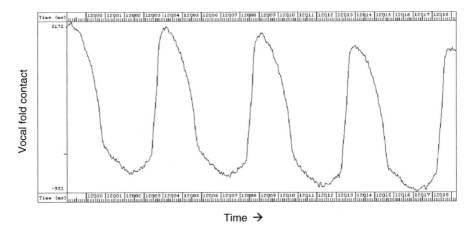

Fig. 9.17 Selected portion of the Lx waveform of boy H aged 12 years, 0 months, singing G3 from a descending slide from G5 to G3

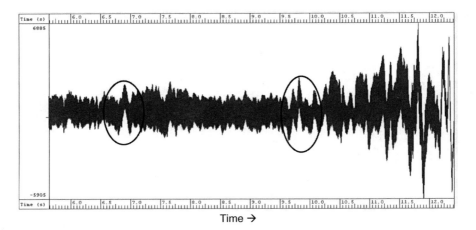

Fig. 9.18 The laryngographic waveform of a two-octave slide showing the two passaggio points marked

this is heard as diplophonia, or two pitches sounding simultaneously. The stronger collisions are heard as a pitch an octave lower than that of the combined collisions; these two pitches are heard at the same time giving rise to the phenomenon of diplophonia. This irregularity occurs at the main register transition point between thick-fold (speech quality) and thin-fold (upper range).

The upper pitches in the recordings of boy H at the mid-point of voice change are surprisingly close to those of the same boy when unchanged. The waveform is not that of falsetto singing, which would typically be a sinusoidal pattern. It appears to be closer to the phonation used by children and adult females at this pitch. It is possible that, as the larynx grows, the boy retains the ability to sing with the soprano

9 Cathedral Choirs in the United Kingdom: The Professional Boy Chorister 141

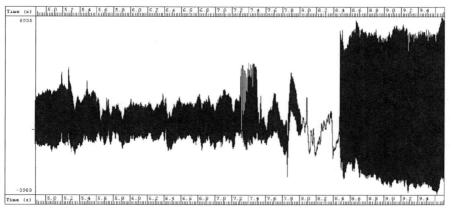

Fig. 9.19 The Lx waveform of boy H aged 13 years 10 months, singing a descending slide from G5 to G3

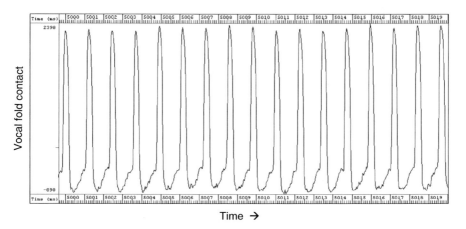

Fig. 9.20 Selected portion of the Lx waveform of boy H aged 13 years 10 months, singing G5 from a descending slide from G5 to G3

sound. Although this has not been longitudinally assessed in boys undergoing voice change, it is known that trained male alto singers use a similar phonation, rather than the pure falsetto used by untrained adult male singers in their upper range.

9.9 Analysis of the Rate of Vocal Fold Closure Over Time

Figures 9.24 and 9.25 show the Lx waveform of the upper pitch range of another boy, Boy C. The superimposed line in pink shows the steepness of the rising part of the curve; this indicates the rate of closure of the vocal folds. The earlier recording,

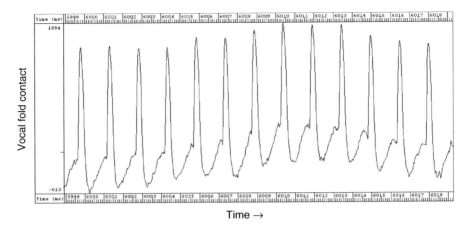

Fig. 9.21 Selected portion of the Lx waveform of boy H aged 13 years, 10 months, singing G4 from a descending slide from G5 to G3

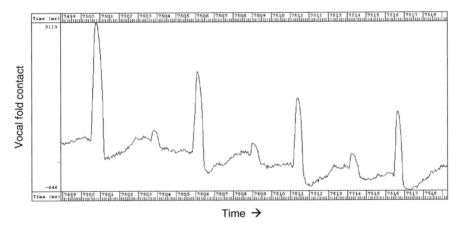

Fig. 9.22 Selected portion of the Lx waveform of boy H aged 13 years, 10 months, at the passaggio point, from a descending slide from G5 to G3

Fig. 9.24, shows a more rapid vocal fold closure. This not only produces a stronger excitation impulse but also boosts the higher frequency spectral component (Howard & Murphy, 2008). This can be seen in the LTAS in Figs. 9.26 and 9.27. The earlier recording with the more rapid closing phase of the vocal folds has a boost of frequencies in the upper range (4000–5000 Hz) which is not seen on the later recording. The voice use of the boy when older was perceived to be more constricted, evidence of this can be seen by the longer closed phase on Fig. 9.26, but it is less acoustically efficient.

The comparisons of the Lx waveform before and during adolescent voice change did not necessarily show any evidence of the emergence of a falsetto phonation in

9 Cathedral Choirs in the United Kingdom: The Professional Boy Chorister   143

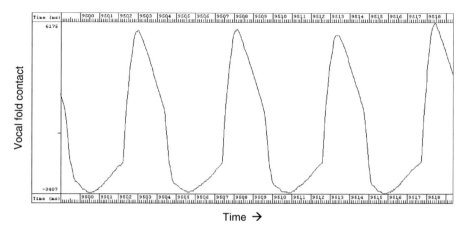

Fig. 9.23 Selected portion of the Lx waveform of boy H aged 13 years 10 months, singing G3 from a descending slide from G5 to G3

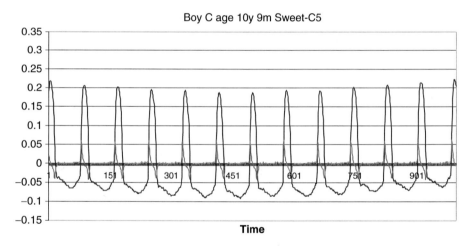

Fig. 9.24 Efficiency of vocal fold closure in boy C at C5, aged 10 years 9 months

the upper pitch range at this stage of development. Cooksey states, however, that in Stage lll of voice change, falsetto phonation is evident in the upper pitch range (Cooksey, 2000). It is possible that the technical skills exemplified by the boys at this stage of their chorister careers enable them to undergo the transition with greater continuity. This may give some insight into the way in which professional male altos use a type of hybrid phonation (Harris, Harris, Rubin, & Howard, 1998), using both falsetto and the thin-fold which tends to be associated with the upper pitch range of children and adult females (Doscher, 1994). This is presumably a learned skill, assuming that the individual has some physical aptitude for this thin-fold phonation. Due to the relatively small number of highly-trained choristers assessed in this study,

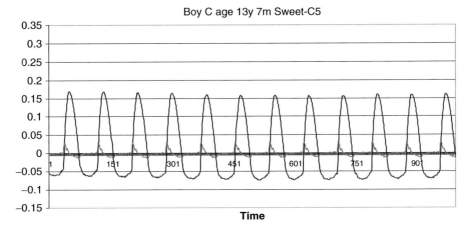

Fig. 9.25 Efficiency of vocal fold closure in boy C at C5, aged 13 years 7 months

Fig. 9.26 LTAS of /i/ vowel on C5, Boy C aged 10 years 9 months

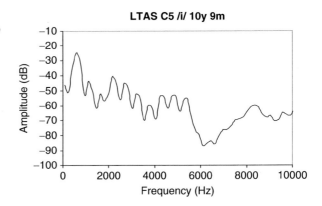

Fig. 9.27 LTAS of /i/ vowel on C5, Boy C aged 13 years 10 months

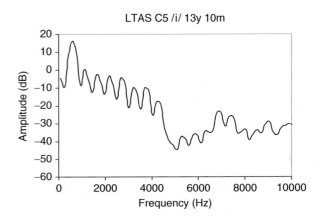

there were only four who were undergoing voice change during the research period. The Lx waveform for each of these four boys was analysed and the same pattern of upper voice phonation was observed. This may not necessarily be the case in all trained choristers, and is unlikely to be the case in less experienced singers.

These findings could inform the practice of singing teachers and choir trainers. The current advice to boys during voice change tends to be to sing in the lowest comfortable pitch range for the duration of this time. These results may suggest that it is possible to maintain a singing voice with a high tessitura, at least for some of the time, during the early stages of voice change, and that the generally given advice may not necessarily apply to skilled boy choristers. This is integral to an ongoing debate between advocates of Cooksey's advice and that of Phillips and Leck. They represent two schools of thought regarding the stages of voice change for males. The first, or 'limited range' school believes that boys' voices change predictably, lowering gradually according to a rather prescribed pattern. Irvin Cooper was the originator of this theory (the 'Cambiata' concept); two of his students continue to advocate this approach: Don Collins (founder of Cambiata Press) and John Cooksey (the 'Eclectic' theory). Cooksey (1992) expands upon Cooper's work and now includes five stages for the male pubertal voice during change. The second, or 'extended range' school believes that boys' voices can change slowly or quickly and may not be limited to a midvoice comfort range of an octave or less during puberty. Frederick Swanson was the originator of this school and contemporary advocates include Leck (2009) and Phillips (1992). The Cooksey system of five stages may be a useful guide for less experienced teachers and singers. It is relatively simple to grasp, and it is unlikely to be misinterpreted. The 'extended range' school may be more applicable to experienced boy singers, who may have a larger accessible pitch range. This would need further research before it could be assumed to be sound pedagogical recommendation.

It is also interesting when cultural and historical perspectives are considered. There are a number of early recordings of boy singers using their upper (soprano) pitch range with a high level of vocal artistry and skill (Beet, 1998). Some of these boys were mid- or post-puberty: this can be heard on the one or two rare spoken interviews with them and it can be seen from photographs. As observed from the Lx data, some boys are able to retain their soprano voices whilst their larynx is growing in power and stamina, especially if these early phases happen relatively fast. The boys on these recordings were reported to have stopped singing when their voices 'broke' (often at the age of 17 or 18). As this event came some time after they had undergone adolescent voice change (probably at the age of 13 or 14 years), it is only possible to conjecture what may have precipitated this 'breaking' and what was happening physically. It is conceivable that the reported 'breaking' was a sudden inability of the laryngeal structures to sustain this thin-fold phonation as the larynx became less pliable in early adulthood. At the time of writing, maintaining the practice of singing in the soprano range after the onset of voice change is not generally popular amongst boys. There is no evidence to suggest whether or not this could be potentially harmful physically in terms of vocal habits persisting into adult singing.

9.10 Conclusion

This study set out to investigate the vocal health and development of intensively trained boy choristers. This was in the context of a relative paucity of scientific research on the singing voices of healthy or 'normal' children and no published research, at the time, in the field of acoustics and psychoacoustics relating to the vocal health or behaviour of children trained in choral singing to a professional level.

Some of the outcomes from the study are:

- Intensively trained boy choristers, despite high levels of vocal loading, have healthier voices than their non-chorister counterparts. Choristers have a higher incidence of low-level vocal dysfunction, suggesting that their voices are slightly fatigued most of the time. They rarely exceed these levels to exhibit higher levels of vocal dysfunction. Choristers probably employ self-regulatory caution with their voice use at all times in order to ensure that they do not exceed certain levels of vocal fatigue. They may also athletically condition their voices to cope with the high vocal loading.
- When measuring detailed voice use of the individual, the Voice Profile Assessment form is the most appropriate; a revised version of this has been suggested in the light of statistical analysis of the data.
- When measuring broad comparisons between groups of this sort, a single-score evaluation of vocal health is most appropriate as the resulting data has sufficient specificity for analysis using SPSS.
- When entering voice change, trained boy singers do not use falsetto phonation in the upper pitch ranges; they use a form of phonation more commonly observed in adult male countertenor and adult female singers – this has implications for voice training during this period of development. When they are actually capable of singing both parts, should they sing soprano or baritone?
- When entering voice change, boys may exhibit attributes of less healthy phonation as a consequence of the rapid growth of the larynx, and not as a result of unhealthy voice use. This has implications for voice assessment practices of voice health professionals and singing teachers.

References

Abberton, E., Howard, D., & Fourcin, A. (1989). Laryngographic assessment of normal voice: A tutorial. *Clinical Linguistics and Phonetics, 3*(3), 281–296.

Arnoux-Sindt, B., Guerrier, B., Alcamo, F., Gabriel, F., Michel, F., & Poulard, D. (1993). *The children's voice: Results of an epidemiological survey on 1120 children undertaken between 1990 and 1993*. Unpublished manuscript.

Artkoski, M., Tommila, J., & Laukkanen, A.-M. (2002). Changes in voice during a day in normal voices without vocal loading. *Logopedics Phoniatrics Vocology, 27*, 118–123.

Beet, S. (1998). The Better Land: Amphion Recordings.

Brandell, M. E. (1982). Psychological/emotional aspects of voice disorders in children. In M. D. Filter (Ed.), *Phonatory voice disorders in children* (pp. 37–59). Springfield, IL: Charles C Thomas.
Carding, P., Carlson, E., Epstein, R., Mathieson, L., & Shewell, C. (2000). Formal perceptual evaluation of voice quality in the United Kingdom. *Logopedics Phoniatrics Vocology, 25*, 133–138.
Capon, J. (2009). Chorister numbers buoyant. *Singing Out*, 1.
Casper, M., Abramson, A. L., & Forman-Franco, B. (1981). Hoarseness in children: Summer camp study. *International Journal of Pediatric Otorhinolaryngology, 3*, 85–89.
Cooksey, J. (1992). *Working with the adolescent voice.* St Louis, MO: Concordia Publishing House.
Cooksey, J. M. (2000). Voice transformation in male adolescents. In L. Thurman & G. Welch (Eds.), *Bodymind and voice* (2nd ed., Vol. 4, pp. 718–738). Collegeville, MN: The VoiceCare Network.
Doscher, B. (1994). *The functional unity of the singing voice.* Lanham, MD: Scarecrow Press.
Green, G. (1989). Psycho-behavioural characteristics of children with vocal nodules: WPBIC ratings. *Journal of Speech and Hearing Disorders, 54*, 306–312.
Harris, T., Harris, S., Rubin, J. S., & Howard, D. (1998). *The voice clinic handbook.* London: Whurr.
Howard, D., & Angus, J. (1996, second edition 2001). *Acoustics and psychoacoustics.* Oxford: Focal Press.
Howard, D., & Murphy. (2008). *Voice science acoustics and recording.* San Diego, CA: Plural.
Howard, D., & Williams, J. (2009). *An investigation of 'ring' in the voices of highly trained child singers.* Paper presented at the PEVOC8, Dresden.
Laver, J., Wirz, S., MacKenzie, J., & Hiller, S. (1981). *The perceptual protocol for the analysis of vocal profiles: Work in progress.* Edinburgh: Department of Linguistics, Edinburgh University.
Leck, H. (2009). The boy's expanding voice: Take the high road. *Choral Journal, 49*(10), 49–60.
Mould, A. (2007). *The English chorister: A history.* London: Hambledon Continuum.
Phillips, K. H. (1992). *Teaching kids to sing.* New York: Schirmer Books/Cengage.
Sala, E., Airo, E., Olkinora, P., Simberg, S., Ulla, S., Laine, A., et al. (2002). Vocal loading among day care center teachers. *Logopedics Phoniatrics Vocology, 27*, 21–28.
Sederholm, E. (1995). Prevalence of hoarseness in ten-year-old children. *Scandinavian Journal of Logopedics and Phoniatrics, 20*, 165–173.
Sederholm, E. (1996). *Hoarseness in ten-year-old children.* Unpublished PhD, Royal Institute of Technology (KTH), Stockholm.
Sederholm, E., McAllister, A., Sundberg, J., & Dalkvist, J. (1993). Perceptual analysis of child hoarseness using continuous scales. *Scandinavian Journal of Logopedics and Phoniatrics, 18*, 73–82.
Shewell, C. (2009). *Voice work, art and science in changing voices.* Chichester: Wiley-Blackwell.
Titze, I. R. (1994). *Principles of voice production.* Englewood Cliffs, NJ: Prentice Hall.
Williams, J. (2004). *An investigation of two German boys' choirs, Leipzig and Dresden, and a comparison with the equivalent London cathedral choirs.* London: Institute of Education.
Wilson, D. K. (1979). *Voice problems of children* (2nd ed.). Baltimore: Williams & Wilkins.
Wiltermuth, S. S., & Heath, C. (2009). Synchrony and cooperation. *Psychological Science, 20*(1), 1–5.

Chapter 10
Singing in Church: The Role of Men in Contemporary Worship Singing

Scott D. Harrison and Daniel K. Robinson

10.1 Introduction

The role of men in the church has undergone substantial change in the last 50 years. Males have held positions of prominence in the Christian church since its inception, often leading to a patriarchal emphasis in structures and practices. Recent attention has focused on the role of women in the clergy, and negative aspects of male priesthood in the Catholic Church. While traditional catholic and protestant movements have dominated the European church, other forms of worship have arisen that provide possibilities for the engagement of males and females in formal settings. Since the Second Vatican Council, Church attendance patterns would appear to have changed, and the much-discussed decline in organised religion, with Altemeyer (2004, p. 77) noting that organized religion has declined greatly in many Western European countries and in North America. What follows, then, is an overview of attendance patterns by men, beginning with trends in North America. The consequential affect on male engagement with singing is then discussed in traditional and contemporary settings. The findings from recent fieldwork in relation to male singing in contemporary settings are presented, along with some strategies for changing the status quo. Underpinning this discussion is the nature of singing within modern Christian worship, and whether men feel comfortable enough to engage in the historically established practice of corporate singing.

10.2 Church Attendance by Men

In North America, the substantial imbalance of sexes in congregations has been noted over the course of three centuries (Engebretson, 2004; Taves, 2002). Lindley (1996), for example, refers to contemporary reports that women vastly outnumbered

---

S.D. Harrison (✉)
Griffith University, Brisbane, QLD 4101, Australia
e-mail: scott.harrison@griffith.edu.au

men in the seventeenth century. In the middle of the nineteenth century, two-thirds of church members in New England were women, according to Carroll (2003). In Canada, 62% of women attend church at least once a month, while the percentage for men is 53% (Gee, 1991). The gender gap is not a distinctly North American one but it is a Christian one, according to Murrow (2005). The theology and practices of Judaism, Buddhism and Islam offer "uniquely masculine" experiences for men, while Christianity does not. Evidence that this is not uniquely American has support in recent surveys in the United States, Canada, United Kingdom, Australia and New Zealand. According to this research, there is an imbalance of males and females in the pews (Lummis, 2004; Duduit, 2005; Mol, 1985; Taves, 2002; Gee, 1991; Hout & Greeley, 1998; Stepp, 2005).

If fewer men are attending church, the reasons for their absence need to be interrogated. Between 1880 and 1920 "muscular Christianity" emphasized manliness (Putney, 2001). This recognized a return to biblical patriarchy and rejected the portrayals of Jesus as having long hair and white robes. Podles (1999, n.p.) however, claims that

> ... contemporary Christianity has lost this masculine sense of a struggle against the forces within oneself, having been watered down to passionate feelings and emotional ecstasies that men find difficult to identify with.

Kunjufu (1994) posits that men don't want to engage in Christianity because they don't want to dress up. There is also the suggestion in Kunjufu's work that sport has a heavy influence in men's lives. This relates to Harrison's work (2005) that intimates men and boys choosing involvement in sport over almost any other activity. Kunjufu recommends scheduling church services around major games, and installing large-screen TVs so men can watch their favourite sports together after the sermon. In New Jersey, one church conducts one service a year at which the congregation is encouraged to wear their football jersey (Drobness, 2009). In a worship environment where 1500 out of a 2000-strong congregation are women, the strategy appears to be attracting more men.

According to Murrow (2005), another deterrent for men is the so-called feminine practice of "singing of love-songs to Jesus, fresh flowers and quilted banners on the walls." The issue of repertoire will be discussed later in the chapter, but the appearance of the church as "feminine" deserves closer scrutiny. Murrow claims "... the church has a reputation as a place for women, weirdoes and wimps. No real man would be caught dead in the church" (n.p.). He goes on to comment that language is a part of the problem, noting that Christian men in particular use words that no "normal" guy would say. In addition, Francis, Kay, and Campbell (1996) found that

> Women more often claim denominational membership, that they pray, read the bible, have religious and mystical experiences, watch religious television programmes, express belief in God, report feeling close to God and derive comfort from religion (p. 11).

This would appear to concur with the views of De Vaus (1984) who observed that women tend to be more religious than men. Francis et al. (1996, p. 12) take this further: "terms such as gentleness, compassion, healing, reconciliation, affectionate, childlike and loyal" are attributes valued in Christian living, but society usually associates these attributes with the feminine. Avoidance of femininity is one of the main ways in which masculinity is maintained. Ironically this notion has origins in the epic sagas of the Greeks and Romans (800–100 BC) that encouraged action, strength, courage and loyalty and such attributes were further entrenched by the teachings of the early Christian church. The monastic tradition of 400–800AD served to further devalue the feminine, while the twelfth century social system emphasized self sacrifice, courage, physical strength, honour and service to the lady. These traditions were embedded in ensuing centuries in Western civilization (see Harrison, 2008).

Music, like the contemporary church experience, is also gendered feminine (Solie, 1993). There are two ways in which singing in church challenges masculinity: once through the feminisation of church, and secondly through the feminine nature of some styles of music. The following passage interrogates the connection between singing and masculinities in the church setting.

10.3 Church Singing

The reluctance of men to sing in church has its foundation in the attendance and participation data for churches described above, and also in the broader concerns related to male singing. According to Koza (1993, p. 50) the lack of desire to sing is based on "discursive binaries that construct females, femininity and homosexuality in the 'undesirable other' category". Koza (1993) also noted that if reliance on rigid definitions of masculinity and femininity continue, along with a devaluation of things feminine, there might be dire consequences for choral programs. The traditional way in which men have interacted with worship has been through unison congregational singing and choral-based music. Mattis (2004) conclude that there is a lack of interest in, or motivation to, participate in group worship of any kind, and it can be argued that singing is one of the main corporate activities in group worship. This is not to say that men don't want to engage in communal activities. Legg (2009) contends that men will happily engage in sports teams, fishing, pub quizzes, paint-balling, DIY projects, curry nights, bowling and going out for a beer: all activities that involve groups. The last of these has been the focus of work in Ireland where Flynn (1993) has questioned the notion that singing is acceptable in pubs while churches "remain silent." In addition, singing at the football is also quite acceptable, though only in a very specific style. Movements such as "beer and hymns" have sought to capitalize on this style of singing (Walker, 2009).

Men have not always been reluctant to participate in worship. In Europe, church leadership in ecclesiastical roles has been the almost exclusive domain of men and there has been an assumption that singing by men was of the highest quality, unencumbered by the timbre of female voices. Recent literature indicates that this may not have been the case. Jerold (2006, p. 78) gives several examples from across the continent including that of a journalist in 1791 who described "... the bungling of the noblest four-part pieces and the terrible aimless screaming and screeching of a Berlin choir". Similarly, Scholes (1959) refers to the church musicians of the late 1700s (in this case castrati) being "made up of the refuse of the opera houses" while in England Reichardt (1785) found that the religious choral singing was "filled with screaming from the most wretched voices." Sixty-five years later, Wesley (1849) called boys' voices a "poor substitute for the vastly superior quality and power of those of women." The quality of the unchanged voice has been thoroughly interrogated by Welch and Howard (2002) who found a high degree of confusability between male and female unchanged voices. This research was undertaken, in part, to interrogate the commonly held belief that boys' voices were distinctive (and superior) in timbre. The quality of voice, and the so-called stigma attached to having females fulfil singing roles in church has therefore been largely overcome through the introduction of female voices into the worship setting in England and continental Europe. This occurs both in lieu of, and in addition to male choral singing.

In America, Gates (1989, p. 37) noted a similar shift:

> ... there has been a marked shift from male to female involvement with public singing from colonial times to the present. Males took leadership roles in public singing and music literacy in early Boston and urged women to sing; today, adolescent and adult males are much less involved with public singing than are females.

Bell's (2004, p. 42) findings are consistent with those of Gates (1989). As noted in chapter one, in her review of the literature to date she found that women singers significantly outnumber the men singers, some by as much as a 2:1 ratio in community-based choirs. Gates (1988, p. 7) also noted that the singing of men in early 1700s was lacking in quality and, furthermore that "the incompetent and contentious congregational singing of the time was undermining godliness" According to primary sources cited by Gates, men were

> ... roundly chastised for singing too loudly, too high, too low, holding pitches too long, using melismas, using more than one tune at the same time, not encouraging women's singing, and being led (by Satan) into contentiousness because they were too ignorant and too stubborn to learn to read music (Mather, 1721; Rowe, 1722; Symmes, 1720; Thacher, Danforth, & Danforth, 1723; Walter, 1722).

Many of these commentators encouraged the singing of women "primarily for religious reasons." By the 1980s, Gates claimed that

> ... male singing has all but disappeared from taverns; singing in gatherings of fraternal organizations and service clubs is perfunctorily engaged in for largely forgotten purposes; and male singing in church congregations and sporting events arguably lacks not only skill but spirited commitment to singing or the social benefits of this activity (p. 40).

The connection between singing in church and singing in the congregation is an interesting one to pursue. Recent research (Legg, 2009) indicates a preference for church songs that are close in style to football anthems. *Onward Christian Soldiers, Guide Me O Thy Great Redeemer, All People That On Earth Do Dwell,*

Amazing Grace and *Dear Lord And Father Of Mankind Forgive Our Foolish Ways*. In a survey of 400 men reported in *Sorted*, other songs were described as "too girly." This comment is reminiscent of the description of musical activities such as playing the flute and singing in choir in the work of Green (1993, 1996) and Harrison (2007). Alternatively, songs like *Onward Christian Soldiers* were described by participants as being "proper macho hymns". Murrow (2005) concurs, stating that contemporary repertoire is suited to women's taste and that the movement away from reformation hymns (those that refer to battle, blood and victory) to the "tender love songs to Jesus" require men to sing lyrics they would not usually sing to another man. The nature of this alternative new contemporary worship singing is worthy of closer examination particularly in terms of genre and style.

10.4 Contemporary Church Singing

The term "contemporary" covers a wide range of potential worship experiences. Robinson (2010) defines the Contemporary worship singer as coming from the western Protestant Christian tradition: one who sings hymns as well as modern praise and worship choruses. In Robinson's work, these individuals operate within five main worship styles: *Liturgical, Traditional, Contemporary, Blended and Charismatic/Pentecostal*. The specific qualities of each of these styles are described in brief here. A more thorough description can be found in Robinson (2010). The *Liturgical* worship style predominantly uses hymns interspersed throughout the overall service. The *Traditional* style also predominantly uses hymns but in a less structured yet in a reasonably predictable fashion. The third worship style, *Contemporary*, is best defined by its use of songs (hymns and choruses) interlaced with scripture and prayer to form a thematic progression which often culminates in the sermon. A fourth worship style, *Blended* worship, seeks to merge both the Liturgical and Contemporary worship styles. The *Charismatic/Pentecostal* worship style encourages the least structured liturgy of all the worship styles and while hymns are sometimes used, the predominant musical style employed is the modern worship chorus. In the contemporary worship environment, music and movement combine to create atmosphere and to connect with contemporary popular culture. Horness (2004, p. 102) defines contemporary worship as employing "modern instrumentation (e.g., guitars, drums, synthesizers, percussion, horns), contemporary musical styles (e.g., rock, jazz, hip hop, rap, gospel), and freshly written or arranged songs (both new choruses and fresh treatments of traditional hymns)." Breward (2001) states that music in this style is "much closer to folk idioms and what people hear electronically" (2001, pp. 373–374) while Robinson (2010) notes that Contemporary worship style will often assemble the songs together to form a 20–30 min set of congregational singing. Repertoire employed in this context is of particular interest. Evans noted that

One criticism levelled at songs ... by older male participants, apart from the secularity of love language involved, is that they are too feminine in construction. As such they become progressively harder for male congregation members to identify with (Evans, 2002, p. 221).

Winslade (2009, p. 34) concurs in relation to the feminine content of songs:

> How many songs do we sing in church that appeal to a feminine motif of love and intimacy that subtly make men cringe or recoil? Sure, those of us who are socialized in the ways of the church understand (or possibly reinterpret) the lyrics, but have you noticed that a growing number of men are not singing with enthusiasm.

Following up specifically on the idea that music is feminine (see Solie, 1993) Geoff Bullock (in Evans, 2002, p. 273) notes that recent performers have

> ... set the standard of intimate involvement that has been followed by many touchy feely guys – in touch with their feminine side. This may be viewed as a continuation of the nineteenth century trend that saw feminine overtones of sexuality and sentimentality emerge in evangelical music.

The extent to which congregational singing fulfils the vision of the Liturgy Constitution of the second Vatican Council which calls for "full, conscious and active participation" (p. 14) is still in doubt. It seems clear that attendees and active participants are predominantly female, and that men do not perceive participation in singing or institutional worship as a masculine activity. Recent commentary by Kimball (2009) supports this:

> ... many churches are male-led and male-dominated. In those churches it is often rare for a female to be on the stage doing anything but singing in the choir or serving as a back-up singer in the band (p. 319).

As part of a larger study, the proportion of males involved in contemporary worship singing was interrogated (Robinson, 2010). In all but one age-group (51–60) the female participation substantially outstripped those of males (Fig. 10.1).

This observation would appear to be at variance from Kimball's inference that the female may serve as a back-up singer or member of a choir. Robinson's data (based on a survey of almost 100 Australian singers) places the contemporary worship singer as predominantly female, singing in a wide variety of styles rock, jazz, hip hop, rap, gospel accompanied by guitars, drums, synthesizers and percussion.

Murrow (2011) blames the lack of participation in singing by men on the introduction of the data projects. The once familiar hymnals and song-books that included a defined canon of material have been replaced by words on a screen. Apart from the inherent decrease in music literacy, worship leaders have used this as an opportunity to introduce new songs each week. Without adequate scaffolding, the congregation finds it difficult to sing songs they've never heard. As Murrow (n.p.) notes "with no musical notes to follow, how is a person supposed to pick up the tune?" As a result a trend is emerging whereby worshippers stand silent as professional musicians play complex instruments, and sing songs that are unknown

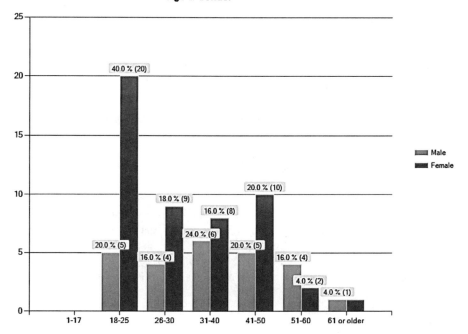

Fig. 10.1 Age and gender of contemporary worship singers

to the masses. Murrow sees this as a final nail in the coffin of men singing in church: singing used to be one of the corporate acts of church, an opportunity for involvement. Its absence creates a problem for church, and for singing.

10.5 Survey Findings

With this conundrum in mind, and taking account of the literature indicating the decline of male attendance at and involvement in church, the authors conducted a survey in March and April of 2010. The survey was used to gather feedback from a cross-section of those involved in contemporary worship. It was an effective way of obtaining data from a diverse pool of individuals. Moreover, the survey's closed and open-ended questions were able to go beyond the descriptive to the interpretive by providing "explanations of the phenomena studied and the patterns of results obtained" (Robson, 2002, p. 235).

Using an online survey tool, a questionnaire consisting of dichotomous questions to a "Yes" or "No" response was combined with the opportunity for comments through open-ended questions. The justification for this process can be found in Jeziorska (1989) who notes:

> We are not dealing with a scientific inquiry done by computers ... there is not one answer to any one question, especially in art. Because of this, the statistical figures of the report are interesting in giving an idea of the general trends, but are not of greater importance than the comments which follow them and which give a clearer picture of what teachers think (p. 3).

The qualitative data gathered in the survey (e.g. in the coding of open-ended questions) were processed using content analysis to extract common themes and trends (Silverman, 2005, p. 160).

In addition to demographic information, the survey interrogated perceptions of gender balance with church attendance, whether Christianity offered masculine experiences and issues of patriarchy in the church. It also broached the subject of male engagement with singing in church, and the genres that are likely to appeal to men within the church setting.

Almost half the cohort were aged 31–40; 16% were 18–25, and a further 16% were 41–50. Most had been attending church for more than 10 years, though 37% had been attending their current church for less than 2 years. A wide variety of denominations were represented in the participants: Baptist, Assemblies of God, Uniting Church and Presbyterian. The worship styles experienced by the participants are of particular interest in relation to this chapter, as represented in Fig. 10.2:

With this context in mind, the perception of attendance at church was explored. Respondents indicated a high level of correlation with the existing data, with male and female participants acknowledging that most attendees are female (Fig. 10.3).

The reasons given for non-participation by men are perhaps of greater significance. Drawing on the literature, a number of categories were presented from

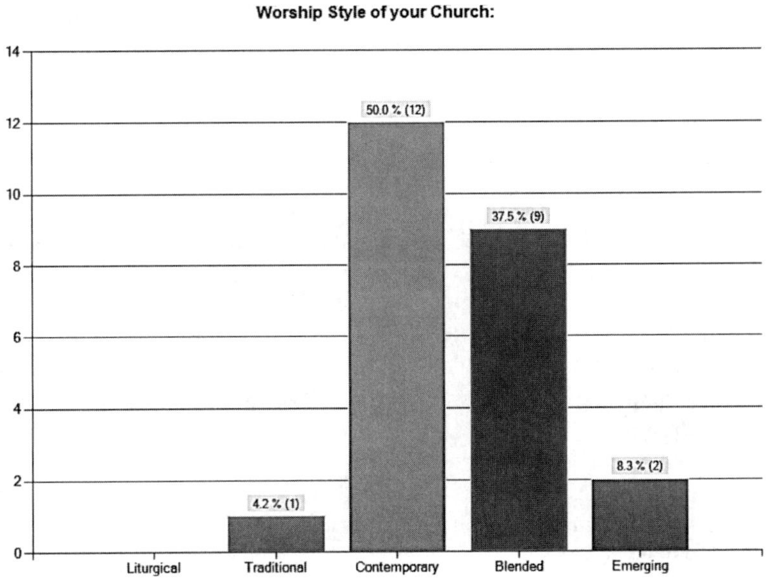

Fig. 10.2 Worship styles

10 Singing in Church: The Role of Men in Contemporary Worship Singing

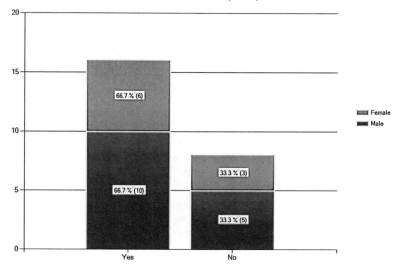

Fig. 10.3 Participation in worship by gender

which respondents could choose. The influence of sport was a clear factor, as was Murrow's (2005) contention that "singing love songs to Jesus" was problematic for men. Other themes from the literature were strongly rejected by the cohort. These included not wanting to dress up and church decorations, as demonstrated in Fig. 10.4.

Participants were then invited to provide open-ended response as to strategies that could be implemented to overcome males' low attendance rates at church. One consistent theme was to have "all-male" events, with comments such as "occasionally focusing on an all male worship and mateship" and conducting "more men's conferences and/or talks." Specifically, one respondent suggested "Something more like a social gathering in a backyard or a pub, which would feel more natural and comfortable for them." The link with the pub responds to Flynn's (1993) earlier contention that singing is acceptable in pubs while churches "remain silent." The connection with "blokey" culture was posited in several other responses, some of them tongue-in-cheek, some not. Responses of this nature included

> *Free beer*
> *More food ... eating as part of the actual service*
> *Cheerleaders, dancing girls...*
> *How about Formula 1 race cars?*

These comments are reminiscent of Legg's (2009) suggestion that men will engage with sports teams etc., but not the communal activities of church. Other comments around this theme called for "speakers on topics that relate to men" and "less

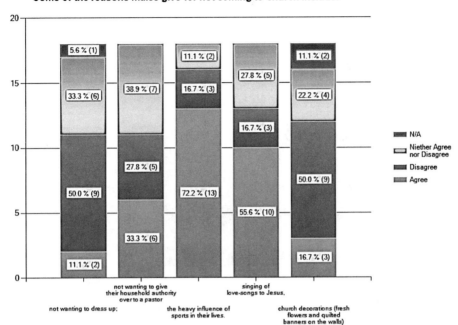

Fig. 10.4 Reasons men may not attend church

sissy emotionalism." This comment appears to connect to the notion of singing love songs to Jesus, a cause for concern by more than 50% of the respondents in Fig. 10.4 above. Specifically focusing on musical involvement, the question of what types of music were likely to appeal to men was asked. As Fig. 10.5 indicates, rock was by far the most popular choice, closely followed by other and pop.

As Horness (2004), Breward (2001), and Robinson (2010) have noted, rock is one of the genres commonly found in contemporary worship settings. The question of why men would choose not to sing in this environment is critical to addressing the paucity of involvement by men in music. Participants provided a great deal of data on this topic, much of which aligns with mainstream thinking about masculinities and music. One even cited "broader socio-cultural influences." Representative comments included:

> There is a stigma associated with singing for many people both male and female, but in Australia may artistic expressions have a stigma for males, i.e., there is a perception that male dancers or singers in certain genres, such as music theatre, are likely to be gay – this stigma flows through to other expression in underlying ways

> The only time non-churched men get together and sing is if they are at a footy game (celebrating a win in the team change-rooms), if they are drunk, or if they are gay. So for many men, the thought of getting together and

10 Singing in Church: The Role of Men in Contemporary Worship Singing

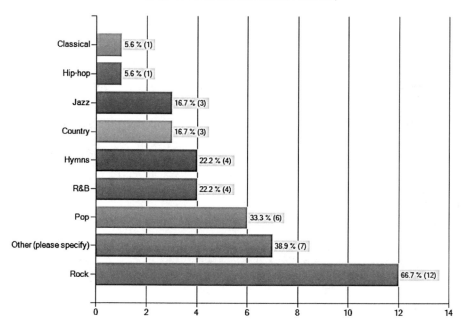

Specifically in relation to music, what types of music do you think are most appealing to men in the congregation? (You may choose more than one)

Fig. 10.5 Music styles appealing to male worshippers

singing songs during a church service (without a footy game, alcohol, or homosexuality) sounds odd.

Lack of cultural emphasis on singing inhibits men from singing in most places...except when inebriated...they are paranoid about being deemed 'sensitive or gentle' and dare note show emotions in public unless it aggressive, argumentative or brash. They feel that singing is not a very masculine thing to do.

Some comments related to more musical reasons, such as the vocal range or a lack of confidence in their own ability to sing. Others related this confidence to the pedagogy: "songs not being 'taught' very well" while some noted "a fear of others hearing they are a bad singer." This relates to Ashton and Davis' (2002, p. 107) remark in which they noted "It is worth looking 'round a Guest Service congregation during a hymn and noting how many adult males are not singing."

Most comments, however, focused on the relationship of alcohol and sport evident in the literature, and a lack of appropriate role models:

There is no other place in our culture where men sing together – at least when they are sober

Where else do you do this unless you are drunk/or chanting (often tunelessly) at a sporting event?

Lack of role models, being in the minority

Looking and sounding silly

Fear of intimacy and looking weak

Good bloke role models as song leaders

They are afraid or think they would look 'stronger' if they just stand there and don't sing

One particularly poignant comment noted: "They don't sing much anywhere else ..." This perception relates to the broader role of singing in society, particularly in schools as Chapman (2006), noted is recognising the shift in western cultures to

> ... an elitist activity – for the talented rather than the community. The tragic loss of school-based singing during the past three decades has served to distance children from this vocal heritage (p. 1).

Similarly, it appears singing in churches is left to the talented, and not for the assembly at large. This devalues singing and, as one participant commented means that men "often do not have a full understanding of its importance; personally and corporately."

In order to address the lack of male involvement in singing in contemporary worship (and indeed attendance at church at all), participants were asked what strategies might be implemented to assist men in participating in singing in church.

The notion of church as a microcosm of society was raised in this response:

Church is often influenced by social norms but also has the potential to counteract those norms – in certain church settings male vocal leadership is prevalent and acceptable, a number of well known worship leaders and songwriters are male, I would suspect in those environments there may be more acceptance within the church culture for male involvement in singing – I think it is all about culture.

Some participants called for the creation of a comfortable, safe environment, as advocated by Holley (2009) in relation to community singing. One participant noted:

I'm not sure what you can do to force them to like it more, as some will always feel uncomfortable with it. Those who are raised in the church will often gravitate toward it (as they are comfortable with singing and see it as entirely normal, whilst those from outside the church will rarely see it as normal). If they are comfortable, they'll like it ... if not, they'll either just stop singing or they'll stop attending the Sunday service.

Another mentioned bringing about "broader cultural change and creating comfortable environments, both aesthetically and sonically." Others referred to the need for role models, as advocated by Adler and Harrison (2004), Harrison (2007) and Hall (2005). Strategies included having "one Sunday where men take the leadership of singing" and "formation of a male singing group."

This chapter commenced with the title *Singing in Church*, but what seems apparent from the research and analysis conducted for the chapter is that men do not seem to approach singing for Christian worship as a subset of the whole. As already noted, a visit to the weekend professional football game will bring an opportunity to witness men singing; often enacted while clothed in team colours, beer in left hand while waving a team flag with the right. Corporate singing does not appear to be activated around the sports stadium because of a predefined program. It develops out of a culture of collective enthusiasm which enjoins individuals to a specific statement that declares, "I belong to this team; we belong to this team".

For men in particular, singing in worship should not be approached as a module that can be either inserted or left aside. It would seem that a culture needs to be developed that allows the masculine voice to emerge; naturally interweaved with other forms of worship expression.

10.6 Conclusion

It is clear from the literature and fieldwork findings presented in this chapter that men do not engage in organised religion to the same extent as women, despite a history of patriarchal dominance of the western church. Consequently, males' involvement in music in church is limited, and their capacity to participate in singing is hampered. It would appear that societal forces at play in the general population are, in part, the cause of this trend.

Suggestions for addressing this phenomenon in contemporary worship settings echo strategies employed in the broader community. These include the cautious melding of activities men are known to enjoy: eating, sport and drinking. Repertoire selection, awareness of musical style choices, male-only ensembles and the incorporation of suitable role models are also significant factors in the development of a culture that supports male involvement in contemporary worship settings.

References

Adler, A., & Harrison, S. (2004). Swinging back the gender pendulum: Addressing boys' needs in music education research and practice. In L. Bartel (Ed.), *Research to practice: A biennial series: Questioning the music education paradigm* (pp. 270–289). Toronto: Canadian Music Educators Association.

Altemeyer, B. (2004). The decline of organized religion in western civilization. *International Journal for the Psychology of Religion, 14*(2), 77–89.

Ashton, M., & Davis, C. J. (2002). Following in Cranmer's footsteps. In D. A. Carson (Ed.), *Worship by the book* (pp. 64–135). Grand Rapids, MI: Zondervan.

Bell, C. (2004). Update on community choirs and singing in the United States. *International Journal of Research in Choral Singing, 2*(1), 39–52.

Breward, I. (2001). *A history of the churches in Australasia*. New York: Oxford University Press.

Caroll, B. (2003). *American masculinities: A historical encyclopaedia*. Thousand Oaks, CA: Sage.

Chapman, J. (2006). *Singing and teaching singing: A holistic approach to classical voice.* Oxford: Plural.
De Vaus, D. (1984). Workforce participation and sex differences in church attendance. *Review of Religious Research, 25*(3), 247–256.
Drobness, T. (2009). *Church scores with guys by hosting football Sunday.* Retrieved May 9, 2010, from http://www.usatoday.com/news/religion/2009-12-11-football-men-church_N.htm
Duduit, M. (2005). *Why men hate going to church: Interview with David Murrow.* Retrieved May 9, 2010, from http://www.preaching.com/resources/articles/11550735/page-8/
Engebretson, K. (2004). Teenage boys, spirituality and religion. *International Journal of Children's Spirituality, 9*(3), 63–278.
Evans, M. (2002). *Secularising the sacred: The impact of Geoff Bullock and Hillsong Church on contemporary congregational song in Sydney, 1990-1999.* Unpublished doctoral dissertation, Macquarie University, Sydney.
Flynn, L. (1993). Singing pubs and silent churches: Revisited. *The Furrow, 44*(7/8), 408–415.
Francis, L., Kay, W., & Campbell, S. (Eds.). (1996). *Research in religious education.* Leominster: Smyth & Helwys.
Gates, J. T. (1988). Samual Gerrish, publisher to the 'regular singing movement' in 1720s New England. Music Library Association Notes 45 (September), 15–22.
Gates, J. T. (1989). A historical comparison of public singing by American men and women. *Journal of Research in Music Education, 37*(1), 37.
Gee, E. (1991). Gender differences in church attendance in Canada: the role of labor force in participation. *Review of Religious Research, 32*(3), 267–273.
Green, L. (1993). Music, gender and education: A report on some exploratory research. *British Journal of Music Education, 10*, 219–253.
Green, L. (1996). The emergence of gender as an issue in music education. In C. Plummeridge (Ed.), *Music education: Trends and issues* (pp. 41–58). London: Institute of Education, University of London.
Hall, C. (2005). Gender and boys' singing in early childhood. *British Journal of Music Education, 22*(1), 5–20.
Harrison, S. (2005). Music versus sport: A new approach to scoring. *Australian Journal of Music Education,* (1), 56–61.
Harrison, S. (2007). Where have the boys gone? The perennial problem of gendered participation in music. *British Journal of Music Education, 24*(3), 267–280.
Harrison, S. (2008). *Masculinities and music.* Newcastle upon Tyne: Cambridge Scholars
Holley, P. (2009). The Birralee blokes. In S. Harrison (Ed.), *Male voices: Stories of boys learning through making music* (pp. 156–172). Melbourne: ACER.
Horness, J. (2004). Contemporary music-driven worship. In P. A. Basden (Ed.), *Exploring the worship spectrum: 6 views* (pp. 97–116). Grand Rapids, MI: Zondervan.
Hout. M., & Greeley, A. (1998). What church officials' reports don't show: Another look at church attendance. *American Sociological Review, 63*, 113–119.
Jerold, B. (2006). Choral singing before the era of recording. *The Musical Times, 147*(1895), 77–84.
Jeziorska, W. (1989). *Report on grade piano examinations. What candidates say* (2nd revised ed.). London: European Piano Teachers Association (UK).
Kimball, D. (2009). Emerging worship. In J. M. Pinson (Ed.), *Perspectives on Christian worship: 5 views* (pp. 288–333). Nashville, TN: Broadman and Holman.
Koza, J. E. (1993). The 'missing males' and other gender issues in music education: Evidence from the Music Supervisors' Journal, 1914–1924. *Journal of Research in Music Education, 41*(3), 212–232.
Kunjufu, J. (1994). *Countering the conspiracy to destroy black boys* (Vol. IV). Chicago: African American Images.
Legg, S. (2009, May). Why men don't go to church. *Sorted Magazine*, n.p.

Lindley, S. (1996). *You have step out of your place: A history of women and religion in America*. Louisville, KY: Westminster John Knox Press.

Lummis, A. (2004). Real men and church participation. *Review of Religious Research, 45*(4), 404–414.

Mather, C. (1721). *The accomplished singer*. Boston: Samuel Gerrish.

Mattis, J. (2004). Factors influencing religious non-attendance among African-American men. *Review of Religious Research, 45*(4), 404–414.

Mol, H. (1985). *The faith of Australians*. Sydney: Allen and Unwin.

Murrow, D. (2005). *Why men hate going to church*. Nashville, TN: Thomas Nelson.

Murrow, D. (2011). *Why men have stopped singing in church*. Retrieved July 3, 2011, from http://worship.com/2011/02/why-men-have-stopped-singing-in-church/

Podles, L. (1999). *The church impotent: The feminization of Christianity*. Dallas, TX: Spence Publishing Company.

Putney, C. (2001). *Muscular Christianity: Manhood and sports in protestant America, 1880–1920*. Cambridge: Harvard University Press.

Reichardt, J. F. (1785). Allgemeine deutsche Bibliothek, (Ed. Nicolai). In B. Jerold (2006) Choral Singing before the era of recording. *The Musical Times, 147*(1895), 77–84.

Robinson, D. K. (2010). Teaching the contemporary worship singer. In S. D. Harrison (Ed.), *Perspectives on teaching singing: Australian vocal pedagogues sing their stories*. Brisbane, QLD: Australian Academic Press.

Robson, C. (2002). *Real world research* (2nd ed.). Malden, MA: Blackwell.

Rowe, J. (1722). *Singing of psalms by seven constituted sounds, opened and explained*. Boston: Brady and Tate.

Scholes, P. (Ed.). (1959). *Dr. Burney's musical tours in Europe: An eighteenth- century musical tour in France and Italy*. London: Oxford University Press.

Silverman, D. (2005). *Doing qualitative research* (2nd ed.). London, UK: Sage.

Solie, R. (Ed.). (1993). *Musicology and difference*. Berkeley, CA: University of California Press.

Stepp, G. (2005). *Are men anti-church?* Vision. Retrieved October 15, 2011, from http://www.vision.org/visionmedia/article.aspx?id=141

Symmes, T. (1720). *The reasonableness of regular singing*. Boston: Samuel Gerrish.

Taves, A. (2002). Feminization revisited: Protestantism and gender at the turn of the century. In M. L. Bendroth & V. L. Bereton (Eds.), *Women in twentieth century Protestantism* (pp. 304–324). Champaign, IL: University of Illinois Press.

Thacher, P., Danforth, J., & Danforth, S. (1723). *Cases of conscience about singing psalms*. Boston: Samuel Gerrish.

Walker, D. (2009). *Church Times*. September, 2009.

Walter, T. (1722). *Sweet psalmist of Israel*. Boston: Samuel Gerrish.

Welch, G. F., & Howard, D. (2002). Gendered voice in the cathedral choir. *Psychology of Music, 30*(1), 102–120.

Wesley, S. (1849). A few words on cathedral music. In T. Day (2000). English cathedral choirs in the twentieth century. In J. Potter (Ed.), *The Cambridge Companion to Singing* (pp. 123–132). Cambridge: Cambridge University Press.

Winslade, B. (2009, December). Men and the church: Do they really mix? *The QB, 1*, 34–35.

Part III
Singing in Informal and Community Contexts

Chapter 11
Mutuality, Belonging, and Meaning-Making

Pathways to Developing Young Boys' Competence and Creativity in Singing and Song-Making

Margaret S. Barrett

11.1 Introduction

Engagement in singing and song-like behaviours is evident from the earliest moments of the infant's vocal production. Whilst the intention of these earliest vocal endeavours may be concerned primarily with seeking fulfilment of basic human needs such as food, warmth, care, comfort, and companionship rather than with musical expression, it is here that the formative behaviours of the singer and creative music-maker are lain down (Barrett, 2003, 2006). Significantly, such early vocalisations are inherently social in intention and effect, seeking to elicit response from carers in what has been described as co-operative and co-dependent acts of "communicative musicality" (Malloch, 1999; Malloch & Trevarthen, 2009a; Trevarthen & Malloch, 2000, 2002) between infant and carer-giver.

Studies of infants' and young childrens' singing of known and invented songs (Davidson, 1985, 1994; Dowling, 1984a, 1984b, 1999; Moog, 1976; Moorhead & Pond, 1978; Tafuri, 2008) suggest some general trends in the development of vocal and singing behaviours with children moving from the production of short melodic fragments sustained through vowel sounds (approximately 1 year) to lengthier musical phrases (towards age two) with a focus on words as the primary shaping element. These studies suggest that singing and song-making are ubiquitous for the young child with no apparent differentiation between boys and girls in relation to the early production of song.

Gendered differentiation in vocal behaviours has been reported in children in the early years of schooling (approximately 5 years of age) (Hall, 2005; Mang, 2006; Welch, 2000, 2006a; Welch et al., 1991, 1996, 1997). This body of research has focused on children's singing skill development largely in relation to known song and indicates that boys' singing development lags behind that of girls'. Less is known of gendered differentiation in children's production of invented song.

M.S. Barrett (✉)
University of Queensland, Brisbane, QLD, Australia
e-mail: m.barrett@uq.edu.au

Invented song as distinct from known song may be viewed as a development of the infant's "musical babbling" (Moog, 1976) and a move toward more independent song-making (Barrett, 2006). Invented song-making begins to emerge in young children's early musical activities at approximately 18 months of age, and continues as a form of music engagement through to the early years of schooling. Importantly, this invented song-making is implicated in young children's early identity work as well as their musical development (Barrett, 2010). In this chapter I shall draw on data generated with young children in a longitudinal study of the role and function of invented song-making in young children's world-making and identity work. The chapter provides a case-study of a 3-year old boy focusing on his singing and invented song-making over a 2 year period. Analysis of data provides insight into the uses, contexts, purposes, and musical features of his singing and invented song-making and provides a context for considering the implications of these for the development of young boys' singing behaviour.

11.2 Theoretical Framework

11.2.1 *The Origins of Singing Behaviour*

The origins of singing behaviour lie in the pre-natal auditory and affective experiences of the foetus in the final months of gestation. During this period the foetus is exposed to the mother's auditory world, a world in which she actively engages as sound-maker and listener; and, through the biological media of amniotic fluid, blood, tissue, and the neuroendocrine system, the infant is exposed to the mother's emotional responses to the sounds of her environment (Parncutt, 2006; Trehub, 2001; Welch, 2005). It is here, in the womb, that the pathways of the child's first responses to and engagement with music begin to be mapped out. In the first year of life infants exhibit a diversity of vocal behaviours including crying (at varying intensities, both emotional and dynamic, and for varying purposes), vocalising with vowel sounds, cooing, and increasingly, "musical babbling" (Moog, 1976) and "vocal play" (Papoucek, 1996) that incorporates the vowels, consonants and linguistic nuances of the languages and musical cultures that surround the infant (Meltzoff, 2002). The musical prosody of these early vocal behaviours indicate the infant's sensitivity to and use of pitch, rhythm, and, musical organisation and phrasing (Papoucek, 1996; Tafuri, 2008).

Recent research in the field of Communicative Musicality (Malloch, 1999; Malloch & Trevarthen, 2002) has suggested that the infant is an active communicator and meaning-maker, and that singing and song-like behaviours play a pivotal role in these processes. Communicative Musicality is described as "co-operative and co-dependent communicative interactions between mother and infant" (Malloch, 1999, p. 31). In this "dialogue" between mother/caregiver and infant the musical elements of pulse, quality (the contours of expressive vocal and body gesture (Trevarthen & Malloch, 2002)), and narrative are shaping forces and provide babies with opportunity to "practise the gestures of song and 'ceremonial' movements, and show them off with pride to people they trust" (Trevarthen, 2002 in Malloch & Trevarthen, 2009b, p. 7). What is evident from this body of research is the ubiquitous nature of singing and song-like behaviour in the infant's early life. In short, infants and young children are not "blank musical slate(s)" (Trehub, 2001, 2003); rather, their early years are rich in musical encounters in which they derive and communicate meanings and lay the foundations of the musical structures and vocabulary on which they will draw in their subsequent music-making.

Ellen Dissanayake draws on the notion of Communicative Musicality to propose that "the improvised duets of mother-infant mutuality predispose us to perform in and respond to temporally organised rituals or group belonging and bondedness" (2000, p. 156). She suggests that in these interactions we develop the processes and structures of five psycho-social needs, those of mutuality, belonging to, finding and making meaning, competence, and elaboration. For Dissanayake, it is the last of these, elaboration, that underpins the human capacity and compulsion for art-making. Arising from the improvised duets of mother-infant mutuality these psycho-social needs I suggest are practiced and developed further in young children's invented song-making, and are foundational to their creative work and development (Barrett, 2006).

Whilst there is little evidence that there is gendered difference in the infant's experience of and encounters with music, research findings suggest that the sex of the child may well shape the nature and extent of musical interactions initiated by adults, with a concomitant effect on the developmental trajectory of the child's musical engagement. There is evidence of gendered differentiation in adult responses to infant crying (Boukydis & Burgess, 1982) and to infant facial expression, particularly smiling (Donovan, Taylor, & Leavitt, 2007). This research indicates not only that fathers respond differently to infant crying than do mothers regardless of the sex of the child (Boukydis & Burgess, 1982), but also that mothers adjust their behaviour dependent upon the sex of the child (Donovan, Taylor, & Leavitt, 2007). Further, observation of fathers' and mothers' musical interactions with infants suggests that fathers adjust their performances according to the sex of the infant with female infants eliciting soothing performances of songs whilst male infants elicit more rousing and lively performances of songs (Trehub, Hill, & Kemenetsky, 1997). These findings suggest that further investigation of gendered musical interaction with infants is warranted.

11.2.2 Early Singing Development

As outlined above, studies of young children's singing behaviours have suggested some broad commonalities in infants' and young children's (0–5 years) singing development. Initially infants' and young children's (1–2 years) independent singing appears to be characterised by a focus on short musical phrases or fragments that have clearly identifiable rhythmic and melodic patterns (Davidson, 1994; Dowling, 1999) and evolves into "pot-pourri" (Moog, 1976) or "outline"

(Hargreaves, 1986) songs around 2–3 years of age. These latter draw on the musical and singing cultures in which children live and incorporate aspects of the child's developing command of speech and increasing vocabulary in the use of speech-like vocalisations and chant (Moorhead & Pond, 1978). The notion of cultural difference in children's early singing development is evidenced in research that has explored the vocal output of children from monolingual and bilingual households (Mang, 2001, 2002). Children living in a bilingual household speaking a tonal language (Cantonese) as well as a non-tonal language (English) evidenced a greater use of "intermediate vocalisations", i.e., vocalisations that encompass some of the qualities of speech and song, than did their monolingual non-tonal language peers. For these latter, there was a larger differentiation between speech and song behaviours. These studies have focused primarily on the vocal behaviours of young girls and do not provide insight into the prospect of gendered difference in vocal production and behaviour at this stage of singing development. The studies do however clearly indicate that cultural contextual factors play a significant role in early vocal development.

Findings of a recent longitudinal study of the singing development of Italian infants and young children (0–3 years of age) have troubled some of the taken-for-granted assumptions about the nature and developmental trajectory of young children's singing development (Tafuri, 2008). 70 children and their families participated in the study over a 4-year period initially (commencing in the first trimester of pregnancy). Central to participation in the study was participation in pre and neo-natal group music classes in which the mothers, and their infants and young children, learnt a repertoire of songs, musical games, and instrumental play which were subsequently incorporated into their day-to-day interactions. Data generated included parental diaries and audio recordings of shared (parent and infant) and independent (infant) singing and song-making, and, researcher observations in the weekly group classes throughout the period of the study. The findings suggest that infants' and young children's communication through singing is extensive and varied. Even at 2 months of age infants exhibited a command of ascending, descending and "mixed" glissandi (ascending and descending), ascending, descending and "mixed" intervals (short melodic motifs) and, sounds of same and differing lengths (2008, pp. 56–57). Significantly, when the project participants' musical output was compared with that of a control group it became evident that:

> the babies (aged 2–8 months) who have been exposed to musical experiences during the prenatal and neonatal stages produced vocalizations that we can consider "musical babbling"...vocalizations that appear earlier, in greater number and with greater musical value with respect to those children who have not had such a rich experience. (Tafuri, 2008, p. 58)

The study participants' transition from musical babbling to singing over the ages of 12–24 months approximately reflected the transitions described by Moog (1976) with the appearance of invented songs evident in children's singing around the 18 month mark. Focusing on singing development primarily, the study findings indicated that participant children were able to sing known songs approximately and/or acceptably in tune (Tafuri, 2008, p. 66) at 33–36 months, a finding that challenges reports that sustained in-tune singing is a much later acquisition in children's singing development (Moog, 1976). The main contributing factor to this finding is, the author suggests, "a musically rich family environment (that) provides encouragement as well as praise, interest and attention for each child" (Tafuri, 2008, p. 70). Significantly, in this study there was no indication of gendered differentiation in singing behaviours in study participants.

11.2.3 Invented Song-Making

Children's invented song-making arises from the infant's early communicative interactions with mothers/caregivers in instances of Communicative Musicality, and/or Infant Directed Speech (Papoucek, 1996) and Infant Directed Song (Trainor, 1996). Communicative Musicality and Infant Directed Speech or Song are initiated primarily by an adult with a communicative intention towards the infant or young child. Invented song in its more developed form (approximately 18 months onwards) is a socio-musico-communicative phenomenon initiated by the child rather than an adult and, whilst communicative in intention does not necessarily involve a communication with a physically proximate other. Invented singing and song-making may be directed at the self rather than others, and can function as a means of world-making and identity work (Barrett, 2010) rather than more overt forms of communication to others. This independent capacity begins to emerge at approximately 6–7 months as a form of musical "babbling" where infants generate original patterns of pitch and rhythm (Moog, 1976; Tarfuri & Villa, 2002; Tafuri, 2008). By the age of approximately 18 months, this babbling also encompasses the generation of distinct melodic patterns (Moog, 1976; Tafuri, 2008). These processes form the basis of children's invented song-making, a phenomenon that is most pronounced in the musical generative behaviours of children aged approximately 18 months to 6 years. The structures of young children's invented songs draw on the musical repertoires they encounter as singers and listeners (Barrett, 2003, 2006; Bjørkvold, 1989; Davidson, 1994; Davies, 1986; Dowling, 1984a; Mang, 2005; Moog, 1976; Moorhead & Pond, 1941/1978; Sundin, 1998; Tarfuri & Villa, 2002; Young, 2004) and evidence continuing generative elaboration rather than the fixed repetition of musical ideas (Barrett, 2006).

Whilst young children's singing and invented song making plays a role in their early language and singing development, a number of researchers have focused on the role of these forms of music-making in expressing and communicating thoughts, feelings, and experience (Bjørkvold, 1989; Campbell, 1998). In a year-long "systematic observation" of children's spontaneous singing and playing, three modes of use of song were identified, those of: *analogical imitation*, where invented song becomes a sound analogue of, and is intrinsic to play; *symbolic representation*, where invented song functions as a means to "tease, report, call, command, ask, reply"; and, *background coloration*, where song accompanies play in a "casual" sense (Bjørkvold, 1989, pp. 68–72). Findings of this study suggest that children's "spontaneous" or "invented" singing is essential to expression and human growth (Bjørkvold, 1989, p. 63) and functions to create contact, communicate, free the imagination, broaden awareness, structure play, socialize, mould individual identity, and establish cultural identity (Bjørkvold, 1989, pp. 80–83). These functions resonate with the findings of other studies of children's song-making (Campbell, 1998, 2002) where children's song-making was categorized as a means to; emotional expression; aesthetic enjoyment; entertainment; communication; physical response; enforcement of conformity to social norms; validation of religious ritual; continuity and stability of culture; and integration of society (2002, pp. 61–64).

The musical narratives of young children's invented songs reflect their emotional states and interests, providing insight into the children's relationships and experiences of people, objects, and events in their daily lives (Barrett, 2003, 2006). Children's invented song-making can function as a means to self-regulation in which children use song "to establish the parameters of their worlds, and to interpret and understand their interactions in and with these worlds" (Barrett, 2010). In their invented song-making young children produce original musical meanings as well as re-produce those they encounter in their home cultures (Barrett, 2003, 2006, 2010). There has been increasing interest in the study and analysis of the "everyday" experience of young children (Tudge, 2008; Barrett, 2009) as a means to deepen understanding of young children's learning and life. Music and invented song-making is a pervasive feature of many young children's lives, yet it is often overlooked in investigations of young children's engagement with their worlds. As a child-regulated activity, invented song-making holds potential to provide insights into the singing and vocal behaviours of young children, and the function of these behaviours in their thought and activity, as it reflects those issues of immediate interest to the child and draws on the individual child's musical understanding and skills. In what follows an account of the singing and invented song-making of a 3 year old boy will be presented in order to explore the meanings of such musical activity in his life and, to consider the implications of such meanings and activity for young boys' singing participation and development.

11.3 A Case – Study of a Young Boy's Singing and Invented Song-Making

11.3.1 Research Approach

The larger study[1] from which the present case is drawn aimed to explore the meaning and function of singing and music-making in young childrens' (aged 18–48 months) identity work (Barrett, 2009, 2010). 18 child – parent dyads[2] were recruited from two settings, a *Kindermusik* programme[3] (12 dyads) and a day-long childcare centre (6 dyads). Jay, the focus of this case-study was recruited from the *Kindermusik* program, which he had joined several weeks prior to his recruitment to the study aged 37 months. Whilst his participation in the *Kindermusik* program

11 Mutuality, Belonging, and Meaning-Making   173

was short-term (one 15 week semester commencing August 2006), Jay and his family contributed data to the study for approximately 2 years (commencing August, 2006). To provide some insight into Jay's day-to-day music engagement the family recorded a video-diary of Jay's music-making and maintained a weekly written diary on a one-page pro-forma (weekly overview) documenting briefly key aspects of Jay's musical activity including the nature of the activity, the location of the activity, those present, and Jay's emotional state. Two interviews with Jay's mother Erica (August 2006 and February 2007) and continuing informal email interactions provided opportunity to explore her perceptions of Jay's engagement with and use of music, her interpretations of the meanings of his music-making, and relevant contextual information concerning those musical events recorded in the video and weekly diaries. Observations in the *Kindermusik* setting and interviews with the *Kindermusik* teacher provided insight into Jay's music-making in settings other than that of the home, and served as a means to triangulate data and interpretations. Erica submitted 13 weekly overview diaries over the period (7 in September–October 2006; 3 in February 2007; 3 in May–June 2007). For the period August 2006–April 2008 Erica submitted 47 separate video episodes totaling 216.05 minutes of video footage. From these rich data the following narrative account of Jay's singing and song-making has been developed.[4]

Jay's Musical narrative

When I first met Jay aged 3 years and 2 months he had only been attending Kindermusik for 6 weeks. In our first interview, Jay's mother Erica told me he "spends a lot of the day dancing round, singing made up songs . . . . And he has a guitar he's had for about 2 years. He loves to, not play it, but he loves to make music with his guitar. Whenever he hears music on the CD player or sees something on the television the first thing he does is he runs and gets his guitar and sits in front of the television or sits in front of the CD player and plays along" (Mother, Interview 1).

Reviewing video footage throughout the period of Jay's participation in the study I observe many instances of his "guitar" playing. His first "guitar" is a sturdy ukelele and Jay displays an assured strumming technique, the instrument slung low, the neck angled down, his right hand maintaining a steady, rhythmic strum. He accompanies his singing, and that of others, marking the beat, and prominent rhythmic patterns in his playing. Although he is given a full guitar for Christmas (2006), he continues to play the ukelele over the next year, alternating this playing with attempts to play the larger instrument. Erica attributes Jay's love of the guitar and singing to his participation in the Song Circle at the local library: "He's watched Jennifer at music play the guitar. He's been going on Monday mornings there since he was 16 or 17 months old so he's always seen her play, but that's the only influence he's had. I guess he sits there and watches her for an hour a week, so he probably has picked it up" (Mother, interview 2). I note that Jay's father also picks up the ukelele and the guitar occasionally to strum along with Jay's singing and dancing, supporting and encouraging his son's music-making.

Whilst the "guitar" is Jay's favourite instrument, he can make an instrument from anything. Two egg cartons, struck together, accompany his song "Here we are in the kitchen".

Fig. 11.1 In the kitchen

Jay is absorbed in and by music, "it's just an integral part of his life" (Mother, Interview 1) his mother comments. Music marks his routines, his moments of quiet, his moments of exuberance, his communication with others, his moments with himself. "He spends a lot of the time," says his mother, "a lot of the day, he's just free forming around the property. And I notice sometimes he's

11   Mutuality, Belonging, and Meaning-Making   175

just running. He was doing laps and he was singing as he was doing laps.... Quite a free existence" (Mother, Interview 1).

Jay's mother has captured one of these moments on video, and I sit in my university office watching a small figure, clad in blue gumboots, jeans and a bright red jumper flash through the gum trees and the tall grasses of the family property, singing along to himself. He comes to rest by a stone wall, draws breath, and starts to sing again. Swinging his arms in alternation for emphasis his songmaking works through fragments of "Old MacDonald," references the middle section of "Rudolph the Red-Nosed Reindeer," and works to a triumphant exclamation with both arms raised to the sky. I can't quite discern the words, but note there's a lot of syllabic play around "bum" sounds.

"*I sing a lot too,*" his mother continues, "*along to things, and we'll dance and sing*". In one memorable instance Erica and Jay dance together to Australian Crawl's[5] cover of a Cold Chisel classic, "Khe Sahn". Erica knows all the words and sings and claps as they dance. They stand still to play air guitar to the lead break, and Erica cues Jay back into the chorus, counting out loud, "*one, two three, four*". Jay delights in the dancing and interaction with his mum and joins in with his version of the words.

Erica continues "*And he doesn't necessarily sing in a structured manner to music. He does sometimes but he prefers to make up his own songs just to do with a running commentary on what he's doing or just nonsense sounds, which he's a bit into at the moment. I keep telling people he can talk. They don't actually think that's English. It's his own language.... Sometimes he just picks up his guitar and dances around and makes up a song and sings a song ... he'll take something that's said or what's happening and he'll make a song out of that*" (Mother, Interview 1).

Waking up early one Saturday morning, excited about playing with his Dad at the weekend, he sings "*I'm in the bed, rolling in the sea*" (October 2, 2006: diary). In the bath with his baby brother, he makes up a song "*I like peace, I like quiet*" as he helps wash Adam (September 30, 2006: diary). On another bath night, he sits on the floor as Adam is bathed, playing the xylophone and singing "*Moon, moon, shining and silver,*" relaxed, his usual exuberance softened (September 20, 2006: diary). Adam *features in many of his songs, including "Adam's boat hat song" (September 12, 2006: diary) and "I'm playing with Adam the baby in the bush" (October 10, 2006: diary). Erica notes in the diaries that some mornings Jay will join her in bed and sing "I love being at this house". She notes that his mood is thoughtful as he sings the song over and over (February 26, 2007: diary).*

Jay sings in anticipation of events, making songs up about "Smiley Cookies" whilst waiting for something to eat (February 27, 2007: diary). Whilst Jay and Adam are playing outside in the rain he sings elatedly "Adam's walking in puddles"! The tempo and volume of the song increases as the boys jump, feet close together, into the puddles forming in the garden (March 01, 2007: diary and video). And he often hums and sings whilst playing in the gravel pit with his diggers.

Jay's mother describes this singing commentary as "... not really thoughts and feelings, he's not that deep (she laughs affectionately). It's a bit to do with Adam. He'll talk to Adam and sing as he's talking to Adam and he'll comment on things he's doing... (he'll sing) ... Adam's a cheeky monkey. You get a lot of him singing Adam's a cheeky monkey and hello Adam" (Mother, Interview 2).

Erica has captured one of these episodes of singing commentary. Early one morning Jay dressed in pyjamas is seen swinging a length of tinsel suspended from the Christmas tree. Adam, seated in a high chair watches intermittently, as he bangs a spoon against the table-top and grizzles. Unaware of his mother filming in the background Jay is singing phrases of "Bob the builder" quietly to himself. He pauses and turns to see his mother. "Hello" he says, and returns to swinging the tinsel. "Baby crying" he muses aloud, then launches into song on the text Baby Crying.

This song finished he pauses momentarily, before starting to sing a song about a telephone ringing. The length of tinsel now becomes the phone as Jay holds the end up to his ears, alternating from side to side. His movements echo the beat of his singing. Adam is now transfixed by his brother, the tapping and grizzling silenced.

The episode continues as Erica asks "How about Jingle Bells?" Jay shakes his head. "Because it's Christmas?" she prompts. "No" Jay responds. "I'll sing a chair song". "Go for your life" Erica responds, and Jay sings a "chair" song to the melody of Jingle Bells.

11 Mutuality, Belonging, and Meaning-Making 177

Fig. 11.2 Baby crying now

Telephone Ringing

Fig. 11.3 Telephone ringing

Chair Song

Fig. 11.4 Chair song

Jay's invention of song draws on familiar songs, as he revisits and elaborates on musical favourites. "A song he loves at the moment is 'You've got a friend in me' which is the end of Toy Story, which is a movie that he watched a couple of times a few months ago. He fell in love with, just loves the whole Buzz and Woody thing. He makes variations on the song. He's taken that song and he changes the words and changes the tune, and he mixes it up and changes the tempo. That's a song he really likes, and I found it on a CD and he does listen to that song. Every couple of days he asks to hear it" his mother comments (Mother, interview 2).

When he is not inventing songs Jay sings medleys of favourite songs. I am struck by Jay's phenomenal memory for song. At the age of three he sings from an extensive repertoire, sure in the melodic line and with perfect retention for words. Jay's singing occurs as company to himself as he stands on his bed to watch the rain falling outside his window, or, to gatherings of family members and friends who prompt him to sing yet another song. Jay is only too happy to comply with the requests of the latter. "He loves a singing session with the grown ups" Erica notes (Mother, interview 2) and the video diary captures many moments when various family members and friends gather in the lounge-room to sing through favourite songs. These include Bob the Builder, The Bear Went Over the Mountain, See-saw Margery-daw, Kookaburra Sits in the Old Gum Tree, Wheels on the Bus, It's our Time, Grandfather's Clock, One Little Duck, Old MacDonald, Postman Pat, Once I Caught a Fish Alive, Twinkle, Twinkle, Little Star, Five Little Ducks, Morning Town Ride, Jingle Bells, Brumby Jack, I've been Working on the Rail-Road.

Jay's repertoire reflects the many places of his music-making: the Kindermusik sessions, "family sings", and, the Song Circle at the local library. A strong social bond has arisen between members of this group and a small group of mothers and their children "go to each other's places" (Mother, interview 2). Some of these visits are captured on video and Jay is quite happy to entertain the group singing, dancing and playing his collection of instruments. These include a small keyboard, maracas, djembe, and the ever-present "guitar"; all presents for Christmas and birthdays. The mothers clap along and encourage his singing and dancing, suggesting further songs, and applauding enthusiastically.

Jay will sing to any-one, even Oscar, the family cat, who is serenaded with Jay's version of "Three Blind Mice" (October 20, 2006: diary). Adam, a ready and receptive audience, follows his brother's musical moves, listening intently, shrieking with delight, babbling along, and echoing his brother's vigorous activity. Erica comments on the ways in which the boys communicate in and through music: "Adam loves music, loves Jay's music... he dances to it and moves to it and bounces... Adam really enjoys (it) and then Jay feeds off that so they'll often dance and sing together and well Adam won't sing cause he's tiny but" (to Adam, seated on her knee) "you can dance to Jay's singing, you can dance!" Erica turns back to me "Jay may not realize that Adam's interacting but Adam will be following behind him clapping or laughing or just taking notice of him".

Jay's mother has captured the two of them one morning, Adam seated on the floor gurgling happily as Jay sings and dances through four verses of "Kookaburra Sits." Jay revels in the attention of his audience, stepping around the living room in time to his singing, alternately clapping for emphasis or gesturing from side to side. By the second verse he is jumping, feet poised together to mark the beat to the line "Pants on Fire." Verse three requires a deeper, growly voice as he leaps from foot to foot turning in circles on the living room floor. Verse four is the "big finish," marked by a return to jumping on the spot, and a ritardando on the last line. A vocal flourish concludes the performance, as he sings the final word "be" from the bottom to the top of his range, and raises his arms into the air to shadow the movement of the pitch. Adam squeals with delight as Jay, the modest performer, strolls to the French windows to observe casually to his mother, "It's a nice day Mum." As his mother notes "He likes a big finish" (Mother, interview 2).

Jay is well-versed in the songs and actions of the Wiggles, accompanying his singing with a sure and steady marking of the beat with feet and hands, his whole body alive with the music. The habit of energetic dance continues and he is often captured dancing and clapping to his mum's recordings of country, bluegrass, and folk favourites.

The soundtrack of Jay's life is constant, varied, and woven into the family routines and practices. "Well the last couple of days we've put on quite a lot of Dolly Parton," says his mother. "Today, for instance. Yesterday we played some

Dolly Parton and Aretha Franklin. Yesterday and today he just asked for the Kindermusik CD which I hate but he had that on a lot of the morning .... I don't listen to commercial radio. I don't want to sound pompous but I listen to Radio National so the radio is not really a source of music as such but um yes some contemporary music – Missy Higgins and that sort of genre. It's quite eclectic. He has quite an eclectic mixture in the day it'd be hard to [pause]. Yes and my father lives next door to us and he has a lot of music as well, stuff that I grew up listening to and he also plays a lot for Jay. Also for Jay he plays a lot of classical which I don't really play. Not that I don't like it I just don't play it. But he purposely plays that to Jay .... Oh yes he likes the Wiggles but we don't have any CDs because we haven't got around to getting any. I've got a few Playschool CDs. He likes those Playschool CDs, and I think mainly classical CDs and he does listen to the afternoon shows but there's nothing explicitly music in those ones. He doesn't mind an ad. Loves an ad" (Mother, Interview 1).

Music has always been important in Jay's mother's life. "I used to play the flute when I was younger, used to play a lot of music, sing and I haven't done that for years. But we have a lot of music in the house and my husband enjoys it too but not in any creative capacity really. Just the CDs these days. I sing with Jay and we dance around and that sort of thing. Yes every day there'd be some sort of music in the house .... I still love really daggy music. Steeleye Span and all these very daggy ... growing up I had a lot of that sort of thing, a lot of that music my parents played. Since I've grown up I've actually gone and found the CDs and played them .... It was Ry Cooder that sort of thing as well and Gordon Lightfoot, the folk stuff .... I've bought them all myself which is really sad, and now Jay likes it!" (Mother, Interview 1).

Jay's mother describes her childhood experiences with the flute: "I started playing when I was about 8 or so .... I considered going to the Conservatorium but my parents talked me out of that, not being a good career. But they've since said they really regret doing that, and I probably wouldn't have pursued it anyway, but I've played for a lot of years but I haven't for about 10 years now" (Mother, Interview 1).

Later in the year, in the midst of family preparations for lunch, Jay stands in the lounge-room strumming his ukulele with a steady beat, stomping from side to side like the best of rockers. "De, de, de, goodbye, Play mu-sic, play mu-sic" he sings, whilst his 6-year-old cousin, Lachlan, blows on the harmonica. "I can play, I. Can. Play" he continues with emphasis, before putting the ukulele on the table as Lachlan walks away. "Are you going to play us a song Jay? What music were you playing mate?" prompts his dad. Jay returns to pick up the instrument and heads towards the kitchen where Lachlan is raiding the 'fridge. Jay begins strumming the guitar, hitting his stride as he reaches the kitchen bench. "In the kitchen, ki-ki-kitchen, In the kitchen, in the kitchen, oh, oh, ooh," he sings, "In the kitchen, in the kitchen." As the family prepare sandwiches around him, and Lachlan removes various items from the 'fridge, Jay adds "Cookie time, Cookie time, we're gonna have Coo-Kie -Time."

Whilst Jay's interactions with his baby brother Adam are often conducted in song, so are those with his mother. The latter occur most frequently in the morning, in the kitchen and often revolve around food. "It's a food song", announces Jay one morning as his mother switches on the video camera, and he begins to sing "yes yes, yes yes, yes yes, yes yes, I like my food". He sings at the top of his voice, dancing from leg to leg, only to stop suddenly. "What's that music?" he asks, as a Bach Partitia for solo violin plays in the background. "It's a violin" Erica responds. "What's that music?" he asks again, standing still, listening intently. "That's just a piece of music for the violin, some-one's playing the violin". His curiosity satisfied, Jay launches into a riff on "Yes Yes", alternating with a riff on "No no".

Breakfast and food are forgotten entirely as Jay jumps up and down on the spot singing the riffs in alternation. "Would you eat your breakfast please?" Erica asks. Jay pauses briefly, looking at her, gauging the mood, before returning to a riff on No no. "So that's a no, then?" inquires Erica. "Yes yes, yes yes, yes yes, yes yes, no no, no no, no no, no no" responds Jay, dancing all the while. Erica follows up "No, seriously, would you eat your vegemite bars please"? Jay, playful, a mischievous grin on his face comes close to the camera singing his "No, No," refrain.

Fig. 11.5 No no yes yes

A few days later, Jay is in the kitchen early in the morning, strumming his ukulele, singing quietly to himself, "Yummy, yummy, yummy. Yummy, yummy, yummy." As Oscar the cat, stalks the bench searching for a quiet spot to sit and wash, Jay begins to hum "Twinkle, Twinkle" meditatively, marking the rhythm of the words on the ukulele. Gradually, the momentum builds as he transfers his attention to a shaker, transformed into a microphone, and launches into a full-voiced rendition that draws heavily on the stylistic conventions of R&B. Oscar pauses mid-wash, to regard Jay with feline outrage, before returning to his ablutions.

Jay doesn't need an audience to make music. Filming from the stairwell in the family home, his mother has captured his meditative strumming of the guitar as he sings through his favourite, "Old MacDonald." He plays with the words ("had a bull-dozer"), the tempos, the rhythms and embellishes the melody before he falls silent, clutching the guitar, lost in thought or imaginary music.

For Jay, life is music, music is life.

11.4 Commentary

The narrative account presented above provides some insights into the rich resources of music and learning that Jay draws on in his singing and song-making. Jay has been exposed to models of singing and positive music engagement throughout his life. These have included his mother, whose love of music is evidenced in her singing, dancing, and listening to music, his father who listens attentively to and accompanies his singing, and "Jennifer" who leads the Song Circle at the local library. Jay's attempts to emulate these individuals' music-making are supported and encouraged by family and friends, and the material resources (instruments, sound recordings) for extending his music-making, are readily available. Music accompanies every activity of Jay's daily life, including eating, bathing, playing with his baby brother, accompanying his play, and comforting him when alone. When considered through the lens of Dissanayake's (2000) psycho-social needs Jay's music-making serves as a means to establish mutuality with others, to identify and belong to a social group, to find and make meaning, to gain musical and social competence, and to elaborate on musical materials and ideas. Jay's interactions with others are underpinned by song, both known and invented, which he uses as a means to establishing relationship, mutuality and belonging (see for instance his many interactions with Adam and his mother). Jay uses song to make and communicate meaning, evidenced for example, as he sings in bed of a morning with his mother "I love being at this house". Jay's musical competence is evident in his capacity for sustained in-tune singing, his solid rhythmic sense and his capacity to accompany himself, marking both beat and rhythm. Singing also provides Jay with a means to strengthen social competence – as evidenced in his playful interaction with his mother over the eating of breakfast. Jay's use of invented singing and song provides evidence of his capacity for elaboration on his own and others' musical materials and ideas in singing and invented song.

11.5 Concluding Comments

The richness of singing in Jay's life suggest that he will arrive at school with established competence in singing and music-making, an extensive repertoire of known song, and a capacity for invention. Jay's experience does not support a view that boys' singing development lags behind that of girls'. What might be the factors that have supported Jay in his positive all-encompassing approach to singing and music-making and the development of competence in many facets of early music-making? I return to Tafuri's study and her identification of the significant role the family plays in young children's musical development. As with the children in her study, Jay's early life has been spent in 'a musically rich family environment (that) provides encouragement as well as praise, interest and attention' (2008, p. 70). To this I would add the creative use of music as a means to establish mutuality with others, to identify and belong to a social group, to find and make meaning, to gain musical and social competence, and to elaborate on materials, ideas, and feelings. Jay's invented singing is responded to and taken up by others as a valued means of engaging in musical relationship, and a valid form of musical expression and engagement. Perhaps these are the factors that support young boys' competence and creativity in singing and song-making?

Notes

1. This study was funded by the Australian Research Council through the Discovery Grant Program, Grant no DP0559050.
2. Initially 20 dyads were recruited. 2 dyads withdrew from the study in the first weeks of engagement. For one dyad the data generation procedures were too time-consuming, whilst another cited family difficulties (resulting in divorce) as the reason for withdrawal. Of the 18 dyads that continued in the study involvement with data generation varied from 12 to 36 months.
3. *Kindermusik* programs provide interactive music experiences for parents and children. In weekly classes participants learn a varied repertoire of songs, dances and movement games, engage in interactive listening experiences, and joint instrumental exploration and group play. Extension experiences are available by purchasing CDs, books, and instruments for use in the home.
4. An earlier version of Jay's narrative was originally published in Barrett, M. S. (2007). "Surface and depth": Generative tensions for a "comprehensive" view of music education. *Music Education Research International, 1*, 25–41. Reprint with permission by Center for Music Education Research, University of South Florida, Tampa, U.S.A.
5. *Australian Crawl* and *Cold Chisel* are Australian rock bands.

References

Barrett, M. S. (2003). Meme engineers: Children as producers of musical culture. *International Journal of Early Years Education, 11*(3), 195–212.

Barrett, M. S. (2006). Inventing songs, inventing worlds: The 'genesis' of creative thought and activity in young children's lives. *International Journal of Early Years Education, 14*(3), 201–220.

Barrett, M. S. (2009). Sounding lives in and through music: A narrative inquiry of the 'everyday' musical engagement of a young child. *Journal of Early Childhood Research, 7*(2), 115–134.

Barrett, M. S. (2010, in press). Musical narratives: A study of a young child's identity work in and through music-making. *Psychology of Music*. http://pom.sagepub.com/content/early/2010/10/14/0305735610373054

Bjørkvold, J. (1989). *The muse within: Creativity and communication, song and play from childhood through maturity* (W. H. Halverson, Trans.). New York: HarperCollins Publishers Inc.

Boukydis, C. F. Z., & Burgess, R. L. (1982). Adult physiological responses to infant cries: Effects of temperament of infant, parental status, and gender. *Child Development, 53*(5), 1291–1298.

Campbell, P. S. (1998). *Songs in their heads*. Oxford: Oxford University Press.

Campbell, P. S. (2002). The musical cultures of children. In L. Bresler & C. Marme Thompson (Eds.), *The arts in children's lives: Context, culture, and curriculum* (pp. 57–69). Dordrecht: Kluwer.

Davidson, L. (1985). Tonal structures of children's early songs. *Music Perception, 2*(3), 361–374.

Davidson, L. (1994). Songsinging by young and old: A developmental approach to music. In R. Aiello with J. Sloboda (Eds.), *Musical perceptions* (pp. 99–130). Oxford: Oxford University Press.

Davies, C. (1986). Say it till a song comes: Reflections on songs invented by children 3–13. *British Journal of Music Education, 3*(3), 279–293.

Dissanayake, E. (2000) *Art and intimacy: How the arts began*. Seattle, WA: University of Washington Press).

Donovan, W., Taylor, N., & Leavitt, L. (2007). Maternal sensory sensitivity and response bias in detecting change in infant facial expressions: Maternal self-efficacy and infant gender labeling. *Infant Behaviour and Development, 30*, 436–452.

Dowling, W. J. (1984a). Development of musical schemata in children's spontaneous singing. In W. R. Crozier & A. J. Chapman (Eds.), *Cognitive processes in the perception of art* (pp. 145–163). Amsterdam: North-Holland.

Dowling, W. J. (1984b). Tonal structure and children's early learning of music. In J. Sloboda (Ed.), *Generative processes in music*. Oxford: Clarendon Press.

Dowling, W. J. (1999). The development of music perception and cognition. In N. D. Deutsch (Ed.), *The psychology of music* (2nd ed., pp. 603–625). London: Academic.

Hall, C. (2005). Gender and boys' singing in early childhood. *British Journal of Music Education, 22*(1), 5–20.

Hargreaves, D. J. (1986). *The developmental psychology of music*. Cambridge: Cambridge University Press.

Malloch, S. (1999). Mothers and infants and communicative musicality. *Musicae Scientiae, Special Issue*, 13–18.

Malloch, S., & Trevarthen, C. (2009a). *Communicative musicality: Exploring the basis of human companionship*. Oxford: Oxford University Press.

Malloch, S. & Trevarthen, C. (2009b). Musicality: Communicating the vitality and interests of life. In S. Malloch & C. Trevarthen (Eds.), *Communicative musicality: Exploring the basis of human companionship* (pp. 1–11). Oxford: Oxford University Press.

Mang, E. (2001). Intermediate vocalisations: An investigation of the boundaries between speech and song in young children's vocalisations. *Bulletin of the Council for Research in Music Education, 147*, 116–121.

Mang, E. (2002). An investigation of vocal pitch behaviours of Hong Kong children. *Bulletin of the Council for Research in Music Education, 153/154*, 128–134.

Mang, E. (2005). The referent of children's early songs. *Music Education Research, 7*(1), 3–20.

Mang, E. (2006). The effects of age, gender, and language on children's singing competency. *British Journal of Music Education, 23*(2), 161–174.

Meltzoff, A. N. (2002). Elements of a developmental theory of imitation. In A. N. Meltzoff & W. Prinz (Eds.), *The imitative mind* (pp. 19–41). Cambridge: Cambridge University Press.

Moog, H. (1976). *The musical experience of the pre-school child*. (C. Clarke, Trans). London: Schott.

Moorhead, G. E., & Pond, D. (1978). *Music of young children*. Santa Barbara, CA: Pillsbury Foundation for Advancement of Music Education. (Reprinted from works published in 1941, 1942, 1944, and 1951).

Papoucek, M. (1996). Intuitive parenting: A hidden source of musical stimulation in infancy. In I. Deliege & J. Sloboda (Eds.), *Musical beginnings* (pp. 88–112). Oxford: Oxford University Press.

Parncutt, R. (2006). Prenatal development. In G. E. McPherson (Ed.). *The child as musician: A handbook of musical development* (pp. 1–31). Oxford: Oxford University Press.

Sundin, B. (1998). Musical creativity in the first six years. In B. Sundin, G. E. McPherson, & G. Folkestad (Eds.), *Children composing* (pp. 35–56). Malmö: Malmö Academy of Music, Lund University.

Tafuri, J. (2008). *Infant musicality: New research for educators and parents*. Farnham, Surrey: Ashgate Publishing Limited.

Tarfuri, J., & Villa, D. (2002). Musical elements in the vocalisations of infants aged 2–8 months. *British Journal of Music Education, 19*(1), 73–88.

Trainor, L. J. (1996). Infant preferences for infant-directed versus noninfant-directed playsongs and lullabies. *Infant Behavior and Development, 20*, 83–92.

Trehub, S. E. (2001). Musical predispositions in infancy. In R. J. Zatorre & I. Peretz (Eds.), *The biological foundations of music: Annals of the New York Academy of Sciences* (Vol. 903, pp. 1–6).

Trehub, S. E. (2003). The developmental origins of musicality. *Nature Neuroscience, 6*(7), 669–673.

Trehub, S. E., Hill, D. S., & Kamenetshy, S. B. (1997). Parents' sung performances for infants. *Canadian Journal of Experimental Psychology, 51*, 385–396.

Trevarthen, C., & Malloch, S. (2000). The dance of well-being: Defining the musical therapeutic effect. *The Nordic Journal of Music Therapy, 9*(2) 3–17.

Trevarthen, C., & Malloch, S. (2002). Musicality and music before three: Human vitality and invention shared with pride. *Zero to Three, 23*(1), 10–18.

Tudge, J. (2008). *The everyday lives of young children*. Cambridge: Cambridge University Press.

Welch, G. F. (2000). Singing development in early childhood: the effects of culture and education on the realisation of potential. In P. White (Ed.), *Child voice* (pp. 27–44). Stockholm: Royal Institute of Technology.

Welch, G. F. (2005). Singing as communication. In D. Miell, R. MacDonald, & D. J. Hargreaves (Eds.), *Musical communication* (pp. 239–259). Oxford: Oxford University Press.

Welch, G. F. (2006a). Singing and vocal development. In G. E. McPherson (Ed.), *The child as musician: A handbook of musical development* (pp. 311–329). Oxford: Oxford University Press.

Welch, G. F. (2006b). The musical development and education of young children. In B. Spodek & O. N. Saracho (Eds.), *Handbook of research on the education of young children* (2nd ed., pp. 251–267). Mahwah, NJ: Lawrence Erlbaum.

Welch, G. F., Rush, C., & Howard, D. M. (1991). A developmental continuum of singing ability: Evidence from a study of five-year old developing singers. *Early Childhood Development and Care, 69*, 107–119.

Welch, G. F., Sergeant, D. C., & White, P. (1996). The singing competences of five-year-old developing singers. *Bulletin of the Council for Research in Music Education, 127*, 155–162.

Welch, G. F., Sergeant, D. C. & White, P. (1997). Age, sex and vocal task as factors in singing 'in-tune' during the first years of schooling'. *Bulletin of the Council for Research in Music Education, 133*, 153–160.

Young, S. (2004). Young children's spontaneous vocalising: Insights into play and pathways to singing. *International Journal of Early Childhood, 36*(2), 59–74.

Chapter 12
Communities of Singing Practice in the Fiji Islands

Joan Russell

12.1 Background

My interest in the role of community in fostering singing competence (Russell, 1991, 1992, 1997, 1999, 2001, 2002) has its origins in my experience as a child in a family of music makers. Neither my four grandparents, nor my parents, nor their siblings had formal music lessons yet they all could either, or both, play instruments by ear, and sing in tune, and they could harmonize *ad lib*. They learned through immersion in the melodic, rhythmic and harmonic idioms with significant others in their social circles. By the age of 6 I had absorbed the logic of tonal harmony and voice-leading through early and frequent immersion in the singing of my mother and aunt, who rehearsed their songs at home for performances on the vaudeville stage. The sounds of voices singing in harmony, and of the fiddle and piano drumming out traditional tunes for the sheer pleasure of making music together, nurtured my ongoing, lifelong participation as a member of a global community of musical practice. These early experiences established my identity as a musical person. Tonal harmony became my musical language, and my immersion in the musical language of my family laid the foundation for my later studies in music. I came to conceptualize my family as a "community of musical practice". Wenger's (1998) notion of "community of practice" offers a useful framework for understanding how we are socialized into developing singing competence and positive attitudes towards singing through immersion in practices that are held to have value by significant members of our communities.

12.2 Learning to Sing in Communities of Singing Practice

The concept of community of practice as a site of learning is central to Wenger's (1998) social theory of learning which was derived from his study of workplace practices. This theory, which rests on four premises may be adapted to any field

---

J. Russell (✉)
McGill University, Montreal, QC, Canada
e-mail: joan.russell@mcgill.ca

which is characterized by "practice" as distinct from theory. These premises are as follows: (1) we are social beings, and this fact is a central aspect of learning; (2) knowledge is a matter of competence with respect to valued enterprises – such as singing in tune (Wenger actually uses this example); (3) knowing is a matter of active participation in valued enterprises; (4) the ultimate purpose of learning is to be able to engage with the world in a meaningful way. Meaning, practice, community and identity are key concepts in Wenger's theory. Meaning refers to our experience of life and the world, and practice refers to our shared historical and social resources. Community refers to the social configurations in which our enterprises are defined as worth pursuing, and our participation is recognizable as competence. Identity has to do with the ways in which learning creates personal histories for us in our communities. "Practice" – characterized by mutual engagement, joint enterprise, and shared repertoire – is the source of coherence of community.

According to Wenger, communities of practice exist as constellations, or clusters, having in common mutual engagement, joint enterprise and shared repertoires of knowledge and skills. An individual or group may be a member of more than one community of practice within a constellation of communities of practice. For example, the practices, performance standards, expectations, goals, repertoire and skills shared by boys in a boys' choir are similar to those shared by members of a girls' choir. Both choirs are part of a larger constellation of communities of musical practice that includes any organized group that comes together to perform music, such as adult choirs, and amateur or professional orchestras. In short, the boys and girls are members of a global community of practice, a community that includes any group of musicians who find musical performance a meaningful way to experience the world, who share historical and social resources in an enterprise that is defined as having value, in which participation is recognized as competence, and through which the personal histories of individuals in their communities are created.

A musical event is defined here an act of planned or spontaneous singing, a joint enterprise, where participants mutually engage in singing shared musical repertoire. Musical events are constitutive of communities of musical practice, and singing competence is defined as the abilities of carrying a tune and singing in harmony. In this paper, instances of Fijian singing are situated conceptually as musical events occurring in communities of singing practice – or sites of learning, where Fijian children absorb the repertoire, singing skills, musical languages and attitudes towards singing that are displayed by significant others in their social circles.

What piqued my interest during two visits to Fiji – in 1989 and 1998 – was the skill, enthusiasm, frequency and lack of self-consciousness with which children, youth, men and women sang. I noted particularly the ability of ordinary citizens to harmonize *ad lib* in a variety of social situations. In a small church in a village far from any large-sized town on Viti Levu, the largest of the more than 300 islands that constitute the Republic of Fiji, I was moved by the singing of the 30 or so men and women who made up the Fijian choir. The choir's singing of the introductory anthem was exceptional. With strength in the men's voices, the sound was rich and the voices well balanced. Phrasing, intonation, changes of key and tempo were executed expertly, yet there was no conductor visible to the congregation, and the singers, singing with heads bowed and eyes closed took their cues the breaths and the voices around them (and, no doubt from subtle visual cues from their leader). Also impressive was the singing of the congregation. During the hymns – which are written to accommodate women's and men's untrained singing voices – each member of the congregation, including myself, was able to find a comfortable place for his or her voice, yielding four-part harmonizations *ad lib*. My immersion in this experience led me to wonder: How did such large numbers of people achieve singing competence? How did they learn new repertoire? These broad questions led to more focused questions that guided my observations: Who sings? What do they sing? When do they sing? Why do they sing? How do they sing? I began to collect vignettes, or snapshots: musical moments that formed grew into a collage of describable musical behaviours.

The population of the Fiji Islands consists of two major groups, separated by ethnicity, language and religion. Approximately half of the population are of Indian sub-continent origin, originally brought to Fiji by the British in the nineteenth century to work in plantations as indentured labourers. There is a scattering of other ethnic groups, but these are small in number. The other approximately half of the population are indigenous Fijians and Rotumans, descendents of the original inhabitants of the Fiji Islands. This group is thought to have emigrated some 3,500 years ago from Melanesia and Micronesia (Clunie, 1986; Wright, 1987). Their descendants form a more or less coherent cultural group in terms of language, religion, history, social organization, belief systems, values and social practices. This paper focuses on the singing practices of this latter group.

12.3 Methodology

I used the tools of ethnography – participant observation, purposeful conversation and document analysis. I sang with Fijians and witnessed singing in organized and social settings – church services, choir practices and school assembly, and on informal occasions – an afternoon on a hillside with a Fijian couple, and a boat ride with school children. I travelled on local buses with Fijians, ate meals and slept in a Fijian home on a small island off the Korolevu coast. Places visited included Namake, Tagaqe, Suva, Vatualalai and Vatulele. I visited Fijian schools and chatted with a professor of music at the University of the South Pacific's music department, attended a rehearsal of the Royal Fijian Police Band and chatted with the music director who had received music training in Canada. I taught a music lesson in a Fijian primary school. While writing my field notes, questions arose: Why was singing was so widespread? How did these communities support the development of singing confidence and competence? I raised these and other questions, which I sought to answer by means of conversations with Fijians in positions of musical leadership. A Fijian primary school teacher explained that music in Fiji is not taught formally as a subject in schools, and there are no courses or examinations in music in teacher education programs. What, then, could account for widespread singing skills and knowledge of repertoire? I chose to participate where possible, talk to people, gather information and make notes.

Through purchases, borrowings and recordings, I acquired a collection of hymn books, song books, video – and audiotapes and compact disks. A preliminary analysis of these items and of my field notes revealed that there was a range of vocal genres and these could be associated with age, gender and social context. Literature on Fijian life (Ravuvu, 1983; Veramu, 1992; Wright, 1987) provided information on Fijian social history, organization, practices, beliefs and values.

Good's (1978) seminal research provided information on the history, function and performance practices of Fijian *meke*, and its role in contemporary Fijian society provided background on its place in Fijian society. An analysis (Russell, 1992) of video recordings of pre-European traditional *meke* revealed the close relation of singing, poetry, movement and instrumental accompaniment. It revealed that singing in four parts, both quasi-tonal and non-tonal is a feature of this traditional ritual performance in these islands.

The snapshots presented below are instances of singing events – exemplars under the umbrella of musical practices. Each snapshot features mutual engagement, joint enterprise and shared repertoire – in short, the "practice" that is the source of Wenger's notion of coherence of community. I chose each vignette to illustrate in miniature a "community of singing practice" occurring in a particular context of time, place and circumstance. Each is understood as mediating children's socialization into a singing community and consequent membership in Fijian society.

12.3.1 Snapshot: A Primary School

Children and their teachers in grades 1–8 congregate in one room to begin each day with prayers, singing and announcements. On this, the morning of my first visit, the words to a new hymn are written on the board. The children sing the hymn in unison, referring as needed to the written text. Their teachers and headmaster join in the singing. From time to time I hear an adult voice – perhaps an older student, perhaps a teacher, attempting to harmonize.

In this community of practice the younger children are learning a new melody by listening to and singing with their teachers and the older children, some of whom are their siblings and cousins. Through repetition of known repertoire and learning new songs together the school community builds a common knowledge base of what Elliott (1995) calls "tones for us". The snapshot suggests that singing in school on a regular basis promotes children's identity as members of a "school" community of practice.

When singing, dynamics has a social, as well as musical meaning.

On the afternoon of my first visit some 100 children from grades 4–6 are packed tightly into the assembly room, seated on the floor, waiting for me to teach them a song. Samuela, the headmaster, sits on a chair at the side of the room, along with other teachers. I suggest that the children sing a song that they know, and I promise to teach them a new song afterwards. Without hesitation, an older child chooses a song and starts it off. The children begin to sing one of "their" songs. After a few moments, Samuela barked a command and immediately the volume level increased significantly; apparently their singing was not sufficiently enthusiastic. In this community of singing practice, enthusiasm, expressed through volume, is valued. Neither the singing nor the enthusiasm appeared to be negotiable.

12.3.2 Snapshot: A Secondary School

I am sitting in the teachers' lounge across from Brother Théophane who tells me about the after-school volunteer choir at the Marist School for Boys in Suva. He tells me proudly that these teenagers memorize sophisticated works from the western choral repertoire, mentioning as examples, works of Handel and Vivaldi. They perform these works in an annual choral festival where hundreds of Fijian singers gather to show their singing prowess. Describing the singing practices in his school, in the wider community, and in the small, remote villages where the Methodist churches are venues for social and spiritual life and choir practices can go on until 1 and 2 o'clock in the morning, he observes that "singing *is* the religion!".

In this secondary school, a community of singing practice provides a space for adolescent boys to participate in a global community of musical practice through the performance of western choral canon. Participation in the annual choral festival these male students enables participation in an enterprise that is seen to have value by hundreds of singers from different regions of the Fiji Islands.

12.3.3 Snapshot: A "Micro" Family

It is a sultry day in Suva, the capital of Viti Levu where I am waiting for a bus. Two little boys – around 5 or 6 years old – and their young parents are waiting with me in the hot sun. As we wait, their mother begins to sing softly. The tune sounds to me like a hymn although it could be a folk song with a hymn-like melody. Soon, their father joins in, harmonizing *ad lib*.

Through their spontaneous singing in a non-formal, public place these parents model a community of singing practice in the presence of their children, acquainting them with both repertoire and the idioms of tonal musical language. In addition, they are modelling a positive attitude towards singing.

12.3.4 Snapshot: Family Worship

As I make my way to Thursday evening choir rehearsal through the darkening village on the main island, I pass a dwelling where about 15 people are gathered for their regular Thursday evening "family" worship. They are seated on the floor of the large receiving room. Through the open windows drift the sounds of voices, singing hymns in harmony.

In this typical Fijian village, where many people are related, an extended family constitutes a community of musical practice. Children of such households absorb the musical language of tonal harmony in situations of family worship practiced by significant adults in their communities.

12.3.5 Snapshots: Church Services

At Sunday morning services at several rural Methodist churches, and an evening service at a large evangelical church in Fiji's capital city, Suva, I join in the singing of the hymns that are part of the order of service. Hymns are written to accommodate untrained voices of all ranges and skill levels. Regardless of location and size, congregation members are able to harmonize *ad lib*.

Church communities of singing practice provide a space for women's high and low voices, men's high and low voices. Singing in harmony provides "a place for every voice" (Russell, 1997).

12.3.6 Snapshot: Before the Service

In the tiny concrete Methodist Church in a small village on the west coast of Viti Levu, pre-adolescent boys are squeezed into a single pew, waiting for the service to begin. A handful of early parishioners wait also, on the other side of the aisle. The boys chat quietly. Gradually their voices get louder, and they begin to giggle and nudge one another. From across the aisle a woman parishioner reprimands the restless boys in a loud voice and they become quiet. After a few seconds, they begin to sing what sounds to me like hymn tunes. Their voices are confident, and they know the words.

12.3.7 Snapshot: An Island Village

On Vatulele, a small island off the Viti Levu coast, about a dozen primary school boys and girls appear at the shore where Captain Ulai is preparing his small fishing boat which will ferry them down the coast to their village school. With Sami, the village chief, directing the embarkation, all the children are soon safely on board. Perched on the railings and the wheelhouse like colourful birds, the children draw upon their shared repertoire of songs, singing one after another during the 15-minute trip. They all sing, and they all know the words. Captain Ulai tells us that Sami directed the parents to have their children meet us at the boat and to sing for us as we motored down the coast.

Sami's actions – which are non-negotiable – teaches the children that singing has important social value; it is a way of expressing hospitality to visitors. In this village community of singing practice, the children draw on their repertoire and singing skills to discharge a social obligation on behalf of the community.

12.3.8 Snapshot: Boys to Men

Four young boys perform a "war *meke*" for tourists and fellow students in a primary school classroom. Brandishing wicked-looking clubs and spears they engage with mock ferocity in false combat with one another, with occasional warlike lunges towards the audience which is seated along 2 walls of the classroom. The students chant the rhyming couplets at the top of their lungs with a power reminiscent of the Maori *haka*. An adult performance of a war *meke* might be to entertain, intimidate, celebrate or impress, but in this representation there is much hilarity as everyone understands that these gestures and these verses are telling a story, and the young boys are emulating their fathers, uncles, cousins. One of the younger of the four boys occasionally strays in the wrong direction or does the wrong action, and with a quick glance at one of the older boys he quickly gets back into the routine. In a few years some of these boys will be expected to join with other Fijian men in their communities to perform *meke* for tourists or traditional celebrations.

I note that the warlike actions and chants are not sanitized or cleaned up for children. This *meke* has real meaning; it is valued by significant others in their social lives.

12.4 Discussion

The church. Singing and religion are closely connected in Fiji, where more than half of the ethnic Fijian population is affiliated with the Methodist church – an institution with a history of congregational singing, which has been prominent in Fijian social and spiritual life since the middle of the nineteenth century. Brother Théophane talked of Methodist choirs that rehearse two or three times per week, sometimes well past midnight, providing models of commitment to singing. His observation that "Singing *is* the religion", hints at the power of singing to contribute to community coherence. Most ethnic Fijians live in villages, some in remote mountain areas, some on small islands accessible only by boat or light plane. In these locations, many of which lack electrical power, entertainment and social life depend upon the initiative of villagers. These realities undoubtedly contribute to the commitment to singing and the maintenance of communities of musical practice. Churches are scattered throughout the islands, providing a location and a context where spiritual and social needs converge and young people learn sacred repertoire, musical idioms and singing behaviours and attitudes by immersion in the practices of significant members of their communities.

Authority. Individuals have obligations to meet the expectations of family and community. In Fiji, authority is vested in certain individuals. Kalawa, lay preacher and assistant choir leader in one village escorted me to and from two choir practices during the week, introduced me to choir members, accompanied me on the bus to a primary school and introduced me to the headmaster. On these occasions, when there were opportunities for conversation, he explained something of the nature and scope of the authority of village chiefs. He told me that if an individual does not attend the family worship he or she can be obliged by the chief to attend. Authority is also vested in other adults who are not the children's parents. The headmaster's command to sing louder and the reprimand of the woman in church elicited an immediate, appropriate response from the children. The village chief's directive to the children to sing during the boat trip was carried out with enthusiastic singing. The events witnessed here suggest that singing is not a matter of choice for young people. Nor it is a matter of choice for older people. Kalawa made me aware of this in a conversation we had during my second visit. I asked him about choir membership, thinking of the difficulties some directors in my city have getting sufficient singers together for services. He replied, "If the chief says you have to sing, you have to sing." Thus, choirs are assured of having sufficient numbers for Sunday services, choir festivals and competitions, and family worship services are assured of sufficient numbers to sing the hymns.

The group vs the individual. In the first visit, in 1989, I heard no solo singing, and among the dozens of cassettes of local music available for purchase I saw none featuring solo singers. In a follow-up visit in 1998 I saw only two cassettes featuring a solo singer. It is safe to suggest, therefore, that group singing is valued over solo singing, a value that I believe is reasonable as an assumption that group singing is a necessary condition for the development of singing competence, especially singing in tune, and in particular singing in harmony. It is also the basis for the maintenance of constellations of communities of singing practice.

Repertoire. Through repetition, and with the leadership of older people in various communities of practice, new hymns and songs are learned and added to the repertoire. Hymns are sung in church, in school, at family worship and at spontaneous moments by men, women, boys and girls. School songs are sung by children both inside and out of the classroom. Anthems are sung by choirs in church, by school children, community and church singing groups at choral festivals and choir competitions. The repertoire is learned under the guidance of a leader who may or may not have had formal training. Solfa syllables and a system of rhythmic shorthand are printed under the words in some hymn books and other choral works, and anthems may be laboriously copied out by hand, photocopied and circulated. Using these syllables, choir members are able to learn anthems quickly – relying less on rote learning – that have changes of tempo, key and metre. I attempted to find out how they have learnt to read music by this method. I speculate that as there is no formal training in music in Fijian schools, the knowledge is passed along non-formally, a mode of learning described by Fijian ethnographer Veramu (1992), an immersion process well known in all non-traditional, non-formal communities of musical practice.

Belief in ability. Blacking (1995) maintains that the ability to sing is a basic human characteristic. A gentleman in the choir at Tagaqe echoed Blacking's words: "We were born to sing". My experience leads me to agree with both Blacking and my Fijian acquaintance, and to argue that communities of singing practice enable the development of the potential for singing we are born with (Russell, 2001). Children who participate in communities of musical practice are more likely to carry such a belief through adolescence and into adulthood. This belief is in contrast to the countless individuals in my own communities who have assured me that they have no musical ability.

Sites of learning. Children who are members of a community of singing practice have confidence in their singing. They learn new material quickly, and are able use it for social purposes. One example of this is the children singing on the fisherman's boat. Another example occurred when I taught the primary school students on Viti Levu to sing Li'l Liza Jane. I then asked them to step the beat, use their silent voices, and clap the rhythm of the lyrics. They responded enthusiastically and learned the song and the tasks quickly. Many of these schoolchildren lived in the village where I attended church and rehearsed with the choir. When small groups of children saw me around the school or walking through village they greeted me by striking up a chorus of Li'l Liza Jane. Even the pre-schoolers knew the song by the next day. When singing is a community's language, songs are currency.

When innovation meets tradition. While the students at the primary school were quick to master the various tasks, my attempt to get them to improvise movements while singing was less successful. The movement task, I thought, was fairly simple: sing the song, step the beat in any direction they wished, stop when they got to the repeated phrase and clap the rhythm of the lyrics. The improvisational component was to walk in any direction they wished. This task seemed puzzling to them: they persisted in trying to walk in straight lines all together, in tight group formation.

Because there were no subsequent opportunities to pursue improvisatory activities with the students, it is impossible to know how they might have responded over time, with practice. In a community of practice where traditions are replicated, and where individual expression is less important than group collaboration, children may be less predisposed to improvise, or to push boundaries of what is familiar to them. The potential for learning new ways of doing and thinking might be constrained by Fijian traditions and respect for authority. On the other hand Fijians might welcome new ways of singing and moving. After this session several classroom teachers approached me and expressed their desire to know more about teaching music, for although they could all sing, they had no training in music pedagogy. One teacher expressed the belief that one could not teach music without instruments. This belief may be a factor in discouraging children, youth and adults from seeing singing as an important human activity. Might strict adherence to tradition be one of the conditions that foster a strong singing culture? How do communities balance preservation and development?

12.5 Conclusions: Wenger's Four Pillars

The snapshots presented here may be viewed from the perspective of the four pillars supporting Wenger's notion of community of practice:

We are social beings and this fact is an aspect of learning. Children who sing regularly, frequently, and with skill in important social contexts with significant others such as peers, relatives, teachers, and village leaders absorb attitudes and learn repertoire and skills.

Knowledge is a matter of competence in enterprises which are valued. Singing competence means knowing the words and melodies, and singing with appropriate enthusiasm. As children enter into adolescence and adulthood, competence in singing increases.

Knowing is a matter of participating in the pursuit of valued enterprises. Singing is not an option for children; they are expected to sing, and to sing enthusiastically. Singing thus contributes to the formation of one's social identity.

Engagement with the world as meaningful is the ultimate purpose of learning. Brother Théophane observed that church choirs sometimes rehearse past midnight. A choir member at states categorically that Fijians are "born to sing." I observe the commitment with which Fijians of all ages sing and I conclude that singing is a meaningful way to experience the world.

12.6 Post-industrial Schooling

In many post-industrial countries, school communities are made up of culturally, linguistically and economically diverse populations with diverse histories, value systems, religious practices and beliefs, and so forth. Unlike Fiji, innovation and individual expression is valued and boundaries between and within disciplines are more porous. There is more distraction, more cash available and greater access to commercially-produced musical products. Many adults and adolescents prefer to watch others sing than to sing themselves, believing that they lack the necessary skills. Although group singing, school choirs and bands, and garage bands, flourish here and there (Campbell, 2002), ensemble singing is not a required practice in schools. Few schools have daily assembly where students start the day by singing together. If children do not attend a church, summer camp or other social institution where singing – whether planned or spontaneous, formal or informal – is practiced, and if classroom teachers decline to sing with their students believing that this need will be taken care of by a music specialist (who might see the children for short periods of time during the school week, and might or might not place singing at the core of the music curriculum), and if parents do not sing with their children, children may grow up believing that they cannot sing. The fewer the number of communities of singing practice that children have access to the less likely they are to see themselves as singers who develop into adults who sing in tune and are able to harmonize, who value singing and who model singing behaviours for younger community members. Identifying the features of successful communities of singing practice offers the possibility of adopting any that might be adapted to our own particular community situation. Creating opportunities for adults and children to sing together regularly and frequently for significant social purposes is one way to create a community of singing practice.

References

Blacking, J. (1995). *Music, culture and experience: Selected papers of John Blacking*. Chicago: University of Chicago Press.
Campbell, P. S. (2002). The musical cultures of children. In L. Bresler & C. M. Thompson (Eds.), *The arts in children's lives: context, culture, and curriculum* (pp. 57–69). Dordrecht: Kluwer.
Clunie, F. (1986). *Yalo i Viti: A Fiji museum catalogue*. Suva: Fiji Museum.
Elliott, D. (1995). *Music matters: A new philosophy of music education*. New York: Oxford University Press.
Good, L. (1978). *Fijian Meke: An analysis of style and content*. Masters thesis, University of Hawaii.
Ravuvu, A. (1983). *The Fijian way of life*. Suva: Institute of Pacific Studies of the University of the South Pacific.
Russell, J. (1991). *Music in Fiji*. Research paper presented at the annual conference of the Canadian Music Educators Association, Vancouver.
Russell, J. (1992). *Music in Fiji*. Unpublished monograph, University of Hawaii.
Russell, J. (1997). A place for every voice: The role of culture in the development of singing expertise. *The Journal of Aesthetic Education, 31*(4), 95–109.
Russell, J. (1999). *Features of a "singing culture" and implications for music education: Toward a cultural theory of music education*. Research paper presented at the American Educational Research Association, Montreal.
Russell, J. (2001). Born to sing: Fiji's "singing culture" and implications for music education in Canada. *McGill Journal of Education, 36*(3), 197–218.
Russell, J. (2002). *Sites of learning: Communities of musical practice in the Fiji Islands*. Bergen: International Society for Music Education.
Veramu, J. C. (1992). *Let's do it our way: A case study of participatory education in a rural Fijian school and community*. Suva: Institute of Pacific Studies of the University of the South Pacific.
Wenger, E. (1998). *Communities of practice: Learning, meaning and identity*. Cambridge: Cambridge University Press.
Wright, R. (1987). *On Fiji Islands*. Markham, ON: Penguin Books Canada.

Chapter 13
The Sounds of Gender: Textualizing Barbershop Performance

Richard Mook

13.1 Introduction

The view of barbershop singing as a process of interpretation, rather than a product, provides an important series of challenges to scholarly analyses of barbershop music that until recently have placed a disproportionate emphasis on lyrics, contest rules, and written arrangements, as opposed to musical and gestic content, while obscuring the song interpretation that barbershoppers use to give their songs meaning (Liz Garnett's recent book notwithstanding). Other studies that harness the voices of barbershoppers to explore the cultural work of the hobby have not used this data to create persuasive analyses of barbershop performances. For example, Gage Averill uses fieldwork to document the importance of "ringing chords" and camaraderie for barbershoppers, but his analyses of songs are based almost entirely on lyrics, and take no account of how performers might interpret the score (Averill, 2003).

By contrast, this chapter will document how one group of contemporary barbershoppers create meaning in their music through song interpretation, allowing the performers to inform more directly current scholarly debates about gender in this predominantly male genre. Specifically, fieldwork data and writings by barbershoppers will show how the Sounds of Liberty Barbershop Chorus in Philadelphia, Pennsylvania learns music and understands its meaning using their own process of song interpretation. This core vocabulary for discussing song interpretation informs an analysis of two performances by the Sounds of Liberty from 2001 and 2002. In this analysis, I argue that musical performance enables the male singers in the group and their female director (a rarity in the barbershop world) to create meaning and perform a range of gendered identities that sometimes challenge the neoVictorian traditions of the hobby.

This argument was inspired and informed by my experiences as a participant-observer with the Sounds of Liberty between March of 2001 and May of 2003, when

R. Mook (✉)
Arizona State University, Tempe, AZ, USA
e-mail: richard.mook@gmail.com

I recorded rehearsals, meetings, and performances, conducted individual interviews with members of Philadelphia Chapter of the Barbershop Harmony Society, and participated fully in its activities. In addition, I visited other chapters in the Philadelphia area, practiced with quartets from other chapters, and participated in division – and district-level competitions. While my status as a white male made my participation easier (only men are allowed to join the Barbershop Harmony Society as singing members, and the organization remains overwhelmingly white), my age set me apart from the group in important ways. When I joined the Chapter at age 24, I was by far its youngest member: most of the men were old enough to be my grandfather. There existed a class and educational divide between Philadelphia's barbershoppers, many of whom were retired from blue-collar occupations, and me, an academic at an Ivy League university. Unlike most members of the Philadelphia chapter, I was not born and raised in the Philadelphia region, but in rural Vermont. Finally, at the time I lived not in the Northeast section of the city, but across town in West Philadelphia, an area that only one other member travelled through regularly. My experience of the chorus therefore differs significantly from those of its members, and I do not claim that any of the members share my conclusions or agree with my argument. Nonetheless, the issues raised in this chapter are of current importance to the Sounds of Liberty.

13.2 Emotional Voicings: Song Interpretation and Meaning

The Sounds of Liberty learns songs in two basic phases. First, the group learns the words and music of the arrangement using sheet music and instructional tapes (often called "learning tapes"), and by imitating specially trained "teaching quartets" during rehearsal. This variety of methods is necessary because more than half of the group is musically illiterate; for these members, sheet music functions mainly as a set of lyric cues. With notes and words mostly learned, the group begins an explicit effort to localize or particularize the song by adding choreography and interpretation, or "interp." At this second stage, the chorus begins to invest the song with meaning and emotion. Eric Jackson, who directed the Sounds of Liberty in both 1980 and 1999, wrote a series of articles for the *Harmonizer,* the national magazine for the Barbershop Harmony Society, in 1982 which details the process of interpretation that the Sounds of Liberty followed at that time, and continued to follow in 2003. Written for barbershoppers in a conversational style, with many anecdotes, examples, and inside jokes, this eight-part series presents a detailed method and a model for how to interpret barbershop songs. Jackson views the performer as an intermediary between a composer with an emotional message and an audience that is seeking emotional stimulation:

> So somewhere, someone just got kissed by the girl he wanted to get kissed by. He can't believe it. He is ecstatic, thrilled. He can write music, so he does. He writes, 'Yes, sir! That's my baby, No sir! Don't mean maybe, Yes, sir! That's my baby now!!' He means it! The song is trivial, unimportant, but the feelings are real. The human experience is real. The human experience is never trivial. The song is a wonderful opportunity to communicate his experience (Jackson, 1982)

Jackson then complicates this stance by asserting that the original, emotional message of the composer is beyond reach. The performer, he asserts, must study the song, and decide on what "emotional content" he or she should perform for the audience: "*You* select the main emotion, and *you* decide what the song is about for *you* as the performer". Since the goal of the barbershop performer is to communicate emotion (an emotion chosen by the performer) to an audience, Jackson argues doggedly throughout this series that "technical" performance decisions, i.e. tempo and dynamics, should be derived from the performers' emotional sense of the song.

After an overview of this basic thesis in the first segment, Jackson guides his reader through the process of song interpretation by modelling the development of two contrasting interpretations of the barbershop standard "The Story of the Rose (Heart of My Heart)." His divides this process of interpretation into eight steps as follows:

> Step 1: Determine the main emotional content of the song
> Step 2: Identify the climax of the song
> Step 3: Organize the song into logical emotional phrases that move toward and set up the climax
> Step 4: Select volume levels for the song, based on the emotions you want to communicate
> Step 5: Select tempos for the song, based on the emotions you want to communicate
> Step 6: Learn the volume and tempo plan AND THE EMOTIONAL CONTENT ASSOCIATED WITH THE DEVICES YOU HAVE SELECTED [emphasis original]
> Step 7: Sing the song and recognize what parts are working and what parts are not working
> Step 8: Make revisions in the plan, based on the emotional message you wish to deliver. Don't tinker with devices.

Jackson assumes (safely) that most of his readers will be familiar with this song, a barbershop standard. He therefore provides only the text of this song at three points during the article without any score. In doing so, he also attempts explicitly to defamiliarize the lyrics by disassociating them from the melodic content, in order to open up new interpretive ideas for the reader. This radical generic shift provides Jackson's readers the opportunity to step back from their established bodily memory of "Heart of My Heart" – its timing and dynamics, or the contour of its melody – by viewing it as a poem. Performers should then physically reshape the song, bending and smoothing its musical contours to fit the emotional plan, avoiding "block dynamics" or "sudden" changes in tempo. In Jackson's normative portrayal of song interpretation, barbershoppers should use emotion to discipline and coordinate their performing bodies. He thereby defines and focuses the place and function of embodiment in barbershop performance. Disciplined by an emotional plan, the performer's body serves as a mailman by delivering an emotional message, in musical form, from the performer to an audience.

Jackson's article, the title of which was also the title of a major judging category at competitions, participates in an established tradition of didactic articles on barbershop song interpretation in the *Harmonizer*. Earlier articles of this type were intended largely to calm debates within the Barbershop Harmony Society about the merits of contests. Though no longer controversial, barbershop contests were a topic of heated debate in the mid-twentieth century between "traditionalist" barbershoppers, who formed an interest group in 1949 that was dedicated to "woodshedding," or improvising harmonies informally without the aid of arrangements, and others who supported contests as a means to perpetuate (and referee) a codified barbershop style.

A number of articles since Jackson's present the relationship between performer, song, and audience in a manner similar to Jackson's. For example, in a piece written just prior to a major revision of contest judging categories in 1993 describing the proposed "Presentation" category, Larry Ager and Rob Hopkins describe the relationship between a performer's emotional message and their use of musical and visual devices (or "techniques") as follows:

> Within the limitations of the composition and its arrangement, which are themselves gifts to the performer, a singer seeks elements that he can use to best convey his message and that of the song. Such elements are called techniques, and they are critical (Ajer and Hopkins, 1992).

Ajer and Hopkins, like Jackson, assert that the performer should use the bodily act of singing in the service of emotional delivery in order to move the audience emotionally. Similarly, a more recent article by David Leeder, a presentation category judge and coach, follows the sequence outlined by Jackson of beginning with an emotional message and then "tailoring" one's performance to suit that message (Leeder, 2001).

Jackson's first term as director of the Sounds of Liberty ended in 1980, 2 years before these articles appeared in the Harmonizer. He later returned in 1999 as co-director, and was instrumental in recruiting Jane to direct the group. Moreover, his approach to song interpretation still held some currency among members of the Sound of Liberty in 2002. In an interview, David, the chapter choreographer, cited Jackson by name as someone who could elicit effective, emotional performances from the chorus by challenging them to perform different emotional "voicings":

David: I believe firmly that if you have a plan to your music, first you decide how – what kind of music this is going to be, what kind of song is it going to be. Is it going to be a rhythm song, is it going to be ... and then you decide where the emotional content is going to be in that song, and then you make sure that the lead can sing – or the lead group – can sing it comfortably, and the bass group can sing the lower notes within their range and then you work from there building emotional content. Eric – were you there when Eric took over first?

Mook: No.

David: The first thing he did was he said, "all I want is beautiful, musical singing. I want the sound to be – we should sing in a beautiful, musical way." And he got us somewhat in touch with that emotion through other ways – you know, there are a million ways to get in touch with your emotions. He got us through these [in a soft voice] nice and easy exercises that he'd start us off with. When he'd warm us up he'd say [with different inflections] "Hi there! Hello there! How ya doin'!" And he'd go through different facial expressions, and we would repeat ... And there were all these different emotions that he went through and that was his warm-up. His warm-up was bringing different emotional voicings and getting us to [in a high voice] work the high area and [in a low voice] work the low area. And he would work the lower section and work the upper section. And this was all to get in touch with something here, in your heart – in your gut or in your heart, and it connected it to that emotional content ... That was all designed to get emotional, genuine singing.

Jackson's concepts of emotion and "character" provide a core vocabulary that the members of the Sounds of Liberty use to evaluate barbershop performances. To clarify this important vocabulary further, I have created the following definitions of three key performance terms using evidence from transcriptions of rehearsals, interviews, and coaching sessions recorded during 2001 and 2002, offering direct quotes where applicable. Though not a comprehensive list, these terms and their definitions encompass the most important ideas that circulated in the Sounds of Liberty concerning performance and interpretation. Many of these, especially character and emotion, show a clear affinity to Jackson's ideas and methods.

13.3 Character

As in theatre, *character* is the role that barbershop singers seek to perform in a given song. It encompasses the singer's response to the situation presented in the song and all of the song's emotions. Performers often communicate character by telling a hypothetical story about the song's subject, his/her past experiences, immediate responses, and hopes or fears for the future. Many refer to character as an emotional "plan," which charts the various emotions that performers will have to project during a song. Several of my informants discussed "character planning" as ideally linked to the entire rehearsal process, from selecting the piece and teaching it to the chorus to designing choreography:

Jane: [The Sounds of Liberty] doesn't get into *character* very much. And we should –that's another step up that we should be working on. Alexandria [the best chorus in the Mid-Atlantic District] has *big-time* character things. When they learn a song, they have the *characters* and the *emotions* and everything already on paper before they even see the song. And we talk about it once or twice a year.

13.4 Emotion

The performed emotions in a song can change from moment to moment, depending on the character developed by the chorus director or the quartet. Emotion can be "real," meaning the performer empathizes with the character or connects song with his/her past experiences and emotions, or "fake," meaning contrived or "put into" the song. Either one will do in performance, as long as it is convincing and all performers are "in the same place" emotionally, or sending the same emotional message. Such coordinated emotional delivery, experienced barbershoppers argue, is necessary for uniform vocal production, blended sound, and ringing chords[1].

13.5 Personality

Personality is the manner or style of a quartet or chorus that is constituted by their group sound, the ways that they interpret songs, and the kind of presence that they project to an audience. Quartets with clear personality convey emotion authentically and are thereby more engaging and entertaining to their audiences than quartets that "just ring chords". For a quartet to project their personality to the audience, they have to perform emotionally, and their emotional efforts have to be coordinated through a unified character. One interviewee named three different international-level quartets and described their unique personalities in turn:

David: Rural Route Four had this personality... you sit down and listen to them and you feel like you are in their living room listening to your family sing ... Whereas Acoustix, they had this personality where they were completely in charge, they were in control, they were power freaks ... The Gas House Gang, they have this personality of being absolute consonant musicians – perfect musicians, where if they do a little flare they all do it *together* ... They are doing little flares in the music ... and everybody does it so that it rings throughout that entire swipe. And that's not easy to do, let me tell you. But they do it so well that it has this boy-choir sound, this youthful, energetic sound.

Emphasizing the importance of personality for the barbershop audience, he explained: "Each [group] has their own thing that works for them and you've got to get in touch with that and let that come out. And the audience can tell."

Songs performed by the Sounds of Liberty were interpreted by Jane and David, both of whom would then explain the character and emotions of each song after the group had learned the notes and lyrics. By expressing these emotions through choreography, gesture, and facial expression, individual members then worked to make the interpretation their own. In the longer run, chapter leaders sought to develop the personality of the chorus by regularly emphasizing the importance of interpretation and key terms like character and emotion in rehearsal and warm-ups. Though the

Sounds of Liberty was often unsuccessful in performing effectively under the model outlined by Jackson, Jackson's views still informed the group members' ideas of a good barbershop performance. His ideas structured the ways that the chorus members thought about what their music meant, both to themselves and to listeners. The following analysis compares two Sounds of Liberty interpretations of a single song in order to document how song interpretation creates musical meaning in barbershop performance.

13.6 "Running Wild": A Comparative Analysis

As the new director of the Sounds of Liberty, Jane chose the song "Running Wild" by Joe Grey, Leo Wood, and A. Harrington Gibbs (1922), and arranged by Freddie King, in 2000 as a competition showpiece in part to challenge the group. With its three key changes, use of extreme registers in all parts, and fast tempo, the arrangement demands tremendous effort on the part of any ensemble. Its status as a competition piece meant that more rehearsal time was spent to bring it to the "next level" of excellence. Special coaches were also brought in to improve the song by fixing "problem areas" and refining the group's emotional delivery. The performances that I analyze here were taped at the Sounds of Liberty's annual show in April of 2001 and a dress rehearsal in April of 2002. These recordings of the group on its "home turf" performing a song that they have rehearsed relentlessly show the Sounds of Liberty at their best. Comparing these two performances is a useful exercise because the interpretation of "Running Wild" underwent significant revisions early in 2002 that draw out how issues of gender impact song interpretation in the Sounds of Liberty. After reviewing the first interpretation and the ideas that informed it, I will argue that the Sounds of Liberty used the song to comment on itself as an all-male barbershop chorus with a female director. The second interpretation, I will argue, enabled the director and chorus members to perform different gender roles that reflected larger changes in the gender politics of the chapter between 2001 and 2002.

The 2001 version of the choreography for "Running Wild," written by David, punned on the lyrics by creating from the start an impression of a group that had "lost control." The front row of the chorus was taught to bolt forward on the first note of the four-bar introduction, run around the director, and back to their original positions in time to begin the first chorus, though in practice the maneuver could not be completed until the seventh bar of the chorus. During this chaotic opening Jane stepped back from the group, gesturing towards those running past with outstretched hands, and shrugging her shoulders in mock resignation. The second phrase of the chorus brought a return of stability, as Jane began directing the song and the front row had ceased its chaotic running. The transition from chaotic opening to stable chorus is audible in recordings of this performance, as the beat and pitch are less certain and less unified when Jane is not directing.

Throughout this introduction and first chorus, all members of the group were performing the song by attempting, with varying degrees of success, to adopt its rebellious emotional content and project that sense to the audience. For the verse, David designed a dramatic change. Here, the director and two members of the chorus altered their roles from performing the song to performing a dramatic role. Jane turned to face the audience and stepped forward, flanked by two members of the front row, each holding a romantic gift (flowers and candy). Each man, in turn, offered Jane the gifts during the lyric "once I was full of sentiment, it's true". Jane's flattered gestures then changed to surprise and dismay, as her suitors threw down the gifts and stomped on them in front of her during the lyric "but now I've got a cruel heart". Separated from the rest of the group by both physical location and choreographed gesture, they became characters in an imaginary drama that lay outside the words of the song, an allegorical development of what the song's lyrics might look like if performed by two disgruntled suitors and the former object of their affections.

The choreography of the second chorus mimicked that of the first, though the movements of the performers were intended to be even more dramatic and enthusiastic. For the difficult tag that concluded the song, the choreographer planned a mad rush off the risers and towards the audience by the entire group. The tag required that the tenors ascend chromatically from high G-flat to a "post," or held pitch, on the tonic (high C) while the lower parts completed a long, chromatic voice exchange ending on the final chord (see Example 13.1). Because one of the tenors was chronically sharp on the final post, while the lower parts tended to lose pitch during their accompanying chromatic passage, the final chord of the song was most often horribly out of tune. The exertion of rushing off the risers exacerbated this problem by distracting the performers and preventing them from hearing each other.

This first interpretation of "Running Wild" was informed primarily by the gender differences between Jane (the director) and the rest of the chorus. In fact, these differences prompted Jane to select the song for the chorus repertory in 2000. As she noted in an interview in 2002:

> I think it's good to have a song, if you're going to have an opposite gender director, I think it's good to occasionally have a song to play off of it and have fun. And I went looking for that. But now it's not [about that] as much [with the new choreography].

According to Jane, the gendered roles in this interpretation of "Running Wild" highlighted Jane's unique position as a female member of the Sounds of Liberty.

Example 13.1 Tag of "Running Wild" as arranged by Freddie King

13   The Sounds of Gender: Textualizing Barbershop Performance   209

Furthermore, gender was an important factor in choosing songs for the chorus repertory more generally because of the demands that song interpretation placed on each performer. As Jane later explained, she only chose songs that both she and the chorus could relate to emotionally, and this meant excluding some pieces that she believed might have worked well with an older or male director.

Jane: We were working with Tom [an arranger] and we had emailed back and forth trying to find a song, a ballad, for contest. And "Now is the Hour" – do you know that song? From 1909 or whatever? There are some songs that I just cannot get into. And he had started that thing where if you put the song into Finale [a computer notation program] you get the song for free. I put it on Finale and I listened to it and I just didn't like it. [laughter] I didn't like the song. There's not too many songs I don't like.
Mook: You couldn't get into it. What does that mean?
Jane: I couldn't find the emotion in it. If I can't put emotion in it, I'm not going to expect my 40 guys to put emotion into it. Even with the gender thing, I'm not going to give my all if I don't have emotion. So that's very important to me.
Mook: How does the "gender thing" fit into that?
Jane: Well, it was more of a guy song. You know, that is a guy song. And they might have been able to – since it is an older chorus and that was another reason why they [the former directors] chose it for me, being there were so many older guys they could relate to the war thing and all that. [Jane, by contrast, was one of the few chapter members under age 50] But I couldn't. So . . . I won't direct a song, especially not in contest, that I can't at least pretend the emotion for, [and] I just couldn't with that one.

The shift in this performance of "Running Wild" from performing within the group in the chorus to performing "about" the group in the verse required different tasks for each individual involved. When I asked Jane to describe her own experience of that moment in the song in her own words, she responded:

Jane: Before I used to be like "oh boy, here comes my part! I get to turn around." I felt it was my chance to be different, to stand out a little bit, which I'm bound to do anyway, hmm. I enjoy the theatrical experience of what I got to do and all the emotions that I got to play when they were doing their thing with the candy and the flower. It was fun.

These comments about the importance of gendered performance for this interpretation of "Running Wild" can provide a starting point for a scholarly critique of this performance. The emotionally charged encounter between a feminine, female director and two designated members of the chorus, marked musically by a key change, carries an important interpretive function; it is, to borrow from Clifford Geertz, a kind of "deep play," or "a story they tell themselves about themselves" (Geertz, 1972). In this case, they also share that story with their audience. Though Jane is "bound to stand out anyway," as she put it, in my view, she plays a more feminine role in the verse than it did in the chorus. I read Jane's role as requiring a shift as she moves from the more masculine subject position of the chorus and its character to the more feminine role of rejected "gal" in the verse. When I asked Jane to respond to this reading she agreed with it, adding "especially because of the way we used to do it, where David and Joe came out and gave me the presents and stomped them and stuff, because then I had to become very female."

For the two "suitors," however, the situation was different. No change in the gendering of their performance or break in their character was necessary, only a willingness to strut momentarily and enjoy the spotlight. They paid no attention to each other on stage; rather, the focus of their efforts remained on showing off their "cruel hearts" to Jane. The masculinity that these two men performed was a unified one, informed by the group standing with uncharacteristic stillness behind them, as if they were acting as representatives of the group rather than as individuals. The suitors became the voice of a communal, masculine rejection of Jane's performed femininity.

Gender politics in the Barbershop Harmony Society as a whole helped to shape this interpretation of "Running Wild" by the Sounds of Liberty. The Society did not formally allow women to perform as directors until the early 1990s. In 2001, Jane, the group's first female director, had been on the job for only one year, and the transition from an all-male to a mixed-gender environment was still in process.

To summarize, this performance mapped the changing roles of women in the Barbershop Harmony Society onto Jane's performance as a director. I argue that during the verse, the Sounds of Liberty is represented by the two men up front. They ultimately reject Jane in her feminine role and allow her to return to the traditionally masculine role of barbershop chorus director, and to the masculine subject position of the song. At the return of the chorus, Jane once again becomes, as she sometimes put it, "one of the guys". The choreography and interpretation of this song, while entertaining the audience, also punned on the gender politics of the Sounds of Liberty, reflecting the changing gender dynamics and sexual politics of the Society as a whole.

Because the Sounds of Liberty did not fare well with this song in the 2001 division competition, which was held just after the show in April, the leaders made a number of changes to the interpretation, arrangement and choreography of "Running Wild." This second version of "Running Wild" was recorded at the last regular rehearsal before the 2002 annual show. I have chosen to analyze this rehearsal because the recorded picture and sound are clearer than the recording made at the 2002 show itself.

Though the changes to the interpretation and choreography of "Running Wild" were prompted by problems with the group's sound, they also had important implications for the song's meaning. The running of the front line during the introduction and the bass melody passage in the second chorus were cut and replaced in the first instance with regimented group choreography and in the second with improvised choreography. The second chorus also received some focused attention from coaches during the following year because the background parts had lost their sense of rhythmic unity and pitch centre. In this second chorus, the upper three parts arpeggiate a triad at a low dynamic level. Performing this passage in tune required unified vowels and attacks, a difficult feat during improvised choreography. Even after extensive coaching the problem persisted in the dress rehearsal from April of 2002, such that Jane had to shout "take it easy" during that passage. They abandoned the scramble off of the risers at the end in favour of an entirely conventional "outboard hand sweep," with the goal of preserving the group's pitch center in the final, climactic moments of the song. After a gruelling, largely unsuccessful rehearsal of the chromatic ending to the tag, a coach cut the passage, replacing it with a simple three-chord progression (see Example 13.2).

Perhaps the most profound musical and choreographic modifications came in the verse. Even after weeks of rehearsal, the modulation that introduces this section proved too difficult for the group to perform at full tempo. Jane therefore introduced a dramatic *ritard* through the modulation, followed by a fermata on the dominant of the new key. The group then performed the verse at a much slower, more deliberate tempo, with a second fermata and free, speech-like interpretation during the modulation that ends the verse. Taking advantage of this slower tempo, David replaced the "drama" between Jane and her "suitors" in the verse with a sequence of regimented choreography that all members of the chorus memorized and performed together. The entire group was told to point accusingly at Jane during the lyric "no gal, I mean just what I say". Then the group was also coached to slap their heads and change their vocal tone during the lyric "wonder how I got that way" from a full, forward tone to a heavy, throaty, clumsy one, as if to say "duh!"

While these revisions effected before April of 2002 helped to improve the sound of the song, they also had strong implications for the interpretation, and thus the meaning of the song for the Sounds of Liberty. In the 2001 performance, the audience was directed by the drama in the verse to observe the interactions between Jane and her two disgruntled suitors. In the 2002 clip, however, the entire chorus stood in sudden opposition to the director, providing a more forceful rejection. For Jane, the moment required a far more limited change in the gendering of her performance: she never turned around, stopped conducting, or stepped outside the narrative of the song. As she related to me in an interview:

Example 13.2 Tag of "Running Wild" as arranged by "Mark" and "Jane" (2002)

Jane: Now the way we've got it, I don't switch [gender] as much now because I'm not turning around, I'm not to the audience, and I just let them do this thing at me [points] and I just [gestures] take it, yeah.

Though Jane's femininity was less pronounced in this performance, her role as director was still very much at issue. The hierarchy that characterized the director-chorus relationship in most barbershop songs suddenly reversed as the chorus rebelled, their gestures suddenly telling the director what to do. This new interpretation facilitated a temporary reversal of authority within the group which the audience (and judges) were expected to experience as entertaining.

In 2001, the song did not really have a character for the group on the risers, aside from an excited man suddenly liberated from women. The new, revised choreography of 2002 carried with it a character that embodied a distinctive vision of masculinity and age for the performers. Mark, the hired coach who simplified the tag for the group, was instrumental in developing this character and communicating it to the Sounds of Liberty. He led a coaching session six weeks before the 2002 video clip was filmed. I reproduce an account of it from my field notes at length in order to show how Mark communicated this new character to the group.

Tuesday, 2/19/02

Mark: Anyone watch the Flintstones? We're supposed to be like Fred: utterly convinced that we have control, that we know about the problem and it will never happen again – until the next time! We've been vulnerable before . . . [he mimicked the choreography designed for the lyrics "once I was full of sentiment, it's true," standing to the side, with his hands on his hips, and a pleasant smile on his face.]

Mark: How many of you guys have never had this happen to you?
[No one raised his hand.]

Carl: We're married. We're not fooling anyone here!
[Laughter filled the room. As a single graduate student, I felt a bit left-out by the comment.]

Mark: but never again!
[He transitioned into the choreography for the next lyric – "but now I've got a cruel heart" – clutching his outboard fist to his breast with a stoic expression.]

David: [in the front row, hand on heart] "Solemn vow."

Mark: Yeah, so we all put our hands in, slap each other on the butt, and go out there.
[Mark then explained to the group that if they acted more enthusiastically and had more fun the audience would "get it too." He also asserted that being "in the same place" emotionally and interpretively was necessary for the song to work. It would lead to a correct tone, better blend, good singing, and unity of sound.]

To create this interpretation and communicate it to the chorus, Mark offered a specific mode of masculinity and life-phase for the group to perform. An element of irony came into play: the audience was supposed to understand that, despite the best efforts of the character, problems with women *would* happen again. Mark coached the Sounds of Liberty to overact the part, to appear "cocky" and "over-confident," and to offer a picture of someone "like Fred Flintstone" who only *thinks* that he has control of his life. The ironic stance that Mark instructed the group to assume was not intended to make the barbershoppers parody the character, but to create internal contradictions, depth, believability, and even vulnerability. The masculinity that the group offered in this song came complete with a physical situation, an age, and a weakness.

With this new character and choreography, and modified arrangement, the 2002 performance tells a very different story, one shaped by the events that occurred within the group between April of 2001 and April of 2002. After the group's disappointing performance at district competition in 2001, many members of the Sounds of Liberty expressed concern about Jane's choice of the song, which they thought to be too difficult and wrong for the group. Frustrated by its disappointing contest scores, the entire ensemble pointed at Jane during the song, asserting: "No gal will ever make a fool of me. No gal; I mean just what I say!" Yet, as she was a seasoned veteran of the group by spring of 2002, Jane's femininity was less of a topic. She performed consistently "in the song" in 2002, as the director, without stepping outside the subjectivity of the song, or turning around to face the audience.

13.7 Conclusion

These performances of "Running Wild" provide an example of how different song interpretations can change the meaning of a musical work for barbershop performers and their audiences. While the director's femininity was an important factor in the early interpretation of the song, it became less pronounced after the group was forced to make changes for musical reasons and she gained their acceptance. Age also functioned in this process, as "older" members strove to limit the choreographic demands on the group, while "younger" members (like David) sought to preserve them.

To conclude, song interpretation provided the Sounds of Liberty with an opportunity to localize and particularize their repertory, perform a range of identities, and position themselves in the context of changing gender roles in their umbrella organization. Viewing barbershop performances as processes, as opposed to products, clarifies how song interpretation creates meaning for barbershoppers on musical and gestic levels.

Note

1. I explore the physical dimensions and gendered implications of this choreographed, emotional delivery elsewhere. See Mook (2007).

References

Ajer, L., & Hopkins, R. (1992). What's the presentation category all about? *Harmonizer, 52*(5), 36.
Averill, G. (2003). *Four parts, no waiting: A social history of American Barbershop harmony.* New York: Oxford University Press.
Garnett, L. (2005). *The British Barbershopper: A study in socio-musical values.* Aldershot: Ashgate Press.
Geertz, C. (1972). Deep play: Notes on the Balinese cockfight. *Daedalus, 101*(1), 1–37.
Jackson, E. (1982). In-ter'pre-ta'tion. *The Harmonizer, 42*(3), 10.
Leeder, D. (2001). Lay the groundwork for interpretation. *The Harmonizer, 56*(4), 10.
Mook, R. (2007). White masculinity in Barbershop quartet singing: 1900–2003. *Journal of the Society for American Music, 1*, 453–483.

Chapter 14
Icelandic Men, Male Voice Choirs and Masculine Identity

Robert Faulkner

Even though I had trained as a professional singer and been actively involved with choral and solo singing since childhood, I found myself compelled to dramatically rethink singing's role in everyday life, and singers themselves, following my migration to Iceland in 1986. I spent the next 20 years living and working in a remote rural community in the north east of the country where singing enjoyed a very different kind of function and occupied very different kinds of spaces from those I had known in the UK previously. I soon became musical director of a local male voice choir, *Hreimur* or *Accent,* a position I enjoyed for nearly 20 years, and during the last 6 years of that tenure, I also undertook a research project that investigated the role of singing in these men's lives, not just in the male voice choir, but also in everyday life in general (Faulkner, 2006). The study was formulated by a multi-disciplinary spanning of the social sciences of music, with a strong emphasis on a music psychology of individuality, developed from Jonathan Smith's Interpretative Phenomenological Analysis (Smith & Osborn, 2003). In addition, the study included ethnomusicological, sociological and historical investigation with the aim of producing a multi-perspective view of Icelandic men and singing. This chapter examines the emergence of the male-voice choir movement, first in Europe, and then in Iceland, whilst keeping a particular eye on gender identity and masculinity in historical and cultural contexts. The chapter then goes on to examine contemporary men in the Icelandic male voice choir *Hreimur* or *Accent,* and to provide an interpretation of their accounts of how singing works for them in regulating Self and in negotiating masculine identity at personal and collective levels.

The point has been made widely in feminist literature that men have been disinclined to engage reflexively with what it means to be a man or with gender identity in general. Instead, such writers argue, there is a tendency for men to accept what is seen as the hegemonic masculine order as something ahistorical, universal and even natural. When challenged by feminists and early men's studies writers who dared to

---

R. Faulkner (✉)
University of Western Australia, Crawley, WA, Australia
e-mail: robert.faulkner@uwa.edu.au

enter a field widely seen as a feminist prerogative, the minor crisis of identity about what modern men were expected to be provoked a strong mythopoetic defence. Robert Bly's Iron John (1990) is the most obvious example, with its insistence on archetypal, fairytale versions of manhood where male hardness appears unambiguous and non-negotiable. If there is no place for softness in maleness, is there a place for song? And if there is, must these songs inevitably be those of mythopoetic Weekend Warriors (Kimmel & Kaufman, 1994) engaged in conflicts real, fantastical or, at least, sporting? Is this, essentially, what the male voice choir tradition is – a series of reiterated performances by men that are from Mars, and whose gender identity is built around variations on a theme of *Men of Harlech* or Gounod's *Soldier's Chorus*? If men sing songs that suggest rich and highly expressive emotional lives, are they men at all?

In questioning a unary view of men, gender, songs and singing, it may be helpful to consider that singing is not simply about the representation of gender identity, but that it *genders* identity by virtue of the meanings ascribed to singings and songs. If then, as Russell's earlier chapter in this book reports, Fijian men believe that they are "born to sing", then they clearly use singing to gender identity in fundamentally different ways from the professional boy choristers that Williams discusses in her chapter, or the young children in many mainstream Western schools, as Hall illustrates here and elsewhere (2005). So whilst, in a global world, gendering identity through song may appear to have become a standardised process with homogenized and even hegemonic outcomes, there is still enough diversity for us, following the example of Connell's seminal writing about male identity in general (1995), to ask for a consideration of plurality. In thinking then of masculinities, men's songs and singings, it may even be the case that individual men configure complex, contradictory male identities by virtue of assorted vocal behaviours in wide-ranging social and cultural contexts. After all, if James (1890) is correct that we have as many social selves as there are people whose opinion we care about, might it not also be true that we have many singing selves? Singing in a male voice choir is quite probably only one of those selves and even in that limited setting, as we shall see, the notion of a singular, consistent identity is hardly sustainable.

Unfortunately, as far as I am aware, no comprehensive study of the modern male voice choir movement exists. In its absence, there is probably a tendency to assume a level of homogeneity amongst men's singing groups that can be seen as constituting a singular cohesive *movement* when the reality may be far more complex. The German male choir tradition, which is most significant in terms of the Icelandic experience, began in the late eighteenth and early nineteenth centuries. It pre-empted the emergence of male voice choir traditions in the UK that were often built, in Wales especially, around industrial settings and influenced by the emergence of Presbyterian chapel singing, by almost a century. Nevertheless, the nationalistic themes, evident in the Welsh male voice choir tradition, and widely seen as a key construct in hegemonic masculinity, had earlier been central to the mainland European tradition, as it spread throughout northern Europe and eventually to Iceland itself.

Much earlier, in the middle of the eighteenth century, men's singing groups had been founded amongst the English middle and upper classes with very different social, musical and political concerns. Such groups tended to focus either on the performance of the older madrigal, as in the Madrigal Club, founded in 1741, or of glees, like the Noblemen and Gentlemen's Catch Club, founded in 1761 (Smith & Young, 2010). It was this tradition that appears to have led to the establishing of similar glee clubs in the USA. Indeed, many of the men's singing groups founded in the UK around the turn of the twentieth century, and now known as Male Voice Choirs, appear to have been originally known as Glee Clubs, Glee Unions or even Glee Parties. Obviously, all these groups shared the notion of exclusive men's clubs and homo-social conviviality, even if their political agendas were a good deal less explicit than their mainland European counterparts.

The importance of conviviality and gleefulness had been evident too in the emergence of two socially fairly distinct German male voice choir traditions: one was built around academic institutions and the educated classes, whilst the other, the more working-class *Leidertafel,* quickly became so widespread that by 1839 a national union was founded (ibid.). This date coincides with the arrival of German migrants in Australia and their founding of *Leidertafel* there, notably the *Adelaide Leidertafel* 1858, which claims to be the second-oldest continuing choir in Australia (Adelaide Leidertafel 1858, 2002). Similar *Leidertafel* were organised by Germans who went to live in the USA, thus the impact of German migration on the emerging choral life of the *new* worlds, and on the gendering of vocal behaviour there, was very significant indeed. It illustrates clearly, as other examples in this book have, how reducing identity to component parts like gender without due consideration of the interaction of other elements – like ethnicity, nationality, class and age – is to fail to understand the complex nature of human identities.

It was these same German traditions that most obviously influenced the emergence of organized male-voice singing throughout Scandinavia. In terms of repertoire, glees and drinking songs contrasted with more serious works often emphasizing romanticism, nationalism and the rural idyll. Composers like Brahms, Kücken, Mendelssohn, Schubert, Schumann and Silcher all produced music specifically for men's groups ranging from informal male quartets to large choral groups. Early male voice choirs in Scandinavia, for example, the university male voice choir in Lund, Sweden (*Lunds Studentsångförening*) founded in 1831, initially often performed the same German repertoire. In Finland, similarly, it was the German émigré, Pacius, who formed the *Akademiska Sångföreningen* in Helsinski, in 1838. Pacius even composed what was to become the Finnish national anthem for these same men's voices – voices that became hugely significant in reforming and mobilizing national identity in the struggle for independence from Russia. In Norway, *Den norske Studentersangforening* was founded in Oslo in 1845, and in Denmark, once again, it was a university male voice choir, known simply as the Copenhagen University Choir or *Studentersangforeningen*, founded in 1839, that claims to be Denmark's oldest formal secular choir. In all these institutions, for "students" read "male students": it was to be several decades before any of them accepted their first female students. In France, male-voice groups, known collectively after the 1830s as

Orphéon, emerged from the choral movement associated with the annual National Festival celebrating the French Revolution (Smith & Young, 2010). In England meanwhile, as its nineteenth century history clearly illustrates, nationalist fervour, calls for revolution and songs of equality, remained a good deal less audible than they were in mainland Europe.

Two themes appear salient here for understanding the role men singing together played in the configuration and representation of nineteenth and early twentieth century masculine identity: firstly, and common it seems to all these movements, was the notion of homo-social recreation and *glee*ful behaviour – men's clubs; secondly, homo-vocal activity was often about more serious men's business – the creation of national identity and unity, and the struggle for independence, democracy and equality. Initially this was very much an intellectual movement, centred round university life, but it was quickly matched by emerging working class singing groups.

If Kantian aesthetics and claims about the purity (and superiority) of instrumental music enabled Western musicians and musicologists to largely ignore music's power as a political, cultural and gendering force – eventually challenged by Adorno (1976) and other cultural theorists and music sociologists – even this brief history of European male-voice choirs implies that the power of song as a political and social force was never far from men's minds or motives as they met together to sing. Rousseau, one of the key enlightenment philosophers, whose work was inspirational for both the French and other European revolutions, had, in fact, already articulated a pragmatic relationship between, on the one hand, democracy and the voice of the people, and, on the other, collective singing's potential to arouse a moral feeling or awareness of others, and its power to create links between individuals that were the basis of community (Simon, 2004). Simon's discussion of Rousseau's writings about the role of collective singing reminds us how useful his philosophical ideas are for understanding the origins of choral singing in modern society and its function. As we shall see, Rousseau's hypothesis resonates strongly with Icelandic men's accounts of singing's power to configure social life and create community.

Superficially, the introduction of male voice choirs in Iceland appears to follow a predictable route. Whilst studying in Denmark between 1837 and 1840, Pétur Guðjónsson witnessed choral singing – in all probability the Copenhagen University Choir – and was so impressed that when he returned to Iceland he introduced singing to the school curriculum at the Lærða skóla (for boys) in Reykjavík, where he was Headmaster. He raised support for the purchase of an organ for the cathedral in Reykjavík and then became its first organist and choirmaster. Whilst this initiative led to the first public concert in Iceland in 1854, predictably given by a male voice choir under Pétur's direction, it was, to begin with, as it had been in Germany, a movement of the educated class in Reykavík – a kind of bourgeoisie. With amazing speed though, male voice choirs sprung up all over Iceland and very quickly it was ordinary, self-educated people in remote rural areas and towns who took possession of a remarkable musical revolution, not just in the area of secular male voice singing, but in church music too. Space precludes a detailed justification for claims about the extraordinary nature of this change, but several points are essential to understanding the level of transformation of musical behaviour that ensued. Grasping contemporary Icelandic musical life, and especially the singing lives of the men we are about to consider, is impossible without some further contextualization.

The first point is that prior to Pétur Guðjónsson's initiative it is fair to say that several centuries of musical development had essentially passed Iceland by. At the height of the Icelandic Commonwealth in the twelfth and thirteenth centuries, Icelandic clergy studied all over Europe. A French priest, Rikini, was even engaged at the Cathedral of Hólar in north Iceland, just south of the arctic-circle, to support a liturgical and musical tradition that was in all probability very similar to that found in European monastic life (Ingólfsson, 2003). As Ingólfsson has illustrated, two-part polyphony, more usually known as "quint-singing" or "tvisöngur", subsequently dominated sacred and secular song in Iceland for 400 years until Guðjónsson's return from Denmark with three- and four-part harmony and classical tonality. Whilst, as Ingólfsson carefully explains, the relationship between the written and oral traditions is complicated and the notion of 400 years of complete isolation is not sustainable, it is clear that a quasi-improvisatory practice of singing in parallel fifths, often converging, crossing and ending again on a fifth, did survive as common everyday practice well into the twentieth century (ibid.).

Another vocal tradition unique to Iceland relates to the Epic song or *kvæðaskapur* and the performance of narrative metrical tales, *or rímur*, whose extant texts date back to the fourteenth century (Steingrímsson, 2000). Subject matter could be pre-existing sagas, romances or novels, and the *rímur* were typically declaimed within a limited melodic range of around a third. Expert kvæðamenn and even ocassional women appeared to enjoy almost professional status and would move from farmstead to farmstead accepting hospitality in return for recitations at the "kvöldvaka" or "evening wake". Typically, the extended family and labourers would be working, mending nets, spinning and sewing, whilst listening to these stories and joining in with the closing notes of phrases or *dillandi* of each verse (ibid.).

Both these traditions were subject to vitriolic condemnation by the emergent educated Reykjavík classes from the middle of the nineteenth century and well into the twentieth century. They were dismissed as unmusical and grotesque noises not worthy of the name song (Ingólfsson, 2003). Others followed Pétur to Europe and especially, since Iceland was still under Danish rule, to Copenhagen. Returning with three and four part vocal and keyboard skills, repertoire, and even harmoniums, they travelled around this sparsely populated and remote country, where the only means of transport was by horse or boat, with a missionary zeal for their new found choral faith. Men's choirs and church choirs (which were increasingly allowed to include women) sprung up everywhere. In the area of north east Iceland where the male voice choir *Hreimur* is located, the first harmonium arrived during the last quarter of the nineteenth century. Yet within 50 years there was a harmonium on nearly every other farm – all of which were over-crowded, pre-industrial, turf farmsteads (Jakobsson & Páll, 1990). In 1880 a men's choir begun rehearsing in Reykjadal in South ingeyarsýslu, initially to sing for church services and replacing the former *tvísöngur* tradition. In many ways this choir is the oldest local forbearer of *Hreimur* itself.

But it was not just new musical styles, repertoire or even classical tonality and form that were brought back from studies in Copenhagen and elsewhere in Europe. Icelandic students, who were primarily the sons of landowners or officials, returned with the seeds of a nationalist revival. Their call for a restoration of Iceland's former glory was part of an emerging pan-Nordic identity in which Icelandic language, sagas and mythology were foundational because of their perceived authenticity. In Iceland meanwhile, the hardships that had been and were continuing to be endured by ordinary Icelanders were, by any standards, extreme; they included natural disasters of extraordinary proportions, bubonic plaques, smallpox epidemics and famine. The population of this remote North Atlantic island had remained fairly constant at around 50,000 since the Middle Ages. The 1783–1784 Láki eruptions – the largest in Europe in modern times – had reduced the population by something like 20%. Indeed, the impact of the Láki eruptions on climate, harvests and health all over Europe are now seen as a contributing factor to the increasing unrest that led to the French Revolution in 1789 (Wood, 1992). Even as Iceland's musical revolution got underway nearly a century later, further eruptions in 1875, and a series of extremely severe winters in the 1860s and 1880s, added to levels of despair that saw widespread migration across the North Atlantic to Canada and the USA. It was against this background that calls for national renewal found cultural expressions – if not really effective political ones.

The importance of literature in the emerging nationalist movement, and of the *Sagas* in particular, cannot be stressed enough. Because of the extremely high levels of literacy that had been maintained amongst the general population, key cultural values were transmitted through the written Icelandic word with its long tradition dating back to the *Sagas*. Alongside this was a strong oral tradition built upon a collective consciousness around the *Sagas*. Ironically then, the emerging vocal and choral styles were modelled upon, if not simply imported wholesale from European romantic traditions. It was these recent imports, or local imitations of them, that facilitated the collective (male) re-iteration of those values and key texts that articulated Icelandic virtues, history and identity.

Political change was a good deal slower than musical change, and although concessions were won, first with the reconstitution of the Icelandic *Alþingi* as a consultative assembly in 1843, it was more than 50 years before Iceland secured home rule, in 1918, and full independence was only achieved in 1944. With full independence, and the influence of Allied occupation during Second World War, came modernization of the Icelandic fishing fleet, and a social and economic revolution of extraordinary proportions. By the 1990s Iceland was consistently ranked among the leading nations in the United Nations indexes for quality of life – configured with measures for education, standards of living, health service, longevity, and so on – and even topping the league table published in 2005 (Watkins, 2005). Three years later, the Global Financial Crisis saw the total collapse of Iceland's only recently privatized banking system, with devastating consequences for the nation's economy, that remain, at the time of writing this chapter, largely unquantifiable.

Returning briefly to nineteenth century Icelandic scholars in Europe, there can be little doubt that they brought back with them a vision of song as a tool for national renewal that clearly echoed Rousseau's ideas about music and the power of collective singing to create empathetic and moral communities. Guðjónsson, and others, like Helgason, were explicit about the power of song to transform family, local and national life. Helgason's (1875–1888) preface to his widely used collection of 4-part songs followed a by now familiar script: Iceland has neglected "singing" for too long and "sowing in this unploughed field" – note the rural analogy – "would ensure Iceland a bright future". The men involved in this vocal revolution believed that they were engaged in a social and political engineering project too – one that would galvanise and mobilise the nation. Whilst there are records of occasional women's choirs and, more often, mixed choirs – usually linked to the church – engaging in public performances, it is quite clear that male voice choirs dominated the public arena, and continued to do so for most of the twentieth century (Björnsdóttir, 2001). Nevertheless, older men in my study made it very clear that the vocal revolution was as much a domestic one as a public one, and in domestic settings very different configuration of gender identity were often at work, as singing *gendered* identities in ways that even contradicted public versions.

With no university in Iceland until 1911, the nationalist movement in Iceland was denied an important building site for the construction of national identity. But other movements like the KFUM (Christian Fellowship for Young People) founded in 1899, the emerging youth movement and sporting associations, along with the brass band movement that led to the founding of community music schools, all mobilized physical activity (especially Icelandic wrestling, athletics and swimming), music, drama and literature, as key agents for national renewal. Indeed, it was through the KFUM, that one of Iceland's oldest surviving and most prestigious male-voice choirs, *Föstbræður*, was founded, going on to make Iceland's first commercial record in 1930. By this time, formal male voice choirs or *karlakór* were a nation-wide phenomenon in Iceland, and the Icelandic Union of Male Voice Choirs had already been established in 1928.

Hreimur has made six long play recordings since it was founded in 1974. Previously, there were several male voice choirs in this part of the country, but as travelling became easier and television begun to impact recreational patterns after its introduction in 1966, numbers declined. At the time of my study (2000–2006) the choir had well over fifty members who came from the fishing and service town of Húsavík, and from surrounding rural communities and hamlets. Typically, members were small-holding sheep and dairy farmers, a wide range of skilled manual craftsmen, lorry drivers, white collar workers at both clerical and managerial levels – including a sales director of a leading international fish processing company and a county director of education – a specialist senior consultant at the local hospital, several students at technical college and retirees. Whilst the men's ages ranged between 18 and 80, the average age was around 50. Some members lived more than 100 kilometres apart and they drove twice a week to rehearsals, usually held between the months of October and May, frequently in difficult winter conditions.

The rest of this chapter turns to contemporary men's experiences of singing in male voice choir – *Hreimur*. The extent to which such singing can properly be called "informal" is debatable: for men in *Hreimur*, singing covers a range of settings along a continuum of formal and informal settings – from highly formalised concerts, to rehearsals, to informal gatherings at members' birthday parties or at other community events. Themes that were central to nineteenth century male voice choir identity still appear to have salience in contemporary settings, so that men's choirs continue to perform dual roles as sites for *glee*ful homo-socialisation on the one hand, and as a site for the construction of national identity on the other. But, as we shall see, members of *Hreimur* configure and present forms of masculinity through contemporary singings and songs that are a good deal more complicated than this: local vocal versions of manhood simultaneously confirm some and contradict other kinds of traditionally accepted male behaviours and the meanings that are made of them.

Having secured Icelandic independence more than 50 years ago, the expression of nationalist sentiment might have been expected to dwindle. This is not the case however: a large proportion of the male voice choir repertoire continues to be made up of the romantic music written for it in the first half of the twentieth century. The following translated extract is one of the most commonly performed examples of this kind of repertoire, with its portrayal of nature, so central to Icelandic identity, and an emphasis on Icelandic traits of industriousness (especially in farming, but not, interestingly, in fishing) and resilience, and a strong romanticisation of the former glories of the Icelandic commonwealth:

> From the ocean rise Iceland's peaks
> With fire in its heart, . . .
> We speak the Icelandic language,
> Honour God, the nations soul,
> And our ancient forefathers . . .
>
> As long as the sun rises,
> The moon silvers the glacier,
> And honour is esteemed,
> Shall the people cultivate the land
> And the flag fly . . . over Icelandic settlements.

It is ironic that farming communities and images of an Icelandic rural idyll were privileged over fishing communities in the construction of Icelandic nationalist identity (Durrenberger & Pálsson, 1989). Whilst it had traditionally been farmers that were seen as the keepers of authentic Icelandic ideals and protectors of its literature, it was the export of fish and the endeavours of fisherman on the perilous North Atlantic and Arctic oceans that bought the remarkable transformation of economic and social life. *Hreimur* does sing some repertoire associated with the sea and fishing – typically these are lively so-called "fisherman's waltzes" with harmonica accompaniment that relate to the mixed sex social life, and particularly to dances or balls, associated with the various "herring adventures" of the twentieth century, and especially to those of the late 1950s and 1960s that some of the men in *Hreimur* would have experienced. Unlike most other male voice repertoire, these songs may be explicitly concerned with heterosexual themes as men anticipate returning to harbour after successful and often long fishing trips and going to a celebratory ball,

14 Icelandic Men, Male Voice Choirs and Masculine Identity

where, according to one popular example frequently sung by *Hreimur* – *Síldarvalsin* or "*Herring Waltz*" – the "local girls will be plentiful and captivating".

Whilst the songs *Hreimur* sings are not often so explicitly concerned with heterosexual relationships, there is a long history of men's singing being seen as having potential as aesthetic sexual display. Indeed, in the thirteenth century book of law (Grágás, 1980), men were actually prohibited from singing to another man's wife. The popularity of male voice choirs – although it has undoubtedly diminished over recent decades – still depends extensively on women's support. And whilst, as in a good many men's clubs, the men's partners may be particularly supportive in all kinds of roles, many women in the community claim to enjoy listening to male voice choirs especially. As one of the men says, with some justification:

> I know lots of women ... they just want to listen to men's voices, to male voice choir recordings. They never want to listen to a women's choir or even a mixed choir, men's voices that's what they want to listen to, go absolutely mad

Men only clubs are frequently theorised as places where men objectify women and their sexual display. If this is true of male voice choirs in Iceland, then it is more likely to be true in non-sexual madonna-like terms through the construction and representation of an Icelandic mountain women figure, rather like the Swedish *Moder Svea* or Finish *Suomi neito*. This symbolic figure of nature and the maternal – *fjallkonan* – who gives birth to Icelanders, was created (by men) as a national personification. She first appears as an idea in a poem by Eggert Ólafsson, son of a farmer and former student at Copenhagen University, in the middle of the eighteenth century and, subsequently, she appears in nationalist poetry throughout the nineteenth century. I have written elsewhere about repertoire relating to this *fjallkonan* figure and its relationship to the objectifying of motherhood in songs sung by *Hreimur*, both in formal concert and at informal events to thank partners for their support, in honour of women collectively, or of an individual woman on, say, her birthday (Faulkner, 2006). Whilst clearly, as artists' impressions of the *fjallkonan* illustrate, this image is about the display of women, the image is concerned with qualities of resilience, tirelessness, courage, beauty and devotion and there is no sense of sexual display or availability.

Songs that *Hreimur* sing in honour of this version of femininity are popular with men in the choir and audiences alike. It is probably no coincidence that they share expressive qualities with a good deal of repertoire that is concerned with the representation of Icelandic nature – not the typically violent volcanoes or desolate black deserts and glaciers for which Iceland is famous – but of a less dramatic, romantic rural idyll of green pastures and woodland, sparkling springs and waterfalls from mountain sides. Typically, these are qualities not much in evidence except for a short-lived summer season where, this far north, the sun does not set for 2 months. What I have in mind here are songs, always sung a capella, that are typified by soft, often relatively slow moving and sustained 4-part harmony. One of the most popular is typical of the appropriation of German repertoire mentioned earlier. The original German poem, in particular the high German version (*Ännchen von Tharau*) by Herder, is a love song of devotion and passion, and widely sung by German male voice choirs following Silcher's composition of a new song to it in 1827. In contrast, the Icelandic poem sung to Silcher's song, written by Guðmundur Guðmundsson around the turn of the twentieth century, is a text in praise of an Icelandic rural idyll:

> The evening's gentle breezes
> Kiss every pasture.
> Summer has arrived
> And the countryside is warm
>
> The sun bids farewell
> Behind the blue mountain ridge,
> And smiling in its reflection
> Are beautiful green meadows.
>
> Tell me what wonderful sights
> Your eye seeks
> On this Icelandic evening
> In the beautiful countryside.

Men in *Hreimur* consistently say that it is songs like this that provide peak aesthetic experiences (Faulkner & Davidson, 2004).

> Take The Evening's Gentle Breezes: we have to sing it in a richly loving way, gentle and beautiful. Yeah, I think that's it, that softer side. To be in control of such a beautiful song, when you can feel that every note feels pure and clean. It can be sung so magically beautifully by a male-voice choir. It's among the most beautiful things you hear. And you're singing together and some bell starts ringing!

> that feeling for singing in harmony ... this sound, the harmony you land inside of ... pulled along in the sound

> You feel much better in harmony with others. Then you get that kick. That's how it is supposed to be

The embodied experience of "being *in* harmony" suggests that singing like this configures a special kind of community and a special kind of relating and communicating: it provides a unique balance of Self-to-other ratio, not just in musical and vocal terms (see Ternstrom & Karna, 2002) but in social, physical and psychological ones too. This is surely an example of what Rousseau meant by singing's potential to create community by arousing a sense of connectedness that is moral and empathetic (Simon, 2004). As one of the men explains:

> The men's choir is quite unique I think; it is a remarkably sympathetic and unified group ... really, really close knit and cohesive

It seems no coincidence therefore, that given the opportunity, whether at informal gatherings, in intervals at dances and so on, these men will organise impromptu singing sessions where traditional male codes of permissible physical proximity are compounded by touching, hugging, close eye contact and even the touching of faces. It is indisputable that alcohol may play some role here, but it is not by any means a perquisite to this kind of intimate song-making.

This is not to deny that men in *Hreimur* enjoy singing songs that conform more closely to "hard and heavy" versions of masculine and national identities. Soldier's choruses by Verdi and Gounod, Wagner's *Sailor's Chorus* from *The Flying Dutchman,* and *Men of Harlech* have all been sung by *Hreimur.* There are Scandinavian versions too, like Grieg's epic *Landkjending,* Cantat for Male Voice Choir and Orchestra Op 31 (*Sighting Land*) which *Hreimur* has sung with full orchestral accompaniment, and Icelandic equivalents exists in the form of songs like *Úr útsæ rísa íslandsfjöll* mentioned earlier, and, more explicitly, in works for male voice choir like Pall Ísólfsson's (a student of Max Reger) *Brennið þið vitar* (*Light the Watchtowers*) – again with full orchestral accompaniment. Interestingly, and perhaps even uniquely, Iceland has no armed forces. Its struggle for independence was a peaceful one and significantly there is no obvious sign of resentment towards the Danes, their former colonial rulers, as, say, in the case of Finland towards Russia.

It would be untrue to say that violence is non-existent in this society, but in the communities where *Hreimur* is based, it is rare, and normally takes the form of an occasional drunken brawl after a ball. Nevertheless, there are still elements of competition in local vocal events – either in rehearsals, where voices (Tenor 1; Tenor 2; Bass 1; Bass 2) engage in banter about the relative merits of other voice-groups, or in informal settings where alcohol aided competitions for singing the highest and loudest are not uncommon (Faulkner & Davidson, 2006). But these competitions afford only passing status and all kinds of strategies are used to keep individual men from assuming permanent positions of power. Whether they are soloists in the choir, the conductor himself, or just individuals who have given the impression of superiority, other choir members will use quickly composed humorous rimes to remind those individuals of a social and personal equilibrium that is demanded of all. Such balance comes from a strong sense of equality and a widespread belief in the specialness of all Icelanders (Durrenberger, 1996) that frowns upon the idea that individuals have the right to think of themselves as more special than others. In choral singing for example, an individual's first responsibility is about blending and not being at all noticeable as an individual, but contributing to the whole.

It is also noticeable that there is a total absence of the kinds of competitive singing events that are integral, say, to barber shop traditions in the US (Stebbins, 1996), nightsong, or *isicathamiya* in South Africa (Erlmann, 1996), or the *Eisteddfod* traditions of Wales and Australia. In Iceland, choirs will often visit each other and even hold large choral festivals: men's choirs are no exception. On the contrary, men's choirs frequently provide hospitality (with very significant help from their partners) for their "söngbræður" or "song brothers" – male voice choirs from other parts of the country. There will be an element of rivalry in these meetings, both in terms of singing at concerts themselves, but also in the social events that nearly always follow and in the use of rimes as humorous sparring matches. Local identity will become key in such contexts (Faulkner & Davidson, 2006) and, in fact, the male voice choir *Hreimur* sees itself as representing the local county and being an important element in its collective identity, as other male voice choirs do in Iceland in other regions.

The county of *Thingeyjarsýslu,* where *Hreimur* is located, produced several important writers in the romantic and nationalist movement, both in terms of political discourse and poetic literature. It was also the site of the first farmers' co-operative movement in Iceland, founded in 1882, which helped to break trade monopolies and establish a different economic foundation for agriculture. Such developments may well have had some significance for other local cultural practices. Local poets and composers, including past and present members of *Hreimur* have provided and continue to provide repertoire portraying local natural landmarks that have been sung into local personal and social identities. Reflecting the high level of cultural participation, not just in singing, but in other musical activities, the visual arts, and drama in particular, no special qualifications are deemed necessary to compose songs or poetry. Two local figures did however pursue composition studies overseas – in the 1940s *Árni Björnsson* studied composition at the Royal Northern College of Music in the UK, and much more recently *Örlygur Benediktsson* studied composition at St. Petersburg Conservatorium where he composed one of the most challenging pieces that *Hreimur* has sung to date. Indeed, that task may have proved too much for the choir had it not been that the composer was a *Thingeyinga*, the son of one of the present members of *Hreimur,* and former pupil of its conductor – me. Ownership and relatedness clearly matter hugely in questions of motivation and identity. *Thingeyinga* are renowned for a strong sense of independence and, stereotypically, they are even accused by other Icelanders of being immodest. It is not a view I have held, and men's intolerance of immodesty within the group challenges this assessment. Even the best singers in the choir, and there are several of outstanding ability, are not immune from the expectation to put the group before self-interest, nor from barbed verbal reprisals should they fail to do so.

This light-hearted ethos is typical of many of *Hreimur*'s rehearsals and social events. Whilst there is no doubting their serious intent to sing as best they possibly can, and the great lengths they go to in pursuit of high vocal and choral standards, humour is a strong element of social interaction. Light-hearted songs or glees themselves are not in abundance in *Hreimur*'s concert repertoire though there is, for example, a fairly extensive collection of Carl Michael Bellman's Swedish drinking songs and parodies in popular local usage. Unlike much of the imported song repertoire, these are direct translations from Bellman's renowned and often explicit lyrics. Interestingly though, these are far more likely to be heard at hetero-social community events, like the annual Midwinter feast or orrablót or at *Hreimur*'s social events, than in any formal music setting.

Men's jokes and verbal sparring are often seen as typical of men only clubs (Fine, 1987) and the rimes that men in the choir regularly compose can easily be seen as falling into this kind of "matey" homo-social behaviour. Nevertheless, the jokes tend not to be sexually explicit. It is possible that two factors may have regulated behaviour: firstly, wives or partners usually accompany men on major tours, and, secondly, the choir's accompanist and assistant conductor has often been a woman. Her role, and more especially men's view of it, is, I have suggested, closely associated with ideals about the *fjallkonan* or *mountain woman* outlined above, that precludes over-stepping certain moral boundaries (Faulkner, 2006).

Hreimur has a large European network of *"söngbræður"*, having toured widely and given concerts in Finland, Norway, Germany, Switzerland, Austria, Italy, England and the Faroe Islands. This follows a long standing tradition of Icelandic Male Voice choirs as foreign ambassadors that started early in the twentieth century with tours to both Scandinavia and the USA. Early accounts of those tours, which were normally men only affairs, are explicit about the semi-official envoy status that male-voice choirs assumed (Björnsdóttir, 2001). Even though nearly a 100 years has passed since those first trips, and *Hreimur* has always encouraged partners and wives to join them on overseas tours, there is still a very strong sense of being representatives of *Iceland*. It is not uncommon for Icelandic cultural attachés, consuls and even ambassadors in respective countries and cities, to support these tours and attend concerts. At such overseas concerts, the partners or wives of *Hreimur*'s members typically attend in Icelandic national costume and the choice of repertoire has distinctive patterns that are significant for discussion here.

When I arrived in this location, I was shocked to discover that resistance to the older Icelandic vocal traditions, discussed earlier, was fierce and widespread. At the time I was ignorant of the context, but quickly came to appreciate that the legacy of late nineteenth century and early twentieth century cultural cleansing was still impacting musical tastes and values: nowhere was this more so than in relation to "quint" and "epic" song. "Quint singing" in particular seems to have been associated with former poverty-filled times. Whilst *Hreimur*'s members were resistant to singing in any language other than Icelandic, even though most Icelanders today typically learn two or even three foreign languages, the same conservatism could not be said about the music itself. There was no compunction about singing a wide range of imported music and musical styles alongside the copious amounts of Icelandic romantic repertoire that was composed in the early twentieth century, or more popular music that had arrived and flourished in Iceland since the Second World War.

Even though Danish, traditionally Iceland's second language, was the language of access to university education and official administrative positions, it seems that it was never a language of song. With the exception of a couple of Danish drinking songs, few Danish songs are sung locally. Even globalisation and popular culture, which has seen English recently replace Danish as Iceland's first foreign language, has failed to challenge the assumption that Icelandic men should sing in Icelandic. Coincidentally or not, it is interesting that whilst international female artists *Björk* and *Emiliana Torrini* have both embraced English, the all-male band *Sigur rós* has enjoyed huge international success whilst continuing to sing mainly in Icelandic or in an invented language for their title-less album known as ( ).

That I have influenced musical taste here is undeniable. The tradition of including two or three idiosyncratic Icelandic "quint-songs" in programmes for overseas tour or for guests, especially dignitaries or visiting male voice choirs from overseas, is nevertheless, clearly recognisable in Icelandic Male Voice choir traditions earlier in the twentieth century long before my arrival. *Hreimur* have adopted this practice too, though in the case of some individuals, this was a begrudging concession only made, I suspect, as a courtesy to me following my insistence that this particular genre was of unique cultural and musical value. In the area of language too, changes have occurred, so whilst Icelandic is still absolutely the language of everyday song here – even popular song – the choir has broadened its repertoire to include occasional songs in Italian, German, Latin, Finish, Maori and English. Nevertheless, translating foreign texts is still a popular pastime for several members of the choir, so that songs by Poulenc and Schubert, from Estonia and Canada, and many others, have been subject to the same kind of local appropriation that has been typical of the Icelandic male voice movement since its inception.

A striking feature of discussions with men in *Hreimur* was their ability to articulate the key role that singing in the choir and in everyday settings at work and home, alone or in the company of others, played in self-regulation. These findings emerged at the same time as Tia DeNora (2000, 2003) was writing about music's everyday function and theorising about the changes that musical events effect, by developing Adorno's seminal work on music's potential as an agent for change. The men in my study reported in their diaries, and in extensive interviews, detailed accounts of a wide range of vocal events where singing is clearly seen as an agent of change and purposefully applied to facilitate it. There are a multitude of purposeful song changing possibilities: entraining the body and mind to physical tasks; creating special kinds of social and psychological networks and connectedness at micro family levels and macro community ones; helping identify self in the environment; and facilitating catharsis from life's minor stresses and anxieties, to much more catastrophic and live changing events. Men talk about "singing themselves away from anxieties", "sedating" themselves and others:

> ... soothing other people, influencing other people, that's incredible influence that that person has.

In this sense men *art*fully employ singing as a kind of self-therapy. As one of them memorably remarked when reflecting upon the tragic death of his brother many years ago:

> There was no sort of help in those days in that sort of crisis, so, so you just sang. And like with x who commited suicide just last year. Singing still works!

Connell's argument that individuals construct and perform a range of masculine identities or masculinities that are dynamic and fluid, and may be anything but consistent (Connell, 1995), finds resonance in this account of male voice choirs – in particular of their development and present agency in the lives of contemporary Icelandic men. The constructs of this particular kind of vocal behaviour are diverse indeed: remnants of the pan-European nationalist movement; Rousseau philosophy and political thinking; an Icelandic renaissance; a long struggle for independence; a new political, social and economic order; dominance of public vocal space; the love of singing soft and gentle songs in 4-part harmony; close, even tender physical proximity; an idealised – but certainly not sexualized – vision of women; and a clear and deliberate practice of self-therapy and everyday regulation through the taking of vocal action. It is hard to reconcile such diversity in a consistent idea of masculine identity. In examining briefly the roots of the male voice choir movement in Europe and the specific Icelandic experience in historical and present day settings, it is clear that singing has gendered identities that conform much more closely to the plural and fluid masculinities of which Connell speaks than to any notion of ahistorical maleness. This is not to deny that elements of hegemonic masculinity are alive in some of the vocal displays reported here, but it is to argue for multi-perspectival views of phenomena like masculine identity and song in authentic contexts, which is the ambitious aim of this book as a whole.

A deeper study of these Icelandic men's vocal lives reveals an astonishing richness of musical experience that is configured by a wide range of songs, styles and musical behaviours that do all kinds of gendering and identifying work at individual and collective levels. Following on from Butler's seminal notion of gender's performativity (Butler, 1999), Connell illustrates how it is the values and meanings ascribed to repeated actions that configure masculine identity (Connell, 1995). For these Icelandic men, singing is one of those repeated actions, and in the Icelandic context, the repetition of some of those actions for over 100 years has ascribed very specific values and meanings to them. Meanings, values and beliefs about male identity are *en*songed as it were. Nevertheless, the stories of male voice choirs in Europe and Iceland, and the stories of *Hreimur*, and of individuals in it, have clearly shown that those meanings and values are open to renegotiation and reconfiguration.

Whilst the first public performance of the men's choir in Reykjavík in 1854 marked a significant vocal re-gendering that set a pattern for establishing some core constructs of collective public masculine identity in Iceland, singing always has the potential to confirm this configuration or challenge it. New songs, or news ways of singing may make that reconfiguration of identity more dramatic, as they did in Iceland in the nineteenth century, but every repeated singing – in formal concerts or in private settings – has the potential to effect change in individual or collective identities. Singing's engendering power, like singing itself, is dynamic, fluid and temporal, even when performances become traditional enough, through their repeated performance, to give the appearance of permanence. The illusion that comes from this process of *traditionalisation* and naturalization is possible by virtual of encores of a limited performance repertoire or genres where participants are complicit in denying the possibility of transformation or translation of meaning. We have seen how this is true in some of the practices that male voice choirs have typically engaged in, but we have seen too how transformation has occurred. Artifacts themselves – songs – may remain unchanged for generations, even centuries, but their social practice and gendered meaning may undergo transformation and translation. Similarly then, masculine identities are always contextual and provisional: they are tied to meanings about specific practices in specific times and locations. The meaning that is made of men's singing practices in contemporary northern Iceland – by the men themselves, by the local community, by national and international audiences, and by me – confirm the possibility of a wide ranging repertoire of masculinities and illustrate singing's role in the performance of complex and even contradictory forms of it.

References

Adelaide Leidertafel 1858. (2002). *A history of the Adelaider Liedertafel 1858*. Retrieved February 17, 2010, from http://www.alt1858.org/index.htm

Adorno, T. W. (1976). *Introduction to the sociology of music* (E. B. Ashton, Trans.). New York: Continuum.

Björnsdóttir, I. D. (2001). Hin karlmannlega raust og hinn hljóðláti máttur kvenna: Upphaf kórsöngs á Íslandi. *Saga, 39*, 7–50.

Bly, R. 1990. *Iron John: A book about men*. Reading, MA: Addison-Wesley.

Butler, J. P. (1999). *Gender trouble: Feminism and the subversion of identity*. New York: Routledge.

Connell, R. W. (1995). *Masculinities*. Cambridge: Polity Press.

DeNora, T. (2000). *Music in everyday life*. Cambridge: Cambridge University Press.

DeNora, T. (2003). *After Adorno: Rethinking music sociology*. Cambridge: Cambridge University Press.

Durrenberger, E. P. (1996). Every Icelander a special case. In G. Pálsson & E. P. Durrenberger (Eds.), *Images of contemporary Iceland: Everyday lives and global contexts* (pp. 171–190). Iowa City, IA: University of Iowa Press.

Durrenberger, E. P., & Pálsson, G. (1989). Forms of production and fishing expertise. In G. Pálsson & E. P. Durrenberger (Eds.), *Images of contemporary Iceland: Everyday lives and global contexts* (pp. 3–18). Iowa City, IA: University of Iowa Press.

Erlmann, V. (1996). *Nightsong: Performance, power and practice in South Africa*. Chicago: University of Chicago Press.

Faulkner, R. (2006). *The vocal construction of self: Icelandic men and singing in everyday life*. Unpublished Doctoral dissertation, University of Sheffield, UK.

Faulkner, R., & Davidson, J. W. (2004). Men's vocal behaviour and the construction of self. *Musicae Scientiae: The Journal of the European Society for the Cognitive Sciences of Music, 8*(2), 231–255.

Faulkner, R., & Davidson, J. W. (2006). Men in chorus: Collaboration and competition in homosocial vocal behaviour. *Psychology of Music, 34*(2), 219–237.

Fine, G. A. (1987). One of the boys: Women in male-dominated settings. In M. Kimmel (Ed.), *Changing men: New directions in research on men and masculinity* (pp. 131–147). Newbury Park: Sage.

Grágás. (1980). *The Codex Regius of Grágás with material from other manuscripts* (Vol. 1) (A. Dennis, P. Foote, & R. Perkins, Trans.). Winnipeg: University of Manitoba.

Hall, C. (2005). Gender and boys' singing in early childhood. *British Journal of Music Education, 22*(1), 5–20.

Helgason, J. (1875–1888). *Söngvar og kvæði* (Hörpuheftin). Reykjavík, Söngfélagid Harpa and Jónas Helgason.

Ingólfsson, Á. H. (2003). *"These are the things you never forget": The written and aural traditions of Icelandic Tvísöngur*. Unpublished doctoral dissertation, Harvard University, Cambridge, MA. UMI 3091584.

Jakobsson, G., & Páll, H. J. (1990). *Fiðlur og tónmannlíf í Suður-ingeyjarsýslu*. Reykjavík: Jakobsson and Jónsson.

James, W. (1890). *Principles of psychology* (2 Vols.). New York: Henry Holt and Co.

Kimmel, M. S., & Kaufman, M. (1994). Weekend warriors: The new men's movement. In H. Brod & M. Kaufman (Eds.), *Theorizing masculinities* (pp. 259–288). Thousand Oaks, CA: Sage.

Simon, J. (2004) Singing democracy: Music and politics in Jean-Jacques Rousseau's thought. *Journal of the History of Ideas, 65*(3), 433–454.

Smith, J. A., & Osborn, M. (2003). Interpretative phenomenological analysis. In J. A. Smith (Ed.), *Qualitative psychology* (pp. 51–80). London: Sage.

Smith, J. G., & Young, P. M. (2010). Chorus (i). In *Grove Music Online*. Resource document. Oxford Music. Retrieved February 27, 2010, from http://www.oxfordmusiconline.com:80/subscriber/article/grove/music/05684

Stebbins, R. A. (1996). *The Barbershop singer: Inside the social world of a musical hobby.* Toronto and Buffalo: University of Toronto Press.

Steingrímsson, H. (2000). Kvæðaskapur (Icelandic epic song]. In D. Stone & S. L. Mosko (Eds.). Reykjavík: Mál og mynd. Retrieved October 15, 2011, from www.music.calarts.edu/KVAEDASKAPUR/Chapter%20V.html

Ternstrom, S., & Karna, D. R. (2002). Choir singing. In R. Parncutt & G. E. McPherson (Eds.), *The science and psychology of music performance: Creative strategies for teaching and learning* (pp. 269–284). New York and Oxford: Oxford University Press.

Watkins, K. (2005). *Human development report 2005*. New York: United Nations Development Program.

Wood, C. A. (1992). The climatic effects of the 1783 Laki eruption. In C. R. Harrington (Ed.), *The year without a summer?* (pp. 58–77). Ottawa, ON: Canadian Museum of Nature.

Chapter 15
Singing, Wellbeing and Gender

Choristers in Australia, England and Germany

Stephen Clift, Grenville Hancox, and Ian Morrison

15.1 Introduction

Singing in community groups, choirs and choral societies is one of the most widespread forms of active musical participation in many Western societies (Chorus America, 2009), although the picture does vary from country to country. Durrant and Himonides suggest for example, that in Greece 'the whole concept of community singing is culturally foreign' (1998, p. 61). Nevertheless, throughout the world, enormous numbers of people regularly come together to sing, motivated primarily by a love of music and the expressive activity of singing itself. Singing together is a social and creative activity, which has intrinsic value and rewards for those who participate and for audiences too. While active participation in instrumental music requires both talent and substantial dedication, singing as a form of music-making is open to everyone, giving amateur singers access, with skilled guidance, to the pinnacles of choral music in the Western classical tradition. This is illustrated very well by the BBC Radio 3 and English National Opera's 2009 'Sing Hallelujah' project which invited choirs to sing the Hallelujah Chorus during November or December that year. From across the UK, 450 choirs registered with the project, and some of them can be heard in a short compilation film (BBC, 2009, Search 'Sing Hallelujah'). The range of songs available for groups to sing extends well beyond the classical repertoire of course. Before Christmas 2009, a guest editor on the BBC Radio Four 'Today' programme, asked choirs to send in recordings of a favourite piece. The BBC was 'inundated' with all kinds of music from choirs across the country, and the samples can be heard through their map of the 'United Kingdom in song' (BBC, 2010, Search 'United Kingdom in Song').

Beyond the intrinsic value and pleasure attached to singing is there any evidence for real and measurable impacts on the health and wellbeing of those participating?

S. Clift (✉)
Sidney De Haan Research Centre for Arts and Health, Canterbury Christ Church University, Canterbury, Kent, UK
e-mail: s.clift@btinternet.com

Could indeed, there be risks for health and wellbeing attached to this activity? Since the early 1990s the questions of health benefits associated with singing, and the role of singing as a form of music therapy for people with compromised health, have attracted increasing attention internationally. Clift, Hancox, Staricoff, and Whitmore (2008) report a systematic mapping and review of research on singing, wellbeing and health, focusing on non-clinical research (i.e. excluding music therapy). Clift, Nicol, Raisbeck, and Morrison (2010) have updated this review focusing specifically on studies of group or choral singing, and extending the scope to include music therapeutic interventions for specific health conditions. These reviews are drawn upon here to provide a selective and critical overview of research studies on the possible benefits of group singing for men and women.

The need to be critical is highlighted by the many unsubstantiated claims about singing and health made in newspaper reports and postings on the web, and by eminent musicians and distinguished academics. Thomas (2010) claims that singing can prevent colds and flu, and Pomfret (2009) states that singing leads to endorphin release. The UK Singing Ambassador, Howard Goodall, suggests that singing can help childhood asthma (Dougary, 2007) and Levitin (2008) claims that oxytocin is released when people sing together, giving rise to feelings of 'group spirit.' Unfortunately, however, none of these claims is supported by a robust body of research.

This chapter begins with an overview of studies involving existing community choirs and singing groups or which have established singing groups for purposes of research. It will be shown that a significant limitation of the existing corpus of work is a lack of attention to gender as a possible factor relevant to the experience of singing and its perceived relevance for wellbeing. The chapter will then present an outline of a cross-national study involving experienced choristers in Australia, England and Germany, which explored systematically gender differences in the perceptions of the influence of choral singing to subjective wellbeing and health.

15.2 Research on Singing, Wellbeing and Health

Drawing on the work of Clift, Hancox, Staricoff et al. (2008) and Clift, Nicol, Raisbeck et al. (2010), Table 15.1 reports the existing corpus of research on the potential value of group singing for wellbeing and health published since 1985. Information is given on the country in which the study was undertaken, date of publication, principal objectives pursued, the character of the group and setting investigated, the methods used and the main conclusions drawn. Twenty-three sources were located through a systematic search strategy, reporting twenty-two distinct studies. Most of these studies were undertaken in English-speaking or Nordic countries, and with only one exception (Wise, Hartmann, & Fisher, 1992), all have appeared since 2001. Some of the research is focused on 'traditional' choirs and choral societies (e.g. Ashley, 2005; Beck, Cesari, Yousefi, & Enamoto, 2000; Latimer, 2008; Sandgren, 2009); others evaluate groups established in particular

15 Singing, Wellbeing and Gender

Table 15.1 Studies considering the effects of amateur group singing on well-being (community singing groups, groups established in special settings and groups set up for research purposes)

Source	Objectives	Context	Sample	Method	Findings
Ashley 2005 England	Explores experiences of singing	Choir of a major city centre church	18m Ages: 10–14	Ethnographic case study, participant observation, diaries, interviews, thematic analysis	Personal wellbeing, self-esteem, sense of meaning, purpose and empowerment in the context of macho gender stereotypes
Bailey 2002, 2005 Canada	Explores experiences and benefits of singing	Choir established with homeless men, choir in disadvantage community, traditional choirs in affluent communities	Homeless 7m Ages: 45–62 Disadvantaged 3f, 5m Ages: 43–64 Affluent 7f, 1m Ages: 24–59	Interviews and group discussion, thematic analysis	Emotional effects of singing similar irrespective of training and social status: energy, relaxation, emotional release, joy. Themes of cognitive stimulation, group participation and audience reaction relevant to both marginalised and middle class singers, but have different meanings
Bailey 2003 Canada	Assesses experiences of singing, listening to music with others and listening alone	Participants recruited from three choirs	165f, 47m Mean age: 49	Questionnaire to assess five holistic health effects of music in different contexts	Singing given higher ratings than listening for: improves mood, exhilarating activity, achievement, creative and gives a high

Table 15.1 (continued)

Source	Objectives	Context	Sample	Method	Findings
Beck 2000 USA	Effects of singing on IgA and cortisol levels in saliva	Professional choir, two evening rehearsals and one performance of Beethoven's *Missa Solemnis*	23f, 18m Ages: 25–62	Non-controlled pre-post singing assessments of sIgA and cortisol	sIgA increased during rehearsals and performance; emotional experience during performance predicted sIgA increase. Cortisol decreased in rehearsal and increased in performance
Clift 2001 England	Explores perceptions of the effects of singing	University choral society, student, staff and community members	Qualitative study 84 Questionnaire 74f, 16m Ages: 18–69	Qualitative study, written answers to questions on benefits of singing, content analysis. Questionnaire based on qualitative study. Factor analysis to identify components	In the qualitative study, 84% identified possible health benefits: lung function, breathing, improved mood, stress relief. Majority identified social and emotional benefits from singing. Six components identified from survey: wellbeing and relaxation, breathing and posture, social benefits, spiritual benefits, emotional benefits, effects on heart and immune function. Women expressed greater wellbeing benefits.

Table 15.1 (continued)

Source	Objectives	Context	Sample	Method	Findings
Cohen G 2006 USA	Effects of singing on health, social activities and service utilisation	30 professionally led singing workshops and 10 performances over 1 year	Intervention 70f, 20m Mean age: 79 Control 61f, 15m Mean age: 80	Non-randomised controlled study. Intervention and control groups comparable at baseline. Baseline and 1 year assessments using a battery of measures	Intervention group had higher ratings of health, fewer doctor visits, less medication use, fewer falls and health problems, than control group
Cohen, G 2007 USA	Effects of singing on measures of health, social activities and service utilisation	30 professionally led singing workshops and 10 performances over 2 years	Intervention 56f, 12m Mean age: 80 Control 42f, 18m Mean age: 81	Non-randomised controlled study. Intervention and control groups comparable at baseline. Baseline, 1 and 2 year assessments using a battery of measures	Intervention group had fewer health problems and less use of medication than control group. Overall, singing group showed trends towards better health and controls
Cohen, M. 2007 USA	Explores experiences of singing	A joint inmate-community volunteer choir in a minimum security male prison	Inmates 20m Ages: 21–53 Volunteers 24m Ages: 35–82	Questionnaire, participant observation, interviews, use of documentary material, grounded theory based analysis	Social bonds and working cooperatively; joy and peak experiences; sense of achievement, pride, broadened perspectives and increased self-worth. Some evidence of frustration and sadness.
Cohen M 2009 USA Study 1	Effects of singing performance and listening to singing on well-being	Male prison inmate choir performing inside the prison, control inmate group listening to the performance	Intervention 10m Ages: 23–60 Control 10m Ages: 22–44	Non-randomised controlled study. Well-being measure completed before and after performance	Increase in well-being for both groups. No difference in change between singing and listening control group

Table 15.1 (continued)

Source	Objectives	Context	Sample	Method	Findings
Cohen M 2009 USA Study 2	Effects of singing performance and listening to singing on well-being	Male prison inmate and volunteer choir performing outside the prison, control inmate group did not attend the performance	Intervention Choir inmates 23m Ages: 19–60 Choir volunteers 25m Ages: 23–78 Control Inmates 10m Ages: 22–44	Non-randomised controlled study. FWell-being measure completed before and after performance by singing group. Completed by control group on same day	Increase in well-being for the singing group. No change for the control group
Hillman 2002 Scotland	Explores the perceived effects of singing on quality of life and wellbeing	Community choir for people in retirement	60f, 15m	Questionnaire assessing quality of life, health and wellbeing before joining the choir and at time of survey	Improvements to general quality of life, emotional wellbeing and understanding of singing. Value of singing for coping with bereavement, maintaining physical health and wider social engagement
Jacob 2009 Canada	Explores reasons for singing and perceived effects	Non-auditioned university choir,	9 Ages: 18–25	Semi-structured interviews, thematic analysis	Community and social bonding, personal and group achievement, stress relief, improved mood

15 Singing, Wellbeing and Gender 239

Table 15.1 (continued)

Source	Objectives	Context	Sample	Method	Findings
Kreutz 2004 Germany	Effects of singing and listening to singing on mood, IgA and cortisol in saliva	Amateur choir, rehearsal of Mozart *Requiem*	23f, 8m Ages: 29–74	Experimental study, singers acting as own controls in listening condition. Pre-post measures of mood, sIgA and cortisol	Positive mood increased after singing but not listening. Negative mood decreased after singing but increased after listening. sIgA increased after singing but not listening. No change in cortisol with singing, but decreased with listening
Lally 2009 Australia	Assesses effects of a singing workshop on wellbeing	30-week singing workshop for older people	26 Ages: 51–83	Participant observation, focus groups, questionnaires, interviews, case studies, thematic analysis	Perceived improvements in physical fitness, flexibility and stretching, improved mood, relaxation and self esteem, improved social wellbeing, sense of group solidarity, improved singing voice and confidence, feeling more creative
Latimer 2008 USA	Explores the role of singing in gay identity and wellbeing	A gay men's chorus	Questionnaire 87m Ages: 41–45 Qualitative study 30m	Survey followed by 2-year participant observation study, interviews, documentary material, Interpretative phenomenological analysis	Reasons for participation: Enjoyment, socialising, feelings of community, enhanced self-esteem, supporting coming out. Singing supported a positive gay identity

Table 15.1 (continued)

Source	Objectives	Context	Sample	Method	Findings
Louhivuori 2005 Finland and South Africa	Assesses contribution of singing to social capital	Community choirs, church choirs, youth choirs and senior choirs	500+	Questionnaire on motivations, relationships and communication in the choir, impacts of choir membership	Satisfaction of individual and social needs, building of social networks and feelings of community, friendships, emotional benefits, self confidence
Rohwer 2009 USA	Explores perceptions of singing	Two high school choirs	42f, 15m	Written accounts of the choral singing experience	Friendship and social support, musical development, effort and achievement, life enhancing and life changing
Sandgren 2009 Sweden	Effects of singing on well-being for men and women	Participants recruited from 11 choirs in the Stockholm area	152f, 60m Ages: 19–90	Uncontrolled single group study with assessment of emotional states before and after a regular rehearsal	Greater increases in positive emotional states for women than men: alert, proud, content, satisfied and glad. No differences for changes in negative emotional states
Silber 2005 Israel	Explores links between choral processes and the needs of women prisoners	Women's prison choir	7f Ages: 17–35	Ethnography, participant observation, video, interviews, discussions with staff	Increased sensitivity to others, cubing aggression, enhancing trust, group support, self-control, empowerment, self esteem, all linked to processes on three levels in the choir

15 Singing, Wellbeing and Gender 241

Table 15.1 (continued)

Source	Objectives	Context	Sample	Method	Findings
Soutcott 2009 Australia	Explores experiences of singing	Choir of older people that performs for care home residents	8f, 2m	Phenomenological study, discussion, interviews, documentary material, interpretative analysis	Enhanced sense of purpose and meaning, positive social relationships, personal growth, service to the community
Tonneijek 2008 The Netherlands	Explores experiences of singing	Amateur choir	4f, 2m Ages: 45–58	Participant observation during rehearsals, interviews, interpretative analysis	Personal growth and purpose, sense of wholeness, unity with others, transcends daily life, distraction from daily worries
Wise 1992 USA	Assesses the role of singing in the lives of older people	Retirement community choir and non-singers in the same community	Choir 49 Mean age: 64 Non-singers 47 Mean age: 65	Survey of singers and non-singers in same retirement community, measures of life satisfaction, alienation and self-actualisation	Singers had sung throughout life and continuation provided achievement, social status, socialising and group membership which contributes to successful aging
Zanini and Leao 2006 Brazil	Explores experience of singing in a therapeutic choir for the elderly	Extension university students registered for twelve 90 minute choir workshops	25f, 1m Ages: 58–91	Session feedback, audio-visual recordings, individual interviews, professional commentary on video recordings	Singing as a means for self-expression and self-fulfilment, songs revealing inner subjectivity, self-confidence of participants, expectations for the future

contexts for their potential value social or in terms of rehabilitation (e.g. Bailey & Davidson, 2002, 2005, choir in a homeless shelter; Cohen (2007, 2009), Silber (2005) choirs in a prison setting; Lally (2009) choral workshops for older people, and in one case, choirs which ran over a period of 2 years were specially established for research purposes (Cohen, Perlstein, Chapline, Kelly, Firth, & Simmens, 2006, 2007).

With respect to the samples investigated, a number of points are striking. Firstly, only two studies have considered the value of singing for children and young people (Ashley, 2005; Rohwer & Rohwer, 2009). Where age ranges are given it is clear that they are quite broad, but with a marked bias towards people in midlife or above. Five studies in fact are specifically concerned with older people in retirement (Cohen et al., 2006, 2007; Hillman, 2002; Southcott, 2009; Wise et al., 1992; Zanini & Leao, 2006). Secondly, many of the studies involved very small samples. In some cases, this reflected the small size of the choirs involved (e.g. Silber, 2005, included only seven female prisoners in her study from a small prison choir). In other cases, however, limited numbers of participants volunteered from quite large choirs (e.g. Jacob, Guptill, and Sumsion (2009) interviewed only nine singers form a university choral society, and Tonneijck, Kinebanian, and Josephsson (2008) interviewed six participants from a large community choir). In all of these studies, individuals have voluntarily joined choirs, because of their interest in music and singing, and one would expect a generally positive attitude towards singing and its value. Given that small samples are then volunteering to participate in a research study, there is clearly considerable scope for additional biases affecting the accounts they give.

A further bias in existing studies is also apparent when the sex composition of the studies is examined. Column four in Table 15.1 reports the sample size. If a single number is given this indicates that the author(s) did not report the sex composition of their sample. This is true for four of the studies (Jacob et al., 2009; Lally, 2009; Louhivuori, Salminen, & Lebaka 2005; Wise et al., 1992).[1] Seven studies include single sex choirs. Ashley (2005), Bailey and Davidson (2002, 2005), Cohen (2007, 2009), and Latimer (2008) deal with boys and men, while Silber, 2005 deals with women. This leaves twelve studies in which details are given of the numbers of men and women, and in all of these studies, women out-number men, sometimes quite considerably. It is clear therefore that the findings reported by these studies may well reflect more 'feminine' experiences and beliefs about the contribution of singing to wellbeing and health, than those held by men. Only two studies in this corpus explicitly compared men and women. Clift and Hancox (2001) administered a specially constructed questionnaire to assess choristers' experiences of singing and a Principal Components Analysis revealed an initial strong factor labelled 'wellbeing and relaxation.' Comparing males and females, they found a statistically significant difference on this first component, which suggested that women experience greater wellbeing effects from singing than do men. In line with Clift and Hancox (2001) finding, Sandgren (2009) also reports that positive emotional changes associated with singing are stronger for women than for men.

The studies summarised in Table 15.1 also differ considerably in terms of the methods employed and the kinds of data gathered. Many of the studies are described as qualitative and exploratory, utilising interviews and specially devised questionnaires. Others are experimental in character and have employed previously standardised scales to assess mood, wellbeing and health, together with more objective indicators and bio-markers relevant to wellbeing.

15.2.1 Qualitative Studies of Singing and Health

Small-scale qualitative studies and descriptive surveys have identified a range of social, psychological, and health benefits which singers feel they gain from singing (reviewed more fully in Clift, Hancox, Staricoff et al., 2008; Clift, Nicol, Raisbeck et al., 2010). While such studies are difficult to synthesise to draw precise conclusions, similar themes appear repeatedly. Most studies, for example, report that singing can be mood enhancing (Clift & Hancox, 2001, 2010; Clift, Hancox, Morrison et al., 2010; Bailey & Davidson, 2002, 2005), even to the point, of producing feelings of 'euphoria' or a 'singer's high' (Jacob et al., 2009). Singing brings people together and helps to create a sense of group identity, social support and friendship (Clift & Hancox, 2001; Latimer, 2008; Southcott, 2009). Singing can help to develop skills, self-confidence, self-esteem and a sense of achievement (Bailey & Davidson, 2002, 2005; Silber, 2005). Singing is also a physical activity which is both 'energising and relaxing' and can help to relieve stress and tension (Bailey & Davidson, 2003; Jacob et al., 2009; Tonneijck et al., 2008). Singers commonly believe that singing helps to improve breathing and lung capacity, improves voice quality and promotes good posture (Clift & Hancox, 2001; Clift, Hancox, Morrison et al., 2009). Because of the cognitive demands associated with singing, the activity can also serve to distract attention from personal worries (Tonneijck et al., 2008). Several studies also identify a strong spiritual dimension to singing for some choristers (Clift & Hancox, 2001; Latimer, 2008; Tonneijck et al., 2008).

15.2.2 Experimental Studies of Singing and Health

Three studies have measured mood, emotional state or wellbeing of participants before and after singing, using standardised instruments (Kreutz, Bongard, Rohrmann et al., 2004; Cohen, 2009; Sandgren, 2009). In each case, the broad hypothesis under test was that singing enhances positive mood/emotions and a sense of wellbeing. There is some support for this hypothesis, but effects sizes are generally smaller than might be expected from the evidence of qualitative studies (Kreutz et al., 2004; see Clift, Hancox, Staricoff et al., 2008 for a discussion).

Two studies have undertaken physiological monitoring of individuals, before, during and after singing, to assess bio-markers assumed to have relevance to wellbeing and health (Beck, Cesari, Yousefi et al., 2000; Kreutz et al., 2004). Both measured the effect of singing on salivary immunoglobulin A (sIgA), an antibody which is part of the immune system defending against respiratory infections. Measures were also taken of cortisol, a hormone which plays a significant role in the body's responses to stress. Both found an increase in sIgA in response to singing, but findings were mixed with respect to cortisol. While significant increases in sIgA suggest increased immune system activity it is unclear whether such changes have any significance for health. Firstly, no data are presented on how long such changes are sustained after singing. Secondly, no evidence is presented to show that the level of changes has any real clinical significance with respect to an individual's resistance to infection. And thirdly, given the context of group singing, the change may have come about because singers are breathing energetically in close proximity to one another. In other words, the heightened immune response may be a direct response to an increased risk of respiratory infection.

Cohen, Perlstein, Chapline et al. (2006, 2007) report the only study to assess the value of group singing over a substantial period of time, using standardised measures of health and indicators of health service utilisation. In a controlled but non-randomised study, healthy elderly people engaged in singing activities for 30 weeks a year over 2 years, were compared with a 'comparison group' who received no form of intervention except the assessments involved. The outcomes of the study at the end of the first year appeared to be quite remarkable:

> Results obtained from utilizing established assessment questionnaires and self-reported measures, controlling for any baseline differences, revealed positive findings for the intervention such that the intervention group (*chorale*) reported a higher overall rating of physical health, fewer doctor visits, less medication use, fewer instances of falls, and fewer other health problems than the comparison group. The intervention group also evidenced better morale and less loneliness than the comparison group. In terms of activity level, the comparison group experienced a significant decline in total number of activities, whereas the intervention group reported a trend toward increased activity. (Cohen et al., 2006, p. 726)

Despite the admirable features of this study, Clift, Hancox, Staricoff et al. (2008) identify a range of significant problems with data presentation, analysis, use of significance levels and the way in which conclusions were drawn from the results. For example, no account was taken of substantial attrition rates over 2 years. Apparent floor effects on some of the measures employed were not acknowledged. Furthermore, a very liberal 10% level was used for judging significance of changes, raising the risks of type 1 errors. In addition to these technical issues, Cohen et al. do not address the possible role of study demand characteristics which may have substantially biased questionnaire completion. Thus, while the study does provide some evidence of health benefits for older people from choral singing, Clift, Hancox, Staricoff et al. caution against accepting Cohen et al.'s findings at face value.

15.3 A Cross-National Study of Choral Singing and Wellbeing

The second half of this chapter presents some of the findings from a major cross-national survey of choral singers exploring the connections between singing, wellbeing and health (see: Clift, Hancox, Morrison et al., 2008, 2009, 2010; Clift &

Hancox, 2010). The purpose of the study was to build upon the foundation of work already undertaken, particularly the initial study by Clift and Hancox (2001), and provide a basis for future research. The central aim of the study was to assess singers' perceptions of the effects of choral singing on wellbeing and health, and consider the relationships between these beliefs and information on health-related quality of life assessed by the World Health Organisation Brief Quality of Life Questionnaire (the WHOQOL-BREF).[2]

Choirs in Australia, England and Germany were recruited into the study by research teams in the three countries. This was done essentially on a basis of convenience, and most of the large choirs in the local areas were approached with a request to participate.[3] The sample consisted of 1124 choral singers drawn from 21 choral societies and choirs in England (N = 633), Germany (N = 325) and Australia (N = 166). In England, a sample of choristers involved in an on-going community singing project for elderly people also participated. The overall response rate was 61%. All the choirs are mixed sex and most sing major choral works from the Western Classical repertoire from the fifteenth to twentieth century. Some choirs sing a more eclectic repertoire including well known songs from musical shows and films. Only six of the 21 choirs are auditioned and the remainder are open. Several of the choirs have been established a long time. The *Stuttgarter Liederkranz* in Germany is the oldest choir in the survey, founded in 1824, followed by the English *Ashford Choral Society* founded in 1857, and *The Queensland Choir* in Australia set up in 1872. Societies that have continued in existence for this length of time indicate their appeal from the nineteenth to the twenty-first centuries. There are also some recently established choral societies and choirs in the study: the German *Ensemble ad libitum Stuttgart* was formed in 2002, and *The Silver Singers*, Gateshead, England and *The Esplanados*, Brisbane, Australia were set up in 2005.

15.3.1 The Questionnaire

A questionnaire was designed for this survey in English and translated into German for the German participants. It was structured in three parts. The first part asked for personal information and details of the respondents' involvement with music and singing. The second section focused specifically on the effects of choral singing and started with three open questions on the effects of singing on quality of life, wellbeing and health. These open questions were then followed by 24 statements about choral singing using items defining the first major 'wellbeing and relaxation' component reported by Clift and Hancox (2001) and items from the 'Singers' Emotional Experiences Scale' devised by Beck et al. (2000). The instruments devised by Clift and Hancox and Beck et al., could be criticised for including only positively worded items, which could help to reinforce a positive response bias. In the present questionnaire, therefore, twelve items were positively worded and twelve negatively worded, and participants responded on a 5-point Likert scale from 'strongly disagree' to 'strongly agree.' The third section of the questionnaire contained the WHOQOL-BREF. This was designed to assess four major life quality domains:

physical (e.g. How much do you need medical treatment to function in your daily life?), psychological (e.g. How much do you enjoy life?), social (e.g. How satisfied are you with the support you get from your friends?) and environmental (e.g. How satisfied are you with the conditions of your living place?). The questionnaire has been widely used internationally and has high levels of reliability and validity. It was considered especially suitable for a cross-national survey as official WHO versions of the questionnaire are available for use in Australia, Germany and the UK. Findings from the WHOQOL-BREF are not reported in this chapter (See Clift, Hancox, Morrison et al., 2008, for details).

15.3.2 Sample Characteristics

Comparisons of the demographic and biographical characteristics of the national samples revealed interesting differences. For example: the proportion of women to men was higher in the English sample (3:1) compared with the German and Australian (2:1). The English sample was also older on average, but in all countries a clear majority of choristers were aged 50 or older. Figure 15.1 is an image of some of the members of *The Silver Singers*, an English community choir that meets in *The Sage Gateshead*. This gives a very good indication of the average age and the sex composition of the English choirs in the study.

More than 50% in each national sample reported having had a higher education and those with no more than secondary education were in the minority in all countries. Current employment patterns for the Australian and German samples were fairly similar, whereas the English choristers included a higher proportion of retired people. The pattern of employment and retirement in the three samples closely reflects their age distributions. Participants were also substantially white and reported substantial previous experience of choral singing.

15.3.3 Analysis of the 'Effects of Singing' Items

A central objective pursued in this survey was the construction of a suitable scale for measuring the perceived benefits of singing for wellbeing and health. The 24 items included in the questionnaire were based on the first factor emerging from the analysis undertaken by Clift and Hancox (2001), supplemented by items from Beck et al. (2000) (The full set of items is given in an Appendix to this chapter). As noted above, Clift and Hancox found a significant sex difference on this first factor indicating that women reported stronger wellbeing effects from singing than did men. The cross-national survey provided an opportunity to determine whether this same difference appeared in a larger more diverse sample of choristers.

The total data set was subject to Principal Components Analysis and the first component emerging was very substantial, accounting for 36.2% of the total variance, and defined strongly by items related to a sense of happiness, wellbeing and health, positive mood, reduction in negative feelings and quality of life. The

15 Singing, Wellbeing and Gender 247

Fig. 15.1 Members of *The Silver Singers*, The Sage, Gateshead, UK

remaining three factors were small by comparison. Component two was defined by three positively worded items identifying negative aspects of choir membership. Component three was defined weakly by four items, two of which were negatively worded. Component four, interestingly, was defined by the two spiritual items included in the questionnaire.

Following this initial analysis with the total sample, the first principal component was extracted from samples of men and women in each national group. This analysis showed that consistently high loadings (in excess of 0.6) were obtained across all six groups for the same 12 statements on singing (eight positively worded and four negatively worded).

Table 15.2 First principal component for six countries by sex groups (12 items)

	Total sample	English Men	English Women	Australian Men	Australian Women	German Men	German Women
Makes me feel a lot happier afterwards	0.75	0.74	0.73	0.66	0.83	0.72	0.78
Singing gives a positive attitude to life	0.74	0.74	0.74	0.68	0.78	0.72	0.74
Singing has improved well-being/health	0.74	0.68	0.77	0.76	0.81	0.71	0.69
Singing releases negative feelings	0.73	0.74	0.75	0.69	0.82	0.71	0.73
Singing helps make me a happier person	0.73	0.72	0.78	0.78	0.74	0.69	0.68
Singing doesn't give me a 'high'	−0.70	−0.71	−0.71	−0.74	−0.61	−0.73	−0.67
Choir positively affects quality of life	0.70	0.66	0.75	0.64	0.66	0.74	0.60
Relaxing and helps deal with stress	0.69	0.61	0.70	0.67	0.70	0.66	0.74
Doesn't release negative feelings in my life	−0.69	−0.72	−0.68	−0.65	−0.74	−0.67	−0.65
Singing makes mood more positive	0.69	0.68	0.71	0.71	0.71	0.71	0.60
Doesn't help general emotional well-being	−0.67	−0.69	−0.68	−0.44	−0.75	−0.73	−0.62
Singing gives no deep significance	−0.65	−0.65	−0.65	−0.68	−0.63	−0.66	−0.69
Variance accounted for	50.1	48.4	51.9	46.2	53.8	49.5	46.7
Cronbach alpha	0.91	0.91	0.92	0.89	0.92	0.91	0.90

Principal Components Analysis was re-run with these 12 items and the results are reported in Table 15.2. It can be seen that the initial component accounts for over 50% of the total variance represented by these items. A summed scale constructed from these items (with the negative statements reverse scored), had high Cronbach alpha values for internal consistency for the total sample and for each sub-group. The consistency of the findings is especially striking given that the German groups were responding to the items in German.

15.3.4 Country, Age and Gender Comparisons

Table 15.3 reports data from the singing scale by country, sex and age group. Cell means are consistently within the range 46–52 out of a maximum possible score of 60. Clearly, there is a wide consensus among choristers that singing brings benefits for subjective wellbeing and quality of life. Country and age group differences are minimal, but a marked main effect emerges for sex, with women scoring just over 2 points on average above men (F = 11.7, df = 1/1028, p = 0.001).

Differences in the whole sample between women and men are presented graphically in Fig. 15.2. This shows clearly the variation that exists with both sex groups, but indicates that the distributions for both groups are negatively skewed, and that for women there is a clear ceiling effect. Given also that the mid-point on the scale is 36, it is clear that the large majority of both men and women are well above the mid-point and are essentially in agreement that singing gives rise to positive feelings of wellbeing. However, many more women give very high scores on the scale compared with men, and the overall mean differences between men and women are partially accounted for a higher proportion of women who express consistently strong views about singing.

Table 15.3 Singing scale descriptive statistics for country by sex subgroups

Age		England Men	Women	Australia Men	Women	Germany Men	Women	Total Men	Women
Up to 50	Mean	47.2	50.1	48.3	50.0	48.9	50.0	48.3	50.0
	Std.	6.8	7.3	6.2	7.2	4.5	6.0	5.7	6.7
	Dev. N	18	76	18	46	28	82	64	204
51–60	Mean	46.7	50.9	51.8	52.2	48.5	49.0	48.4	50.6
	Std.	8.1	6.2	4.8	6.5	7.0	7.2	7.3	6.6
	Dev. N	26	107	13	30	17	55	56	192
61–70	Mean	48.9	50.5	49.7	50.1	46.0	49.5	47.9	50.2
	Std.	5.9	6.4	6.1	6.1	7.8	4.8	6.8	6.6
	Dev. N	48	184	14	22	42	47	104	253
71+	Mean	48.5	49.1	47.2	50.4	44.2	49.6	47.5	49.2
	Std.	7.1	7.3	3.5	9.9	7.8	4.8	7.1	7.2
	Dev. N	42	82	6	5	42	8	61	95
Total	Mean	48.1	50.2	49.5	50.7	47.0	49.5	48.0	50.1
	Std.	6.8	6.7	5.6	6.9	7.0	6.6	6.7	6.7
	Dev. N	134	449	51	103	100	192	285	744

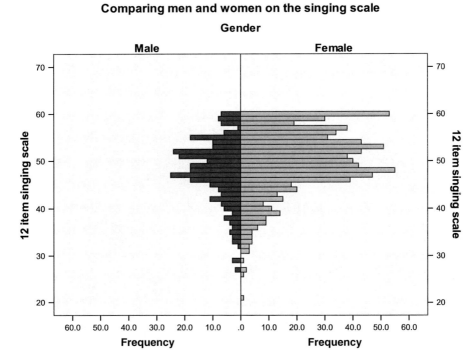

Fig. 15.2 Comparative histograms of the distributions of scores on the singing scale for the total sample of men and women

15.3.5 Gender Differences in Response to Individual Singing Items

As the analysis reported in the last section reveals a significant sex difference on the singing scale (but no country or age group differences), it is of interest to examine responses of men and women to the component items of the scale as this may give further insights into the source of significant differences overall.

Table 15.4 gives the percentage frequency distribution of responses to each of these items, ordered according to the strength of the sex difference for positively worded and negatively worded items. Essentially, substantial majorities of both men and women agree or strongly agree with the positively worded items, and disagree or strongly disagree with the negatively worded items. Cells with low frequencies are combined for the purposes of statistical analysis, and comparisons reveal particularly marked sex differences for five items.

Women were more likely than men to strongly agree that singing makes them feel happier, makes their mood more positive, helps improve wellbeing and health, and helps them relax and deal with stress. Similarly, they were more likely to strongly disagree that singing doesn't help to release negative feelings. These findings also underline the fact that the overall mean difference between men

15 Singing, Wellbeing and Gender

Table 15.4 Gender differences in response to singing items

	Strongly disagree	Disagree	In between	Agree	Strongly agree	Chi-square df = 2
Positively worded items						
Makes mood more positive						
Male	0.0	1.3	13.0	50.3	35.3	26.5***
Female	0.1	0.9	6.3	42.1	50.6	
Relaxing and helps deal with stress						
Male	0.3	4.3	16.1	55.5	23.7	22.7***
Female	0.8	1.9	10.5	49.1	37.8	
Makes me feel a lot happier afterwards						
Male	0.0	1.7	17.3	52.0	29.0	21.8***
Female	0.5	1.0	10.1	45.2	43.0	
Has improved wellbeing and health						
Male	0.0	8.1	16.8	58.4	16.8	17.4***
Female	0.4	4.3	15.6	50.6	29.2	
Releases negative feelings						
Male	1.3	6.0	18.1	59.5	15.1	13.5***
Female	0.4	2.9	16.9	54.7	25.1	
Helps make me a happier person						
Male	0.0	2.4	15.8	50.8	31.0	8.8**
Female	0.3	1.1	10.7	49.9	38.0	
Positively affects quality of life						
Male	0.3	1.0	6.4	51.2	41.1	n.s.
Female	0.4	0.3	5.3	45.7	48.4	
Gives a positive attitude to life						
Male	0.3	3.0	13.7	55.5	27.4	n.s.
Female	0.4	2.4	11.2	51.5	34.6	
Negatively worded items						
	Strongly disagree	Disagree	In between	Agree	Strongly agree	Chi-square df = 2
Doesn't release negative feelings in my life						
Male	15.2	48.1	22.6	13.1	1.0	20.6***
Female	27.9	44.1	18.2	8.5	1.1	
No deep significance compared to other things						
Male	23.2	41.1	19.2	15.8	0.7	14.0***
Female	32.1	42.6	13.3	10.9	1.1	
Doesn't give me a high						
Male	31.0	47.6	13.9	6.8	0.7	11.0**
Female	41.5	42.6	10.1	5.1	0.8	
Doesn't help general emotional wellbeing						
Male	36.6	46.6	10.7	5.0	1.0	7.3*
Female	44.1	44.2	7.5	2.9	1.4	

and women reflect the greater willingness of women to 'strongly' agree with positive statements about singing, whereas men are more inclined simply to 'agree' with them.

15.4 Discussion

The present survey was designed on the basis of a careful review of previously published research in order to address some of the obvious limitations of earlier studies.

More research is needed before strong evidence-based claims can be made for the value of singing for wellbeing and health. The existing corpus of research on this issue lacks a common approach to health and wellbeing. Little attention has been given to developing a coherent model of the mechanisms by which singing could affect health. Many studies are exploratory and involve very small samples. Few well-controlled experimental studies have been undertaken. Little attempt has been made to build a body of knowledge in a coherent way. Nevertheless, the research published so far does give promising indications in support of the hypothesis that 'singing is good for health.'

In the present study, the decision was made to build upon an earlier study (Clift and Hancox, 2001) on the perceived benefits of choral singing, in a more ambitious, larger-scale investigation involving multiple choirs in three countries. A mixed-method approach was adopted in studying choristers' experiences of singing, through the use of structured items drawn from previous studies (Clift & Hancox, 2001 and Beck et al., 2000), and open questions so that respondents could express their own views. Large sample sizes would ensure that factors such as sex and age could be investigated for their impact on experiences of singing.

In relation to reported experiences of singing, the findings from the survey are highly consistent with Clift and Hancox (2001). Large majorities of choral singers perceive singing to be beneficial to their health and wellbeing, but there is a minority who do experience singing in this way, particularly with respect to their physical health. There is also confirmation that women in general endorse the emotional and wellbeing benefits of singing more strongly than men. Further qualitative research is needed to explore this finding in further depth, to determine whether it reflects a gender difference in the willingness of men and women to express their feelings strongly, or whether there is something more fundamental at work in the character of women's and men's emotional experiences generated by singing. Physiological monitoring of men and women during singing may well provide some answers here. In the introduction, the claim made by Levitin (2008) that group singing leads to the release of oxytocin was questioned, but nevertheless, this may point to an important difference between men and women. Oxytocin is released in women during childbirth and breast-feeding and is implicated in the processes of maternal bonding. The same hormone is released in fathers too, and has the same biological functions, although not so strongly. A fascinating future study would involve monitoring oxytocin release in men and women during singing and relating this to their subjective experiences. Research has also shown that 'chill' experiences in listening to self-selected music are associated with objective indicators of emotional arousal and also dopamine release in the brain (Salimpoor, Benovoy, Longo et al., 2009; Salimpoor, Benovoy, Larcher et al., 2011). It would be of considerable interest to monitor chill experiences during choral singing to discover whether they are more frequent and more intense among women than men.

This study also has further limitations which should be acknowledged. The study is based on convenience samples of choral societies and choirs within defined geographical regions. The choirs were certainly varied in character, but by and large the singers involved were white, well educated, very experienced in choral singing and of a high average age. Further studies are needed to extend the nature and range of singing groups investigated (in terms of nationality, culture, age, repertoire etc.), to assess the generalisability of the findings reported from this study.

More importantly, the survey is cross-sectional in design and essentially provides a descriptive account of the self-rated health and wellbeing of choristers and their perceptions of singing. The results are consistent with the underlying hypothesis that group singing has health benefits, but it does not rigorously test this idea. Further experimental studies, replicating and extending the work of Beck et al. (2000), Kreutz et al. (2004), and especially Cohen et al. (2006, 2007), are clearly needed.

Despite, its limitations, it is argued that this study represents a substantial step forward in the developing field of research on singing and health. The authors hope that it will help to contribute to the development of a progressive programme of research to fully explore and test the notion that 'singing is good for you!' A strong evidence base is essential if health professionals and services are to take the potential value of singing seriously, and actively promote opportunities for more people to come together and sing.

Acknowledgements Thanks to all our participants, and to Prof. Donald Stewart, Prof. Gunter Kreutz and Ms. Bärbel Hess, for assistance with data gathering.

Notes

1. Discounting the initial qualitative survey reported by Clift and Hancox (2001), which provided the basis of a structured questionnaire subsequently administered to choristers.
2. For details of the WHOQOL-BREF see: http://www.who.int/substance_abuse/research_tools/whoqolbref/en/ Accessed 26 June 2011
3. In addition, in England, a large community choir based in The Sage, Gateshead, in the North East of the country were invited to participate.

Appendix

24-item 'Effects of Singing Questionnaire' used in the cross-national survey (each item responded to on a five-point scale from 'strongly agree' to 'strongly disagree')

1. Singing is something I really look forward to each week
2. Coming to the choir and singing can help to make my mood more positive than it has been during the day
3. Singing has little or no spiritual significance for me personally
4. Singing is something that helps to make me feel a lot happier in myself afterwards
5. Taking part in singing generally has no effect on my energy levels or alertness at the time of day we sing
6. I find singing helps me to relax and deal with the stresses of the day
7. Singing doesn't really help to improve my general emotional wellbeing
8. If I am feeling worried about anything, singing doesn't really help me to put these worries out of my mind
9. Singing helps to give me a more positive attitude to life
10. I wouldn't say that being in a choir and singing is a very important part of my life
11. Singing helps to make me a happier person
12. For me, singing doesn't serve as a way of releasing negative feelings about other aspects of my life
13. I often feel exhilarated during or after participating in a performance by the choir
14. I wouldn't say that singing is an activity that has made me physically healthier
15. Singing helps to give me a sense of personal identity as a musician and performer
16. Singing doesn't give me the kind of 'high' some people talk about
17. I enjoy singing but it is not something that has a deep significance for me compared with other things that are important in my life
18. I feel singing has helped to improve my general sense of wellbeing and health
19. Being in the choir and singing is sometimes a source of frustration for me
20. Singing usually helps to release any negative feelings I have hanging around from the day
21. Singing in the choir is a time when I have the strongest sense of a spiritual dimension to life
22. There are ways in which for me singing could be damaging to aspects of my wellbeing and health
23. Being in a choir makes a positive contribution to my quality of life
24. Being in the choir is a commitment that is sometimes a source of stress or difficulty in other areas of my life

References

Ashley, M. (2005). Singing, gender and health: Perspectives from boys singing in a church choir. *Health Education, 102*(4), 180–186.

Bailey, B. A., & Davidson, J. W. (2002). Adaptive characteristics of group singing: Perceptions from members of a choir for homeless men. *Musicae Scientiae, VI*(2), 221–256.

Bailey, B. A., & Davidson, J. W. (2003). Perceived holistic health effects of three levels of music participation. In R. Kopiez, A. C. Lehmann, I. Wohther, & C. Wolf (Eds.), *Proceedings of the 5th triennial ESCOM conference*, 8–13 September 2003, Hanover University of Music and Drama, Germany.

Bailey, B. A., & Davidson, J. W. (2005). Effects of group singing and performance for marginalized and middle-class singers. *Psychology of Music, 33*(3), 269–303.

Beck, R. J., Cesari, T. C., Yousefi, A., & Enamoto, H. (2000). Choral singing, performance perception, and immune system changes in salivary immunoglobulin A and cortisol. *Music Perception, 18*(1), 87–106.
Chorus America. (2009). *The Chorus Impact Study*, Chorus America. Retrieved on June 26, 2011, from http://www.chorusamerica.org/
Clift, S., & Hancox, G. (2010). The significance of choral singing for sustaining psychological wellbeing: Findings from a survey of choristers in England, Australia and Germany. *Music Performance Research, 3*(1), 79–96. Retrieved on 26 June 2011, from http://mpr-online.net/
Clift, S., Hancox, G., Morrison, I., Hess, B., Stewart, G., & Kreutz, G. (2008). *Choral singing, wellbeing and health: Findings from a cross-national survey*. Canterbury: Christ Church University. Retrieved on June 26, 2011, from http://www.canterbury.ac.uk/centres/sidney-de-haan-research/
Clift, S., Hancox, G., Morrison, I., Hess, B., Kreutz, G., & Stewart, D. (2009). What do singers say about the effects of choral singing on physical health? Findings from a survey of choristers in Australia, England and Germany. In J. Louhivuori, T. Eerola, S. Saarikallio, T. Himberg, & P.-S. Eerola (Eds.), *Proceedings of the 7th triennial conference of European Society for the Cognitive Sciences of Music (ESCOM 2009)* Jyväskylä, Finland.
Clift, S., Hancox, G., Morrison, I., Hess, B., Kreutz, G., & Stewart, D. (2010). Choral singing and psychological wellbeing: Quantitative and qualitative findings from English choirs in a cross-national survey. *Journal of Applied Arts and Health, 1*(1), 19–34.
Clift, S., Hancox, G., Staricoff, R., & Whitmore, C. (2008). *Singing and health: A systematic mapping and review of non-clinical research*. Canterbury: Canterbury Christ Church University. Retrieved on June 26, 2011, from http://www.canterbury.ac.uk/centres/sidney-de-haan-research/
Clift, S., Nicol, J., Raisbeck, M., Whitmore, C., & Morrison, I. (2010). Group singing, wellbeing and health: A systematic review. *UNESCO Observatory E-Journal, 2*(1). Retrieved on June 26, 2011, from http://www.abp.unimelb.edu.au/unesco/ejournal
Clift, S. M., & Hancox, G. (2001). The perceived benefits of singing: Findings from preliminary surveys of a university college choral society. *Journal of the Royal Society for the Promotion of Health, 121*(4), 248–256.
Cohen, G. D., Perlstein, S., Chapline, J., Kelly, J., Firth, K. M., & Simmens, S. (2006). The impact of professionally conducted cultural programs on the physical health, mental health, and social functioning of older adults. *The Gerontologist, 46*(6), 726–734.
Cohen, G. D., Perlstein, S., Chapline, J., Kelly, J., Firth, K. M., & Simmens, S. (2007). The impact of professionally conducted cultural programs on the physical health, mental health and social functioning of older adults – 2-year results. *Journal of Aging, Humanities and the Arts, 1*, 5–22.
Cohen, M. (2009). Choral singing and prison inmates: Influences of performing in a prison choir. *The Journal of Correctional Education, 60*(1), 52–65.
Cohen, M. L. (2007). Explorations of inmate and volunteer choral experiences in a prison-based choir. *Australian Journal of Music Education, 1*, 61–72.
Dougary, G. (2007, April 28). A song for everyone. *The Times*. Retrieved on June 26, 2011, from http://women.timesonline.co.uk/tol/life_and_style/women/body_and_soul/article1714652.ece
Durrant, C., & Himonides, E. (1998). What makes people sing together? Socio-psychological and cross-cultural perspectives on the choral phenomenon. *International Journal of Music Education, 32*, 61–71.
Hillman, S. (2002). Participatory singing for older people: A perception of benefit. *Health Education, 102*(4), 163–171.
Jacob, C., Guptill, C., & Sumsion, T. (2009). Motivation for continuing improvement in a leisure-based choir: The lived experiences of university choir members. *Journal of Occupational Science, 16*(3), 187–193.
Kreutz, G., Bongard, S., Rohrmann, S., Grebe, D., Bastian, H. G., & Hodapp, V. (2004). Effects of choir singing or listening on secretory immunoglobulin A, cortisol and emotional state. *Journal of Behavioral Medicine, 27*(6), 623–635.

Lally, E. (2009). The power to heal us with a smile and a song: Senior well-being, music-based participatory arts and the value of qualitative evidence. *Journal of Arts and Communities, 1*(1), 25–44.

Latimer, M. E. (2008). Our voices enlighten, inspire, heal and empower. A mixed methods investigation of demography, sociology, and identity acquisition in a gay men's chorus. *International Journal of Research in Choral Singing, 3*(1), 23–38.

Levitin, D. (2008) *The World in Six Songs: How the musical brain created human nature*. London: Dutton.

Louhivuori, J., Salminen, V.-M., & Lebaka, E. (2005). Singing together – A cross-cultural approach to the meaning of choirs as a community. In P. S. Campbell, J. Drummond, P. Dunbar-Hall, K. Howard, H. Schippers, & T. Wiggins (Eds.), *Cultural diversity in music education: Directions and challenges for the 21st century* (pp. 81–94). Bowen Hills, QLD: Australian Academic Press.

Pomfret, E. (2009). Credit crunched? Then lift up your voice. *The Times*, 24 January. Retrieved June 26, 2011, from http://entertainment.timesonline.co.uk/tol/arts_and_entertainment/music/article5573830.ece

Rohwer, D., & Rohwer, M. (2009). A content analysis of choral students' participation perceptions: Implications for lifelong learning. *International Journal of Community Music, 2*(2&3), 155–262.

Salimpoor, V. N., Benovoy, M., Larcher, K., Dagher, A., & Zatorre, R. J. (2011). Anatomically distinct dopamine release during anticipation and experience of peak experiences in music. *Nature Neuroscience*. Published online 9 January.

Salimpoor, V. N., Benovoy, M., Longo, G., Cooperstock, J. R., & Zatorre, R. J. (2009). The rewarding aspects of music listening are related to degree of emotional arousal. *PLoS One, 4*(10), e7487.

Sandgren, M. (2009). Evidence of strong immediate well-being effects of choral singing – With more enjoyment for women than for men. In J. Louhivuori, T. Eerola, S. Saarikallio, T. Himberg, & P.-S. Eerola (Eds.), *Proceedings of the 7th triennial conference of European Society for the Cognitive Sciences of Music (ESCOM 2009)*, Jyväskylä, Finland.

Silber, L. (2005). Bars behind bars: The impact of a women's prison choir on social harmony. *Music Education Research, 7*(2), 251–271.

Southcott, J. E. (2009). And as I go, I love to sing: The Happy Wanderers, music and positive aging. *International Journal of Community Music, 2*(2&3), 143–156.

Thomas, T. (2010). The choral cure. *The Independent*, 12 January. Retrieved on June 26, 2011, from http://www.independent.co.uk/life-style/health-and-families/features/the-choral-cure-1864774.html

Tonneijck, H. I. M., Kinebanian, A., & Josephsson, S. (2008). An exploration of choir singing: Achieving wholeness through challenge. *Journal of Occupational Science, 15*(3), 173–180.

Wise, G. W., Hartmann, D. J., & Fisher, B. J. (1992). Exploration of the relationship between choral singing and successful aging. *Psychological Reports, 70*, 1175–1183.

Zanini, C. R., & Leao, E. (2006). Therapeutic choir: A music therapist looks at the new millennium elderly. *Voices: A World Forum for Music Therapy, 6*(2). Retrieved on June 26, 2011, from https://normt.uib.no/index.php/voices/article/viewArticle/249

Part IV
Singing in Popular Music Contexts

Chapter 16
"But I Can Write Songs Okay": Male Voices in New Zealand Alternative Rock

Matthew Bannister

16.1 "But I Can Write Songs Okay"

Writing about New Zealand pakeha (white settler) society in the 1950s, Bill Pearson claims that the "ordinary man":

> will not even sing as he feels: he either assumes a mocking rhetorical tone (to let listeners know he does not take his voice seriously) or he consciously imitates the star who popularised the song ... he is performing a tepid act of devotion to someone else's performance which is public property and must not be violated (1974, p. 13).

New Zealand/Aotearoa shares with other settler cultures such as Australia and the Western US a history of representations of tough, pioneering, white masculinity as emblematic of the emergent nation; "artistic" activities like singing have tended to be marginalised as feminine (Phillips, 1987; Connell, 1995, pp. 185–194). Pearson characterises pakeha (see King, 1999) culture as puritanical, dour and inexpressive, generally suspicious of public performances of emotion outside of a few exceptional sites of "male bonding" (such as pubs and sports clubs). New Zealand culture has become more pluralist and multi-cultural since the 1950s, but taboos around public singing by white men are still strong. There is less of an emergent male choir movement, compared to, say, Australia (Rickwood, 2010; Harrison, 2007). However, other aspects of pakeha male "pioneer" culture, such as amateurism and DIY, have provided alternative routes towards music-making (Phillips, 1987, p. 18).

In the late 1970s, punk rock "arrived" in New Zealand, and its philosophy of amateurism, simplicity and DIY proved amenable to local conditions, giving rise to a body of music that is now frequently identified as uniquely local (Churton, 2000, p. 32). Independent record labels, for example Flying Nun Records, set up by Roger Shepherd in Christchurch in 1981, documented the scene (all the artists cited here recorded for that label). The distinctiveness of this new local music was associated with extreme amateurism: bands like the Clean were lauded by New

---

M. Bannister (✉)
Waikato Institute of Technology, Hamilton, Waikato, New Zealand
e-mail: Matthew.Bannister@wintec.ac.nz

Zealand rock writer Campbell Walker for having "no background, bugger all gear, no singing ability" (quoted in Mitchell, 1996, p. 218). Appropriation of punk DIY values by local musicians served a number of functions: identifying with an established pioneering tradition, emphasising self-reliance, and concurring with rock values of authenticity through home-made, non-commercial modes of production (Keightley, 2001). The discourse of amateurism had an enabling effect – if technique no longer had to be "learnt", then local cultural production could be freed from its perceived reliance on (overseas) tradition and inherited models. However, the DIY ethos was mainly empowering for white men, overlapping with broader discourses of cultural power: rock authenticity, authorship and Romantic/modernist models of artistry.

The relation of gender to musical participation is a central question for all researchers of music as a cultural practice. In classical music performance and music education, Scott Harrison has highlighted how gender limits or enables participation in musical performance, particularly for males (Harrison, 2007). He argues that boys participate less, are choosier about what instrument they play, are especially reluctant to sing, and that these are "perennial" problems. In popular music performance, women are under, or mis-represented, and the bulk of scholarship focuses on why this is the case, and how it can be remedied (Bayton, 2006; Coates, 1997). Nevertheless, this apparent distinction may mask underlying continuities across the musical domain in terms of gender theory. For example, Lucy Green acknowledges that the gendering of musical performance roles in secondary school education may favour girls, but also argues that when it comes to composition and writing new material, boys are perceived as superior (Green, 1997). Greater female participation in, for example, classical music performance does not significantly challenge the way that its value is predicated on a canon of great male authors. So even if the "voices", instrumental or vocal, are performed by women, the overall "voice" is still masculine. While it is possible, and in fact essential, to distinguish these two different types of voice, I would suggest that conventional Western musical and artistic discourse tends to conflate them, and this applies as much to popular as classical music. This in turn affects the ways that many male singers in popular music understand their voices as "in service" to their songwriting.

In this chapter I use interviews with male singers involved in popular music scenes as a way of fleshing out critical analysis, allowing male voices to be heard reflecting on their own practice, while also interpreting them according to music/gender theory and popular music discourses around gender. The overall thesis is about how singing is positioned within gender discourse and in the field of popular music, with particular reference to a local New Zealand "scene", the "Dunedin Sound" and an international genre, alternative guitar rock (Bannister, 2006). "Voice" is theorised from a number of perspectives – participant's experience of their voices versus audience perceptions; as a generic aspect (e.g. the way that vocals sound on a recording) versus live performance, and especially the ways that voices interact with performance conventions in a particular "scene" to create meaning, for example, through the connection of voice with authorship.

The scene/genre distinction is important because whereas genre tends to emphasise formal stylistic features, "scene" is much more open to the ways that meaning is created in interaction between musicians, audiences and situations, in particular cultural and economic circumstances (Straw, 2005). "Scene" also provides the opportunity to consider the way that global and local music cultures interact, as opposed to "community", which tends to presume a more unified local tradition of music making. This is especially relevant for popular music, in which emergent global genres interact and are formed out of particular local scenes (Straw, 2005). Eighties alternative guitar rock can be viewed as an transnational genre within popular music, but it can also be viewed in terms of individual particular "scenes" that contributed to the genre's emergence.

My case study is the New Zealand 1980s "Dunedin Sound", a scene in which I participated in as a band member, recording for Flying Nun Records, whose roster included bands such as *The Clean*, *The Chills*, *The Verlaines*, *Sneaky Feelings*, *The Bats*, *The Puddle*, *Straitjacket Fits* and *The Jean-Paul Sartre Experience*. Alternative music scenes similar to and contemporaneous with New Zealand's in the UK, US and Australia have produced *REM* (US) and *the Smiths* (UK), as well as "cult" acts such as *The Pixies, Dinosaur Junior, Sonic Youth, Husker Du, Sonic Youth* (US); *My Bloody Valentine, The Wedding Present, Orange Juice* (UK) and *The Go-Betweens* (Australia). The genre has also influenced "grunge" acts like *Nirvana*, *Britpop* (most obviously *Oasis*), the garage rock revival (e.g. *The Strokes*), post-rock acts like *Mogwai*, and "new" folk (*Devendra Banhart*).

The obvious unifying factor in 1980s alternative music is its "independent" mode of production, that is, working through small local record companies, not multinationals, a trend that began with punk rock (Hesmondhalgh, 1999). In terms of musical style, there is a punk influence (amateur singing, low production values, loud guitars), a tendency towards the 60s instrumental line up of electric guitars, bass and drums (also true of much punk music), and a standard personnel of young white men, creating an overall "jangly", "echoey" sound, with vocals low in the mix. "Classic" 60s pop song structures predominate: "Guitar jangle... low-tech production ... a shared aesthetic which emphasized the primary importance of the song, and valorized the roughness of the music" (Shuker, 1998, p. 104). "There wasn't a Dunedin Sound, except that the bands recorded on the same equipment and possessed the same feel. We all shared a love of good songs and a loathing of stage personas and such" (Martin Phillipps, quoted in McGonigle, 2005).

Punk's rallying cry "Anyone can do it!" catalysed a huge growth in independent music production in the early 1980s. Amateurism was both a necessary feature of the genre, and one of its founding ideologies. Professional performance and "slick" studio production were suspect; post-punk musicians made a virtue out of necessity by favouring "rough", "live", locally produced sound and performance as more authentic, because (supposedly) less mediated than its mainstream, commercial counterpart (Bannister, 2006). However, the concept of "authenticity", namely that the integrity of a musical performance depends on its immediacy, dates back to Walter Benjamin's "aura" and had been a key strategy for differentiating "rock" from "pop" within popular music discourse since the 1960s,

(Keightley, 2001). At the same time, alternative culture was contradictory: while proclaiming that amateurism and localness gave rise to immediacy, originality and innovation, it took musical inspiration from recordings of iconic 1960s rock acts, some mainstream (*The Beatles, The Byrds*) and some "cult" (*The Velvet Underground* and 60s "garage" rock, an early form of punk), hunted down in secondhand record shops. Alternative guitar rock was both backwards and forwards looking, and this contradiction also informs its relation with gender.

Feminism was an important cultural influence on punk, encouraging female participation (*The Raincoats, The Slits, The Au-Pairs, Poly Styrene, Lydia Lunch*). By the early 80s gay, "gender bending" or androgynous stars such *Boy George, Annie Lennox* and *Prince*, or genres such as New Romanticism, were increasingly part of the pop mainstream. However, 80s alternative rock featured few female musicians (and even fewer singers), and little overtly gay or androgynous performance. Alternative rock performance styles were instead influenced by the feminist critique of machismo: "masculine", sexist or "rockist" styles of performance, "explicit, crude, and often aggressive expression of male sexuality ... cock rock performers ... [who] constantly seek to remind the audience of their prowess ... mikes and guitars are phallic symbols ... vocal styles involve shouting and screaming" (Frith and McRobbie, 1990, p. 374). Alternative musicians reacted against these stereotypes' mainstream connotations, avoiding overt performance of gender and sexuality onstage. Some claimed that indie represented a "feminization" of rock, whether through "lo-fi" recording approaches, or the "vulnerability" of male indie musicians, for example in their vocal stylings (DeRogatis, 1996, pp. 13–14; Gilbert, 1999, pp. 44–45; Grajeda, 2002, pp. 242–244). Sarah Cohen's ethnographic study of indie music making in Liverpool highlights non–macho performance styles:

> The lead singer of *Cast* ... holds his guitar tight up to his chest ... in a manner that conveys a youthful fragility and earnestness ... enhanced by the clarity of his voice and the way he stretches up his neck to the microphone ... The sounds produced by bands like *Cast, Space* and *The Lightning Seeds* suggest a masculinity that is rather soft, vulnerable and less macho, aggressive and assertive, less threatening and explicit than that promoted by many styles of heavy rock or metal, rap or funk. The lyrics suggest "fragile masculinity – men who are lost, confused and betrayed" (1997, pp. 26–29).

Alternative performance tended towards casualness, lacking "a show" in the usual sense, tending towards a folk aesthetic of immediacy. It was a "group" approach, in which no member was highlighted, minimising the element of display. The performers tended towards scruffy uniformity, passivity, and "a minimal display of musical prowess" (Hesmondhalgh, 1999, p. 38). Displays of instrumental virtuosity were rare. Vocals in 80s indie or alternative rock tend to be indistinct, partly because they are low in the mix, like punk (Laing, 1986, pp. 53–54). Even when the vocal is "mixed up", it tends to avoid expressive devices like glossolalia, melisma, sudden changes in tone, rhythmical subtleties – devices associated with vocal virtuosity and African-American music. A matter-of-fact or deadpan tone is frequent. Robert Scott (the Bats): "I'm a bit reticent, tend to give the minimum of what the song needs." Some *Flying Nun* singers (and guitarists) eschewed the use of vibrato.

I conducted a series of interviews with singers from *Flying Nun*/Dunedin Sound bands of this period: George Henderson (*The Puddle*); David Pine (*Sneaky Feelings*); Graeme Downes (*The Verlaines*); David Kilgour (*The Clean*); Robert Scott (*The Bats*). All were white males resident in Dunedin in the early 1980s. I have also drawn on published interview material with other Dunedin musicians such as Martin Phillipps (*The Chills*) and Bruce Russell (*The Dead C*). The dominant gender discourse in New Zealand was (is?) the "Kiwi bloke", a tough, working-class, pragmatic, sporty, laconic, rural stereotype. Bruce Russell: "I faced some antagonism as a young person in Dunedin, because I was a student and there was some . . . aggro towards students and 'poofters'" (quoted in Burch, 2009). So was singing regarded as unmasculine? Graeme Downes: "I never considered it on a gender level at the time but . . . I had normal guy strengths to fall back on [playing soccer and cricket]. I was never teased about coming to school with an oboe or violin under my arm either. But . . . there was a lot of anti student, punk and contra Springbok tour violence around the time. Singing in a rock band registered as abnormal in a broader cultural context for sure." David Kilgour: "I was too shy to sing at school. Being a boy, probably."

What of influences? Only Graeme Downes and Robert Scott had formal musical training, and not in singing. Most respondents had sung a bit at home, in church or at school. George Henderson: "I didn't find it easy to sing in tune. I sang in school assemblies (Southland Boys). I liked singing strong tunes. Familiarity made it easier . . . I wasn't brought up to sing." David Pine: "I sang in church every Sunday. But after performing in a musical in standard four (age 9–10) I didn't perform in public again till my first gig with *Sneaky Feelings*" (at 19). Alternative rock encouraged amateur voices, although clearly this is also true of rock more generally, and many role models cited by respondents echo this: "Lou Reed, Bob Dylan, obviously 'bad' singers" (George Henderson); "Dylan, Van Morrison, Neil Young. Tonal things influenced me (I didn't have a hope in hell of emulating Van Morrison melodically)" (Graeme Downes); "John Lennon, Gram Parsons, Neil Young, Randy Newman" (David Pine). Interestingly no punk vocalists are mentioned, George Henderson commenting: "Punk singing was aggressive, and I found that restrictive." Perhaps the association of aggression with machismo was significant here.

When I asked how or why respondents started singing in a rock context, many answered that they were inspired by seeing other local bands perform, although David Pine stated that he wanted to emulate the sounds of records that he liked, and for David Kilgour it was about "[being] vinyl junkies, pure love of music" and making home recordings with his brother Hamish. But when Kilgour saw early Dunedin punk band *The Enemy* in 1978, he thought: "This is what I'm gonna do." All stated that they sang primarily because they wrote songs. "I wrote songs so I had to sing them. I didn't enjoy it; it was the part you'd rather not do, the 'poor cousin' . . . but necessary to get the words out" (George). "I got the job because I wrote the songs" (Graeme). "I was writing most of the songs; no one else was going to sing them" (Robert). This approach could be termed instrumental or pragmatic: singing was necessary because they wrote the material and no one else was volunteering.

The emphasis on necessity suggests that these singers didn't particularly like their voices, and indeed they heard themselves as "shaky", "pitch imperfect", "not powerful" and "limited". These impressions were confirmed to a degree by audience/critical feedback. "We played a gig in Germany and afterwards a guy came up to me and said: 'You write so well but you do not sing in tune, surely it is not so difficult?'" (David Pine). "Terrible singer. You've improved" (George). Early reviews of Flying Nun bands sometimes commented adversely on vocal quality: "Scott's fleeting pop melodies ... [are] given a distinctively naive twist by his slightly atonal, nasal vocal delivery. To some that's his charm and to others it's irritating" (*Rip It Up* review of *The Bats'* "By Night", October 1984, quoted in Davey and Puschmann, 1996, p. 16). "'Platypus' seems to feature vocals from a volunteer from the audience" (*Rip It Up* review of *The Clean's* "Tally Ho", September 1981, quoted in Davey and Puschmann, 1996, p. 35). Graeme confirms these impressions but also notes that it was not a major issue:

> It was a very supportive scene at the time, which was more focused on the song than the performance, so I don't remember too many adverse comments. That doesn't mean I was any good – I know I wasn't. I have a massive insecurity about my voice that lingers still, but I've got to know it and have mastered the unruly beast that I started with pretty well.

Robert: "[There was] not a lot of critiquing going on. We were out of tune, but people liked the energy, they weren't worried about tuning." Another issue affecting vocal performance was the quality of PAs (vocal amplification) and especially foldback (monitor speakers onstage so singers can hear themselves). Monitors were often inaudible, drowned out by electric guitars and drums, and this affected vocalists: "I used to sing falsetto a lot of the time because I couldn't hear myself otherwise" (George). Robert: "I sing low at home [when songwriting] so I often have to transpose up for live [performance]." Graeme: "Some of [my] early songs had very small ranges ... because I simply couldn't control the muscles very well to stay in tune." A degree of self-consciousness about singing is not surprising, given that much popular music is recorded and produced to a high technical standard by professionals. Although alternative music did not emphasise technical standards, they still became an issue when local acts approached commercial radio. "The programmers predicted the end of society ... if they were forced to play that terribly amateur NZ stuff" (Martin Phillipps, quoted in McGonigle, 2005). But of course, this very same amateurism could also be interpreted from alternative perspectives as proving authenticity, through vulnerability – a "bad" voice is an honest voice. This ties in with the idea that indie masculinities presented themselves as more honest, because more fallible, less powerful, than traditional rock masculinities.

All singers interviewed also played guitar, unsurprising in that they are also songwriters. George commented, on the subject of live local bands: "The fact that they were not just singing but also playing guitar was important." David Kilgour: "Being onstage was terrifying enough [without singing]." David Pine: "Given the nakedness of singing, the guitar is a form of clothing. With a guitar, you can be one of the band." In contrast, a dedicated vocalist usually focuses audience attention as the "front person". David Pine: "The whole idea of a separate singer went against the 'anti-star ethos'" (which was part of indie culture). "Everyone knew that singers were prats and show-offs, like Mick Jagger and Bob Geldof. Singers had to jump around and put on a show. In Dunedin, standing still was the acceptable mode of performance" (Bannister, 1999, p. 20). There were few dedicated vocalists (i.e. non-instrument players) in the Dunedin Sound. Internationally, some indie groups did have front persons, such as Morrissey of the Smiths or Michael Stipe of REM and perhaps consequently these groups went on to enjoy a measure of commercial success. This association of singer/front persons with commercialism requires further comment.

The importance of a singer/front person for commercial success in popular music relates to discourses around individual "stardom". Groups are harder to market because of the lack of individuation (unless they are *vocal* groups, e.g. *The Spice Girls*, *Boyzone* etc). The vocal is the central and loudest feature of most pop singles, which is consistent with a visual emphasis on the "star". Rock tends to emphasise instruments more: "the notion of the band or group is central to rock music ... in contrast to pop music, with its focus on the vocalist, backed by anonymous studio musicians" (Clawson, 1999, p. 101). In live performance, the front person/vocalist is subject to the audience gaze to a greater degree than other performers – he/she is commodified and also sexualised, a feminine position (Green, 1997; Mulvey, 1989). Popular music videos exemplify this: women performers sing; men may sing but also play. Women rarely play instruments, that is, manipulate technology, as this detracts from the gaze. Men generally avoid the gaze, unless they are fronting. Rock (as opposed to pop) videos are often "performance" clips, that is, they show the band playing together, as a collective, often dressed either casually or fairly uniformly (e.g. the ubiquitous black leather), often not even looking at the camera (which enhances authenticity by suggesting documentary). Thus they avoid individualisation. Men appear in a wider range of roles and genres than women, who are mainly confined to pop/R&B.

Although videos are not necessarily representative of popular music practice, there are significant continuities in terms of gender. Generally, men in popular music have more flexibility in what they can do, for example, singing styles. Women are generally expected to be "good singers", and the genres in which they are prominent generally require a professional sound. Male singers don't have to be so accomplished, especially in genres which emphasise expression rather than skill. Additionally, in rock, the strong link between authorship and voice can make voice individually, personally expressive (precisely because of its "human" quality) in a way that is denied to the "professional" pop singer, who is often perceived as a mere interpreter of someone else's material, or a puppet manipulated by the industry.

This discussion of how singing is positioned in popular music discourse aids my interpretation of how my respondents think about singing. Being a singer exposes one to the gaze and this is an undesirable, feminised position. It also goes against the alternative scene's "anti-star" ethos. Playing guitar deflects the audience's gaze; it "clothes you". It imparts seriousness and implications of authorship. Finally it allows you to be part of the band. The band is a homosocial male collectivity united by a common goal, which is normative in the public domain (Sedgwick, 1985). Thus the "anti-star" ethos of alternative rock can be interpreted as reinforcing normative gender roles – men working together as a homosocial collectivity, directed towards the ends of artistic (rather than commercial) success, with the common job of delivering content.

The vocal therefore becomes just another instrument contributing to the overall performance of the song, which is seen as central, as the main event: "The scene at the time ... was more focused on the song than the performance" (Graeme). "The song was the main thing for us" (David Pine). When asked about vocal influences, Robert responded that it was the "songs rather than the vocal style" of performers that he identified with. This "song" discourse is has become part of the critical consensus around the Dunedin Sound: A 1996 compilation of "Forty years of Dunedin Music" entitled "But I can write songs okay" implied the primacy of composition above other factors. In *Anything Can Happen*, a 1989 TV documentary about Flying Nun, the theme of "good songs" ("not necessarily played that well") is repeated by a number of interviewees, including UK music journalist David Cavanagh and label head Roger Shepherd.

Simon Frith (2008) states that the identification of performer with song in rock discourse tends to collapse the distinction between them. Singing is heard as a direct expression of the singer's thoughts and feelings, and this is a key plank of rock's "authenticity" and immediacy – the idea that the performer "really means it". The voice of the singer is identified with their inmost self, but in the process other issues are overlooked. The voice does not guarantee "presence" – it is a medium, not a transparent bearer of meaning. Interestingly, most respondents had never been interviewed about their voices before, indicating perhaps the invisibility of the voice in popular music discourse. Songs have not always been identified with their performers – in pre-rock popular music (e.g. Tin Pan Alley), songwriting and performing were much more demarcated, but as rock emerged, critics strived to legitimate it through auteur theory: rock music expressed a personal vision, but one that was not identified with the voice so much as the "authored" combination of musical elements: "The criterion for art in rock is the capacity of the musician to create a personal, almost private universe and express it fully" (Landau, 1972, p. 15).

In classical music, the relation of performer and musical composition is, in a sense, the reverse of rock, because we hear primarily not the voice of the performer, but that of the composer (Frith, 2008). There is an illusion of transparency (the technical skill of the performer facilitates a satisfactory realization of the composer's intentions, which are manifest in the score). This is both unlike and like rock discourse: different in that the performer and the composer are not the same person, but similar in its emphasis on the text/song, independent of all other mediating, performative and situational factors. This emphasis on text rather than performance reveals the affinity of rock with classical, high culture, "art" values. The ideology of classical music depends strongly on a mind/body split, in which we hear music primarily as the expression of the composer's "genius". Lucy Green reads gender into this situation:

16 "But I Can Write Songs Okay": Male Voices in New Zealand Alternative Rock

... with composition it is *a metaphorical display of the mind* of the composer which enters into delineation ... Whilst we listen to music, it is not just the inherent meanings that occupy our attention, but also our idea of the composer's mental processes ... The masculine delineation of music is articulated through ... the cerebral control of knowledge and technology which is implicit in the notion of composition (1997, pp. 84–85, 216, italics in original).

The song is equivalent to the score; the composer is king.

The mind/body split also extends to how performers perform. At a classical concert, the orchestral players must minimise bodily display, remaining static at all times, apart from the movements necessary to play. They can't tap their feet or sway to the music – such bodily expression is only permissible for soloists and the conductor. The orchestra is like a machine that translates the intellectual concepts of the composer into music.

The alternative rock scenes I have examined show some continuities with the gendered classical model just described. The group typically "underperform", avoiding "show" and this can be read as invoking a discourse of seriousness and high art. The bodies of the performers are de-emphasised through the team approach and the lack of individualising elements. There is a general suspicion of commercialism, which is associated with the feminisation of mass culture (Huyssen, 1986). Vocals, associated with the body, are a necessary evil; a means to an end. Alternative rock can be described as an "art world", both in Bourdieu's sense of an avant garde that reverses mainstream values to produce cultural capital (integrity over money); but also in the more traditional sense of high culture that values intellect, formalism and "the canon" (Bourdieu, 1993; Hibbett, 2005). Indeed art and high culture references feature in the work of a number of Dunedin bands (*The Verlaines*, *Sneaky Feelings*, *The Puddle*) as well as in alternative rock more generally (*The Smiths*, *The Go-Betweens*). Moreover, in the nearly 30 years that have elapsed since the heyday of the Dunedin Sound, its popular critical reception has tended towards legitimisation and institutionalisation, largely by drawing on traditional discourses of authorship: "Graeme Downes shows he is still one of this country's most adventurous and accomplished songwriters" (Bollinger, 2008). "*The Puddle's* George D. Henderson has an almost shamanic knack for neatly concise pop songs" (Dass, 2008). In a review of David Kilgour's collaboration with local poet Sam Hunt, Nick Bollinger (2008) makes the link between voice, authorship, high art and popular music explicit: "You could say both artists have made careers out of being themselves. Each discovered at a young age the thing he was apparently put on this planet to do: in Hunt's case, making poems; in Kilgour's, playing thrilling guitar. And each quickly established a voice that was uniquely and recognisably theirs, something most poets and guitar players never achieve in a lifetime". That is, the value of the Dunedin Sound is now primarily understood in high cultural terms – a canon of artists and works comparable to local canons of fine art, literature or film. The lack of any other frame of reference perpetuates a discourse of Romantic/modernist heroic individualism so that agents, in turn, may come to understand themselves in these terms. But this approach elides the contributions of other "voices" and enabling factors in the scene: other musicians in the bands, audiences, critics, venues, influences and the specific historic and cultural circumstances (such as the formation of the Flying Nun label, which happened in Christchurch, not Dunedin) which produced the music and made it meaningful.

Rock writers Simon Reynolds and (in New Zealand) Matthew Hyland are critical of this auteurist "good song" approach (Hyland, 1990; Reynolds, 1990). Taking their cue from Roland Barthes, they read "voice" in alternative music as connoting nostalgia for presence, for a centre and guarantor of meaning, a master signifier. Extrapolating from Barthes' comments about "the grain of the voice", they emphasise sound or noise (abandon or *jouissance*) over clear articulation of melody or lyrics, which tends towards the reassurance of *plaisir* (Barthes, 1990). The questioning of the "master narrative" of voice/presence leads to a gender reading of traditional rock as phallocentric. Alternative rock, they argue, should subvert the traditional hierarchy of voice and instrumentation, producing a chaotic flux in which traditional western binaries of form/content, noise/voice, male/female are dissolved, resulting in "androgynous ... queer rock" (Gilbert, 1999, p. 43). In Dunedin, Bruce Russell's band *The Dead C* produced white noise guitar music which was marked by some similarities of approach – an experimental attitude to guitar playing and amplification, minimal, atonal vocals, producing "unstructured" music, "freed" from conventional dictates of melody, harmony, meaning etc (although the music still has a beat) with the ideological aim of breaking down "conventional modes of listening and thinking" (Butt & Russell, 1993). Ironically, "voice" is now understood as phallocentric, the opposite of voice as feminine.

How effectively do such developments address issues around gender and voice in alternative rock? Feminist critiques have pointed out that while alternative rock may have provided a thrill of "feminine otherness" for men, the scenes associated with it remained just as exclusively male in terms of performers, audiences and overall ideology, and that indie's construction of male "vulnerability" appropriated "feminine stereotypes as a male aesthetic credential, rather than empowering women" (Goodlad, 2003, p. 138). Russell's experimental approach links mode of production and meaning, but overlooks the diverse ways that music can be interpreted by audiences. The poststructuralist reading of Reynolds et al. reverses the conventional valorisation of intellectual, authorial voice by emphasising instead grain, physicality and sound over meaning and presence. The conventional hierarchy is reversed, reifying "feminine" noise, grain, non-sense over "masculine" authority and meaning. But this is simply substituting one idealisation for another. The "character" of a musical text does not determine its meaning, which is always negotiable according to context, audience, mode of production etc.

In this chapter I have discussed how male voices are understood by performers and audiences in an alternative rock scene. The bodily aspects of voice tend to be disavowed and are instead associated with the mind – the "vision" of the author. In the same way, in performance, the body is disavowed through a style of "non-performance" and avoidance of the gaze. Although alternative performance styles reject aggressive and vulgar displays of rock machismo, masculinity is still affirmed through a quasi-classical discourse of individual authorship, which simplifies the complex meanings of the scene by reducing it to a list of classic "songs", written by individuals. Post-structuralist readings critique this intentional model, de-centring and questioning "voice" and its connection with "song", which led to new readings of gender in relation to the genre. But privileging sound/noise/grain over structure/meaning/voice overlooks how music is socially and culturally situated, especially in terms of questions of performance and audience, and thus simplifies questions of affect. While there is no doubt that it can produce such connotations for some, there is no direct way of linking these insights to broader audience responses. There is no such thing as a pure voice, unmediated by social discourse. Emergent movements such as male choirs therefore need to continually consider how they position themselves in relation to dominant discourses around gender and music.

References

Bannister, M. (1999). *Positively George street: A personal history of Sneaky feelings and the Dunedin sound.* Auckland: Reed.

Bannister, M. (2006). *White boys, white noise: masculinities and 1980s indie guitar rock.* London: Ashgate.

Barthes, R. (1990). The grain of the voice. In S. Frith & A. Goodwin (Eds.), *On record: Rock, pop and the written word* (pp. 293–300). New York: Pantheon.

Bayton, M. (2006). Women making music: Some material constraints. In A. Bennett, B. Shank, & J. Toynbee (Eds.), *The popular music studies reader* (pp. 347–354). London and New York: Routledge.

Bollinger, N. (2008, January 12–18). A decent heathen. *NZ Listener.* Retrieved January 20, 2010, from http://www.listener.co.nz/issue/3531/artsbooks/10288/a_decent_heathen.html

Bourdieu, P. (1993). The field of cultural production: Essays on art and literature. New York: Columbia University Press.

Burch, J. (2009). The Dead C. *Mountain Fold Music Journal, 1*(2) (pages unnumbered).

Butt, D., & Russell, B. (1993, December 15). *Heaven on earth is always a beguiling prospect.* Retrieved January 20, 2010, from http://www.audiofoundation.org.nz/articles/discourse/heaven-earth-always-beguiling-prospect-dialogue-between-danny-butt-and-bruce-russ

Churton, W. R. (2000). *Have you checked the children? Punk and post-punk music in New Zealand, 1977–1981.* Christchurch: Put Your Foot Down Publishing.

Clawson, M. (1999). Masculinity and skill acquisition in the adolescent rock band. *Popular Music, 18*(1), 99–114.

Coates, N. (1997). (R)evolution now? Rock and the political potential of gender. In S. Whiteley (Ed.). *Sexing the groove: Popular music and gender* (pp. 50–64). London: Routledge.

Cohen, S. (1997). Men making a scene: Rock music and the production of gender. In S. Whiteley (Ed.), *Sexing the groove: popular music and gender* (pp. 18–34). London: Routledge.

Connell, R. W. (1995). *Masculinities.* Berkeley, CA: University of California Press.

Dass, K. (2008, August 23–29). Voodoo rocker. *NZ Listener.* Retrieved January 20, 2010, from http://www.listener.co.nz/culture/music/voodoo-rocker/

Davey, T., & Puschmann, H. (1996). *Kiwi rock.* New Zealand: Kiwi Rock Publications.

DeRogatis, J. (1996). *Kaleidoscope eyes: Psychedelic rock from the 60s to the 90s.* Citadel: Secaucus.

Frith, S. (2008). The voice as a musical instrument. In M. Clayton (Ed.), *Music, words and voice: A reader* (pp. 65–71). Manchester and New York: Manchester University Press.

Frith, S., & McRobbie, A. (1990). Rock and sexuality. In S. Frith & A. Goodwin (Ed.), *On record: Rock, pop and the written word* (pp. 371–389). New York: Pantheon.

Gilbert, J. (1999). White light/white heat: jouissance beyond gender in the Velvet Underground. In A. Blake (Ed.), *Living through pop* (pp. 31–48). London: Routledge.

Goodlad, L. (2003). Packaged alternatives: The incorporation and gendering of "alternative" radio. In S. Squier (Ed.), *Communities of the air: Radio century, radio culture* (pp. 134–163). Durham, London: Duke University.

Grajeda, T. (2002). The "feminization" of rock. In R. Beebe, D. Fulbrook, & B. Saunders (Eds.), *Rock over the edge* (pp. 233–254). London: Duke University.

Green, L. (1997). M*usic, gender, education*. Cambridge: Cambridge University.

Harrison, S. (2007). A perennial problem in gendered participation in music: What's happening to the boys? *British Journal of Music Education, 24*(3), 267–280.

Hesmondhalgh, D. (1999). Indie: The institutional politics and aesthetics of a popular music genre. *Cultural Studies, 13*(1), 34–61.

Hibbett, R. (2005). What is indie rock? *Popular Music and Society, 28*(1), 55–78.

Huyssen, A. (1986). Mass culture as woman: modernism's other. In T. Modleski (Ed.), *Studies in entertainment: Critical approaches to mass culture* (pp. 188–199). Bloomington, IN: Indiana.

Hyland, M. (1990, September). In defense of surreal guitars. *Stamp, 13*.

Keightley, K. (2001). Reconsidering rock. In S. Frith, W. Straw, & J. Street (Eds.) *Cambridge companion to pop and rock* (pp. 109–142). Cambridge: Cambridge University.

King, M. (1999). *Being pakeha now: Reflections and recollections of a white native*. Auckland: Penguin.

Laing, D. (1986). *One chord wonders: Power and meaning in punk rock*. Milton Keynes: Open University.

Landau, J. (1972). *It's too late to stop now: a rock and roll journal*. San Francisco: Straight Arrow.

McGonigle, D. (2005). In love with those times: Flying Nun and the Dunedin Sound. *Stylus Magazine*. Retrieved December 8, 2009, from http://www.stylusmagazine.com/feature.php?ID=1567

Mitchell, T. (1996). *Popular music and local identity: Rock, pop and rap in Europe and Oceania*. London: Leicester University.

Morris, S. (Producer) (1989). *Anything can happen*. New Zealand: TVNZ.

Mulvey, L. (1989). *Visual and other pleasures*. Bloomington and Indianapolis, IN: Indiana University.

Pearson, B. (1974). *Fretful sleepers and other essays*. Auckland: Heinemann.

Phillips, J. (1987). *A man's country? The image of the pakeha male – A history*. Auckland: Penguin.

Reynolds, S. (1990). *Blissed out: The raptures of rock*. London: Serpent's Tail.

Rickwood, J. (2010). Taking the piss? Australian blokes and a cappella choirs. In S. Brunt & K. Zemke (Eds.), *What's it worth? "Value" and popular music: Selected papers from the 2009 IASPM Australia-New Zealand Conference* (pp. 55–63). Dunedin: IASPM.

Sedgwick, E. K. (1985). *Between Men: English literature and male homosocial desire*. New York: Columbia University Press.

Shuker, R. (1998). *Key concepts in popular music*. London: Routledge.

Straw, W. (2005). Communities and scenes in popular music. In K. Gelder & S. Thornton (Eds.), *The subcultures reader* (pp. 494–505). London: Routledge.

Various Artists. (1996). *But I can write songs okay: Forty years of Dunedin popular music*. [CD]. New Zealand: Yellow Eye Music.

Chapter 17
Southern Masculinity in American Rock Music

Jason T. Eastman

17.1 Introduction

Minutes into the very first interview of my dissertation research I asked my musician informant, "How can I tell the difference between southern rock and regular rock?" He smiled politely but in a somewhat annoyed and condescending voice replied, "You can't; all rock is southern". Quick reflection immediately revealed my question contained an oxymoron. Rock-n-roll, and all music considered quintessentially American for that matter, originates in the southeastern part of country (Malone & Strickland, [1979] 2003). This region includes both the coast states remembered for the English, aristocratic-like agrarian economy built almost entirely on slave labour and the rugged, isolated Appalachian mountain region settled by fiercely independent Scots-Irish immigrants.

Historically, the strict patriarchy and feudalistic social hierarchy of The South meant underclass men experienced persistently high levels of marginalization and economic hardship. Expressing these experiences endemic to the region, southern artists produced the blues, gospel, jazz, and country music that is not only now central to the American songbook but also spread around the world partially because of these musics' ability to communicate the plight of oppression many across the globe experience. Musical voices communicate the shared southern sacrifice and hardship, as well as the good times with the close-knit communities and relationships with God the southern region of the United States (U.S.) is known for. Ever since the rise of first mass and now digital media, all United States citizens of all regions have come to claim southern music known around the world for their own.

But musical styling aside, what about the culture attached to southern music and its relation to U.S. society more generally? During another interview I asked a musician how to differentiate Southern culture from the larger American culture and he reiterated a Malcolm X quote by saying, "You just know you're in The South when you cross the Canadian border". While the civil rights leader was referring to

---
J.T. Eastman (✉)
Coastal Carolina University, Conway, SC, USA
e-mail: jeastman@coastal.edu

systemic racism found not just in The South but the entire country, this musician went on to explain how "ya'll think ya won the [civil] war, but since then we've been taking over incognito". This point was personally affirmed to me a few months later when I auditioned for a band in Niagara Falls, New York. While driving to the audition I was so far north I could literally see Canada across the river, but upon my arrival the rebel battle flag, the highly contested and controversial symbol of The South, hung behind the drum set. I asked who was from The South, only to receive the response, "No one, we just love southern rock". Thus, while northern culture is equated and conflated with U.S. culture generally, perhaps all Americans are slightly more southern than they realize – or more southern than they would like to admit because the region both historically and contemporarily is stereotyped as ignorant and backward (Eastman & Schrock, 2008).

17.2 Southerness as Masculinity

I spent the last half decade exploring those who boldly and proudly express a "self-declared" southerness in contemporary southern rock music. I find this southern rebel identity is best conceptualized as a form of masculinity that poor, white men from all around the country embrace as a means to protest the presumably non-southern, middle-class manhood associated with the status quo. Marginalized men unable to meet the status-quo ideals of the middle class turn to southern musicians for clues how to define their own manhood in alternative ways, often by protesting and defining themselves in comparison to the educated, economically successful urban men of the middle class that set the hegemonic standard of what all Americans should strive to be (Eastman & Schrock, 2008).

In embracing a self-declared 'southerness,' poor and working class men reject the presumably northern, middle-class definitions of manhood built upon the institutions of work and education. Instead of claiming power through their jobs, rebel men create a façade of empowerment through drinking, using drugs, brawling with each other, and sexually objectifying women. This enables southern men to meet hegemonic masculine ideals (Connell, 1987) or to personally signify a power and dominance central to U.S. men – a power most middle class men claim through their careers and material successes. That is, while most men empower themselves through their acquired resources and authority, poor and marginal men lack assets and power. Since men unable to affirm their manhood become subject to especially influential informal sanctions such as being labelled feminine or homosexual, marginalized men must either accept assaults to their masculine ego or develop alternative strategies that convince both themselves and others they are dominant and in control. In the case of lower class men, hegemonic masculinity is achieved by protesting the normative conventions of the larger culture (Connell, 1995), which is what southern rockers do in embracing a southern rebel identity that stands in stark contrast to the middle class, generalized male.

Historically, men's use of a southern rebelliousness to empower the masculine self by protesting the 'northern' status quo has been a mainstay in the U.S. almost since the country's founding. Prior to the Civil War, southern masculinity stood in stark contrast to northern masculinity as southern men publicly defined their manhood via strict adherence to protestant values and personal mastery. While northern men adapted to industrialization and competitive capitalism to embody a 'self-made manhood' (Rotundo, 1993; Kimmel, 1996; Bederman, 1995) built on American individualism, the pre-Civil War masculinity of The South remained closely aligned with the communal manhood of the colonial era in which men claimed honour and mastery via family, faith, civic duty and domination of lower class others including the poor and racial minorities.

Many classic explorations of southern culture illustrate both the centrality of public prestige to southern men and the ways men achieved this honour and mastery by affirming independence. W.J. Cash ([1941] 1991) describes the quintessential southern man as individualistic, independent, and resentful of authority. Bertram Wyatt-Brown (1986) writes of a southern honour defended through public displays of mastery and violence, while in private these men engaged in drinking, gambling, fighting, dueling and keeping company with prostitutes. These deviant behaviours allowed southern men to empower their masculine selves by proving they were controlled neither morally nor physically by anyone (Glover, 2004). While there were always cultural differences between the American North and South (Friend & Glover, 2004), as the 19th century progressed, southern men increasingly defined themselves in opposition to the "Yankee" men who they would eventually be defeated by on the battlefield. In fact, strong arguments can be made that the political, economic and cultural disagreements between the American North and South escalated into war partially because of the strong connections between masculinity, nationalism, and the southern code honour must be defended even through violent militarism (Nagel, 2005).

During Reconstruction after The South's loss in the U.S. Civil War, two different, somewhat contradictory southern masculinities were practiced throughout the southeast. Men strived to reclaim the all-important honour they had lost on the battlefield while they replaced the mastery previously allotted via the now defunct institution of slavery. Southern men began claiming honour, pride and self-esteem by publically adhering to Christian faith, family and community while also engaging in public violence and aggression (like lynching) to affirm their mastery and defend their status (Friend, 2009). And even though these two masculinities are seemingly contradictory to each other in many ways, they were often practiced in tandem as both are ultimately strategies to empower the self by allowing southern men to view "themselves in opposition to what they describe as urban, industrial, liberal, corrupt, effeminate men of the north (Friend, 2009) [x]."

Following the U.S. Civil War southerners experienced a century of racial apartheid that only ended, at least formally, after extensive and extended grassroots social movements demonized the region as the source of the country's cold war ills. Today the region is still stereotyped as culturally backward, with exaggerated prejudices built upon very real regional factors such as high rates of rural poverty, strong individual commitments to evangelical, fundamental protestant sects, and conservative politics that resist change. Because of these commitments to traditional culture, the region still retains a rigid patriarchy and feudalistic class structure of "haves" and "have nots," which sustains and reproduces a masculinity centred on power, honour, and individuality.

17.3 Southern Masculinity in Rock Music

The vast majority of U.S. men are not musicians, and even fewer are vocalists. Thus, many American men do not express themselves artistically and instead look to others for aesthetic representations that help them understand their own place and purpose in the world. Men are especially likely to turn to vocalists who not only express with everyday language, but also use the emotive aspects of their voice and stage presence to communicate what words alone cannot. Furthermore, in the culture industry musicians are more than performers; they are also personas and thus become more than just expressers for other men but also serve as role models who portray an idealized identity and masculinity that few if any men can embody themselves.

Many musicians still explicitly maintain a southern identity by drawing upon the traditional south in their music and adhering to the centuries old tradition of defining their own manhood by rebellious acts and protesting the middle class masculine conventions central to American culture more generally (Eastman & Schrock, 2008). However, the question still left unanswered is whether these southern rebel strategies that affirm a masculine self are present in other genres of rock-n-roll where singers and musicians do not blatantly claim a southern identity, but still embrace a southern songwriting tradition and rocker identity. Or in other words, while it is widely recognized rock music has traditionally been, and continues to be, the music of young men, does this mean rock-n-roll still retains its southern themes of masculine empowerment via rebellion?

In the following survey of sociological research, I find that while rock music evolved into many different genres since its inception in the 1950s, most rock-n-roll musicians (especially singers) still implicitly express a southern-like manhood. In expressing a masculinity based on rebellion, they also serve as masculine role models for their fans, many of whom are men marginalized by their class or age. In embracing the music as more than art but also an identity, these audiences thus use rock music and its southern strategies of masculine empowerment that compensate for their lack of resources and prestige and instead stake claim to dominance and mastery through rebellion.

17.4 Masculinity and the Dawn of Rock-n-Roll

The first genres of rock music emerged during the 1950s when the U.S. created a period of adolescence with the institution of compulsory secondary education. Stylistically 50s rock music traces its roots to what *Life Magazine* author Richard

Goldstein (1968) called the "unholy alliance" of country and blues that occurred during the latter half of the decade. Called "rock-a-billy" through a combination of slang for the blues and the white "hillbillies" who crossed racial lines and embraced the Black music, rock exploded out of Memphis as Sam Phillips' crew of artists that included Jerry Lee Lewis and Johnny Cash recorded and toured under the Sun Music label. As one of the first popular performers who borrowed Black performers' styles and made sexuality a centrepiece of stage presence, Elvis was especially influential in shaping the masculinity and performance styles of the rock artists who followed in his wake. Not only was his sexuality shocking to a conservative postwar nation, Elvis also broke middle class taboos by putting the centuries-old practice of poor Whites and Blacks creating music together on the national stage (Betrand, 2004).

While not all 50s rock artists were as flamboyant as Elvis on stage, almost all abandoned the classic, standoffish performance style of white musicians that distanced performers from audiences. Instead, rockers borrowed the more energetic and emotive Black performance style that would become the standard for following generations of rock musicians. Rock-a-billy artists' "sensual performing style was as much an expression of stereotypical masculine imagery deeply embedded in southern working-class as it was a violation of conventional middle-class standards ... which effectively implanted much of the working-class culture of the south in the nation at large" (Malone & Strickland, [1979] 2003, p. 106). Thus, ever since rock's inception performers have used their stage presence to affirm and empower their masculine self by challenging and rebelling from the status conventions of middle class society.

17.5 The 1960s

During the 1960s rock music became central to the new left or "hippy" counter culture. The movement was cultural and musically experimental, and through this process rock music lost some of its southerness. Experimentation opened up new ways for male musicians to present masculinity to an entire generation of middle-class youth. Young men who were disillusioned by the extremely conservative and materialistic world of their parents rebelled en masse against a rigid social structure prescribing social conformity across almost all aspects of life. The counter culture rebelled and defined itself against the postwar technocracy, a form of social organization in which modernization and rationalization pervaded all aspects of public and even personal life (Roszak, 1969). Progressive politics, peace, tolerance, non-western religions, free love and drug use as enlightening experiences all became central to the nationwide counter culture (Howard, 1969; Yablonsky, 1968) and its rock music. Embracing an identity constructed almost entirely by rejecting the middle-class status quo or being everything the previous generation was not, the counter culture's masculinity was constructed as a complete juxtaposition of the white, militaristic, capitalistic, patriarchal manhood of the previous 50s generation.

In the hippy subculture, men valued "cooperation over competition, expression over success, communalism over individualism, being over doing, making art over making money, and autonomy over obedience" (Flacks, 1971, p. 129). But more generally, in rejecting both the world and the manhood of their fathers, "hippy men" rebelled against the power and dominance central to both hegemonic and southern masculinity. Thus, 60s men of the new left used a southern strategy of rebellion to embrace a manhood that was anything but southern.

The rejection of larger society and its masculinity was readily apparent in the music and performance styles of new left artists. At the beginning of the decade, musicians like Bob Dylan borrowed heavily upon the folk music of the Great Depression to inspire the next generation of protest politics. The 60s folk singers never presented themselves as models of American masculinity like Elvis, and the rejection of hegemonic individualism is even more readily apparent in the acid rockers' communal performances of the late 1960s. These artists harmoniously infused instruments and vocals, a practice which stood in contrast to the more patriarchal style of southern performers known for a vocal 'front man' supported by nameless, seemingly faceless backing musicians and elaborate stage designs that drew attention away from the artists themselves to the expressive form they created.

Thus, in surveying the 1960s, we see the new left followed in the long-standing southern tradition of defining one's identity via rebellion from the status quo, though in other ways rock-n-roll temporarily lost its southern, masculine roots as hippy men embraced traits often considered feminine (peace, love, tolerance, understanding, pacifism, etc...). Still, southern men's traditional masculine rebellion against the economics and culture of the middle class was a strategy used by new left men a century later to define an independent masculine self. Hippy men and the counterculture more generally protested the status quo they found themselves surrounded by, including the traditional hegemonic ideals of power and dominance alongside the social institutions (education, family, military, economy etc...) built upon that idealized form of manhood. Furthermore, the antiauthoritarianism and nonconformity of the 60s subcultures stand in stark contrast to southerners who embrace a community founded more on conformity to a marginal identity and community, thereby being deviant while also suppressing individuality by not readily accepting any and everyone.

The rebellion of the 1960s is readily apparent in musical critiques of the 60s counter culture from southern artists who presented themselves not as rebels, but as part of the status quo. In an ironic transition of cultural roles, the southern musicians began to present themselves as rebel traditionalists in a rapidly changing world in order to stand against the new masculinity they thought was becoming a new status quo to reject given the prolific spread of hippy youth culture. For example, Merle Haggard's country song "Okie from Muskogee" undermines hippy men's masculinity by chastising their sandals, long-hair and antiwar sentiments. In this same song, Haggard also sings of his own pride to embrace southern/midwestern manhood.

17.6 After the 60s

While rock music evolved greatly during the 1960s it never lost the southern tradition that claimed youth masculinity via a protest of adult, middle class virtues. However, the cultural experimentation and "feminization" of U.S. men that occurred throughout the 1960s was short lived as a more traditional masculinity quickly retook centre stage in rock music. The youth cultures of rock-n-roll reclaimed forms of masculine rebellion closely aligned with the southern masculinity at the roots of not just rock, but all forms of U.S. manhood based on personal empowerment through achieving honour and mastery. The men who wrote and performed rock music used rebellion as alternative means to achieve hegemonic, masculine empowerment. Marginalized youth, especially those from the lower classes that had little optimism in a secure future, found their own insecurities expressed and overcome by the next generation of male vocalists.

While Woodstock is often remembered as the capstone event of the 60s counter-cultural revolution, music critics Greil Marcus ([1989] 2003) and Jim DeRogatis (2003) both stress how another 1969 concert was more indicative of what rock would become. The same year as Woodstock, *The Rolling Stones* performed a free concert in Altamont, California, just outside the epicentre of the original hippy movement in San Francisco. The band hired the Hell's Angels motorcycle gang as their security, a group who shared hippy's love of sex and drugs but clashed frequently over politics because of the riders' nationalistic, pro-war conservatism. As the Rolling Stones played, the crowd became unruly and violent, and after an extended and intensive period of chaos the Hell's Angels stabbed and killed an attendee.

Both the motorcycle gang and *The Rolling Stones* led by Mick Jagger, who uses Elvis-like, sexually charged stage moves, rejected the passivity and peacefulness of hippy masculinity while using the sex and drugs of the counterculture to substantiate their own claim to masculine power. In the new rock music, everything was old again. By the dawn of the 1970s drugs and alcohol were no longer used to expand the mind, but to get high. Musicians and fans transformed sex as an expression of compassion into the chauvinistic objectification of women. And no longer would the "better man" shy away from conflict as passivity was rejected while violence and the threat thereof were equated with individual empowerment. In this context, musicians went from communicative artists to popular entertainers in which many built their masculine image through the hedonistic indulgence of 'Sex, Drugs and Rock-n-Roll' (Frith, 1978) that many listeners interpreted as individual behaviors they could use to empower their own selves.

17.7 1970s

As the socially-conscious, communal protest politics of the 60s new left receded, The South and the individually based southern masculinity began to retake its place back at the forefront of American rock. In some ways, the American southern rock movement of the 1970s and the European hard rock counterparts were backlashes against the new left counterculture of the previous decade. In musically moving back to the country and blues roots of the music, these movements resurrected the region's writing and performance style by highlighting individual singers and musicians through songs with open spaces that unlocked opportunities for vocal and instrument solos. This new musical approach can even be seen in group names like *The Allman Brothers*, *The Marshall Tucker Band* and *The Charlie Daniels Band;* labels that highlighted individuals over the collective group rarely appeared in the counter culture new left since they go against the communicative, cooperative values of the subculture. Furthermore, these bands explicitly embraced their southern roots as "southern rock music was marketed with a self-conscious southerness unknown even at the height of the rockabilly craze" (Malone & Strickland, [1979] 2003, p. 113). Proudly displaying the highly controversial confederate flag, southern rockers like *Lynyrd Skynyrd* lyrically celebrated their agrarian, patriarchal homeland and culture with songs about drinking, womanizing, using drugs, and fighting juxtaposed with expression of faith and family. A similar movement occurred across the Atlantic as British hard rock bands like *AC/DC* and *Led Zeppelin* revived blues guitar styling while celebrating a working class masculinity defined by antagonizing the middle-class status-quo. In revitalizing southern rebellion, musicians around the world embraced the deviance of rock music as a way to empower their own selves, thereby affording men who lack resources and authority strategies to substantiate their claims via hegemonic authority and success in the capitalist marketplace.

Through the 70s, rock music performers and audiences further embraced the masculinity of the U.S. south as hard rock evolved into the metal music that even more explicitly uses rebellion to empower the individual masculine self. Deena Weinstein ([1991] 2000) describes metal music as Dionysian, putting forth a depiction of reality that allows fans to suspend the troubles of everyday life through indulgence in all that is pleasurable – including uninhibited and uncommitted sex and mind altering substances. But while these practices certainly involve recreation and catharsis, metal musicians and audiences also use these behaviors to empower themselves, thus explaining why the music is so popular with working class, white men and alienated youth who increasingly find themselves marginalized and without a means to claim masculine pride via their jobs. Even one of the most well-known and celebrated music sociologists Simon Frith agrees that Deena Weinstein "persuasively argues" the core of heavy metal is power, and musicians have the ability to "empower" a social group who lacks clout because of institutional barriers (Frith & Street, 1992). Others also agree, like Robert Gross (1990) who surveys 172 symbols on jewellery in an advertisement from a metal magazine and found the pieces include but are not limited to electric bolts, skulls and skeletons, along with a vast collection of Egyptian, Biblical and Occult symbols such as pentagrams, pentacles, inverted crucifixes and crescent moons. These symbols empower the self through shocking imagery; few fans actually practice Witchcraft or Satanism as a religion. Jarl Ahlkvist's (1999) survey of album covers reveals similar findings about empowerment, often through dark imagery, though he adds how masculinity is further defined through the sexual objectification of females as "depictions of women in heavy metal music are almost universally sexist and in some cases, misogynous. Women are represented as one-dimension sex objects, the embodiment of evil, or childlike virgins" (p. 134). Thus, the darkness and evil expressed in metal is first and foremost about individual, personal empowerment – not a literal worshipping of the devil or call for violence and suicide as some critics of the music proclaim (Gross, 1990; Strasburger, 1998).

Metal music is especially attractive for nihilistic and alienated young men because the music is loud and powerful (Arnett, 1991b), and the musicians who perform metal use their stage presences to heighten these musical expressions. Guitars are almost always distorted and often tuned down while vocalists use classical-like styles to explore both high and low ranges seldom used in other genres of rock. These musical practices occur over a steady, constant blues beat thrusting like a running machine which cannot be stopped. Stage movements like the head bang mimic violence while other musicians simulate sex with microphone stands and instruments. Opera-like vocals of long, extended notes at extreme ranges allow musicians to embrace and express this power. Ritualistic concert experiences symbolically instil the experience of personal power and mastery (Paul & Caldwell, 2007) while they protest the status quo. This means that while metal is quite removed from its southern roots, like most genres of rock music, metal entails the same traditional southern practice in which men claim their masculine honour and mastery by defining themselves in opposition to the middle class and presumably northern power elite.

17.8 1980s

While heavy metal styles diversified as the genre evolved through the remainder of the century and into the next, the masculine empowerment via rebellion borrowed from the men of southern history remains constant across the different types of metal. For instance, the pop metal that grew out of the Los Angeles underground through bands like *Mötley Crüe* or *Poison* revolves around masculine empowerment via rebellion from middle class conventions (Walser, 1993; Rafalovich, 2006). This genre is often called "hair metal" because male musicians feminized their appearance with teased hair and make-up while sexualizing their stage acts with overly acrobatic dance moves. Still, these rockers held true to the traditional southern practice of drinking, using drugs, espousing violence and sexually objectifying women to signify hegemonic masculinity. In glamorizing their hedonistic lifestyles, these rock stars made their fans want to be them.

In the music underground, many subgenres of metal including thrash, speed and doom evolved by rejecting the popularized style of the mainstream in favour of a more aggressive, raw sound. These artists partially rejected the hedonism of the mainstream and focused more on lyrical critiques of larger society through songs of violence, death, destruction and the occult. They also expressed a manhood their fans could embrace because it empowered the masculine self through rebellion. Dark and nihilistic, the singers of this metal often use a low, angry voice to make the emotive fury expressed in metal sound all the more threatening – a style especially attractive to "adolescents who need to express rage against a society that has left them helpless and without a vehicle to define themselves" (Reddick & Beresin, 2002, p. 53).

Across all the hard rock and metal genres that existed throughout the 1970s and 1980s, musicians showed how their fans could use drinking, drug use, sex and other high risk behaviors (Arnett, 1991a, 1992) to both provide a certain amount of catharsis (Paul & Caldwell, 2007) and compensate for their lack of power. Thus, while the metal subculture seems far removed from the south, metal musicians and fans still embrace the century's old southern practice in which men, most of whom have no resources of their own to claim hegemonic ideals, create a façade of empowerment through rebellion. In fact, my own research reveals many contemporary southern metal scenes, like the death metal of North Florida or the swamp metal of New Orleans, explicitly embrace southerness illustrating how metal music is not incompatible with the traditional masculinity of The South.

In the 80s another British working class music called punk found its way to American shores. Even though it came from across the Atlantic, like most genres of rock, punk was blues-guitar based and followed the southern tradition where musicians and vocalists put a rebellious masculinity on public display fans could embody to empower their own masculine selves. Musically, punk is simplistic, raw and fast, with the vocals often fading into the noise of the music except when songs include communal chants similar to those heard at sporting events to create a sense of community amongst fans. Often lacking coherent lyrical meaning, punk music cannot be fully appreciated via recordings and is best experienced in person where the energy of the singer and band is exacerbated with outlandish stage movements.

A founding principle of punk music is a protest of the profit-driven culture industry and capitalism more generally, a practice that invokes memories of the agrarian southerners who rejected the northern industrial economy prior to the civil war. Other elements of southern masculinity are present in punk rock music – especially the longstanding practice of overly aggressive male performers (Frith, 1981). Punk musicians, especially those in the 'hardcore' subgenres, often encourage violence thereby providing an avenue for marginalized men to empower themselves through the aggression innate to hegemonic masculinity. In line with the southern rock-n-roll tradition that was exaggerated in the metal years, punks also embrace drinking alcohol and using drugs as a means to personal empowerment via rebellion. But unlike metal, punk is more explicit and abrupt about distrusting and disrespecting authority (Hansen & Hansen, 1991). Thus, punks (especially the male performers) are much closer to the southern masculine tradition in which men signify their manhood by defining the masculine self in contrast to the status quo through deviance.

Perhaps nowhere is the southern-like, communal rebellion of punk more readily apparent than in the mostly male groups who use the music to embrace and embody a deviant, masculine identity as a collective group. For instance, skinheads who rebel against the racial progress America has made gravitate toward punk music because of the genre's ability to build community through shared musical experiences led by musicians who write songs and perform in ways that emphasize the group over the individual (Baron, 1989). Straight-edge, which is a drug and alcohol free lifestyle, also embraces punk music by instilling a sense of group solidarity through communal rebellion against a society they perceive as over-run by drugs, tobacco and alcohol. This movement does reject the substance abuse long central to rock music masculinity, but straight-edgers perceive themselves as protesting not just a punk subculture but an entire society that glorifies intoxicants. Thus celebrating abstinence empowers their own masculine selves through both rebellion and self-mastery via their ability to resist temptation. But whether punk expresses a substance free lifestyle (Haenfler, 2004; Smith, 2011) or white power (Kimmel, 2005), research shows both subcultures use the rebellion expressed by male performers that double as role models to empower their masculine selves, thereby achieving the hegemonic ideals of the larger American culture via alternative strategies.

17.9 1990s

Musically, the last decade of the 20th century was dominated by the alternative rock inseparably entwined with the 'Generation X' youth culture. Musically, a diverse variety of rock styles fall under the 'alt' umbrella, and most of these styles diffuse the overt masculine sexuality, substance abuse and violence that characterize most other genres of rock. Angst is central to Generation X and 'standoffish' performance styles that entail little if any stage movements reflected this worrisome anguish. Garbled, incoherent and even nonsensical lyrics sunk into a raw sound that only avoided complete chaos because of the simplicity and moderate tempo of the music. Alternative musicians rejected the "rock star" role model common in many genres and instead presented themselves as folk artists, abandoning stage costumes and elaborate show technologies to present themselves as just like one of their fans to heighten the communal experience of live performances. Furthermore, rejection of the rock star status changed the masculinity of Generation X as alternative singers and songwriters reinvented 1960s manhood by rejecting violence and misogyny while embracing individual creativity, expansive knowledge bases, and minimalistic lifestyles.

Generation X is characterized as hiding their pessimism about social reality behind a façade of sarcasm and cynicism (Arnet, 2009). Furthermore, while most genes of rock cater to the working class, the Generation X movement revolved around college-educated, middle-class youth, and thus the subculture and its music had less incentive to promote a means for marginalized men to empower themselves via individual rebellion. Ideologically the music traces its roots to the hippies of the 1960s, evolving through the underground college radio stations that carried forth new left politics through the 70s and 80s (Weinstein, 1995; Kruse, 1993) as bands such as *REM* from the home of southern rock in Athens, *Nirvana* and *Pearl Jam* from Seattle, and the *Smashing Pumpkins* from Chicago emerged from local scenes to rise to national prominence.

Originating from the college-educated class, Generation X and its alternative musician role models abandoned a generalized and often symbolic rebellion from the social whole and instead focused their protests on the white-collar, suburban, yuppie world via academic arguments. Laying the roots of the American wing of the global justice movement, Generation X and its musicians were at the forefront of a critique of corporate greed and American individualism (Moore, 2005), perhaps best symbolized by the ongoing fight over profit margins between the band Pearl Jam and the concert ticket seller Ticketmaster (DeRogatis, 2003). Thus, alternative men were more secure in their masculinity, because like hippy men of the 1960s they originated from the privileged middle class and were confident about secure futures, especially given the good economic environment and global peace at the end of the last century (Arnet, 2009). Furthermore, unlike the working class, 'Generation Xers' were socialized to believe they had the power and the means to change the world as opposed to being instilled with a sense of working-class passivity and acceptance. Led by their alternative rocker role models who voiced critiques against the mainstream with their anger and apathetic filled voices on and off the stage, Generation X borrowed from pre-Civil War southern men and defined their identities by communal challenges against the system in political ways as opposed to using the more common rock-n-roll strategy of affirming individual masculinity by personally empowering the self through individual acts of deviance and symbolic rebellion.

One element of alternative music that sets it apart from most other genres of rock is a rebelling against patriarchy. Generation X is known for relaxing gender norms while making third wave feminism and feminist causes a centrepiece of rock-n-roll (Schippers, 2000, 2002). For example, Eddie Vedder of the band *Pearl Jam* is remembered for his efforts to further pro-choice causes, while Nirvana bassist Krist Novoselic worked on anti-rape efforts in war torn Bosnia. Furthermore, movements like the riot grrls (Garrison, 2000; Rosenberg & Garfalo, 1998) opened up opportunities for female musicians when the 1990s alternative music took a harder edge and evolved into now what is called "indie," short for independent as the music is written, recorded and released without record company support. Thus, by not relegating women into secondary, sexually objectifying roles like that of groupie (Clawson, 1999) alternative rockers rejected the common rock pattern of affirming individual masculinity by oppressing women. However, this egalitarian interactional style was short-lived in mainstream rock; by the end of the decade rock music, musicians, and fans revitalized the southern misogyny central to rock-n-roll since the genre's founding.

17.10 2000s

As the 1990s progressed, mainstream rock returned to its southern roots as the music became more aggressive. Male performers and audiences alike rejected third wave feminism and embraced the violence, substance abuse and sexual objectification of women long central to both rock-n-roll and southern masculinity. During the first decade of the 21st century, American rock-n-roll music increasingly gravitated toward what is often called "nu metal," a sound rock writer Ian Christe describes as created via a "formula that raged with the thunder of heavy metal while swaying to the funky pulse of rap music. Then they struck a compromise between that mixture and the gruesome sonic assault of death metal" (2003, pp. 324–326). The music is also sometimes called "shock rock" because the aggressive music is often accompanied by dramatic stage performances that explicitly express the nihilism and violence often left only anticipated in other genres of metal. Nu metal also relies heavily on grotesque imagery to convey a symbolic rebellion to their mostly male audiences. While most bands do not go so far as shock rock bands like G.W.A.R. who perform in elaborate stage costumes that make the band look like larger-than-life demonic figures from science fiction films, most musicians incorporate symbolism into their rebellious critiques of the middle class status-quo. For instance, goth rocker Marilyn Manson named himself to illustrate the two extremes of America's preoccupation with those of fame, both actress Marilyn Monroe and cult leader Charles Manson. The nine member band Slipknot performs in identical jumpsuits with barcodes to protest the stealing of individuality and identity via the culture industry, commodity fetishism and conspicuous consumption more generally. These stage shows, combined with the music that is metal-like in sound but often borrows the aggressive lyric style of rap, are described as carnival spectacles where musicians (especially singers) promote dissidence and rebelliousness through the experience in ritualistic deviance. Thus, on the surface, even though shock rock seems remotely distant from the rockabilly sung a half century earlier, the centuries old southern practice of affirming manhood through rebellion is still central to this latest incarnation of rock-n-roll.

17.11 Conclusion

It has been long recognized that all of the different rock genres are primarily written by men for men, the music promotes rebellion, and rock still retains the basic southern elements of a blues-driven beat accompanied by melodic guitars and expressive vocals that give lyrics precedence over harmony. However, we seldom recognize the interconnections between these three elements. Just as southern males have done for centuries, musicians use rebellion to outline strategies for their fans to signify a hegemonic masculine self when they lack resources because they are marginalized by class or age. Rock music did lose the hypermasculine elements of its southern roots when artists turned their attention from individual to collective rebellion and protest politics during the 1960s and 1990s. However, the music always returns to the southern rebel tradition as musicians express the plight of marginalized men while giving them strategies to take back their masculinity by protesting the society and culture that affords them little if any opportunities to construct meaningful and successful life histories.

Simon Frith writes "rock is the slipperiness, the power, the idea of 'America' itself" (Frith, 1981, p. 11)," and this survey of the masculine rebellion found in all subgenres of rock-n-roll affirms this. While rock music has undergone prolific changes, the music has historically embodied and expressed basic value contradictions enmeshed in U.S. culture. Since WWII, there has been a value cluster at the centre of ideal U.S. culture espousing individualism, achievement and success through activity and work (Williams, 1965), a cluster of ideals that overlaps with hegemonic masculinity as many American men build their manhood through work and career (Connell, 1987). And while many men, especially middle and upper class men, embrace this modern variant of the protestant ethic and 'self-made manhood,' for centuries now southern music and southern masculinity has provided a readily available critique of this Americanism. This critique has been prominent in rock-n-roll ever since the music's rise to national and international prominence. Throughout rock's history, men who are unsuccessful in achieving the American dream draw upon the alternative ways to substantiate masculinity expressed in rock music to rebel against a cultural logic that emasculates those without access to power and resources (Schrock & Schwalbe, 2009).

References

Ahlkvist, J. A. (1999). Music and cultural analysis in the classroom: Introducing sociology through heavy metal. *Teaching Sociology, 27*(2) 126–144.
Arnett, J. (1991a). Adolescents and heavy metal music: From the mouths of metalheads. *Youth & Society, 23*, 76–98.
Arnett, J. (1991b). Heavy metal music and reckless behavior among adolescents. *Journal of Youth and Adolescence, 20*(6), 573–592.
Arnett, J. (1992). The soundtrack of recklessness: Musical preferences and reckless behavior among adolescents. *Journal of Adolescent Research, 7*(3), 313–331.
Arnet, J. (2009). High hopes in a grim world: Emerging adults' views of their futures and generation x. *Youth & Society, 31*(3), 267–286.
Baron, S. W. (1989). Resistance and its consequences: The street culture of punks. *Youth & Society, 21*(2), 207–237.
Bederman, G. (1995). *Manliness and civilization: A cultural history of gender and race in the United States*. Chicago: University of Chicago Press.
Betrand, M. (2004). I don't think Hank done it that way: Elvis, country music and the reconstruction of southern masculinity. In M. K. McCusker & D. Pecknold (Eds.), *A boy named Sue: Gender and country music* (pp. 59–85). Jackson, MS: University Press of Mississippi.
Cash, W. ([1941] 1991). *The mind of the South*. New York: Vintage Books.
Clawson, M. A. (1999). When women play the bass: Instrument and gender interpretation in alternative rock music. *Gender & Society, 13*(2), 193–210.
Connell, R. (1987). *Gender & Power*. Stanford, CA: Stanford University Press.
Connell, R. (1995). *Mascunlinities*. Berkeley, CA: University of California Press.
DeRogatis, J. (2003). *Milk it: Collected musings on the alternative music explosion of the '90s*. Cambridge, MA: De Capo Press.
Eastman, J. T., & Schrock, D. P. (2008). Southern rock musicians' construction of white trash. *Race, Gender & Class, 15*(1–2), 205–219.
Flacks, R. (1971). *Youth and social change*. Chicago: Markham.
Friend, C. T. (2009). From southern manhood to southern masculinities: An introduction. In C. T. Friend (Ed.), *Southern masculinity: Perspectives on manhood in the south since reconstruction* (pp. vii–xxvi). Athens, GA: University of Georgia Press.

Friend, G. T., & Glover, L. (2004). *Southern manhood: Perspectives on masculinity in the old south*. Athens, GA: University of Georgia Press.

Frith, S. (1978). *The sociology of rock*. London: Constable.

Frith, S. (1981). *Sound effects: Youth, leisure and the politics of Rock'n'Roll*. New York: Pantheon Books.

Frith, S., & Street, J. (1992). Rock against racism and red wedge. In R. Garofolo (Ed.), *Rockin the boat: Mass music and mass movements* (pp. 67–80). Boston: South End Press.

Garrison, E. K. (2000). U.S. feminism – grrrl styles!: Youth (sub)cultures and the technologics of the third wave. *Feminist Studies, 26*, 141–170.

Glover, L. (2004). Let us manufacture men: Educating elite boys in the early national south. In C. T. Friend & L. Glover (Eds.), *Southern manhood: Perspectives on masculinity in the old south* (pp. 22–48). Athens, GA: University of Georgia Press.

Goldstein, R. (1968). The new rock: Wiggy words that feed your mind. *Life, June*, 67–70.

Gross, R. (1990). Heavy metal music: A new subculture in American society. *Journal of Popular Culture, 24*, 119–130.

Haenfler, R. (2004). Manhood in contradiction: The two faces of straight edge. *Men and Masculinities, 7*(1), 77–99.

Hansen, C. H., & Hansen, R. D. (1991). Constructing personality, and social reality through music: Individual differences among fans of punk and heavy metal music. *Journal of Broadcasting & Electronic Media, 3*, 335–350.

Howard, J. R. (1969). The flowering of the hippie movement. *Annuals of the American Academy of Political Science, 382*, 43–55.

Kimmel, M. S. (1996). *Manhood in America: A cultural history*. New York: Free Press.

Kimmel, M. S. (2005). Globalization and its mal(e)contents: The gendered moral and political economy of terrorism. In M. S. Kimmel, J. Hearn, & R. Connell (Eds.), *Handbook of studies of men & masculinities* (pp. 414–431). Thousand Oaks, CA: Sage.

Kruse, H. (1993). Subcultural identity in alternative music culture. *Popular Music, 12*(1), 33–41.

Malone, B. C., & Strickland, D. ([1979] 2003). *Southern music/American music*. Lexington, KY: University of Kentucky Press.

Marcus, G. ([1989] 2003). *Lipstick traces: A secret history of the twentieth century*. Cambridge, MA: Harvard University Press.

Moore, R. (2005). Alternative to what?: Subcultural capital and the commercialization of a music scene. *Deviant Behavior, 26*, 229–252.

Nagel, J. (2005). Masculinity and nationalism: Gender and sexuality in the making of nations. In S. Philip & H. Wollman (Eds.), *Nations and nationalism: A reader* (pp. 110–130). New Brunswick, NJ: Rutgers University Press.

Paul, H., & Caldwell, M. (2007). Headbanging as resistance or refuge: A cathartic account. *Consumption, Markets and Culture, 10*(2), 159–174.

Rafalovich, A. (2006). Broken and becoming god-sized: Contemporary metal music and masculine individualism. *Symbolic Interaction, 29*(1), 19–32.

Reddick, B. H., & Beresin, E. V. (2002). Rebellious rhapsody: Metal, rap, community and individuation. *Academic Psychiatry, 26*, 51–59.

Rosenberg, J., & Garfalo, G. (1998). Riot grrrl: Revolutions from within. *SIGNS: Journal of Women in Culture and Society, 23*(3), 809–841.

Roszak, T. (1969). *The making of a counter culture: Reflection on the technocratic society and its youthful opposition*. Garden City, NY: Anchor Books.

Rotundo, A. E. (1993). *American manhood: Transformations in masculinity from the revolution to the modern era*. New York: Free Press.

Schippers, M. (2000). The social organization of sexuality and gender in alternative hard rock: An analysis of intersectionality. *Gender & Society, 14*(6), 747–764.

Schippers, M. (2002). *Rockin' out of the box: Gender maneuvering in alternative hard rock*. New Brunswick, NJ: Rutgers University Press.

Schrock, D., & Schwalbe, M. (2009). Men, masculinity and manhood acts. *Annual Review of Sociology, 35*, 277–295.

Smith, G. (2011). White mutants of straight edge: The avant-garde of abstinence. *The Journal of Popular Culture, 44*(3), 633–646.

Strasburger, V. C. (1998). Is it only rock 'n' roll? The chicken-and-the-egg dilemma. *Journal of Adolescent Health, 23*(6), 1–2.

Walser, R. (1993). *Running with the devil: Power, gender and madness in heavy metal music.* Hanover, PA: University Press of New England.

Weinstein, D. (1995). Alternative youth: The ironies of recapturing youth culture. *Young: Nordic Journal of Youth Research, 3*(1), 65–71.

Weinstein, D. ([1991] 2000). *Heavy metal: The music and its culture*. London: De Capo Press.

Williams, R. M. (1965). *American society: A sociological interpretation* (2nd ed.). New York: Knopf.

Wyatt-Brown, B. (1986). *Honor and violence in the old south*. Oxford: Oxford University Press.

Yablonsky, L. (1968). *The hippie trip: A firsthand account of the belief and behaviors of hippies in America*. New York: Pegasus.

Chapter 18
"Let Me Know You're Out There!" Male Rock Vocal and Audience Participation

Andy Bennett

18.1 Rock and Its Audience

The emphasis on audience participation in rock performance is undoubtedly born out of the scale of the live rock event. During the so-called British invasion of the US in the mid-1960s, the escalating success of bands such as *The Beatles*, *The Rolling Stones* and *The Who* meant that they were booked to play increasingly large venues, culminating in the Beatles proto-stadium rock events at Shea Stadium and Candlestick Park. As *The Beatles* withdrew from live performance to concentrate on studio work, rock found a new medium in the form of the festival, with events such as Monterey, Woodstock and Isle of Wight featuring iconic performances from some of rock's largest and most successful acts of the day, such as Jimi Hendrix, *The Who* and *The Doors*. During the 1970s and into the 1980s, the size and scale of rock performances continued to grow under the banner of the all encompassing banner of 'stadium rock'.

However, it was not simply the performance arrangements for rock that changed at this point. The physical experience of performing in stadiums at loud volume to legions of fans arguably had a notable influence on the nature of rock music itself – both in terms of its sound, style and also its visual representation. Inspired by the wall of sound they were able to create in the stadium setting, rock bands began aspiring to create an ever thicker and richer sound in the studio. In this respect, *Led Zeppelin* are a good case in point. Sonically speaking, the band's eponymous titled debut album is moulded very much in the British electric blues tradition through which the group's founder, Jimmy Page, had risen to prominence as part of *The Yardbirds* during the mid-1960s. The organ inflections added by fellow band member John Paul Jones add to the album's distinctly sixties' feel. The second *Led Zeppelin* album, Led Zeppelin II, is, by contrast, a move into quite different sonic and musical territory. Recorded while on tour in the US, the album sees Page layering up electric guitar rhythm tracks to create a far thicker sound (something he

A. Bennett (✉)
Griffith University, Brisbane, QLD, Australia
e-mail: a.bennett@griffith.edu.au

would continue to develop and refine on subsequent *Led Zeppelin* albums), while John Bonham's drum sound also becomes noticeably heavier and thicker, featuring the distinctive pounding, and inherently 'live' sounding, bass drum sound that was to become Bonham's signature and central to the *Led Zeppelin* style. Early in their musical career, *Led Zeppelin* thus perfected a sound that was both derived from the stadium setting and made them the quintessential stadium rock band, and the benchmark they set had a significant impact on the direction of rock from that point onwards. By the mid-1970s, a clear trend was developing in rock towards creating a 'bigger' sound in anticipation of performances in stadium settings. For example, the style of British band *Bad Company*, which grew out of the ashes of *Free* (who had a number 1 hit in 1970 with 'Alright Now'), was literally created around the stadium rock aesthetic. Other emergent rock bands of the 1970s, such as *Queen*, *Foreigner* and *Van Halen* followed this trend, writing songs that seemed tailor made for the stadium rock audience.

Stadium rock was duly criticised for what many considered its pompous and pretentious nature. Many claimed that it was out of touch with its audience, an observation that, in itself, sparked a backlash in the form of pub-rock, a precursor to punk. As Laing observes:

> ...the virtue of smallness was taken by pub bands from their memory of the Merseybeat and British R&B era. The size of the bar-room allowed for, even insisted upon, the intimacy between musicians and audience they believed was somehow essential for meaningful music. Pub rock's stance implied that things went wrong for bands when they became superstars and 'lost touch' with their original audiences (1985, p. 8).

The implied distinction between pub and stadium rock here is clear. While pub rock adheres to an ethic of inclusivity, its stadium based counterpart leaves no room for audience involvement. Rather it is suggested, stadium rock audiences are merely passive recipients of a spectacle over which they have no influence and no creative input. Arguably, however, such an assertion overstates, if not misses, a fundamental aspect of the stadium rock aesthetic. For even while the spatial parameters of the stadium rock performance prevent the intimacy offered by the bar or pub setting, stadium rock offers new avenues for audience participation, interwoven within its musical and lyrical textures.

18.2 Sing Along with Me!

> One night when we came off, [the audience] didn't stop singing. They were signing to us, they sang 'You'll Never Walk Alone'. And we all looked at each other and thought, 'something is really happening here, this is a complete interaction'. And that night I woke up in the middle in the night thinking, 'what would an audience do if you gave them permission, what would they do?' They could stamp, they could clap, they could sing something which made them feel they were bonded together. Something which made them feel strong. (Extract from interview with Brian May, *The Seven Ages of Rock*)

The above account by Brian May, guitarist with British rock group *Queen*, describes the inspiration for his writing of the song 'We Will Rock You'. Released

18 "Let Me Know You're Out There!" Male Rock Vocal and Audience Participation 289

on the album *News of the World* in 1977, 'We Will Rock You' quickly became a staple of Queen's live show.[1] The chant-style chorus, achieved in the studio through multiple vocal overdubs contributed by lead vocalist Freddie Mercury and May, together with drummer Roger Taylor, provided a sonic blueprint for the live version of the song in which Mercury led the audience in anthemic song-along style, exploiting the vocal intensity of the mass stadium audience to the full. Even in the studio, Mercury adds the words 'sing it' to the end of the chorus in anticipation of the song's interactive role in a live context.

However, despite May's personal account of his conceptualisation of 'We Will Rock You' as a device for harnessing the audience's desire for involvement in the live event, generically speaking the song fits within a by then already established rock tradition of audience participation. As early as the late 1960s, rock musicians had already begun to solicit participation from their ever-increasing audience, sometimes offering provocative comments as a means of essentially goading the audience to get involved in the performance. A pertinent case in point, and one consigned to celluloid history, is Country Joe McDonald's performance of his song 'Fixin' to Die Rag', a hard-edged satire on the fate of young Americans being drafted into the US Army to fight in the Vietnam War, at the 1969 Woodstock festival. As depicted in *Woodstock: The Movie* (see Bennett, 2004a), having initially caught the audience's attention with his now legendary call and response 'Gimme an F, gimme a U, gimme a C, gimme a K, "what's that spell?", [2] McDonald leads the audience in a chorus that depicts with a dark humour the fickle attitude of many of those serving in Vietnam and their lack of empathy with the socio-political context in which the war was being staged (see Whiteley, 2004). Mid-way through the song, McDonald interjects with a retort on the audiences' failure to fully engage with the chorus:

> Listen people I don't know how you expect to ever stop the war if you can't sing any better than that. There's about 300,000 of you fuckers out there. I want you to start singin'. Come on (*Woodstock: The Movie*, 1970).

Although signalling a point made in response to a specific era of foreign policy in the USA, semantically, McDonald's dialogic engagement with the audience assisted in establishing a convention of practice that successive generations of rock performers would continue to exploit and refine.

Thus, to return to the example of *Queen's* 'We Will Rock You' (a song recorded some 8 years after the original Woodstock festival) even as a studio track this possessed a critical architecture for audience involvement gleaned from existing examples of this rock tradition; indeed, *Queen's* by then famous multiple vocal overdubbing technique is self-consciously used in the track to mimic the mass voice of the audience in anticipation of live shows to follow. Other rock groups had little difficulty in replicating this formula, writing songs with signature hooks designed as a means of instantly orchestrating audience participation in the stadium context. *AC/DC's* track, 'For Those About to Rock' from the album of the same name (Atlantic, 1982), mimicking as it does a discourse of combat, acts as a rally call to a chorus of fans only too willing to exploit the opportunity afforded by the song to join in with it during live performance.

18.3 The 'Live' Album

If audience interaction has become a central aspect of the make rock vocal aesthetic in the concert setting, then equally technology has allowed for its traces to flow back to the recording studio. In the autumn of 1981, Canadian rock band Rush released their second live album, *Exit Stage Left* (Mercury, 1981). The Liner Notes for the album contain an intriguing entry that reads thus: "A special tribute to the Glaswegian Chorus for the background vocals on 'Closer To The Heart'. Nice one, folks!" Possibly one of the first times that audience participation had been listed on the Liner Notes of a live album in this way, this reference also bespeaks another significant aspect of audience participation in the live rock event. Since the release of the *Beach Boys'* album 'Pet Sounds' (Capitol, 1966) and *The Beatles*' 'Sergeant Pepper's Lonely Hearts Club Band' (Parlophone, 1967) the emphasis on studio technology had been growing. As Frith observes, the studio became an important intermediary in the music production, allowing producers the luxury of 'mak[ing] records of ideal not real events' (1988, p. 22). Although Frith is referring here primarily to the production of studio created music, studio technology also offers significant creative license in the production of studio music. In 1976, following the release of their first live album 'All The World's A Stage', *Rush's* bass player and vocalist Geddy Lee was interviewed by Toronto's *Globe and Mail* newspaper. Lee noted that some overdubbing had been required when remixing the live tapes, adding that "other well-known concert albums have had some studio wizardry performed on them" (Banasiewicz, 1988).

Interestingly, such accounts seldom reflect on the use of the audience itself a resource inherently ripe for creative re-working and re-positioning during the production of a live album. Yet the techniques for capturing the voice of the audience, as part of the overall live ambience of the rock concert, have long been in place. At concerts that are being recorded for possible inclusion, in whole or in part, on a live album, as much care goes into the positioning of microphones to capture off-stage sound as the sound on-stage. This allows for maximum manipulation of such sound sources during the post-concert production of the live album, a technique that is often used to dramatic effect – often to create a cosmetic effect, rather than to faithfully document the audience-artist interaction during the actual concert performance. A pertinent example of this is heard on *Thin Lizzy's* 'Live and Dangerous' album (Vertigo, 1978). The album begins and ends with a predominantly male audience chanting 'Lizzy' followed by three rapid handclaps in soccer terrace fashion. Although in all likelihood comprising authentic audience recordings from concert tapes recorded for the album, the 'Lizzy' sequence has been edited, processed and creatively repositioned to provide dramatic 'intro' and 'outro' sequences for the album. Simultaneously, such a positioning of the 'Lizzy' sequence transforms it into a primary text – a means through which *Thin Lizzy* audiences can identify and assert their role and place within future live performances of the group.

Over the course of the late 1970s and early 1980s, the inter-weaving of the audience within the text of the live album became increasingly commonplace and was used to achieve a range of different effects. On their 1977 live album 'Status Quo

Live' (Vertigo, 1977) British blues-boogie band *Status Quo* effectively enshrined their cover of the *Doors*' 'Roadhouse Blues', already an on-stage favourite, as the centrepiece for audience-group interaction during *Status Quo's* live performances. This is involved a relatively simply, yet seductive, process of creative license which involved re-mixing of the popular 'Quo' chant, again a popular purview of *Status Quo's* then predominantly male audience, so that it assumes a central place in the stereo mix. The chant is then used throughout the middle sequence of 'Roadhouse Blues' during which the chugging boogie shuffle of the two guitars and bass drops in and out at two bar intervals to allow drummer John Coughlan to lead the *Quo* chant with a tight, 4/4 bass, snare, and hi-hat syncopation. This part of the song also provides a platform for lead singer/guitarist Francis Rossi to announce, and prepare the audience for, what he refers to as 'the bit', during which he leads the band through a scratch rendition of a traditional Irish reel. The combination of band-audience rapport re-presented here is a particularly compelling example of the way in which the live album has been used as a vehicle for the mediation of a band-audience relationship. *Status Quo*, a very popular live group since the early 1970s, have long-enjoyed a particular form of relationship with their audience built around a straight-forward approach to song-writing and a down-to-earth-attitude among members of the band. The live version of 'Roadhouse Blues' contained on 'Status Quo Live' is very much a testament to this relationship.

The live album has also pertinently served to invest apparently spontaneous outpours from audience members with currencies of legitimacy and longevity. This section began with a reference to the *Rush* song 'Closer To the Heart' as it appears on the group's second live album *Exit Stage Left*. Not purposely written with the intention of soliciting audience participation, the song is rather an example of the more erudite lyric writing that grew out of the progressive rock scene of the early to mid-1970s (see Macan, 1997). However, due to Rush's decision to feature this particular live cut of the song on the *Exit Stage Left* album and to position the audience's contribution high in the mix, 'Closer To the Heart' subsequently became an onstage favourite with band and audience alike. Subsequent live versions of the song, such as that featured on Rush's *Grace Under Pressure Tour* video (1985, Anthem/Mercury Records) demonstrate the extent of fixity between audience, song, and context that can often be achieved though the live album's role as a sonic document.

As the above example illustrates, from the early 1980s onwards video technology began to add a critical new dimension to the role and significance of audience participation in the context of the live performance. In essence, audiences had been a key aspect of popular music in a television and cinema context since the 1950s when, as Shumway (1992) observes, clips of artists such as Elvis Presley and *The Beatles* mixed footage of the performer with footage of the audience. Building on this tradition, rock music in the video age was dominated by what Kaplan (1987) defines as the performance-video aesthetic. Rock videos typically attempted to capture and reproduce the live concert atmosphere, often been shot on stage with a clear view of the audience adopting a role that it had by now become entirely used to and comfortable with. The key difference between rock in the video and pre-video ages was the element of control that could be exercised to, once again, produce 'ideal' rather than 'real' events. The techniques learned from the production of live albums were easily transposed to video production where carefully selected audience shots could be matched up with a soundtrack in which the live-edge of the music was countenanced with the singing, cheering and clapping of the audience. In other cases a studio track could be laid over footage from a live performance, with audience voices added to the mix at particular points for maximum effect. Again, given the long-established tradition of artist-audience rapport in the live concert setting, such cosmetic interventions fold seamlessly into the textual narrative of live rock performance and audience involvement.

18.4 Situating the Audience Voice

Thus far, this chapter has considered a number of empirical examples in an effort to illustrate the ways in which rock groups have endeavoured to incorporate their audiences into live performance through the medium of song. The final section of this chapter will deal with the question of what such examples tell us about notions of ownership as these relate to the rock text and the spatial dynamics of its live performance. Since the early 1990s, the cultural turn in sociological theory has placed increasing emphasis upon the importance of reflexive modernity as a conceptual framework for our understanding of social identity formation (Giddens, 1991). Developing this train of thought, Chaney (1996) has proffered the concept of lifestyle as a means of developing an explanation of how individuals in contemporary societies appropriate objects, images and texts produced by the media and cultural industries, creatively re-working these into individual and collectively articulated lifestyle projects. Drawing upon these conceptual discourses within a framework of what is now increasingly referred to as cultural sociology, a number of writers have begun to ask how we might begin to map and explain the everyday cultural significance of popular music for members of the audience (see, for example, DeNora, 2000; Bennett, 2008). Particularly important here is the notion of ownership as this pertains to musical texts, the performers who produce these, the audiences that consume them and the spaces in which such consumption takes place. Writing in the late 1980s, Simon Frith claimed that there is:

> ... something specific to musical experience, namely, its direct emotional intensity. Because of its qualities of abstractness (which 'serious' aestheticians have always stressed) music is an individualizing form. We absorb songs into our own lives and rhythms into our own bodies; they have a looseness of reference that makes them immediately accessible. Pop songs are open to appropriation for personal use in a way that other popular cultural forms (television soap operas, for example) are not – the latter are tied into meanings we may reject (1987, p. 139).

The individualising quality of music observed by Frith can be set in the context of a range of other leisure and cultural forms and commodities through which individuals are argued to construct individual lifestyles in the context of late modernity. However, as Chaney (1996), drawing on the work of Simmel, argues, such individual lifestyles also form the bedrock for occasions of sociality in later modernity as individuals come together in specific spaces and places to celebrate common cultural tastes and practices (see also Bennett, 1999). In relation to this, the concert hall takes on a significant level of importance though providing a space in which a normally geographically diffuse fan base can assemble en masse to engage in their collective appreciation of a particular group or artist. In this sense, the collective voice of the audience is an important medium, acting as it does as a means though which the audience can instantly connect with the music – easily competing with the volume of the amplification and public address system at critical moments, flowing into the sonic gaps in performance and responding to the pre-planned sequences of audience sing-along or call and response between performer and audience.

In this important sense then, the audience finds a critical medium for collective ownership of the rock text through its vocal engagement with the latter. Earlier in this chapter, it was noted how genres such as punk and pub rock have previously mounted a critical attack on stadium rock for its alleged out-of-touchness with the audience. Through their vocal interaction, however, rock performers and their audiences overcome the potentially alienating dimensions of the large music venue music. Indeed, the audience become as key to the rock performance as the group or artist on the stage; through their vocal involvement in the performance, audiences are able to articulate a collective identity simultaneously asserting their symbolic ownership of the performance. Moreover, the technological positioning of popular music in a late modern context provides a still broader spectrum for the articulation of such audience engagement and ownership in ways that transcend the physical live performance itself. In the context of the live album CD or concert DVD the collective voice of the audience effectively moves beyond the immediate spatio-temporal location of its original utterance, becoming an embedded part of the digitally reproduced, and preserved, live rock peformance.

18.5 Conclusion

This chapter has examined the role and significance of audience participation in the context of live rock performance. This began with an examination of rock's development as a stadium-based music genre, a development that had a significant impact on the volume and scale of rock performances and on the size of the audience. The following section of the chapter considered how rock artists sought to cope with the size and scale of the live rock spectacle in terms of connecting with their audience and offering fans scope for involvement in the performance. One critical medium, it has been shown, was through audience participation in song. The chapter subsequently considered how the very nature of rock song-writing itself shifted to accommodate the new scale and dynamics of audience participation afforded by the stadium setting. Attention then shifted to the way in which the collective voice of the audience voice has moved beyond the concert hall becoming an integral part of the soundscape of the live album. The positioning of the audience as an aspect of the live rock performance medium, it was argued, is now as integral to the practices involved in the production of live albums as the music itself – audience and musical content having become inextricably intertwined. Finally, some consideration was given to what the role and significance of the audience's vocal participation in the live rock performance contributes to a cultural sociological understanding of popular music's everyday cultural significance. In relation to this, it was suggested that audience participation in the live rock performance can be aligned with the symbolic appropriation and cultural 'ownership' of rock texts as an aspect of late modern lifestyle projects.

Notes

1. Indeed at one point in the band's career Queen included two different versions of 'We Will Rock You' in their on-stage repertoire; the basic structure of the album version being worked up into a rebel-rousing riff-based opening song.
2. Although employed to different effect in *Woodstock: The Movie*, where MacDonald's performance is placed mid-way through the film, MacDonald actually performed his solo acoustic set as the opening act at Woodstock. As MacDonald later reported that he used the F-U-C-K chant as a means of voicing his frustration at the audiences' initial lack of attention to his performance (see Bell, 1999; Bennett, 2004b).

References

Banasiewicz, B. (1988). *Rush – visions: The official biography*. London: Omnibus Press.
Bell, D. (1999). Tripping north. In D. Bell (Ed.), *Woodstock: An inside look at the movie that shook up the world and defined a generation* (pp. 266–279). Studio City, CA: Michael Wiese Productions.
Bennett, A. (1999). Subcultures or Neo-Tribes?: Rethinking the relationship between youth, style and musical taste. *Sociology, 33*(3), 599–617.
Bennett, A. (Ed.). (2004a). *Remembering Woodstock*. Aldershot: Ashgate.
Bennett, A. (2004b). Everybody's happy, everybody's free: Representation and nostalgia in the Woodstock Film. In A. Bennett (Ed.), *Remembering Woodstock* (pp. 43–54). Aldershot: Ashgate.
Bennett, A. (2008). Towards a cultural sociology of popular music. *Journal of Sociology, 4*(4), 419–432.
Chaney, D. (1996). *Lifestyles*. London: Routledge.
DeNora, T. (2000). *Music in everyday life*. Cambridge: Cambridge University Press.
Frith, S. (1987). Towards an aesthetic of popular music. In R. Leppert & S. McClary (Eds.), *Music and society: The politics of composition, performance and reception* (pp. 133–149). Cambridge: Cambridge University Press.
Frith, S. (1988). Video pop: Picking up the pieces. In S. Frith (Ed.), *Facing the music: Essays on pop, rock and culture* (2nd ed., pp. 173–220). London: Mandarin.
Giddens, A. (1991). *Modernity and self identity: Self and society in the late modern age*. Cambridge: Polity.
Kaplan, E. A. (1987). *Rocking around the clock: Music television, postmodernism and consumer culture*. London: Methuen.
Laing, D. (1985). *One chord wonders: Power and meaning in punk rock*. Milton Keynes: Open University Press.
Macan, E. (1997). *Rocking the classics: English progressive rock and the counterculture*. Oxford: Oxford University Press.
Shumway, D. (1992). Rock and roll as a cultural practice. In A. DeCurtis (Ed.), *Present tense: rock and roll and culture* (pp. 117–133). Durham, NC: Duke University Press.
Whiteley, S. (2004). 1, 2, 3. What are we fighting 4 ? Music, meaning and the Star Spangled Banner. In A. Bennett (Ed.), *Remembering Woodstock* (pp. 18–28). Aldershot: Ashgate.

Discography

Albums

The Beach Boys (1966) *Pet Sounds*, Capital.
The Beatles (1967) *Sergeant Pepper's Lonely Hearts Club Band*, Parlophone.
Rush (1976) *All The World's A Stage*, Mercury.
Rush (1981) *Exit Stage Left*, Mercury.
Status Quo (1977) *Status Quo Live*, Vertigo.
Thin Lizzy (1978) *Live and Dangerous*, Vertigo.

Singles

AC/DC (1982) 'For Those About To Rock', Atlantic.

Documentaries and Series

The Seven Ages of Rock (2007) BBC Worldwide and VH1.

Films

Woodstock: The Movie (1970) Dir. Michael Wadleigh, USA, Warner Bros.
Videos
Rush (1985) *Grace Under Pressure Tour*, Anthem/Mercury Records.

Part V
Practioner Reflections

Chapter 19
Male Singing in Early Years of School

Miriam Allan

The sociological experience of singing for boys may differ significantly once the boy's personal history; socio-economic status; his parent's education and their religious beliefs are taken into account.

My work with boys has been in Australia in a non-religious format and in the United Kingdom in the cradle of western musical and religious tradition. The primary difference is that the boys in English choir schools (such as Westminster Abbey or St Paul's Cathedral) often come from backgrounds where parents: have a university education; have been exposed to Christian practices; have an understanding and appreciation of the history of the English choral tradition and classical music; and enjoy a mid to high level of economic stability.

The boys I worked with in Australia came from a much wider range of backgrounds and, as religion was not integral to the programme I was teaching, parents chose this program over others offered in the community that did have a religious foundation. I was also the first girl chorister in my local cathedral choir in Australia. It started out because my father sang in the choir and my parents were active in the parish community. Sociologically speaking, the rise of the girl chorister in churches in both Australia and England is fascinating. Where has this left boys? What impact has the introduction of girls had on the recruitment of boy choristers? Are girls the way of the future as they keep their voices longer?

To enhance my observations as both a teacher and former chorister, I have interviewed a number of friends, family members and colleagues about their experiences in choir schools in three countries. I have also spoken with boys who sang extensively in their treble voices, but outside of a choir school and I've gathered the recollections of some former girl choristers – a relatively new phenomenon. These respondents have been given code names to protect their identities: CS for Choir School, SB for Singing Boy and GC for Girl Chorister. Respondents ranged from those who attended choir school in the 1950s to choristers who had finished choir school in 2009.

M. Allan (✉)
Westminster Abbey and Bloxham School, Oxfordshire, UK
e-mail: miriam.allan@mac.com

Singing is inherent in most western religious practices: be it Jewish cantors or "song-leaders" in the charismatic churches. This often the first place boys come into contact with singing. Choral foundations in England are now able to count their music tradition in millennia. The ancient ties between singing and the liturgy enhances the experience for many a listener and it is a formative ground for young singers as they have a captive audience who are often encouraging and enthusiastic. CS03 says his over-riding memories of his time at St Paul's Cathedral, London are of encouragement and thanks from an extremely supportive congregation. Former girl choristers reported that although the congregation may, at first have been resistant, the support they won in the end was heart-warming. CS06, CS03 and CS08 all mentioned that the clergy were specifically supportive, not just of them and their singing, but their families too.

Boys come to choir schools in the United Kingdom via a variety of paths. Commonly one or more of the following –

- it was a path their own father trod (or perhaps another male relative such as an uncle or grandfather)
- they were identified as musically inclined at a very young age
- their parents were attracted by (reduced fee) private education and an education that is not solely focused on academic achievement
- the family has already had Christian experiences and supports the religious nature of the school or is tolerant of it
- an education in a boarding school or day school with extended hours is deemed suitable, reasonable, desirable.

Boys participate in community choirs for a very different set of reasons:

- it is relatively inexpensive when compared to individual instrument tuition and the purchase of instruments
- the time commitment is relatively minor (one afternoon after school per week and performances roughly once per term.)
- it is free of any sort of religious affiliation
- it supports other musical activities children undertake – particularly those who learn piano and their parents (and often their piano teachers) feel participating in a choir will provide them with a social way of making music from the otherwise solitary pursuit of playing the piano
- it provides them with an environment where singing is championed and where there is no stigma attached to a boy wanting to sing. It may even be that boys are praised for their "social strength" in joining a choir.

Social changes, such as the recent, public and numerous revelations of the abuse of children by priests have had an obvious and explicable effect on the recruitment of boy choristers to English choral foundations. GC03 stated explicitly that she would not be sending her children to a school where the church was involved. Coupled with the diminution of the church's standing in both Australia and the United Kingdom, the ability of these historic, long-established institutions to attract the most talented and enthusiastic choristers has been greatly damaged.

A changing attitude to schooling is also having an effect. Parents are looking to move away from a boarding school education to having their children at home. In the United Kingdom, almost every school with an internationally recognised choral foundation is either a boarding school or requires the boys for an extended day – from an early start for rehearsals to a late finish due to evensong or a further evening rehearsal. (Two such examples: New College, Oxford; Magdalen College, Oxford.) Nearly every former chorister I spoke with mentioned that this would be or has been a major consideration for sending their children to choir school and listed the detachment from their parents and siblings as disadvantageous to their choir school education. CS10, CS09, CS03 and CS05 all said that they would be (or are) happy for their sons to be choristers provided it wasn't a boarding school. CS09, CS03 and CS05 who all attended the same choir school, felt very strongly about this, saying they would not consider sending their son to the school they themselves had attended though they were still in favour of choristerships. Sharing their feelings throughout their interviews, they all mentioned the "amazing" choirmaster they had and wished their children could work with him! Clearly the school was not as wonderful as the choir. CS18 mentioned that the choir school education he received was exceptional on an academic level – particularly as the average class size was 7 pupils.

Curiously, for the girls, choristerships were, on the whole, a family affirming affair – many, myself included, becoming involved in singing because of the participation of parents and male siblings. However, it must be noted that the opportunities for girls to be choristers in English choral foundations are still practically non-existent. Most are choristers in a much less formal way or in a "supporting", separate choir which does not require them to attend a specific school.

A primary reason these choral foundations need to be considered socially significant is the environment that they provide for *boys to sing with other boys* – thus removing the stigma of "singing being for girls" or "sissys". At an English school where I currently work as the Head of Singing, one of my first decisions was to start an ensemble for boys with unchanged voices. This was in order to provide those boys who were already keen on singing with an outlet for musical excellence; a quality vocal sound and, crucially, with "mates"- other boys who, like them, like to sing. Although the number of members has never exceeded seven, the impact is already seen in the school. This has meant, as our first year of boys moved into a new vocal experience that they continued to sing and inspire their peers. That impact has sent ripples through the school community and has allowed these boys, at school at least, to enjoy the social freedom of expressing themselves through singing and enjoy the respect of the other boys in the school. Outside of the family, the school society is going to provide a boy with the foundation of his own masculinity and his comfort in participating in all sorts of scenarios – such as singing.

The social support found in choir schools of boys and for boys cannot be underestimated when considering the career destinations these boys might have. Many of those interviewed said, in hindsight, the social support was considerable and they benefited from that. Among those questioned, it was only the most recent former choristers (those aged under 16 years at the time of publication) who mentioned anything about singing being "for girls" and the "relief" of attending a single sex choir school supporting their wish to sing. Perhaps this is indicative of a more recent sociological trend. CS11 said singing being for "sissys" was a commonly held belief at his current secondary school, but he thinks them "ignorant." The remaining people questioned said that this had never been an issue for them. CS10, himself a father of three young sons, is delighted at the talent his boys show but has not enrolled any of them in choir school. This is, in part, due to his desire to keep them at day school, but is also influenced by the way his sons see singing: they see it as something girls do. What is most interesting is that CS10 is a tenor of international reputation and his sons still see singing as something girls do. The Australian respondents mentioned that singing was contrary to the perceived cultural stereotype of Australian masculinity. SB04 said: "I think in the context of the Australian cultural climate at the time, my [positive] experiences were unusual."

British choral foundations, along with similar ones in other countries, including the Tolzer Knabenchor, Wien Sänger Knaben (Vienna Boys Choir) and Drakensberg Boys Choir in South Africa, provide the social support discussed in the previous paragraph and the sort of education which lends itself to a career as a professional musician. (It must be noted here that all three of those choir schools are not affiliated with churches.) Generally, it is required that, in addition to their daily choral work, the boys take lessons on the piano and an orchestral instrument. The breadth of their musical experiences – their ability to transpose; the understanding of part writing; the ability to sing another part other than the melody and the hugely advantageous skill of sight-reading that comes as part and parcel of the English chorister's training are the envy of the many, and make these boys extremely employable musicians as adults. All I spoke with attested to this. A further advantage arises from these musical abilities being combined with the years of training in team-work, performing under pressure with little rehearsal time and being able to rise to the occasion.

Girl choristers are not, at this point in time, getting quite the same breadth of musical education. This is primarily due to schooling and its geography. More often than not, girls are not at choir boarding schools, meaning that the burden of their musical education falls to their parents. This burden may include much travelling and financially providing for instrumental, vocal and theoretical tuition as well as finding the tutors. It also appears that girls I spoke with who were choristers in their early school years do not enjoy the same socio-economic status as many of the boys I interviewed.

Frequently people ask me: why teach children singing? Surely, as their voices mutate and change and they are constantly growing, it is useless? The basics of a singing technique, as I tell my students weekly, do not change regardless of the voice type they develop in adulthood or the genre of music they choose. Questions of postural alignment, support, production and a broad musical education which allows them to find the freedom to express themselves through song (be it extant or their own compositions) are the same when they are seven as when they are seventy. It has been my experience that confidence, both of sound quality and with respect to performance anxiety, is gained through a secure and dependable technique. For a number of the boys I work with who face performance situations ranging from a daily evensong or a school concert to their parents and peers, to live television and radio broadcasts (and in the age of live streaming via the internet, these performances are now live around the world, reaching larger audiences than at any point in history) confidence is essential – as is the dependability of their technique. For the sanity of their directors this is equally essential! About half the former choristers I spoke with had had individual singing lessons, though the frequency and length of these lessons varied considerably. It was also revealed in my research that individual singing lessons are a relatively new phenomenon and are still not standard practice.

Most suggested that they didn't have enough time with a singing teacher – CS04 even went as far as to say that he wasn't always able to put the singing teacher's suggestions into practice in the song school, which frustrated him throughout his choristership. More recent choristers (those from the last 20 years) seemed to suggest that their organists, the traditional choir trainers, were "striving" to integrate the technical language employed by singing teachers into their sessions. The days of organists bearing the entire responsibility of the vocal training and supporting the vocal health of his choristers seem to be behind us. As a singing teacher, this is certainly my experience. Some organists are bringing singing teachers into the song school rehearsals to reinforce unity of language and technique. This shift is, in part, due to availability of information regarding the science of the voice, of singing and an appreciation that change is necessary in order for the English choral tradition not to just survive, but thrive in the twenty-first century. Changes are not limited to the introduction of singing lessons and the training of organists in vocal matters. The modern equivalent of the girl chorister scandal was the appointment of a non-organist to the post of "Master of the Choristers" at a prominent English cathedral. Instead, a professional singer was appointed.

Technically, the teaching of singing to children should demonstrate little difference from the teaching of an undergraduate in a music college. The teaching should be of the highest possible quality. A thorough understanding of vocal physiology and particularly how it will grow and change are essential. Musicianship of the finest calibre should be employed to ensure that the child receives the best possible grounding in musical basics. This is not a babysitting job or just about teaching "songs". Many of the appalling habits picked up in childhood singing are painfully dissected and reconstructed by teachers later. Teach children well and you teach them skills for life. The primary difference is the language used (the KISS policy certainly applies – as does the need for a consistency of language) and the creativity and imagination the teacher might need in order to inspire concentration, application and understanding. For example, football/soccer and cricket metaphors creep into my teaching of boys aged 7–13 years far more than they do when teaching teenage girls. A rewards system is a useful tool – gold stars, stickers, points, A grades etc. mean a great deal to children and keep them motivated. It is rare you see a sticker chart on the wall of a "lecturer" in a university.

A great deal of research has been done in recent years into the vocal physiology of children and I refer you to that excellent work for further detail. It has become generally accepted that the fundamental basics remain the same regardless of the age of a singer. In my work I focus on four main areas as mentioned above:

19.1 Postural Alignment

This cannot be stated strongly enough. Poor postural alignment can be the foundation of so many technical problems that plague children and lead to technical issues as adult singers. Choir directors do not always have the opportunity, when faced with a room full of children, to individually check and correct each child. I find myself saying to students over and over again that their *whole body is their instrument*. Therefore, particularly for children singing in choirs, it is essential that they begin by *turning their whole body to face the conductor*, not just turning their head. That has obvious vocal disadvantages. In her 2006 book *Singing and Teaching Singing*, author Janice Chapman outlines in a case study the serious implications and treatment required in an adult singer who had adopted a poor posture as a chorister in the choir stalls. By only turning his head towards the conductor, he had encouraged his larynx to rise off to one side. As an adult singer this prevented him from accessing the top of his range (Chapman 2006). Manual osteopathic therapy (which is said to be painful and confronting) and 2 years of re-training the muscles resulted in this singer moving forward healthily. But these were 2 years of treatment and retraining that might not have been necessary had better care and attention been paid to his postural habits as a chorister. I have also found the principles of Alexander Technique and Feldenkrais to be most useful. The physical nature of Feldenkrais exercises and the concept of *awareness through movement* rather than just stillness seems appealing to children as well as effective. It also provides them with a frame of reference as to how things feel. When singing in a choir, it is crucial that the child learn to *rely on how singing feels rather than how singing sounds*. That way, they are able to more accurately gauge how well they are or are not functioning. CS09 wrote, that in addition to his weekly singing lesson, the foundations of Alexander Technique, taught alongside his singing lessons, really assisted him and have stayed with him.

19.2 Support

Especially for boy choristers, teaching the foundations of support is vital. The intensity of their work alone, regardless of the vocal demands of any particular piece of music, requires stamina equal to any professional singer. It would be unthinkable for a professional singer to work without support, and why it would be considered unnecessary for children seems utterly ridiculous. The size of opera theatres and orchestras are frequently mentioned in other volumes on teaching singing when discussing the need for a well-supported voice. Consider the size of a cathedral. Consider the amount of sound produced by a cathedral organ. Consider the size of the child.

19.3 Production

Specifically onset, breath management, tongue root tension and diction. There seems to be a misconception that children's voices, particularly those in a religious context, are by their nature breathy. This couldn't be further from the truth. Occasionally, due to pathology or poor technique, a child's voice can be overly breathy. A good singing teacher would work to reduce that. For children who are working as often as choristers, breathiness, which is already vocally exhausting, could become truly debilitating and lead to vocal damage. The benefits of effective breath management and control are obvious and do not need to be extolled here. It is common for singers to attempt to "hear" their own sound by tensing the root of the tongue and feeding the sound back through the jaw back to the ears. This is particularly common in child choristers as they rarely hear themselves alone. This habit can led to significant tension of the vocal apparatus and can reduce the volume and freedom of the sound. Fortunately, it can be dealt with through a series of rather fun exercises. Diction is a word favoured by many choral directors. Rather than encouraging children to "spit out their words" which generally leads to a reduction of support, unwelcome tension and poor breath management, I try to teach children to connect their consonants to the breath (plosives not withstanding) and to connect them to the vowels preceeding and following. This maintains the technique, the quality of sound and gives excellent diction.

19.4 Musicianship

Though not directly related to vocal technique, the stronger the child is musically, the less likely they are to be distracted by it. This is particularly relevant in my work with choristers because of the amount of music they sing each week. Children who are distracted by "getting something right" compromise their technique. They might lean closer to "really look" at the music, disturbing their posture or they might focus completely on the dynamics and neglect to support their voice. The better their musical knowledge, the better their technique.

GC08, CS05 and CS06 detailed the difficulty of "unlearning" the poor habits they had picked up as choristers. CB06 listed the primary disadvantage of his choir school years as the "not being taught to sing properly". Considering the high percentage of child choristers who become professional singers, it seems be even more important that these children receive the best possible technical tuition.

Young children have the adorable (or wretched) habit of asking pertinent questions! As a teacher, I am never more challenged to find new ways of explaining something than when working with children. It is, therefore, one of the richest learning environments I have personally encountered. They may also find it easier to be honest than some older students. This sort of honesty is linked to the emotional state of the child and the trust they place in the adults who teach and care for them. Once they are comfortable with a teacher they proffer all sorts of information. One child once told me that "Daddy purchased a sports car and Mummy says it is because he is having a mid-life crisis!" This sort of information, though highly irrelevant to their singing on the surface, can be an insight into their trust of their teacher and therefore, their willingness to invest in their teacher's instruction. This can lead to terrific results, though the reverse also applies. If they are trying their best and still not achieving the desired result, tears may not be far off.

Although the aforementioned social environment of working with other boy singers (and living with them in the case of boarding choir schools) can have enormous benefits, it can be a highly competitive environment too. As with any competition, someone wins and someone loses. Four former choristers who attended the same choir school within a few years of each other also detailed the outrageous bullying that went on. Anger, hurt and resentment are powerful emotions and have a massive impact on a child's singing. A level of sensitivity and patience that may not be appropriate when teaching adults is certainly required when teaching children.

A common criticism of former choristers is that their singing lacks emotion. CS06 spoke of learning to show no emotion when he was a young chorister, "like a ninja". CS17 feels that a significant disadvantage for him, in his career as an opera singer, has been "shaking off the choir stalls in order to negotiate stage craft." This may seem like a peculiar aspect of musicianship to single out especially when former choristers had no difficulty in listing the numerous advantages of their choristerships. But choristers are often getting through a huge amount of music per week for services, recordings, broadcasts and concerts. Emotional content may be overlooked in favour of accuracy and, as is certainly my experience, vocal health. Questions of being able to support the sound or sing through an entire oratorio with excellent posture and stamina seem to be coming up in the song school more often than dead accuracy. However, it is not my experience that the emotional content of the music (particularly the text) features in rehearsals. I think there are some very sound reasons for this, discounting for a moment the obvious disadvantages. Some of the works that young singers are encountering – such as passions – contain some disturbing imagery, like that of the crucifixion. Connecting children too much to these sorts of images may prove more harmful than occasionally criticising them for a lack of emotional content. To be honest, I hear a dazzling amount of emotion in the sound of most trebles. In fact, a lot of the child's personality and emotional state shines through in their sound. What I don't often see – and in fact, it would be inappropriate in a liturgical situation – is a great deal of emotion on the face of the child. Perhaps this general criticism is actually more a question of *performance skills,* than the ability of the treble to display a range of emotions in their sound.

Enough has been written on the negative side without me adding to it. Mostly, the exploitation of children as labourers for the church, perhaps a feature of a chorister's life hundreds of years ago has now has been replaced with a top quality, preparatory school education.[1] Children who participate in choral singing, both within a faith-based framework and in the community, have been given opportunities to make like-minded friends, explore a magical world of music and often tour to foreign countries. All in all, the most disadvantageous aspect of children singing seems to be the distances their parents needed to drive or, where applicable, being away from their families at boarding school. Even then, most of those I spoke with said this was only one small aspect and that overwhelmingly they adored their childhood.

Another question I am often asked regards the incidence of vocal trouble in young singers. It is not, in my experience, more prevalent in choristers or children who sing and I would refer you to Jenevora Williams' more scientific work on this. Provided the children are well-cared for vocally, physically and emotionally, I have not seen anything which would indicate that they are in more danger of suffering from vocal damage than other children. Working in schools I have heard some rather interesting vocal pathology – and it is mostly from the "sporty" kids who shout a great deal over a lot of noise and over great distances.

One question I asked everyone I spoke to: how did being a chorister affect you and your family. Most mentioned the practicality of Christmas and other festivals. Many mentioned the dedication of their parents. CS13 says his parents "got into the habit of driving thousands of miles each year to attend services and concerts I was singing in – a habit that continues to this day." GC04, GC06, GC08, CS07 and CS10 mentioned the "burden" they must have been for their parents and their cars! And choristers from the 1950s to the present day said it was a brilliant, wonderful experience which gave them so much in addition to music and singing – an appreciation for the arts and culture in general; the team aspect of choral life; working as a unit; the joy of seeing the world from tour buses and aeroplanes; exposure to foreign languages both modern and dead; a comprehension of something bigger than them and the impression that it is a tradition worth preserving.

Similarly the former girl choristers share the love of the tradition and want girls to, quoting GC02, "flourish along side the boys and not replace that tradition." GC05 said that the tradition of boy choristers was "very important" to her, though welcomed the opportunity being extended to girls. A few of those I interviewed were choristers at Salisbury Cathedral which famously introduced girl choristers. Wrote CS13: "Whilst I was in the top year, Salisbury began its girls' choir which shook the place to its foundations. I was always all for it, so long as the choirs didn't mix in a permanent way." GC02, an early girl chorister at Salisbury, wrote: "At first there were lots of people against the girls' choir, but it quickly calmed down." Adding, "they've always been adamant that keeping the boys' and girls' choirs separate is important."

I was in a rare mixed treble line. At first I was the only girl, followed by my sister. Gradually a few additional girls (all relatives of other boys) joined and by the time I finished singing as a treble in my late teens, a separate girls choir had been established. One incident has stayed with me and my sister. Much had been said about the "break" from choral tradition and the introduction of girls. As part of our Cathedral's annual music festival a presenter from ABC radio, organised a blind test of the audience's perception of girl and boy choristers. Safely out of audience view in the organ loft, approximately 12 trebles sang to the assembled mass. (If memory serves, there were roughly the same number of each sex.) After hearing each singer, the audience indicated whether they thought it was a boy or girl. They got every single one wrong. A similar radio experience for GC08 in the UK turned up a similar result (as did Welch et al. – see Chapter 3).

Girl choristers have not so much replaced as complemented the traditional boy treble. I'll leave arguments as to the quality and difference of sound as well as the economic sense (as I've heard it crudely put) of investing in girl trebles, as they keep their voices longer, for another time and place. Regardless, the sociological impact this is having on boys and singing in the early years of school cannot be ignored. The idea of singing being for "girls" among those I interviewed seems to be on the rise, particularly among the younger generation. Fewer people are keen on allowing their own children attending choir school when it is a boarding school. Co-ed schooling now seems to be preferred as well.

And yet, these same people all said that it was one of the best things that had ever happened to them, using phrases like:

- "I have moved house many times since [I left choir school] but my heart is still in that building" CS13
- "It made me a very musical person and opened up a lot more options for my future" CS12
- "I loved every minute" CS19
- "I loved it – there were some amazing moments. I'm truly glad I did it" CS11
- "I enjoyed the sense of being part of something significant which spanned the ages" CS08
- "It has definitely left me as a better, more fulfilled and prepared person" CS04
- "I absolutely loved it and have absolutely no regrets" CS17

Singing in childhood was, for me, overwhelmingly positive, strengthening and affirming. These sentiments have been echoed by all those I interviewed. The number of these former choristers who are now professional musicians is staggering, though in no way surprising. This is not limited to singing either – many are now conductors and instrumentalists of international standing. And this has not changed over the many, many years of experience covered by those I interviewed.

What is changing is the social perception of singing, education and the church. My research and my experience as a teacher point to the rise of singing being unequally gender specific and the need for boys to have a thicker skin (as put by SB03) in order to survive some of the social taunts that may be forthcoming as a publicly singing boy in the community. The number of boys participating in choirs at early school age who are praised for their bravery or courage far exceed similar comments dealt to girls of the same age. Former choristers frequently mentioned how their choir school experiences helped them to win significant scholarships to secondary schools – schools that would have otherwise been unavailable to them. As the social standing of the church has diminished, this is and will continue to prevent ancient choral foundations from recruiting boy choristers.

Incidentally, like many of my fellow church musicians, I am an atheist. However, I am content with my role within the church and view myself as a worship facilitator, which is an important role. I don't have a problem with the church per se, and I am happy if people get their religious kicks out of my music making, which gives me a massive kick anyway.

So said SB03 who, like many of the former choristers I interviewed, continues to work as a professional church musician. The sociological impact of atheistic worship facilitators is clearly outside the scope of this chapter, but is certainly representative of current experience and the continuing diminution of the church. How will this affect church musicians and the support given to them by the church in the future? This could have an irreversible impact on choir schools and the unique education they provide. If my research is indicative of social trends in the wider community, they will also have to re-visit their approach to schooling in order to maintain this tradition– particularly those foundations supported by a boarding school.

A new approach may be required, perhaps one employing the same sort of creativity and imagination I use when teaching children! I am not certain that the English choral foundations are ready or prepared to fight the battle of changing their constitutions to admit girls or disband the schools at which they educated their boys. Nor would I support that. My research seems to indicate that if choir schools tamper too much with the tradition, a wider impact will be felt in the musical community – judging by the number of boys whose singing in early school years leads to a career in music.

Note

1. Readers are encouraged to explore a more detailed history of choir schools and how the education of choristers changed through the ages in Alan Mould's outstanding book *The English Chorister, A History*. Hambeldon Continuum, 2007.

Reference

Chapman, J. (2006). *Singing and teaching singing* (p. 33). San Diego, CA: Plural Publishing.

Chapter 20
The Courage to Sing: Reflections on Secondary School Singing

Anthony Young

20.1 Prelude

Two weeks ago I was supervising the end of a school dance. The continuous contemporary dance music which had been echoing around at deafening volume in the old gymnasium stopped and the crowd spilled out. A large group of older boys reached the doors of the gym and spontaneously launched into an enthusiastic rendition of "Ancient Words", a religious song by Michael W. Smith. They clearly enjoyed themselves and had no hesitation in singing in front of the large group of invited girls from other schools. I did not recognise the boys as belonging to any particular music group or choir in the school. "Ancient Words" was a piece of repertoire they knew from liturgical singing. These boys had developed the courage to sing. In the greater scheme of things it does not matter whether these men join choirs, sing in rock bands, perform in musicals, sing with guitars at the beach or around camp fires, sing along at concerts or sing to their sons and daughters but it does matter that they are given the freedom to do so by enculturation and education. As a secondary school teacher, I believe I have a duty to teach boys to sing and create an environment (an "ecosystem" as mentioned earlier in this text) where it is manly to sing.

At our recent *National Men's Choral Festival*, Dr Chris Kiver, our English born, Australian experienced and American trained and employed guest choral conductor suggested that Australia was advantaged in having a large number of boys' schools. He echoed research which claims that it is easier to nurture male singing in a single sex school setting. I enjoy working in such a setting at present but spent my first 6 years in a public (State funded) co-educational school. Some boys' schools in Australia have strong singing traditions while other traditions have withered away or never existed. Separating genders may help men sing but it does not guarantee

A. Young (✉)
St Laurence's College, Brisbane, QLD, Australia

Griffith University, Brisbane, QLD, Australia
e-mail: AYoung@slc.qld.edu.au

participation. The editors of this text requested that I write a practitioner reflection. On seeing the names of the other contributors of this volume, all of whom I respect, I realised that there was little point in repeating their material. What I can offer are lived examples of how the common themes of this text have been applied in a school to return to men their birthright of being able to communicate through song.

20.2 Context

St. Laurence's College is a large inner-city middle-class boys' school run by the Christian Brothers with students aged from eight to seventeen. Our school fees are one third of those at the neighbouring elite girls' school. Many of the parents have trades or work in small business. The school has no academic, sporting or cultural scholarship program and involves students from a wide range of backgrounds. A small number of our students are indigenous or refugees and a larger number have "special needs". While academic results are good, the school is not academically elite. There is a strong trade and apprenticeship program and the current Music Captain is an indigenous student who is training to be an electrician. He plays 'cello in orchestra and sings Bass II in choir.

Many of our students are "first generation musicians" and we, like many music teachers, have students whose parents do not have musical expectations for their children. The school is run by a church organisation but few of the students and families are regular churchgoers so the students do not benefit from religious singing on a weekly basis. Students coming from State primary schools have had free instrumental and classroom music lessons with specialist teachers once a week. Unfortunately, the majority of our students are from Catholic primary schools and have had very varied experiences. This is the reverse of the situation 40 years ago when religious sisters and brothers in Catholic schools provided powerful musical education throughout the country. In many Catholic schools, these brothers and nuns have not been replaced on retirement.

Accordingly, there are numerous reasons why music and singing would be difficult to cultivate at St. Laurence's. Students come from many different suburbs and feeder schools. There is a comprehensive sporting program. Many travel long distances to get to school and parents are not automatically supportive or expectant. In spite of these challenges there are five Choirs, five Concert Bands, three Big Bands, three String Groups and two Classical Guitar orchestras as well as a number of informal Rock and Pop music groups. The students run a week-long Rock Festival each year.

My first suggestion, then, is not to waste energy complaining about your context. Our Director of Music has a saying which runs: "the grass is always greener where you water it." The energy spent envying the conditions in a neighbouring school can be put into creating success in your own. I recommend working where you are to do what you can.

20.3 Supporting Choral Music in the School

20.3.1 Timing Rehearsals and Broadening the Culture from Within

In Queensland, secondary school choirs rarely rehearse during class time so most rehearsing and performing is done before or after school. Some schools have success with lunch rehearsals but where I work, the breaks are only 30 minutes long. Substantial rehearsal before or after school necessitates developing a constructive and supportive relationship with the sport department and adopting elements of dominant sporting culture of the school.

It has been necessary to carefully appropriate elements of hegemonic masculinity so as to effect change from within the discourse. The dominant construction of masculinity in our culture is to be active and physical so recasting singing as a sport-like activity reaps benefits. Harrison admits, "examples of effective practice in exploring the complementary nature of the two activities are scarce, but isolated instances can provide useful illustrations for . . . improving the plight of music in relation to status and participation" (Harrison, 2005, p. 56). Harrison wisely counsels, "sport can be harnessed as a motivational tool in music, but this needs to be executed with caution so as to avoid entrenching stereotypes" (ibid., p.57). At St. Laurence's as much as possible, music and sport work side by side.

In Australia, the structures of co-curricular music and sport are very similar. Sportsmen train and Musicians rehearse. Sport has games and Music has concerts. This similarity is not confined to Australia. Roe in the United States advises "get the coach to back the choral program if you can" (Roe, 1983, p. 17). Ashley coached rugby himself (Ashley, 2009, p. 94). His boys "are content to go out to primary schools . . . *as long as the lesson they are missing is not double sport*". He advises "boys will sing provided they are not asked to choose between choir and sport, an unfair choice that youngsters should not have to make (ibid., p. 103). Clever and complementary scheduling of singing and sporting activities is therefore essential.

Vocal pedagogue Richard Miller recalls that his high school choral conductor "would identify leading athletes" and "convinced students that being a member of the choral group was as prestigious as being on an athletic team. Her logic was that well-developed bodies would produce relatively mature voices". Miller's "location in the concert choir was between the co-captain of the football team and a leading basketball player" (2008, p. 18). Miller's conductor was effectively recruiting influential sporting peers to the choral program so that it would be an acceptable activity for more of the men.

These activities assist in broadening the concept of masculinity in the school provided the choral program does not become complicit in reinforcing some of the more unsavoury aspects of hegemonic masculinity. We are lucky to have sporting colleagues who value decency and good sportsmanship. They place participation and the achieving of personal bests ahead of beating the opposition. The same values are reinforced in the Music department where we value concerts and festivals with other musicians over competitions. I have found that trying to satisfy the requirements of competitions compromises my ability to make the choral ensembles at our school authentic to our context and membership.

At St. Laurence's, we work closely with the co-curricular sport department to ensure that boys are able to participate as much as possible. "Student sharing" deals are done where a child will miss a rehearsal every second week to ensure continued maintenance of skills in a sports team. Perhaps the standard of each team is a little lower as a result but the balanced development of the child is maintained. It is possible to schedule rehearsals and trainings creatively and our students are involved in Cricket, Swimming, Volleyball, Rugby, Soccer, Cross Country, Athletics, Basketball, Tennis, Australian Rules Football, Touch Football, Water Polo, Debating, Service Learning (community service), Theatre Sports and Chess. Readers will note from the inclusion of Theatre Sports that Drama is already appropriating the language of the discourse of sport.

In Chapter 2, Freer recommends "teachers shift away from an emphasis on continuous participation in choral music". Sometimes, giving a boy a few weeks off at the peak time in his sporting season may yield a life-long commitment to singing. A standard occurrence in my early morning choral rehearsals is boys arriving dripping from Swimming, sweating from Cross Country or smelling from Rugby. It is a powerful message for those boys who struggle to get out of bed for rehearsal at 7.15 am to realise that others were training for at least an hour before they woke up.

Once a working relationship with the sport department is established, we face the same problem as sports coaches. There are lots of other things boys can do other than attend training or rehearsal and many choose to do nothing. Membership challenges have confronted conductors for centuries. English Cathedral choral texts from last century bemoaned the fact that young trebles would leave choirs to work in factories to help support their families. We as conductors need to ensure that rehearsal and performance experiences are more attractive to boys than the alternatives. We must ask ourselves, what are we offering in rehearsals and performances that young men will want?

20.3.2 *Don't Call It a Choir*

Unfortunately there are many negative associations with the word "choir" so at St. Laurence's the choirs are called 'hoods. The largest Tenor-Bass choir is called the Brotherhood. The term has a number of connotations. It links us with the Christian Brothers who founded the school and is clearly male. It obliquely refers to mateship that is considered a core Australian male cultural value. Orwell's novel *1984* is taught in year Eleven English and the Brotherhood is the name of the resistance group in that text. All other choirs are named accordingly. The main groups are the Treblehood for unchanged voices, the changing voice choir (about Cooksey stage three) is called the Little Brotherhood and once voices begin to settle (about Cooksey stage for) boys join the Brotherhood. Voice maturity generally determines which group a child attends. Everyone who applies for membership who is committed to reliably serving the team is accepted save those who exhibit vocal pathologies and need medical assistance. Chamber groups are also auditioned by attendance. The primary school chamber group is called the Reblehood and the secondary school chamber group is called the Big Brotherhood.

I think it matters to boys that they can describe their activities using words which are likely to be accepted by their peers. Over the years, the 'hoods have become an accepted part of school culture and a musical community which protects its own. Indeed, for a bully at a school event, the sight of 150 loudly amplified singers on choir risers in front of a massed orchestra presents a body with which it might not be wise to pick a fight. This perception is enhanced when that bully is surrounded by others who are joining in with the singing.

20.3.3 Build a Culture of Community Singing

If singing is something that is just part of what everyone does, choirs become a natural extension of that activity. We foster community singing at St. Laurence's. This is easier in a "religious" school where there are times in the year when the school undertakes the role of singing congregation but when I worked in state education we developed the whole school's singing of the National Anthem as a community singing event. Unfortunately, in Australia men often stand mute while the Anthem is played. At the State High School we physically separated the boys and girls and they sang together. This was after I had been at the school for 5 years and had taught almost all of the students singing in compulsory music class. Melbourne High School is a secular school (see Chapter 22) that has had a strong community singing tradition for many years.

At St. Laurence's, on the orientation day for new students, the last activity is the teaching of the school song to all the new year fives and eights by the year twelvs. The value of having the most senior men of the school do this in terms of role modelling is obvious (Ashley, 2009, p. 156).

Primary students have a specialist music lesson which is largely voice based once a week and the secondary students all undertake compulsory music in their first year. It is imperative that the students are taught to sing in these classes if they are to sing for the rest of their time in the school.

The Pastoral Head of Year Eight is an Old Boy of the College who performed in the school rock festival when at school. All of year Eight performs a song with their Head of Year in a performance at the school speech night. Again, this becomes a powerful rite of passage for those boys.

I teach new repertoire to the school on a few occasions each year. I work with about 400 students at a time armed with a microphone and tuning fork. We rehearse in the resonant gymnasium mentioned at the start of the article. I find unaccompanied rehearsal the most efficient and teach by singing lines to the students and them singing back. The form of the music taught must be short and the range appropriate and the rehearsals must be fun. The boys generally enjoy the sound they make when singing together and they like getting out of class. The boys are most focussed when the singing rehearsal is before morning tea or lunch. Cooperative behaviour is rewarded by timely access to food. When I started at the school, these rehearsals began as 5–10 minute segments of rehearsal in year level groups.

Repertoire choice is always a challenge but I am often amazed at what boys will sing. This year we revived an old 1970s folk hymn "We are One in the Spirit". I had little expectation of the boys singing it. In desperation I arranged the piece for the worship band in a reggae style. "It went viral". On reflection, I realise the words were accessible, the form was simple and the range was manageable so it worked.

Cultivating community singing brings many advantages. Singing together is joyful. It can powerfully reinforce personal and corporate identity. Everyone has a voice and all can play a part in the enterprise. A singing community will be more understanding of the challenges of singing and is likely to be both a more discerning and supportive audience for choirs and singers generally. This has benefits in the broader community as well as within the school. Graduates of singing communities might expect singing communities for their own children. At St. Laurence's, a number of choir performances in front of peers will be occasions on which the whole student body will also be singing either at assemblies or liturgies. This makes choral singing in front of peers less daunting and in my experience; the one thing to avoid at all costs is embarrassing students in front of their peers.

Good community singing takes great patience, good humour and enthusiasm. You may wait until all your first years are in their final year before you will have a whole school "on side". After that, both maintenance and growth are hard but satisfying work. Satisfaction comes from building a community of participant musicians and a support base for further choral singing and music study.

20.4 Rehearsals

20.4.1 Planning

The core requirement of a rehearsal is that the singers must want to come back and there are plenty of texts and publications that deal with repertoire preparation and rehearsal strategies.

My experience accords with Freer's suggestion that rehearsals take into account the learning styles and behavioural characteristics of adolescent boys. Freer recommends "a change of activity focus or location in the room about every 12 or 13 minutes" (Freer, 2007, p. 29). This accords with current Kodály teaching methodology that recommends that lessons comprise a number of short focuses (Klinger, 1990). This means that rehearsals need to be fast-paced focussed and efficient.

Like many, I prepare for rehearsal by singing each part while playing the others at the keyboard to ensure I have an aural understanding of the music to be taught and of the likely challenges inherent in the piece. I aim to conduct the core repertoire of the season from memory so that I can keep eye contact with the singers. Good conducting is important for less experienced singers as they rely on you far more than highly trained musicians might. I find that if I forget to breathe in a cue, the choir may not sing even if the gestural cue is correct. I try to be organised in my goal setting for rehearsals. Quite bluntly, if I waste a boy's time he will do something else.

20.4.2 Repertoire

I try to have a range of music in rehearsal from simple canons and immediately successful music to more challenging repertoire. If the music is too easy singers will think they don't need to come to rehearsal but if it is too difficult the choir will be demoralised by the tedious work required to produce a respectable performance. I try to keep a balance between detailed technical work within pieces and letting the choir enjoy singing a piece from start to finish. In my context, only the top groups can approach four part men's choral music of the American tradition. The Brotherhood sings in three to four parts. I find that most published men's choral music is too low, too high and too hard and have had the luxury in recent years of having old boys of the choirs undertake composition studies at the local conservatorium. These men have provided us with some relevant, singable and beautiful music.

20.4.3 Activity

Our rehearsals often look sport-like. There are stretches and often the boys begin rehearsal laying down with their knees up in order to undertake accent method breathing exercises like those advocated by Chapman and Morris (2006). "Warm-Ups" are actually technical work designed like a very large group singing lesson and all are accompanied by choreography designed to improve body alignment and breath support while relieving tongue root tension, jaw tension, encouraging good resonance and assisting with passaggio transitions. These movements include bouncing from the knees with hands in the air and the chest open, bouncing on the beat with a skiing motion of the arms, spinning in a circle, stepping on the beat with hands held up and making a frisbee throwing action while singing. These movements are developed from the suggestions of Cooksey (2000, p. 829). There is voice pedagogy and choral methodological support for physical involvement in this context. (Eichenberger, 2001; Castles, 2009, p. 40).

I find it continually necessary to work with beat and rhythm as many boys arrive in secondary school with little skill in this area. This is tragic given that in many cases, the popular music they admire is rhythmically fascinating. The Kodály approach encourages the use of the large limbs for the feeling of the beat. Singing while walking the beat or dancing is a valuable way of developing a sense of the beat in singers. Clapped ostinati, games and the use of the Curwen hand signs are also part of the stock in trade of the Kodály teacher and can make rehearsal rooms far more active places. The continuation of the Kodály games throughout schooling further encourages the allying of sport and singing and Ashley validates the value of singing as "social play" (2009, p. 146).

For a number of years I had no seats in my rehearsal space thereby avoiding the nightmare of trying to get adolescent boys to sit well for singing. I still sit the choirs rarely in our 1 hour and 15 minute rehearsals. In some ways traditional "still" rehearsal methods can allow poor posture, locked knees, locked hips, bad breathing and poor body alignment.

Movement also assists the development of good musicianship. It is always dangerous if a whole section of a choir is relying on the musicianship of a key member to stay in tune. Our technical work includes singing a canon and walking around the room past singers who are holding another part. The movement is enjoyable and the aural challenge helps develop more independent singers.

20.5 Teaching Singing in Rehearsal

I believe teaching singing in rehearsal helps recruit singers as well as improving the ensemble. If you spend time in a practice room helping a rock singer achieve a high note and tell him that this assistance is available at every rehearsal, he may join the group. It can be great for the image of your singing group if the rock singers of the school find membership valuable. Students also value the gift of knowledge about singing. At the end of last year a year Eight boy told me I was the first conductor who had told him how to sing and not just what to sing. I was flattered but saddened by what the student had missed in the earlier years.

I assume the readers of this text no longer need to be convinced of the importance of boys singing through their voice change. I have found the exercises of a number of researchers very valuable. Cooksey recommends vocalising down ward through the falsetto to the lower range of the voice. (2000, pp. 828–829). David Jorlett, Anton Armstrong, (personal observation) and Jerry Blackstone also support the maintenance of the Head Voice with Blackstone advocating extensive use of Head Voice for settling voices (1998).

Cooksey also recommends spoken sighs which glide smoothly from head voice to chest voice (Cooksey, 2000, p. 829). These exercises are commonly used at Westminster Choir College (Haasemann & Jordan, 1991, p. 62). Cooksey suggests that these exercises be refined into descending five note and three passages as the voices develop. We generally sing descending five note patterns in head voice, through the passaggii and into chest voice in each rehearsal. It is important to take care with these exercises to ensure there is not too much tension produced at passaggio points. Ancel, who has had considerable success with changing voices has developed the "loo law" exercise which is part of every rehearsal for changing and settling voices at St. Laurence's (Ancel, 2010). His exercise encourages register transition without tension. I find singing on fricative consonants really useful. Singing with the tongue out on a voiced "th" can simultaneously encourage breath support and relax the tongue and jaw. Work with fricatives has been powerfully developed with the "primal sound" work of Janice Chapman (2006).

In the quest for good intonation I recommend viewing correct intonation as "an achievable challenge rather than a quixotic goal." Welch valuably describes a "continuum" model of singing development as opposed to a deficit model (2000, pp. 704–706) and makes clear the importance of "an environment which fosters" singing "development" (ibid., p. 711) so that students do not become "singing disabled" (ibid., p. 713). Leon Thurman reminds us that the brain learns by "target practice" (Thurman, 2000, p. 196). I try to have aural and vocal solutions for struggling students (Young, 2006, p. 20). Physical and aural training activities including "inner hearing", "silent singing" and training in solfege can be invaluable and provide the "target practice" that adolescent men need.

The foregoing reads as if choir rehearsals at St. Laurence's consist solely of leaping about and making strange noises. We teach vocal technique to the students in the rehearsals so that they know the reasons for and aims of the various movements and sounds. Less than one third of choir members are able to afford individual vocal lessons while a number of others get voice lessons in groups of four. Accordingly, I am the only source of vocal technique advice for many of my singers. In the largest choir, the school voice teacher attends every rehearsal and assists individual students while the rehearsal is running. This helps all concerned and aids in recruiting more private voice students. A good deal of technique can be taught in the first 15 minutes of rehearsal and this time is sacrosanct. The remaining part of the rehearsal is given over to repertoire and the technical work continues in the rehearsal of the music itself. This approach mirrors that of Noel Ancel at the Australian Boys Choir (personal observation). I find that it is imperative that the activities used in the technical work are carried through into the repertoire learning so that good vocal technique is cemented in real contexts.

20.6 Singing in "Classroom Music"

20.6.1 Problems of Definition

During the school day, "Classroom Music" is offered in most Queensland secondary schools as an elective, usually after a "taste" of the subject as a compulsory program in the first year. Choir, Orchestra and Band are not offered for credit. The "Classroom Music" courses in Queensland culminate in the Senior School with "Senior Music" in which students need to show facility in Analysis, Composition and Performance. The concept of "Classroom Music" has been a battleground of conflicting pedagogical approaches and the proliferation of possible learning experiences has marginalized class singing in many schools.

At St. Laurence's we use performance and singing to teach composition and analysis throughout the course. In this way, singing becomes a powerful cognitive tool in the intellectual development of the students in addition to being a compelling means of personal expression.

Teaching music literacy is fundamental so that students are empowered to participate in a range of musical discourses. Literacy in moveable doh, absolute letter names, guitar tabulature, French time names and a number of clefs is taught by singing in context. Sound comes before sign and all literacy is underpinned by strong aural development.

Analysis examples can be taken from any style or culture provided that they are used with cultural sensitivity and an awareness of context and the listeners are prepared for the listening so that they can engage actively and cognitively with the material. This preparation largely involves singing and playing either the material itself or manageable themes and excerpts.

Composition activities flow naturally from the repertoire being performed, listened to and analysed. These compositions are submitted as performances, recordings or on computer generated scores depending on the style, context and genre.

This approach enables the school to satisfy syllabus requirements while still maintaining music making as core to every lesson. Of course many other learning experiences are used, and computer technology is powerfully integrated, but singing is not marginalized.

20.6.2 Repertoire

Music taught is not chosen for its relevance to a particular "unit" but rather, because of its appropriateness for teaching a musical concept. These musical concepts are taught sequentially and are continually reinforced. The practicality of singing of the repertoire is a key consideration at every year level.

Repertoire is chosen which students will be able to vocally master. For example, instead of using "The Erlkonig" to teach Lieder, "Der Muller und der Bach" would be preferred as it has a smaller range. This piece also enables the teacher to teach jump bass, arpeggio, modulation to the tonic minor, the Neapolitan 6th, the use of musical elements to express emotion and the characteristics of Romanticism. The baritone key of D minor works best in year Eleven.

Given the research on the participation of males in singing you could suggest that having so much singing in the Music course is asking for unemployment. However, at St. Laurence's there are healthy numbers of students taking the subject and the senior results are outstanding. Teaching students to sing and teaching intellectually challenging lessons about how music works is successful. Our program starts from scratch, with students learning beat, rhythm and pitch, proceeds sequentially and ends with irregular metres, secondary dominant sevenths and modes.

20.6.3 Lesson Planning

I have found much of the advice about adolescent learning mentioned above is applicable in the Classroom context. Indeed, Kodály is said to have advised that we treat our classes as choirs. In my view it is essential to have the students sing in the first lesson so that they simply assume that singing is part of music class just as addition is part of mathematics. Once this has occurred, provided the environment is supportive and the teaching engaging, the problem of the boys not singing diminishes. At St. Laurence's we normally achieve accurate conscious in tune singing and reading in simple metres in pentatony by the end of the compulsory course. Students can also play pentatonic tunes on the keyboard and guitar and can usually sing their core repertoire in, sol fa, French time names and absolute letter names. We find this provides a good basis for continued singing through the school.

The 50 minute Classroom Music Lessons at St. Laurence's usually comprise 6–7 focusses, each with a review of known material, a new point of learning and a reinforcement of that learning. New musical concepts are taught using strategies which are sequential sets of focusses. In this way, new thought processes are continually reinforced and developed. This approach is supported by research (Bromfman, 2009, p. 61; Thurman, 2000, p. 196) and reflects the use of focus teaching in the Kodaly method where each focus will usually end with a reinforcement stage that is a repetition of the skill learned in a new way (Klinger, 1990). The lessons are not all singing. There is also playing (keyboards, guitars, drums), listening, improvising, composing, using notation and sequencing software, inner hearing, part work, repertoire learning, game playing and dancing.

20.6.4 Head and Chest Voice in Class

Ashley has found "for boys who do not sing, I have reached the conclusion that an introduction to singing has to be through the modal voice" while the "boy voice, in its full range of capability from head/falsetto downwards" will become a "small specialist niche" for those boys who are interested in singing and want to extend themselves. (Ashley, 2009, pp. 168–169). At St. Laurence's, with the luxury of boys who are made to experiment with their voices, I use head and chest voice in almost every lesson. This follows the approach taken by Ancel with the Australian Boys Choir. Clearly, we need to use whatever voice or voices work in our contexts.

20.6.5 Unison Singing Range and Repertoire for Changing Voices in Class

Cooksey finds that "unison singing is possible" but complains that "most published unison songs have pitch ranges that are too wide or the appropriate ones are in keys that force many changing voices into pitch ranges that they are incapable of singing without excess vocal effort" (Cooksey, 2000, p. 824). This presents a problem for me where the singing of scales is essential for the teaching of musicianship and music theory. I use the Queensland Late Beginner sequence of concepts that starts with restricted range and builds gradually. While the teacher may be confronted by students at different stages of voice mutation, good voice teaching coupled with careful choice of keys should enable the teacher to accommodate most changing voice boys (Young, 2006, p. 20). In addition, students with particularly unruly voices and restricted ranges can learn to swap octaves and still participate in tune in class activities without compromising their vocal comfort or development. It is important to remember that during voice change, the voice is not the measure of the mind and very intelligent boys might have voices that are difficult to control.

20.7 Advocacy

On the ubiquitous "Subject Selection Night" you need to adduce valid arguments to parents about why their son should take Music instead of Business, Information Processing Technology, Graphics, Manual Arts, languages and the other creative arts, such as Fine Art, Drama and Dance. Subjects such as Business, Graphics and IT are very tough competitors as they can be seen to directly lead to gainful employment and parents have a strong desire for their sons to keep them in comfort in old age. It is understandable during a mining boom that a parent might prefer their son to be a mining engineer rather than a musician. The music teacher must argue that Classroom Music offers the cognitive enrichment that all mining engineers need and that a mining engineer who is musical will be a much better companion in the parents' dotage.

In these circumstances it is essential to be offering a subject that can compete in academic rigour with the other subjects. On these occasions, the work of the Senior Students is the most compelling for younger students and parents. It is often wise to have older students attend to testify for your subject. I usually play performance videos of current senior students, play samples of the sophisticated compositions on Sibelius software and allow parents to read the substantial analysis examinations written by the students. It is also reassuring to parents to know the illustrious careers being enjoyed by the graduates of the music course.

In the field of boys' singing, successful completion of the Senior Music course ensures that we are graduating literate, analytically skilled, articulate compositionally accomplished singers and musicians. This sort of training should put paid to the cruel joke that a singer at the door "cannot find the key and does not know when to come in".

20.8 Conclusion

We must be the first advocates for Classroom music and Choirs. If we do not have faith in our area as a worthwhile activity, no one else will. The most powerful advocates are the students. Students often join choirs or classes because of the decisions of their peers and those peer decisions rest on our ability to create activities which are appealing whether in the choral context or in the classroom. In my experience, a solid base of community singing can provide a fertile environment for the formation of successful, accepted and supported specialist singing groups (choirs, musical casts, etc.) and for the enthusiastic study by many of musical analysis, composition and informed performance.

References

Ancell, N. (2010). Building voices and concepts. In S. D. Harrison (Ed.), *Perspectives on teaching singing: Australian vocal pedagogues sing their stories* (pp. 155–169). Bowen Hills, QLD: Australian Academic Press.

Ashley, M. (2009). *How high should boys sing? Gender; authenticity and credibility in the young male voice*. Surrey, England: Ashgate Publishing.

Blackstone, J. (Writer), & Blackstone, J. (Director). (1998). *Working with men's voices* [Motion Picture]. Santa Barbara, CA.

Bromfman, J. (2009). Repeating with variety: Implementing motor learning theory in the middle school choral rehearsal. *The Choral Journal, 50*(1), 61–63.

Castles, A. (2009). Oh boy(s)! Ideas for engaging boys in music. *Music in Action, 7*(2), 40.

Chapman, J. (Ed.). (2006). *Singing and teaching singing: A holistic approach*. San Diego, CA: Plural Publishing.

Chapman, J., & Morris, R. (2006). Breathing and support. In J. Chapman (Ed.), *Singing and teaching singing: A holistic approach* (pp. 39–58). San Diego, CA: Plural Publishing.

Cooksey, J. (2000). Male adolescent transforming voices: Voice classification, voice skill development, and music literature selection. In L. Thurman, G. Welch, & J. Ostrem (Eds.), *Bodymind and voice* (Vol. 3, pp. 821–841). Minneapolis, MN: Fairview Voice Centre.

Eichenberger, R. (2001). *Enhancing musicality through movement*. Santa Barbara, CA: Santa Barbara Publishing.

Freer, P. K. (2007). Between research and practice: How choral music loses boys in the middle. *Music Educators Journal, 94*(2), 28–34.

Haasemann, F., & Jordan, J. (1991). *Group vocal technique*. Chapel Hill, NC: Hinshaw Music.

Harrison, S. D. (2005). Music versus sport: A new approach to scoring. *Australian Journal of Music Education, 1*, 56–61.

Klinger, R. (1990). *Lesson planning in a Kodály setting*. Brisbane, QLD: Clayfield School of Music.

Miller, R. (2008). Acknowledging and indebtedness. *Choral Journal, 49*(5), 16–22.

Roe, P. F. (1983). *Choral music education*. Englewood Cliffs, NJ: Prentice-Hall.

Thurman, L. (2000). Human-Compatible learning. In L. Thurman, G. Welch, & J. Ostrem (Ed.), *Bodymind and voice* (Vol. 1, pp. 188–301). Mineapolis, MN: Fairview Voice Centrre.

Welch, G. (2000). The developing voice. In L. Thurman, G. Welch, & J. Ostrem (Eds.), *Bodymind and voice: Foundations of voice education* (pp. 704–717). Collegeville, MN: Voicecare Network.

Young, A. (2006). Classroom strategies for changing voice boys. *Australian Kodály Bulletin, 2006*(1) 17–23.

Chapter 21
The Male Voice Choir in the United Kingdom

Peter Davies

21.1 Background

Histories of choirs and the movement are documented in much greater detail elsewhere. However, in essence, the movement in the United Kingdom can trace its history back into the 19th century and the development of heavy industries in the north and south west of the country and, a little more recently, to Wales. It is a common misconception that Wales saw the start of the movement. As the movement spread and became more popular, choirs started to form outside the industrial heartlands and as late as the latter half of the 20th century new choirs were forming, initially as groups of friends or workmates. Many Police forces started constabulary choirs, some of which still exist today, one still being supported at a professional financial level. A very small number of choirs originated in sports clubs but, surprisingly, knowing how well young males sing on the terraces of both football and rugby pitches relatively few sprang up from this source.

New choirs are still forming. In the "traditional" format, they are forming largely as a result of the amalgamation of older choirs whose numbers have declined below sustainable levels. However, new and exciting choirs are being formed in schools, as part of local authority (and sometimes independent) arts or music centres and a small number as a result of direct intervention and support into schools from traditional male voice choirs. The former category continues the style established many years ago and perpetuates similar repertoire. The latter group is developing new music and styles of singing. Government intervention, in the form of the *Sing Up* (see the evaluation of Sing Up in relation to boys' singing in Chapter 3) and *Youth Music* initiatives have had a major impact on singing, particularly in primary schools.

Prior to some pilot initiatives, singing in schools in any format had been excluded from the National Curriculum for over 20 years. Pressures on teachers led, in all but a few excellent examples, to singing also being lost as an extracurricular activity. Therefore, a complete generation of children had not experienced singing in a group

---

P. Davies (✉)
Cornwall International Male Voice Choral Festival, London, UK
e-mail: peter.davies@abcd.org.uk

setting and, with declining church membership together with the loss of many church choirs, that source of singing training has also been largely lost. The government initiatives listed above, which came about as a result of considerable pressure from organisations representing singers and choral leaders in the country over many years, have led to an explosion of teacher training initiatives, choral leader training, qualifications in choral directing and, as a direct consequence, new and exciting male singing ensembles.

21.2 The "Average" Male Voice Choir in the UK

The English (often all male) UK cathedral choir tradition is not covered in this chapter. Male voice choirs in the UK traditionally sing in four parts: two tenor parts; two bass parts. The harmonies are set approximately over a two and a half octave range centring on the G below middle C. The music is not sung in close harmony (unlike "Barbershop" choruses). Singing is usually accompanied by piano or organ though choirs occasionally sing some unaccompanied items. Very few items, if any, in a normal concert programme are choreographed.

A recent survey of all 478 traditional UK male voice choirs conducted specifically to give a statistical basis to this chapter has given an interesting picture of the movement. Almost 60% of choirs have a membership in excess of 40 (the average membership across all choirs is 48). Basses (including baritones) outnumber the two tenor sections combined and the age range, with a few exceptions is 30–90 plus. Over 40% of all members are in the 66–75 age range with over 80% in the 56–85 age range. These quite alarming statistics have been guessed at before but never proven.

Recruitment is often seen as a major issue. With the average age so high, those who have to stop singing need to be replaced if only for membership to be constant. Age-related illness also has an impact on choirs. An average choir may well have members with Alzheimer's disease, prostate or other cancers, heart illness, age-related disability and, in some cases, lung disease. However, all is not doom and gloom. More choirs have increased in size than decreased though one third have stayed about the same for the last 5 years or so. New member recruitment in these "traditional" male choirs is mainly in the 55 plus age group. (Whereas anecdotal evidence suggests that recruitment in the Barbershop movement is, on average, at a younger age.)

The new breed of male voice choirs now emerging as a result of the initiatives referred to in the Background emanate largely from primary, secondary and (Saturday) music schools. A recent conference in Cornwall for male singing leaders organised by *Sing Up* discussed mechanisms to recognise the special requirements for a younger age group of male singers and ways in which skills and resources of adult male choirs could be used beneficially in their support. These are more adequately described in the Outreach section of this chapter.

Finding appropriate music for these young singers is a challenge. *Sing Up* has a web-based "Music Bank" available to singing leaders. Some young singers are being encouraged to write and perform their own music. The Cornwall International Male Voice Choral Festival has recently decided that music it commissions for the movement every 2 years as part of the biennial Festival will, for 2011, be commissioned from someone with wide experience in encouraging male teenagers to sing.

While the majority of traditional adult choirs (69%) elect senior officers for an annual term, the reality is that most hold positions until they decide to relinquish them. This has led, in some choirs, to a conservatism of approach to new ideas, repertoire and the use of technology to aid learning and for communication. Where senior officers are appointed on strictly fixed terms (and specifically the chairman), in general, a more pragmatic approach to repertoire, technology, the use of rehearsal time, remuneration of the musical team and competition work seems to be evident. A minority of excellent examples do contrast with this generality. This is almost always down either to the charisma of the musical director, the chairman or as the result of an excellent relationship between these two key players driving the choir forward.

Most choirs depend on funds raised through membership and concert performance to survive. Approximately one tenth of choirs receive some form of business sponsorship but over 70% have not received any form of outside funding. Only a very small proportion have successfully applied for funding from the UK National Lottery, Arts Council or other grant giving scheme (5%). Over a quarter of all choirs either make no charge for a performance or only charge "travelling expenses". The average appearance fee appears to be of the order of £150 while only 3% of choirs charge in excess of £400 to appear.

Major travelling expenses of choirs include the musical team (where they are paid), music, rehearsal space and travelling. Travel, while often subsidised from choir funds, is largely paid for directly by members. The average spend on music in any 1 year across all choirs is £381. With music in the UK at least £1-50p per copy and choirs averaging approximately 50 in number, only a maximum of five new copies of music are purchased in any 1 year with nearly half of all choirs introducing it on a termly basis. Where male choirs have been in existence for some time, some of the spend will be used to replace music lost from library stock. Repertoire turnover is markedly less than in mixed choirs, most of which would expect to change repertoire completely at least every academic term.

However, finance apart, the main reason for a slower repertoire change is that most male voice choir members cannot read music, learning everything by rote. More progressive choirs provide learning CDs, tracks for download to MP3 players or websites with access for members only where tracks can be downloaded to computers. These choirs tend to have a slightly faster change of repertoire. A small number of musical directors actively teach the ability to read music either during short "theory sessions" in rehearsal or outside in special sessions.

The music sung is stuck in somewhat of a time warp. With the dramatic rise in the number of male choirs during the earlier part of the 20th century, an explosion of new writing occurred. Many composers of the era wrote for male ensembles and their music seems to have a place in almost every male choir's current repertoire. Much music written for male ensembles prior to 1900 has been lost in favour of a much "lighter" repertoire style.

While there is new writing for the movement which is either commissioned by or submitted to publishers, nearly 60% of all choirs have never commissioned new music and only 5% have commissioned music during the last 12 months (16% within the last 10 years). Much of the music newly published is an adaptation or arrangement of Welsh (sometimes English) hymnody, American spirituals or an arrangement of post war pop songs or of "songs from the shows" in a variety of styles.

Some excellent pieces were commissioned for the "National Male Voice Choir Championship" an annual competition, held in the North of England. In each case the piece, commissioned from eminent composers of the time, was the "set piece" for the competition and compulsory for all entrants. However, bearing in mind that most singers could not read music and with the pieces becoming ever more complex, the competition ceased to attract choirs because of the considerable preparation time require and ceased in 2000. The only "all male voice choir" competition in existence in the UK at present is that held as part of the biennial *Cornwall International Male Voice Choral Festival*. It attracts choirs from across the world as well as showcasing the very best of male voice singing in the UK. Several attempts have been made to introduce all-male voice choir competitions over the years (notably as a separate adjunct to the *Peterborough Festival*). All have succumbed to a lack of enthusiasm.

Llangollen International Eisteddfod attracts many male voice choirs into competition (as one or more classes in a much wider competitive environment). Participation in this Festival is not open, however, choirs being *selected for participation by a panel. The BBC Radio Three Choir of the Year Competition* attracts approximately 10 male choirs but in direct competition with other adult (mixed, single sex and barbershop/harmony) choirs. Smaller festivals and eisteddfodau across England and Wales have male voice classes. The number of choirs participating is quite small with some festivals only having single choirs enter. However, 26% of choirs claimed to have entered some form of competition within the last 12 months. Two thirds of the choirs that had entered competition suggested that the overall experience had been positive, The remaining third described the effect as either neutral or negative.

It is the third that found competition neutral or negative that provides food for thought. It could be argued that dealing with the competitive environment involves managing the expectations of singers as well as excellent training techniques and hours of work. Where members of choirs are led (by sometimes inexperienced directors) to believe that they will "do well", when they do not, the "we woz robbed" mentality prevails and choir members believe that the adjudicators were incorrect, misheard, had favourites (never them), etc. Men in particular seem to have a problem with not winning (though the writer has observed the phenomenon in both mixed and other single sex choir competitions too)! The "taking part" and being given a professional acknowledgement of those things which need attention through adjudication seem to be of little importance for members and leaders of these choirs.

Bearing in mind the very proud histories of success in competition for many choirs during the earlier part of the 20th century (which in some cases are still used 50 or more years on as a sign of the current quality of the choir), it could be argued that they would not wish to compete against "lesser" rivals and be "shown up". In some cases, the musical team simply does not see the value in competition. Some choirs are simply not prepared to put the amount of work in necessary for competition preparation or are "too busy with the concert schedule" to prepare for them. Over half of all choirs have said that they will not be entering a competition within the next 3 years.

The performance schedule for some male choirs in the UK could, truly, be regarded as punishing. A quarter of choirs perform in concert fortnightly while nearly half sing at least every month in concert. However, bearing in mind the slow repertoire change, many will be singing very similar repertoire in successive concerts. The performances are largely in local churches, in aid of local charities (for which many thousands of pounds are raised every year) to audiences whose average size is approximately 140.

21.3 The Choir Music Team, Its Skill Levels, Remuneration and New Developments

In addition to permanent directors and accompanists, two thirds of choirs have assistant directors and half have assistant accompanists. In contrast to the Barbershop movement where every chorus will have section leaders, only one fifth of traditional male choirs have them available to assist in teaching.

The qualifications male voice choir directors hold gives an insight to the overall quality of the choirs in the UK. Almost a third of all male voice choir directors did not study music to any level in school and a further 16% only studied music at school (no figures are available to show to what level at school). A further 18% have a music degree. Only 9% of the directors have both a degree in music and performance qualifications, some of which will have included time spent undertaking choral direction tuition. However, only 2% of the directors of male choirs have professional music direction qualifications.

Until very recently, the UK had no formal choral directing courses either at under or post graduate level. At the time of writing still no university in the UK offers doctoral degrees in choral directing: students having to study in the USA or elsewhere. However, since 1986 the Association of British Choral Directors (to which only 12% of male choir leaders belong),, the Royal School of Church Music, The Royal College of Organists, The Voices Foundation, The British Voice Association, *Sing Up* and a number of private organisations have recognised the need to develop choral leader training. Between them, a large number of seminars, conventions and courses are organised for those wishing to improve or develop their skills. Many are aimed specifically at teachers who, in primary education, rarely have any music qualifications. However a wide range is also available to those involved in choral leadership outside schools who may also have no musical qualifications.

Formal qualification strands are now available through a small number of universities (initially Roehampton, now additionally Chichester and the Royal Welsh College of Music and Drama with MA courses specifically in Choral

Direction). For those who want to study and qualify outside the university context, the Associated Board of The Royal Schools of Music (ABRSM) offers Diploma, Licentiate and Fellowship qualifications in Music Direction specific to the needs of the candidate (e.g. choral or orchestral) and the Royal College of Organists offers a Diploma in Choral Directing (also available to non organists). The Royal School of Church Music, through its "Church Music Skills" programme, currently offers a "Certificate of Affirmation" following study of modules for those leading singing ensembles (among other topics) within a liturgical setting.

Many directors of male choirs (75%) arrange music for their choirs but only a tenth of them have music professionally published. Arrangements are frequently of hymns or popular songs. Few publishers in the UK solely publish music for the genre and, unlike the worldwide Barbershop movement (through both BABS and LABS) no central repository of new items is available. Publishers of male voice choir material tend to rely on archived material. Only two publishers actually distribute new material though new private publications are available. Publishing new music through the internet does not yet seem to have had a great impact on the material available to choirs.

Analysis of the length of service of music directors with a choir leads to some interesting statistics. Just over a quarter have been directing their choirs for 20 years or more while nearly 30% were new in post within the last 3 years. This is a considerable turnover and appears to be as a result of two main factors: mostly the age achieved before retirement (in one case nearly 80); a frustration with the ability to move the choir forward and introduce new repertoire and attitudes (but this is anecdotal evidence obtained in discussion rather than quantitatively observed). The average length in post for the remaining 45% of male choir directors is 8 years.

Financial remuneration for those directing male choirs is generally not good. Many directors undertake the work because they love it and have other means of generating income (or are retired). Well over one third receive an "honorarium" of £1000 a year or less, a further quarter are paid under £2000 while a fifth receive up to £4000 per annum. Only the remaining 3% receive over £5000 per annum.

Of the directors new in post over the last 3 years, only a quarter have no formal choral direction training or other musical qualifications. Generally, they receive low levels of remuneration (£1000 per year or less). Those directors with formal music qualifications and especially those appointed with choral direction qualifications (one tenth of all of those appointed within the last 3 years) receive higher levels of remuneration, in excess of £3000 per year. Anecdotal evidence suggests that when making new appointments, choirs are beginning to realise the amount of work involved heading the music team and have achieved a greater understanding that applicants are not prepared to undertake the work just "for love".

Accompanists, despite additional work they have to undertake in preparation and practice are also poorly remunerated with almost two thirds receiving £1500 per year or less. Only a quarter receive an average of just under £3000 per year. The turnover statistics are broadly similar to those of directors. A slightly greater percentage have been in post 20 years or longer and one tenth have been appointed within the last 3 years. A quarter of accompanists have no formal music qualifications while over half have either a degree in music or performance qualifications. Almost one fifth have both a degree and performance qualifications. Where accompanists are more highly qualified, in general terms they are better remunerated and the skills and qualifications of the directors are also higher.

Despite all the opportunities available, fewer than a quarter of all leaders of male choirs in the UK are involved in any form of professional on-going development. Those that do attend seminars, workshops, courses and master classes almost entirely self-fund. Choirs do not contribute to the cost (but it may be that they are not asked to).

The significance both psychologically and physiologically of warming up at the start of a rehearsal is beginning to be recognised. Fifty-six per cent of choirs commence with warm up activities but with the average amount of time spent on them being under 10 minutes across all choirs. It was not possible to analyse the format, content or complexity of these warm up activities.

These statistics could lead the reader to believe that the male voice choir movement in the UK is dominated by poorly-skilled, ill-paid music directors and accompanists who are poorly supported because of a lack of musical literacy and, therefore, potential leadership "in the ranks". It could also lead to the conclusion that the choirs are not of the best quality. In some cases that is true. However, bearing in mind the medical histories and ages of members suggested above, the slow speed of repertoire turn over and the frequent concert schedule (often to very appreciative audiences), the quality could be described as "good". The UK has a few stunning male choirs led by professional, well paid, dedicated music teams. The majority, however, struggle with recruitment, learning, skill levels and sound production. Nevertheless appreciated by audiences, they do demonstrate problem areas when in concert or competition.

In contrast, those new male choirs emanating from schools and music centres have an average age below 20. They demonstrate high levels of skill with members often fluent music readers. They are usually led by professionally paid and qualified staff, have a very rapid repertoire turn over, use much more recently published or arranged music and are experimenting with new forms of accompaniment (including instrumental ensembles, beat boxes, etc.). Some use sound recording and production technology, PA systems and electronically produced backing tracks. They are wonderfully enthusiastic and bring a totally different dimension to on-stage performance. With an increase in interest in choral singing demonstrated by the visual media across the UK, several of these choirs (notably from Wales) have achieved UK-wide recognition. Outside Wales, the movement is gaining strength particularly in Cornwall, Nottinghamshire, Warwickshire and Berkshire where concentrated efforts by small teams of leaders have brought together large numbers of boys and teenagers to form quite exceptional male choirs.

Perhaps the most outstanding achievement in the establishment of new male singing ensembles is the National Youth Choir of Great Britain in which several male ensembles have been formed across the country. Led by the inspirational Mike Brewer MBE, the choir staff teams have brought together some of the very best young male singers in the country to form a choir which rivals the very best in the world.

21.4 Choir Outreach

With recruitment issues, a high age profile and a reduction in the number of "traditional" male choirs across the UK during the last 10 years, it might be expected that outreach might introduce mechanisms and opportunities for redressing some of these problems. In all but a small minority of case studies given below, that does not seem to be happening. Only 10% have links with schools, cathedrals, other boy/youth male choirs, sports clubs or other outreach activity related to sustaining the male voice movement. Interestingly, there is little correlation between that proportion of choirs and the 12% of choirs that are involved in outreach bursary schemes (two of which are substantial and offer music or singing teaching sponsorship for one or more years at UK universities). However, the bursary schemes are for only one or at most two individuals in any 1 year with a single exception where two singing classes at a local festival are sponsored.

Within the very small proportion of choirs actively engaged in outreach activity, some stunning examples of success can be found. The last part of this chapter gives an outline of many of these successes which fall into two broad categories: recruitment within a similar, possibly slightly younger age range; the development and support of new boy and teenage choirs involving visits to schools.

21.5 Cases

21.5.1 East Anglia

The musical director of a choir in East Anglia could see that his choir, though good, was not growing and was likely to decline. He felt that the choir was largely introspective and, because of a fairly staid repertoire, presented a very difficult learning challenge to potential new members. He also recognised that wherever he went, he could hear men singing (on the terraces at football and rugby matches, in nightclubs and other social venues). He recognised that men do want to sing but were reluctant to join his choir. They perceived it as of high quality, potentially threatening to join because of the very steep learning curve and difficult socially because everyone knew everyone else. With a support team from within the choir, the director instigated a "Come and Sing" project which was intended to attract non-singers. The project was initially resourced from choir funds and started with small numbers. However, word spread quickly through use of media contacts and an excellent marketing campaign in a variety of locations. The group started with basic instruction on how to sing, how to breathe, some fun, unison songs and then moved to slightly more complex material as confidence was gained. Eventually, the group became a training "choir" which was more than twice the size of the original choir. For some time, it ran in tandem with the original choir, eventually becoming self-resourcing.

As the skills of individuals developed, they were transferred to the original choir. The original choir is now one of the largest in the country with 120 active members.

This model has been used by other choirs with differing levels of success. The success of this particular choir can be attributed to five sets of circumstances: the choir director concerned was highly skilled with wide experience of choral direction techniques; the director and his support team had great charisma; the project was time limited; appropriate funding was made available by the choir to ensure all necessary costs were met (including room hire, music team staff costs, music, etc.); clear, achievable objectives were set and during each stage of the project, evaluations of progress were undertaken with feedback effecting change. The project required the musical director and his team to be available outside normal choir rehearsal nights in that, effectively, a new choir was established. The project was fully resourced and the director was remunerated appropriately because choir members and officers could foresee the long term benefits. As a result of the considerable increase in size, other benefits have accrued to the choir including a reduction in the age profile, an increase in repertoire turn over, considerable business sponsorship, larger audiences, a greater recognition nationally, more secure funding for touring and exchange visits and a greater variety of professional skills available (through members) for the wider benefit of the choir.

21.5.2 The West Country

A member of a West Country based choir retired from his post as headmaster of the local secondary school. He had sung with the local male voice choir for some years and recognised that the membership of his choir faced the "usual issues" for male choirs in the UK. He also recognised some of the possibilities that links with the school he had recently left might achieve. At first, he and a few friends from the choir visited the school to sing to small groups of pupils. This soon turned into the opportunity to sing during assemblies, a practice that has been abandoned in many UK schools. In support of the music staff at the school, the group of men attending the school became larger as the enthusiasm of their reception in the school was recognised. While the whole choir is never able to attend during school hours, a reasonable number do. This has resulted in a small number of boys showing an interest in singing and now forming their own, growing, male voice choir within the school. The secondary school choir now performs with the male voice choir. The ultimate aim is that the school choir "feeds" the male voice choir. However, the major benefit is that young men have been introduced to singing which, with continuing nurture, may be something that they never forget and continue wherever their careers take them.

In this case, the skill of the music staff at the school along with the enthusiasm of the male voice choir members (and probably the considerable respect the retired head still retained amongst the staff) enabled the new group to be formed and supported.

21.5.3 Cornwall

The model of adult male choirs working alongside secondary school pupils to encourage them to sing is particularly strong in Cornwall (from where the above example is drawn). In other parts of the county, choirs are also involved in the support of teenage boy choirs, primary school boys choirs and county wide choirs. The recent national *Sing Up* conference was organised in Cornwall specifically because so many primary schools (30 in all) are involved in getting boys singing.

For some years, the *Cornwall International Male Voice Choral Festival* has supported both the Cornwall Boys Choir and specific events aimed at teenage boy singers. At every Festival, visiting choirs (particularly those comprising boys or teenagers) from outside the UK are encouraged, through a planned programme, to visit both primary and secondary schools to encourage boys to sing and demonstrate different national repertoires. In several cases, this has resulted in spontaneous singing by boys in the schools, the opportunity for the development of foreign exchange visits, and an increased awareness of male singing through attending Festival concerts and events.

The Festival is planning a much more ambitious role in the development of a cross-county teenage boys' choir. A co-funding plan will be established which will have three main aims: financial support for a music team at a professional level; the ability to bring in occasional inspirational workshop leaders and ensuring that the choir can be sustained for a period of time pending it achieving a greater level of self funding. It has to be recognised that this may take some time.

In several parts of the UK, local authority music services (and sometimes retired heads of those services) have recognised the need to get boys singing and have made stunning progress in the development of boy choirs. In these choirs numbers have reached well over 100 singers. They are well led by experienced and knowledgeable staff.

21.6 Other Related Issues

The issue of the sort of role model boys need in education has raised much discussion in the UK. A Government move to recruit more male teachers to primary education is widely believed to be because male teachers are appropriate role models. Research reported by Martin Ashley at the recent *Sing Up* conference disclosed that boys don't notice the gender of their singing leaders. What they did notice was the quality of their singing leader. Gender was not seen as important but skill was.

It was also clear from Ashley's research that it is important that schools do not timetable sport directly against singing or other musical activities, that teaching staff understand that singing is actually the ultimate team sport. Boys' singing in UK schools, needs much encouragement. It needs, above all, teachers who understand the importance of singing and do not embarrass potential singers in front of their peers because they, the teachers, feel that sport, for example, is more "boy-like" than singing.

Despite the bureaucracy and important childcare legislation, organisations are still able to make contact with young people to encourage them to sing. Members of an amateur opera group have been able to visit schools on a one off basis to introduce opera to pupils without having to be "CRB checked". This has raised great interest among both boys and girls to the delight of the opera group concerned. It is hoped that members of male voice choirs will feel similarly enthused to sing and encourage pupils in similar circumstances.

21.7 Conclusion

Maybe the 478 adult male choirs in the UK are, slowly, in decline. Some are taking very active steps to ensure longevity. Many (in some cases quite literally!) stagger on in the hope that, like Wilkins Micawber, "something will turn up" in the form of new members. Some show little active concern, regarding their choirs more as a social activity for them and their partners alone.

Many choir members, while concerned about declining membership, seem to have lost the verve and "get up and go" of youth, so do not become involved in active marketing campaigns, visits to schools and other places where younger men meet. Many, of course, are now retired and "do not have the time they had when they were at work". This is an interesting phenomenon in its own right but also speaks of the other priorities which overtake the generation of men singing in UK male choirs.

In the last 5 years alone, four choirs have disappeared in Cornwall (forming two amalgamated choirs) and, nationwide, a further 10 have disappeared. It is true that the industrial heritage which gave birth to the male voice choir movement has largely disappeared in the UK. However, whether it is Manchester United, the Six Nations Rugby games or international sporting events, men sing!

The great joy is that new choirs are forming. They are different, frequently smaller, much younger in age profile and use different styles of accompaniment and presentation. All are directed by inspirational, professionally qualified and remunerated leaders who have dedicated their lives to developing the skills of new male singers, showing them that singing is as challenging, as encouraging, as rewarding and requires as much of the "team spirit" as any sport might.

Male singing in the UK operates at each end of the age spectrum. Those involved in male choirs have much to encourage younger singers with. Those new to singing have much to benefit from the experience in "older" choirs. The UK has an imbalance at present, more adult men sing in male choirs than boys of any age. Largely, men aged between 20 and 45 do not sing at all. Were the UK government to extend the *Sing Up* project into secondary schools in a future phase aimed at getting teenage boys to sing and to develop choral direction skills amongst a greater range of secondary teachers, a completely new generation of choirs would be established and more new singing leaders would emerge. As a male singing leader in the UK, the writer fervently hopes that this will happen and that adult male choirs will become much more involved in sustaining the movement, whatever the shape, repertoire or style that may evolve.

Chapter 22
Giving Voices to Gifted Antipodean Unicorns

Curtis Bayliss and Robert Stewart

> *The soul of Melbourne High School is expressed through its singing.*
> *Principal Jeremy Ludowyke*

Traditionally, learning a musical instrument has been perceived as a "feminine" pursuit and singing even more so. In his study of instrumental choice and gender, Harrison found that the harp, flute or singing were considered the most feminine instruments, with girls making up 90% of those surveyed (Harrison, 2007). Despite such overwhelming odds, there are many prominent examples of boys singing and doing it very well indeed.

22.1 Facing the Challenge

Music is central to the lives of most high-school age boys. However, music education is a marginalised area of the school curriculum, decreasing in popularity as students approach senior school and succumb to pressures to choose subjects perceived to be more useful in the "real world" (McGregor & Mills, 2006). McGregor and Mills articulate a problem faced by many music teachers in today's schools. It is a paradox that in an age when music is so easily available to consumers, it has become increasingly difficult to recruit boys into music programmes. Some authors attribute this phenomenon to family, peer pressure, gender roles or even an adolescent boy's voice change (Harrison, 2009c). Harrison elaborates upon the influence of gender roles or gender role "rigidity" further, calling it the "lack of ability for males to experience femininity as much as females experience masculinity" (Harrison, 2009b). This is a multi-faceted problem that has been addressed by several studies.

C. Bayliss (✉)
Melbourne High School, Albert Park, VIC, Australia
e-mail: bayliss.curtis.w@edumail.vic.gov.au

Many authors (Harrison, 2003; McGregor & Mills, 2006; Roulston & Mills, 2000) share a common view in their writing about the "feminisation" of music, even tying it to the wider perception of music being linked with other feminine areas of study such as languages and the humanities.

Another problem is that often music is not recognized as a viable career option for young men. By extension, it is not always worthy of serious study in secondary years. Anita Collins recognizes seven interconnected elements that influence what she calls a boy's "musical habitat" and within these elements the "relative health of the boy's musical ecosystem is defined" (Collins, 2009). In short, a student's peer group, family, school culture, role models, support from the leadership team and teaching strategies combine to inform the importance of music and singing within the school community.

Of course, teaching style and how music teachers present the subject are vitally important. While no set strategy is advocated for every situation, overall themes in the chosen literature do appear. One thing that all the selected writers agreed upon is the need to make the subject matter as practical as possible. Boys learn by doing; rather than reading an instruction manual, they prefer to use trial and error (Mason, 2009). As a result, endless hours of theoretical learning will only frustrate and disengage boys. Therefore, young men also require lessons that are fast paced and varying; it is suggested that "young adolescents need a change of activity, focus or location in the room about every 12–13 minutes" (Young, 2009). In classroom practice, this also means building on team work, peer relationships and activities that are physical/kinaesthetic, which is supported by "a meta-analysis of educational research in five countries [that] found males to be more kinaesthetically and peer oriented than their female counterparts" (Young, 2009). In the end, passive learning atmospheres will not be conducive to boys' learning styles (Veel, 2002).

The classroom atmosphere itself is one of mutual respect and good humour. Veel stresses that at this stage in their development, young men are testing adult authority and do not respond well to dictatorial classroom management. She advocates allowing the peer group to establish clear guidelines arrived at democratically by the group- developing a

> Behaviour/consequence system ... whereby a non-cooperative behaviour received an immediate negative consequence established by the group ... cooperative behaviour ... would receive a positive reward at the end of the session, to be negotiated by the group (Veel, 2002).

While maintaining a classroom environment that facilitates learning, a music teacher must also balance this with being an advocate *outside* the classroom. Keeping positive relations with various school groups and stakeholders is also important to a successful programme. A supportive principal class (Collins, 2009), good relationships with other faculties, especially Health & Physical Education (Harrison, 2003) and a wider role in the community (Beale, 1991) help to ensure that a strong music programme is valued and perceived as important by students.

22.2 Allowing Everyone Their Own Voice

Situated on a grassy knoll beside Australia's Yarra River, the castle-like Melbourne High School is a selective-entry state government school for 1,380 boys of years 9–12. The oldest high school in Victoria, it is not a specialist music school, but nonetheless regarded as a national leader of singing for boys and is one of the few schools in Australia to run massed singing as a core curriculum subject. It is perhaps the only government school with a voice specialist teacher appointed as Director of Choral Music and the requirement that the four classroom music teachers contribute to choral conducting and choral arranging. These teachers form a team-teaching unit for the whole school singing program.

In this age in which students have few rituals and ceremonies, this secular school has found that collective singing contributes a sense of occasion and can build varieties of humour or levels of *gravitas* in ceremonies. It seems most apt that the students' uniform black blazers feature a gold unicorn that appears to be singing! Group singing, called "massed singing", is the first team building experience requested of the 365 new Year Nine students. Few new students, in any Australian government school, will have been expected to do something of this nature together. Singing is considered a likely indicator of student participation and attitude towards academic work in general.

Singing is part of the liberal-humanist philosophy of developing the "well-rounded" individual. As Principal Ludowyke stated:

> Massed singing is a potent subversion of the strictures of masculinity because it compels young men to collaboratively and publicly transgress the boundaries. Once you have convinced a bunch of young men that it is okay to stand alongside their peers and sing together, and to do so lustily, the barriers and restraints are set aside and, from that moment, anything is possible. (Harrison, 2009a)

The Year 12 students also report singing as an academic respite and cohort realignment, frequently mentioning singing as the catharsis from mounting exam and academic tension. Former Assistant Director of Music, Roland Cropley, outlined the journey of most students' participation in massed singing:

> At first [Year 9] it is very tentative, but eventually most boys make more than a token effort. By Year 12, the enthusiastic involvement, expertise and sheer volume of the singing are astonishing. Most boys eventually take the risk of letting go of their fears and begin to contribute their energy wholeheartedly into learning to make controlled beautiful singing. (Cropley, 2005)

The simple expectation is that all MHS students will sing! Besides the remarkable array of singing heard in the busy corridors, singing at Melbourne High School is organised in three streams:

22.3 Inclusive Singing

In addition to the small amount of vocalization in the core classroom music program for years 9 and 10 and the solfege based work in elective classroom music at years 11 and 12, Melbourne High School also runs:

- An all inclusive massed singing program (which is an expectation) that *every* student will engage in and sing with their year level cohort in the Memorial Hall for one period each week during class-time.
- The House Instrumental and Choral Competition, in which every boy sings for his House, establishing a "singing energy" in the School at the beginning of each year. This exciting and competitive day-long whole-school singing event held in the expansive Melbourne Town Hall in the first term shows the talents of each of the school's four Houses in producing massed singing, chamber choir and instrumental items before three judges and a large audience. The school administration gives this Choral Competition such high regard that the time-table is altered to allow three times for choral rehearsals each day of the first term. Interestingly, the Choral Competition is regarded as part of the responsibility of the Director of Sport (as it is part of the annual House competition, which also includes swimming, athletics, cross country, selective sports, debating and theatre sports).
- Additional educational outcomes of this competition are the workshop training and practical experience given to teams of young choral and instrumental conductors, the skilling of the accompanists, and the notated and tested choral arrangements created by the students.
- Singing, both competitively and as a "taunting" in sport assemblies, is usually a part of the very long running annual exchanges with interstate Schools from Adelaide and North Sydney.
- 350 Year 10 boys also form the choir for the RSL-Legacy ANZAC Day military style open air commemoration ceremony with the School's Military Band at Melbourne's The Shrine of Remembrance each April.
- Music assemblies at the end of each term, before an audience of staff and guests, provide the performance opportunity for the pieces mastered in the weekly sessions. These "in-house" performances also help prepare students for the disciplines and stamina needed for the lengthy whole school singing of the Speech Night performances held in a 6,000 seat venue every November (Fig. 22.1).

Fig. 22.1 Melbourne High School speech night

22.4 Elective Singing

The elective music program is possibly the largest in Victoria. For example, more than 200 students elect Year 10 music and around 700 students participate in ensembles across years 9–12. The reality is that the elective vocal and choral activities are so well supported because the weekly massed singing sessions help generate a school-wide acceptance and culture of singing. Elective singing options are listed below.

- Private voice lessons for about 22 students by a voice teacher.
- Vocal quartets in group voice lessons with a voice teacher for another 12 students
- Participation in "project choirs" such as Finalé Choir (which requires six rehearsals and performance in the annual Winter Concert.
- For over 50 years Melbourne High School has staged high quality annual school musicals, sometimes referred to as "the opera". The musicals have a production time-frame beginning with auditions in November and are staged in mid-May. Included in the preparation over the last few years has been a series of workshops with famous theatrical old-boys and visiting music theatre practitioners. To further assist the development of the students' skills in the musicals, a collaboration is staged each October year with the drama students of scenes and monologues from musicals entitled Moozikal Schmoozikal.
- Some of these projects may also become more attractive to our boys because they are co-operative ventures with our sister school, The Mac.Robertson Girls' High School.
- As part of a cultural involvement programme, students may join the un-auditioned group of about 70 students who sing as the Melbourne High School Chorale or an auditioned close-harmony group of 21 singers with student accompanist – the Melbourne High Singers. The Singers, a pop choir, begun in 1977, is organised as 4 year based TTBB quartets and a leading group of TTBB soloists with a singing accompanist. The chief aim of this group is to present outstanding arrangements by the members of the group.
- A large number of our boys seek even further extension and join Broadway Chorus Australia and the DEET program "Join In the Chorus" or the Melbourne Youth Music summer-schools.

22.5 Student-Driven Singing

These activities vary yearly in support and leadership as the student population changes. There is usually a student-run Barbershop Society and a number of boy-bands (especially near School social events) and much singing with the School's Rock Club. In recent years, students have written and staged their own musicals. Even some of the School's sports groups, notably the rowing and the rugby teams, sing together to raise money and to intimidate opponents! In visiting Tonga recently the School's Rugby team sang a prepared concert for the Prime Minister of the country.

22.6 Beyond the School

Previous Director of Music, Anne Lierse (2002–2010), encouraged a strong research and professional development in her 18 music staff. School staff and students present at international, national and state conferences. Present Director of Music, Mr Robert Stewart, is a Canadian born and European trained voice teacher and choral educator who has led staff and students to gain a more national and international choral perspective and encouraged a review of existing process.

Leading voice and choral specialists from around the world have visited and presented at Melbourne High School including Professor Graham Welch, Dr Adam Adler, Dr Scott Harrison, Dr Richard Gill (a music department patron), Noel Ancell, Robert Edwin, Feldenkrais voice teacher Stephen Grant, and barbershop experts and voice and technology experimentalist Mal Webb. Teachers from around Australia frequently visit to share their singing experiences.

Melbourne High School is a centrally located venue in Melbourne and has co-hosted a number of successful conferences on boys' music education and boys' vocal education. Our students also annually gain Old Boys Association bursaries to attend Choral Conductor Training workshops and National Choral Association summer schools and conferences. As well, the School has an ongoing relationship with two Victorian university teacher training courses for voice and choral and classroom teaching candidates. Melbourne High School is a singing school seeking to share with others.

The rich mix of a long tradition of "expected participation" in House and massed singing together with "elective" singing and instrumental tuition, the varied ensemble options, including high standard school musicals, is remarkable in a school that does not offer music scholarships nor is a designated "music school". The concepts imparted in the music lab and classrooms and the participation as performers and audience do affect students beyond their school life and do impact on the greater Melbourne community. These intelligent young men venture into the world as more discerning music consumers and at best ready to become even more skilled and sharing performers, composers, conductors and educators. More importantly, almost all exiting students leave the school confident to read music and to bravely raise their voices.

22.7 The Future of the Massed Singing Approach

The music staff and principal are keenly aware that real educational and institutional benefits must be gained to justify the inclusion of massed singing in a demanding curriculum as the issue of tradition, whilst it has value, is not the reason that anything survives in the vigorous competition for space in the School's curriculum (Cropley, 2005, p. 175) Currently our requirements for massed singing are:

1. A large hall filled with whole year levels (circa 350 boys per year) seated
2. A pianoforte and accompanist

3. A team of conductors and other teaching staff
4. A microphone and amplification
5. A computer with music score or text projected from a data projector
6. A projection screen
7. An introduction of verbal "focus" from (vice-) principal or year level teacher followed by a rhythmic -based focus activity from a music teacher

Working with such a large group (either 350 or 700 boys at each session), and in dress rehearsals (1,380 students), we need to be constantly looking to head off potential misunderstandings or opportunities for pupil subversion. Conducting a year level chorus or massed singing program takes a few special strategies:

- Keep the language used for directions simple and pro-active
- Maintain the rehearsal pace … allow breaks/respites and then clearly set the return to physical "singing posture" and the objective aim of any repetitions of material in resuming singing
- Keep a sense of humour and positive good-will
- Any process needs to be realistic, manageable and free of any preciousness
- Invite students to make repertoire suggestions
- Repertoire needs to engage and educate … possibly also entertain
- Songs need to be in the right key to suit the particular group
- The diversity of team teaching is extremely valuable
- The presence of non-music teachers is vital in helping to reinforce the focus, participation and discipline amongst the students seated in the Hall
- Try to stir imaginations and emotions with repertoire choice and the passion of teaching style, especially in initial and subsequent delivery of the material

22.8 How Can We Improve the Way We Run Our Massed Singing Program? Some Ideas Recently Discussed by the Music Staff Include

- More extensive conducting training of the team of teaching conductors
- Even greater allowance for student suggestions and arrangements into repertoire selections
- Finding closer relationships of material used in massed singing and in classroom work
- A commitment to performing Australian compositions
- Broaden our language and historical breadth of material
- Diligently engage with even-more pro-active language to foster a richer climate of reward
- Add moments of surprise and the unexpected in our delivery of material
- Increasing physiological-anatomical accuracy about the process of singing
- Various methods of formal reportage and assessments of students efforts in massed singing

- Using rhythmic and focus exercises at the start of each session prior to giving an overview of what we intend to achieve in each session
- Experiments with particular seating configurations of student singers
- Considered approaches to maintaining correct octave singing and sensitivity to Year 9 boys with cambiata voice transition states
- Discipline process for students who do not participate or are disruptive
- The best uses of technology, including improving notation quality, creating a digital store of our projections and using our school internet servers as a remote access point for students to learn and review the music taught in our massed singing sessions
- Allowing student access to guide tracks and video material to help with style and memorization via the internet
- Identifying and consolidating the benefits of our team teaching system
- Greater variety of accompaniment ensembles and instruments
- Drawing on the language and performance skills of our non-music staff
- Examining best practices elsewhere in the world

It is our hope that our young men feel that they own the act of singing in this School. The boys need to explore their individual and collective sounds and learn to love their new and changing voices. The School environment ideally needs support from peers and even from families, however we can only do little to control these influential permission sources.

On the most basic level we must offer great songs to sing, achievable challenges, some fun and humour, and "encouragement" which may sometimes equal a little proactively worded coercion. We consciously promote in our school that singing, in all sorts of guises, promotes community; vocal activity contributes to this diverse School's cultural solidarity, awareness, respect and (especially when pieces and events go very well) self-pride. Singing promotes joy of personal creativity and expression. At Melbourne High there is no audition; no pre-requisite experience or talent are necessary. The students' willingness to participate and bring along an attitude of being ready explore are the all attributes required.

References

Beale, R. (1991). Keeping boys singing. *The Musical Times, 132*(1780), 314–318.

Collins, A. (2009). A boy's music ecosystem. In S. D. Harrison (Ed.), *Male voice: Stories of boys learning through making music* (pp. 33–47). Camberwell, VIC: ACER Press.

Cropley, R. (2005). Rituals, assemblies and singing'. In J. Prideaux (Ed.), *More than just marks: Boys' education* (pp. 174–175). Melbourne, VIC: Pennon Publishing.

Harrison, S. D. (2003). Music versus sport: What's the score? *Australian Journal of Music Education, 1*(1), 10–15.

Harrison, S. D. (2007). A perennial problem in gendered participation in music: What's happening to the boys? *British Journal of Music Education, 24*(3), 267–280.

Harrison, S. D. (Ed.). (2009a). *Male voice: Stories of boys learning through making music*, Camberwell, VIC: ACER Press.

Harrison, S. D. (2009b). Aussie blokes and music. In S. D. Harrison (Ed.), *Male voice: Stories of boys learning through making music* (pp. 4–15). Camberwell, VIC: ACER Press.

Harrison, S. D. (2009c). Music making in adolescence and beyond. In S. D. Harrison (Ed.), *Male voice: Stories of boys learning through making music* (pp. 48–61). Camberwell, VIC: ACER Press.

Mason, S. A. (2009). Talking technology: Boys engaging in music in single-sex and co-educational environments. In S. D. Harrison (Ed.), *Male voice: Stories of boys learning through making music* (pp. 107–123). Camberwell, VIC: ACER Press.

McGregor, G. & Mills, M. (2006). Boys and music education: RMXing the curriculum. *Pedagogy, Culture and Society, 14*(2), 21–233.

Roulston, K., & Mills, M. (2000). Male teachers in feminised teaching areas: Marching to the beat of the men's movement drums?' *Oxford Review of Education, 26*(2), 221–237.

Veel, L. (2002). Motivating middle school boys through music. *The Boys in School Bulletin, 5*(1), 2–5.

Young, A. (2009). The singing classroom: Singing in classroom music and its potential to transform school culture. In S. D. Harrison (Ed.), *Male voice: Stories of boys learning through making music* (pp. 62–78). Camberwell, VIC: ACER Press.

Chapter 23
The Foolishness Came Later: The Foundation and Development of the Spooky Men's Chorale

Stephen Taberner

The foolishness came later. The original idea was somewhat more modest: to assemble a group of men and sing deep, sonorous, resonant songs, in deep sonorous, resonant places. Like somewhat hip, agnostic monks on a roving commission amongst the crypts of the world. This was the original notion for the Spooky Men's Chorale.

The idea arose sometime in winter 1996, when from time to time I'd turn the lights out, light a candle, and listen to Georgian choirs with a glass of wine and a tear in my eye. The sound was raw, elemental and deeply thrilling. It was sung with no ceremony other than that required by the song, and suggested an ancient world which was somehow simpler and more direct than ours: where men were men, and in all probability you had to milk a goat on the morning.

That was the Rustavi Choir, the pre-eminent folkloric ensemble, who sung church songs, hunting songs, and songs about men. There was also, in fact, a mixed choir, the Zion Patriachal choir of Tblisi. This choir was astonishingly adept at creating a whole parallel world of shimmering harmonics which traced their own luminescent path an octave or two above the singing. I would follow them, agape with wonder, and dream.

Men's voices always sounded good to me, so long as they could learn to sing with each other. There's perfectly good reasons for this, of course. The ear is biased towards homogeneity, on the blending of like with like. String or Brass ensembles have a more immediate and easy pull on the ear than, say, a cor anglais, a double bass, a soprano sax and a recorder. A mixed choir presents complexities of blending arising from the confluence of different kinds of voices, and can be more challenging to the ear.

The first formal attempt to form a male voice choir was *The Choirboys*, a bunch of mates who would meet up in Glebe Town Hall, primarily to share repartee, but secondarily to conduct extended masculine vocal improvisations, sometimes musical but always grunty, and thus terrorise the yoga class immediately downstairs. It

---

S. Taberner (✉)
Spooky Men's Chorale, Blue Mountains, NSW, Australia
e-mail: taberner@tpg.com.au

was good clean fun, but essentially a highly enjoyable side alley. It soon became clear that they would prefer to sing actual songs.

When the *Spooky Men* did emerge, they were almost perfectly formed. It was as part of an evening called "This was nearly my life", in August 2001. Basically I called up every guy I knew who could sing and seemed to be a tolerable human being, taught them 3 songs, and asked them to show up wearing black and with an interesting hat.

The three songs were "Vineyard", a Georgian church song, "Georgia", a mock Georgian original, and "The Mess song", an existential rumination on the aftermath of breakfast. The song is by New Zealand's Don McGlashan, and was our first clue as to subsequent directions in relation to humour. The audience's hilarity at our ultimate descent into mock catatonic oblivion was only one of several prophetic moments that evening. Another was the ecstatic response we got before we'd even sung a note: it seemed that even the sight of 15 black clad men preparing to sing was something they'd been unknowingly waiting for, for a long time.

By then we were already noticing the paucity of healthy male choral antecedents. Leaving aside the Georgians for a moment, we'd noted the Welsh and Cornish choirs, the classical traditions, barbershop and the like, or doo-wop and gospel traditions, all documented elsewhere in this volume. Interestingly, most of these traditions seemed to have become fixated on the extremes of the male voice, athletic freaks of contrabasso, tenor or falsetto. There was a distinct lack of blokes singing in the middle range. For an Australian ensemble the repertoire needed to be about something that was a little closer to home than "A Nightingale in Berkley Square", or someone else's blues.

We did some gigs. We learnt a few more songs. It wasn't long before I noticed a few things about working with a choir of men. The first thing was that there were no women there. That seemed to have an interesting effect on the general vibe. Most choirs I'd conducted till that point were mixed voice community choirs, which generally meant they were women's choirs with a few men standing in the corner looking bemused. The women seemed to instinctively understand and promote the notion and reality of choirs as community networks. They were invariably the main shakers and movers, and blissfully exploited the possibilities of the choir for social networking. Meanwhile the guys, who were fawned over like rare gems when they did actually show up, were more peripheral. When there was any kind of drama or conflict, the guys were usually charmingly oblivious to it.

When rehearsals for Spooky Men began, the guys would shuffle around and offer wry comment. This is the art form of sly commentary, in the moment, a collective witty improvisation. Guys seem to love this zone. In the crude and undeveloped form, it's a series of jokes. In its higher form, it's repartee, and there's no limit to its excellence. Of all the things I love about the Spooky Men, maybe it's the repartee I love best. When we tour, waiting at comfort stops, we can stand around at the service station and talk nonsense. When we made our first album, the producer listened to this happy bullshit for a while and then said "I guess this is as close as you guys get to fighting..."

Repertoire began to emerge. One early favourite was a cover of Kasey Chambers' "Am I Not Pretty Enough", which was mostly pointless foolishness gleaned from the sheer improbability of men singing such lyrics. In order to milk the humour properly, however, we began to untangle some of the key antecedents of the Spooky ethos. The song begins with the chorus, so how were we going to approach that? It seemed obvious that we needed to browbeat the audience, point a finger at them and glower. How *dare* they accuse us of not being pretty enough? By the time we reach the second chorus, we are tragic, abject, unashamed losers, heads hanging in hapless asymmetry.

In the early rehearsals, we seemed more intent on shirt changes or whether we'd hold our head this way or that than the actual songs we were singing. That was not to underestimate the importance of the latter. There was a certain sound we were going for, and the Georgians had a lot to answer for in that respect: a rich, full vein of lower frequencies, which required the subsumation of individual honky frequencies, quirks of phrasing, and outbreaks of vibrato. We needed to learn to blend like beasts, and peel back the edgy harmonics to expose the juicy fundamentals underneath.

People *liked* us: that much was clear. We were being guided not just by that, but by what seemed important to dwell upon in the modern male experience. Hence the emergence of the song "Don't Stand between a Man and his Tool"... It's ironic that I wrote the song, because tools and I meet as intimates only in my imagination, mostly: but at least I like the idea of having a magnificent stable of power tools and endless variations of ways to use them.

The work was surprisingly businesslike and lacking in rancour. After a little bit of repartee, the spooks would happily descend upon the task in hand. Unlike in mixed choirs, it seemed to be possible to offer blunt commentary such as "you're flat" without consideration of what might need to be caretaken afterwards. The so-called lack of male emotional sophistication was turning out to be useful after all. We perfected a singing style that was dense, lugubrious, heavy, fat in the bottom end, and also carrying a certain declamatory gravity, hallmarks of what we later came to think of as, in the vocal sense, "Spooky."

What is the purpose of singing, in this context? Absolutely nothing: that is precisely the glory of it. We are no more than a series of grand buffoons making the biggest, fattest, sweetest sound we can. And when it comes down to it, it makes no difference at all.

But let's return to the story. The general response to the Spooky men's existence was moderately ecstatic. In the first couple of years we performed and rehearsed sporadically, appearing from nowhere like some secret cave dwelling gentlemen's glee club. There was a certain relaxed equilibrium, and no particular desire to up the ante, until the National Folk Festival of Easter 2004, held in Canberra. In front of a crowd at the 3,000 seat Budewang, we debut of what we now call the Spooky Theme:

We are the Spooky Men
We dream of mastodons
Practice mysterious handshakes
And we can grow beards if we want to...

Who knows why we thought of Mastodons, but the image stuck. On two levels, perhaps: Firstly, in that their largeness and hairiness and inelegance, they were the best approximation to Spooky Men in nature, and secondly, that in the dream of the hunting thereof, naked and covered in pigfat, we were giving purest vent to male dreams of freedom that had long been concreted over, confined to small toolsheds, or reworked into guidance towards one's kids as they constructed lego towers.

At the National Folk Festival, we became cult heroes. It is worth considering the effect of our Georgian antecedents on all of this. The sound and ethos that we were aiming for was undeniably influenced by all of this in at least three clear ways:

Firstly, Georgian vocal music is inevitably 3 part, which means that chords are often "open", containing, for example, reading upwards, 1-4-5, 1-5-1 or 1-5-2. This means that there is often no third in the scale, by contrast to a typical choral 4 part chord such as 1-5-1-3. The sparseness that results is a direct contributor to the rawness or directness of the perceived sound, compared to the rococo lushness of, for example, barbershop harmony, which inevitably states all important harmony notes.

The second major influence is in the presentation of the voice, which part of the voice you choose to turn into song, and how. Major singing traditions always make a choice in this respect. Folk traditions tend to be raw, amplifying talking, sobbing, or shouting, and making them into song. In our world, the more mannered presentations which are common in classical singing, opera , and barbershop share a more distant relationship with the primal self. There is a certain stylisation, in that the singing in no way resembles the way they would talk, cry or shout. Singing is, in this respect, high art, high artifice, and divorced from the more visceral realities of life.

The Georgians make a different choice, and we attempt to follow them. We stand, open our mouths, and make a sound something like a bunch of men singing, like men. That, of course, implies the third point, which is the way they stand, the pointless grandeur. In all this we aim to sound as heartbreakingly beautiful as we can, whether singing loud or quiet.

The attention we received at the *National Folk Festival* in 2004 gave rise to a series of opportunities to put our music before a wider audience. This included a wide range of festivals in Australia, and three tours of the UK. We made four CDs and produced various lines of merchandise for the public, including t-shirts, bags, teatowels, and badges.

Two songs in particular seemed to touch a good warm zone with the audience: "Dancing Qveen", which was a version of the Abba hit as sung by an inscrutable and gruff Svedish Glee club, and "Vote the Bastards Out." When we hit the right spot, as we did with these two, the audiences would almost bay with pleasure. The socio-pathology of the typical spooky performance became refined over time, after early experiments with Hawaiian shirts and leopard skin loincloths. It became clear that great subtlety could be conveyed within the confines of deadpan. Some men glowered, some gently wallowed in pathos, some quietly beamed like Cheshire cats. The Spookies had the luxury of being able to explore who their spooky self was. We are sometimes thought of as a comedy act. I would vigorously deny that's what we are, preferring instead the idea that whilst we aim to make people cry, we also hope to make them weep too.

One interesting moment in early Spooky history was when we presented our first public workshop, entitled "Sing like a Bloke". When we arrived, we discovered a happily expectant crowd of 150 or so, more than half of them women. We made it a workshop for "blokes of all genders".... and needless to say, many of the women were better at singing like blokes than the blokes themselves. It was grand fun, and we always specified from then on that blokes of all genders were welcome. For many of the men who come along to such events, they come to realise that rather than having any deep and unresolvable issues around singing, they are merely reacquainting themselves with a piece of equipment they haven't used in a very long time. There are amusing errors of calibration, as they either wildly overshoot or scarcely move at all as you try to coax them to a new note. They usually find their range, more or less. It's a kind of anomaly that in our world singing, for men in particular, has been removed from the lexicon of primal and enjoyable activities.

At a forum on men's singing in Brisbane, Australia, a prominent secondary school music educator said that there was a problem of perceived status with boy's singing, and that they should attempt to address this with such strategies as awarding them colours on their blazers. My take is a little different. Until boys' singing consists of something better than tiresomely florid rearrangements of "Bridge Over Troubled Water" delivered with what seems to be a choir sized set of mouthsized plums, then boys will stay away in droves. The Spooky Men went down like a big black stupid bomb at this forum not because they are good, but because they alone seemed to occupy the yawning void thus opened. Here's how to fill the void: mens and boys' choirs could give up singing in pseudo-classical pofflevoice, especially when they are singing pop or rock songs. They could discover the rich zone of possible material that has been written since Simon and Garfunkel, which seems to be the closest we get to contemporary. They could ransack any number of global singing traditions of which Georgian is only one, which has the requisite boof which has been leached from our own. And they could rediscover the joys of highly cultivated stupidity.

At that forum, there were two moments which restored my faith: one, where a choir of ageing men from Adelaide in maroon shirts sang of all things, *Advance Australia Fair* in quavering 4 part harmony, and despite the cheeseball nature of the song, it moved me (and my colleagues) because it was congruent with who these men were and they sung it (and their other songs) with heartfullness; the other was when a boy's choir sang *What shall we do with the drunken sailor* which was hardly inspired material but offered the lads the chance to unleash the masculine vigour which had been till then entrapped in artifice, and the result was liberating for them, and us.

Our own strength, such as it is, is more in the collective, the ability to move as one big black low frequency organism. Not one of us is necessarily possessed of a golden voice, and I don't mind that at all. We are thus forced to find our strength in concert, to learn, as I have said, to blend like beasts, and within and without the musical framework to find a place for our own brand of foolishness, or perhaps seriousness: to in fact, allow ourselves to become closer to whom we actually are.

In all of this, needless to say, I am constantly inspired by the languid, elephantine grace of many of these men that I am proud to count as friends and colleagues. Most of them are engaged in post modern experiments in multiple role holding: worker, dad, partner, tool fetishist ... to which we can add the tantalising and fiendish extra temptation of international folk star ... the goodheartedness, humour and practicality which attends the ensuing juggle and all ensuing tribulations is sufficient to gladden my beating heart, inspire me to some kind of decency, and suggest that after all, we are somehow on the right track.

About the Editors

Adam Adler A specialist in choral conducting and music education, Adam Adler holds degrees from the universities of Western Ontario, New Brunswick, and Illinois. In June 2002, he became the first graduate of the PhD program in music education at the University of Toronto. His current research and lecture efforts include male gender issues in choral music education, as well as GLBT and equity issues in schooling. Adam Adler has taught music in schools across southern Ontario, and is active as a consultant, clinician, composer and arranger; his compositions and arrangements have been performed across Canada and abroad. In 1999, he founded The Margarita Project – a performance-based collaboration between folk artists and choirs that encourages the choral performance of previously unpublished, unarranged and unperformed folk music. He has served as assistant conductor of The Bel Canto Singers of Fredericton and The University of Toronto Symphony Chorus, and as conductor of The Glenhaven Community Youth Choir and The University of Toronto Hart House Singers. Adam Adler presently serves as the founding conductor of the Toronto-based community choir Just Singers – an adult community chamber choir with a mandate for democratic operation, musical growth, and social service.

Scott D. Harrison works at Griffith University where serves as Deputy Director (Research) at Queensland Conservatorium. Dr Harrison has experience in teaching singing and music in primary, secondary and tertiary environments. Performance interests and experience include opera and music theatre as both singer and musical director. From 1988 to 2008, he performed in over 30 productions for Opera Queensland and he continues to sing regularly as a soloist specialising in the works of Bach, Handel, Purcell and Britten. His teaching areas focus on teacher education, research design and gender. His major research areas are music and wellbeing, vocal education, music teacher education and masculinities and music. He has published extensively in the latter field including *Masculinities and Music* (2008) and *Male Voices: Stories of Boys Learning Through Making Music* (2009). Scott also edited Australia's first volume on vocal pedagogy *Perspectives on Teaching Singing: Australian Vocal Pedagogues Singing Their Stories* (2010). He serves on the editorial boards of *International Journal for Research in Music Education* and *Arts and*

Health. Scott is the immediate past President of the Australian National Association of Teachers of Singing.

Graham F. Welch Professor Graham Welch holds the Institute of Education, University of London Established Chair of Music Education and is Head of the Institute's School of Arts and Humanities. He is elected President of The international Society for Music Education (ISME), Chair of International Scoiety for Education, Music and Psychology Research (SEMPRE) and a recent past Co-Chair of the Research Commission of the International Society for Music Education (ISME). He also holds Visiting Professorships at the Universities of Sydney (Australia), Limerick (Eire) and Roehampton (UK) and also at the Sibelius Academy (Finland). He has acted as a special consultant: (i) on aspects of children's singing and vocal development to the USA National Center for Voice and Speech (NCVS) in Denver and the Swedish Voice Research Centre in Stockholm and (ii) on aspects of educational and research development in the areas of arts and music education, curriculum and teacher development to the British Council in the Ukraine and Argentina, the Ministry for Education and Youth in the United Arab Emirates and the National Research Foundation of South Africa. Publications number over two hundred and embrace musical development and music education, teacher education, the psychology of music, singing and voice science and music in special education and disability. Publications are primarily in English, but also in Spanish, Portuguese, Italian, Swedish and Chinese. Graham Welch is member of the editorial boards of the: Journal of Research in Music Education (JRME), Music Education Research (MER), International Journal of Music Education (IJME), Research Studies in Music Education (RSME), International Journal of Research in Choral Singing (IJRCS) and Psychology of Music (PsyMus). His research interests include Musical Development Across the Lifespan, Early Childhood Education, Singing and Vocal Development, Special Needs Education, Psychology of Music, Learning and Teaching in Music, Teacher Education.

About the Authors

Frank Abrahams is professor of music education and director of the Center for Critical Pedagogy at Westminster Choir College of Rider University in Princeton, New Jersey. A native of Philadelphia, Dr. Abrahams holds degrees from Temple University and New England Conservatory. Dr. Abrahams has pioneered the development of a critical pedagogy for music education. This teaching model encourages music teachers and ensemble conductors to adapt instruction and rehearsal technique to address individual differences in learning styles and empowers students to be musicians. For 17-years, Dr. Abrahams was Program Supervisor for Fine Arts in the Stoneham, Massachusetts Public Schools. He is the curriculum facilitator for the Society for Music Teacher Education. Abrahams is senior editor of *Visions of Research in Music Education* and a member of the editorial board of the *Music Educators Journal*. With Paul Head, he is co-author of *Case Studies in Music Education* and *Teaching Music Through Performance in Middle School Choir*.

Miriam Allan was born in Newcastle, Australia and has been based in England since 2003. She has been a soloist with leading orchestral and choral organisations from all over the world. She has been fortunate to work with many of the finest directors and conductors, including Sir John Eliot Gardiner, Lars Ulrik Mortensen, Laurence Cummings, William Christie and Roy Goodman. She appears on numerous recordings, highlights of which include Pinchgut Opera's *Fairy Queen* and *Dardanus*, *The Wonders of the World* with Echo du Danube, Mozart's *Requiem* with the Leipzig Kammerorchester and Gewandhaus Kammerchor. After making her debut with Glydnebourne Festival Opera in performances of Purcell's *Fairy Queen* in 2009, Miriam continued with that production to Paris, Caen and New York in 2010. Miriam is a vocal coach at Westminster Abbey and Head of Singing at Bloxham School, Oxfordshire.

Matthew Bannister is postgraduate theory supervisor in Media Arts at Wintec (Waikato Institute of Technology), Hamilton, Aotearoa/New Zealand. His main research interests are gender, popular music and cultural identity. He wrote his PhD on masculinities in alternative rock in New Zealand and subsequently published a book, "White Boys, White Noise: Masculinities and 1980s Guitar Rock" with

Ashgate (2006). An experienced musician, he has played in groups like Sneaky Feelings, the Dribbling Darts of Love, the Mutton Birds, the Weather and the Changing Same. He has also been involved with men's groups and presently lives in Hamilton with his wife Alice Bulmer and two children, Tom and Albert.

Margaret S. Barrett is Professor and Head of the School of Music at The University of Queensland. Her research interests include the investigation of the role of music and the arts in human thought and activity, creativity and the pedagogy of creative thought and activity, young children's musical thinking and identity work in and through music, and, the meaning and value of the arts for young people. This research has been funded through grants from the Australian Research Council, the Australia Council for the Arts, and the British Academy, and has been published in the key journals of the discipline. Recent and forthcoming publications include: *A cultural psychology of music education* (2011, OUP), *Narrative inquiry in music education: Troubling certainty* (2009, Springer, with Sandra Stauffer), and *Narrative soundings: An anthology of narrative inquiry in music education* (2011, Springer, with Sandra Stauffer). Margaret is President Elect of the *International Society for Music Education* (becoming President in 2012). She has served as National President of the *Australian Society for Music Education*, a commissioner for the Research Commission and elected board member of the *International Society for Music Education*. Margaret is Editor of *Research Studies in Music Education*, and Associate Editor for *Psychology of Music*, and a member of the editorial boards of key journals in the discipline.

Curtis Bayliss is a voice teacher at Melbourne High School and the Victorian College of the Arts Music Theatre course while also maintaining a busy private studio Voicematters. From 1992–1998 Curtis was Music Director of The Australian Children's Choir. Since graduating from Monash University and also from The faculty of Music at the University of Melbourne, he has performed with Opera Australia, The Victorian State Opera, Travelling Light Musicals, CLOC, Whitehorse and The Australian Ballet (as a singer!). He also sings oratorio and is found regularly performing with the accapella jazz quartet BOPeRA. He was the young voice specialist for the Australian Singing Teachers' Association forum on Music Pedagogy. Curtis has voice coached and arranged for The Playbox Theatre, The Bell Shakespeare Company, The Melbourne Theatre Company, Ballarat Opera festival and for many semi-professional companies.

Andy Bennett is Professor of Cultural Sociology and Director of the Griffith Centre Cultural Research. Prior to his appointment at Griffith, he held posts at Brock University (Canada) and the Universities of Surrey, Kent, Glasgow, and Durham (UK) and spent 2 years in Germany working as a music teacher with the Frankfurt Rockmobil project. Bennett specialises in the areas of youth culture and popular music. He is author of Popular Music and Youth Culture: Music, Identity and Place (2000, Macmillan), Cultures of Popular Music (2001, Open University Press), Culture and Everyday Life (2005, Sage), editor of Remembering Woodstock (2004,

Ashgate) and co-editor of Guitar Cultures (2001, Berg), After Subculture (Palgrave, 2004), Music Scenes (Vanderbilt University Press, 2004) and Music, Space and Place (Ashgate, 2004). Bennett is a member of the International Association for the Study of Popular Music (IASPM) and a former Chair of the UK and Ireland IASPM branch. He is also a member of the British Sociological Association (BSA) and a co-founder of the BSA Youth Study Group. He is a Faculty Associate of the Center for Cultural Sociology at Yale University, an Associate of PopuLUs, the Centre for the Study of the World's Popular Musics at Leeds University.

Stephen Clift is Professor of Health Education within the department. He has made contributions to health education and promotion in the fields of HIV/AIDS and sex education for young people, international travel and tourism, and evaluation of the Health Promoting School. His current interests are focused on the contributions of the arts and music to healthcare and health promotion. Together with Grenville Hancox, Professor of Music at Christ Church University, he has recently established the Sidney De Haan Research Centre for Arts and Health. Stephen's ongoing work includes evaluation of the Silver Song Club Project, which organises musical events for elderly people and their carers in association with local choral societies, and the evaluation of Music Start, an innovative project on the Isle of Wight which aims to promote singing and music making in all families on the island with children aged from birth to 5 years.

Anita Collins is a Senior Lecturer at the University of Canberra. She is convener of Music and Arts Education in Early Childhood, Primary and Secondary education. In 2010 Anita was appointed as a Visiting Fellow to the Australian National University and Secretary of the ACT Music Educator Network. Her research interests include boys' music education, thinking styles, conducting and in 2009 she commenced her PhD study with the University of Melbourne in neuroscience and music education. Anita has lead review panels for numerous secondary and tertiary course evaluations and contributed to a number of scholarly texts in the field of Arts education. In 2009 Anita was awarded with the ATEA Research Recognition Award for Early Career Researchers and the UC Faculty of Education Dean's Excellence Award. In 2008 she published Bedrock: Foundations in Music, a text for adult music learners and educators, which she co-authored with Lucas Edmonds.

Peter Davies has been musical director of Huntingdon Male Voice Choir since 1995 and organist and choirmaster of All Saints Parish Church, Sawtry, since 1985. For nearly all his professional life as a teacher, youth worker/officer, community development leader and consultant, he has pursued music as a performer, teacher, composer, arranger, conductor and through study. He has broadcast widely on radio and television with his choirs. For most of the past 13 years, he has been musical director to three choirs, undertaken major administrative roles for the Association of British Choral Directors (ABCD) and fulfilled the demanding role as a consultant of national repute in post-18 education data and systems issues. Mr Davies has delivered specialist workshops to choirs in East Anglia, seminars on male voice repertoire at ABCD conventions and individual piano, organ, singing and accompaniment lessons. In 2002 Mr Davies was co-ordinator and musical director of the National Association of Choirs Group 20 concert in Ely Cathedral and in 2007 became Director of the British International Male Voice Choir Festivals held in Cornwall.

Colin Durrant leads the graduate programme in Music Education at the Institute of Education University of London. He has been Director of Choral Activities at the New England Conservatory in Boston, visiting Associate Professor in the School of Music at the University of Maryland and Principal Lecturer in Music and Music Education at the Roehampton University (formerly titled University of Surrey Roehampton). He has a wide range of choral conducting and teaching experience and, following his doctoral research into the area of effective choral conducting, designed and developed a graduate programme in Choral Education at the University of Surrey Roehampton, the first and only one of its kind in the UK. His book Choral Conducting: Philosophy and Practice published by Routledge appeared in 2003. He is also on the editorial board of the International Journal of Research in Choral Singing. Colin Durrant has led choral conducting workshops in Australia, Hong Kong, Malaysia, Taiwan and the USA as well as in Europe. He currently conducts the University of London Chamber Choir and Imperial College Choir and has been invited to work with the BBC Singers in their outreach educational programme.

Jason T. Eastman, assistant professor of sociology, joined the Coastal Carolina University faculty in 2007. He earned a bachelor's degree in human relations from the University of Pittsburgh in 2000, a master's degree in sociology and a doctorate degree in equality and social justice from Florida State University in 2003 and 2007, respectively. Prior to joining Coastal, Eastman was a graduate instructor at FSU, a lecturer at Buffalo State College and an adjunct professor at Niagara University. His research focuses on Southern rock music and how this music depicts poor, rural white men, and how social inequities across all status groupings are perpetuated through those representations. This project examines race, class, gender, culture, subcultures and the social construction of race, class and gender through cultural practices and representations. His areas of expertise are inequality and social justice.

Robert Faulkner played a leading role in national curriculum development in Iceland in both in general school music and in community/instrumental music school contexts. Robert has been head of a community music school, part-time lecturer in Music Education at the University of Akureyri and the Icelandic Academy of Arts in Reykjavik, and deputy chair of the Icelandic Music Schools Examinations Board since its founding in 2002. Born in England, Robert studied singing at the Guildhall School of Music and Drama in London. Robert completed his PhD at Sheffield University with an investigation into vocal identity and the role of singing in Icelandic men's everyday lives which spans phenomenological psychology, ethnomusicology, music sociology and gender studies. Apart from articles in leading international journals, based both on his PhD research and research investigating children's composing, Robert has also written teachers' handbooks and journal articles in Icelandic.

Patrick K. Freer is head of the music education division at Georgia State University. He has been the Director of Choral Activities at Salisbury University (MD), the Education Director of Young Audiences of New Jersey, and, for 11 years, taught public school music at all grade levels. Dr. Freer degrees from Westminster Choir College of Rider University and an Ed.D. from Teachers College, Columbia University. He is the author of Getting Started with Middle-Level Choir and a frequent guest conductor for all-state and regional honors choruses. Dr. Freer's research is focused on the relationships between teacher language use during middle school choral rehearsals, student experience and student transition to high school programs. He is currently preparing a series of videotapes for middle school choral directors as part of the Choral Excellence series.

Grenville Hancox received his music education at the Birmingham School of Music, University College Aberystwyth and University College Cardiff. Formerly a teacher in secondary schools, his pioneering classroom methods were promulgated through a national project advocating both widening participation and the centrality of music making in the curriculum, both elements underpinning the work of this With a background in Music Education and performance his present research interests have developed from these areas and have resulted in a collaborative project with Professor Stephen Clift concerned with the benefits of singing for well being and supporting his belief in music as an agent for social change. Five years of work have resulted in publications and the establishment of The Sidney De Haan Research Centre for Arts and Health where one of the long term aims is through partnership with the local primary care trust, to provide singing on prescription. Grenville Hancox was appointed Professor of Music in 2000 and was awarded the MBE in the birthday honours list for services to music in 2005.

Evangelos Himonides is Lecturer in Music Technology Education at the Institute of Education, University of London. As a musician, technologist and educator, Evangelos has an ongoing career in experimental research in the fields of Psychoacoustics, Music Perception, Music Cognition, Information Technology, Human-Computer Interaction, Special Needs, the Singing Voice and Singing Development. Publications currently number over thirty-five, in high-profile international journals, such as Psychology of Music, IJME, RSME, Journal of Voice, Logopedics Phoniatrics Vocology and others.

Richard Mook holds a Bachelor of Arts degree with high research in music and religion from the University of Rochester and a PhD in music history from the University of Pennsylvania. He was awarded the Lise Waxer Prize from the Society for Ethnomusicology for his research on the history of barbershop quartet singing, and his research has appeared in the *Journal of the Society for American Music*.

Dr. Mook's current research projects include a book-length study of American quartet singing in the 20th century and a study of hip hop culture in Phoenix. His research interests include race and gender in American popular and vernacular musics. He is the author of Rap Music and Hip Hop Culture (2008).

Ian Morrison has Masters and PhD in Health Promotion and joined the Sidney De Haan Research Centre for Arts and Health in February 2007 to work on a cross-national survey of singing and wellbeing. He has managed the East Kent "Singing for Health" network for mental health service users' for 2 years. The evaluation of this project has shown clinically significant positive changes for the participants. He is now developing and evaluating a network of singing groups for patients with Chronic Obstructive Pulmonary Disease to assess the physical benefits of group singing.

Ioulia Papageorgi is a Lecturer in Psychology and Human Development and a Coordinating Research Officer in the Faculty of Children and Learning at the Institute of Education, University of London. She is also an Associate Lecturer at the Open University. Her research interests focus on the development of expertise, the psychology of performance and performance anxiety. She has worked in research teams for various funded research projects, and has widely presented her work at international conferences and seminars. She has published papers in international peer-reviewed journals and conference proceedings, and has authored a number of invited book chapters. Ioulia is a Chartered Psychologist (CPsychol), an Associate Fellow of the British Psychological Society (AFBPsS) and a Fellow of the Higher Education Academy (FHEA).

Daniel K. Robinson recently completed his Doctor of Musical Arts at Queensland Conservatorium, Griffith University with a focus on the delivery of voice education for Contemporary Worship Singers. He is the principal vocal coach and supervisor of pedagogy for the DJArts Voice Studio. Daniel is heavily involved in the Australian National Association of Singing Teachers, as an executive member of the National Council. Beyond his extensive studio practice, Daniel is a regular guest lecturer at tertiary institutions, voice clinician to contemporary worship singers. He has presented extensively on his ground-breaking research into the Contemporary Worship Singer. Besides Daniel's ongoing research and teaching of voice, Daniel actively travels Australia as a solo independent artist.

Joan Russell is Assistant Professor at the Faculty of Education, McGill University, where she is Director of Music Education. Her research interests include music teacher discourse and practice, the development of music teacher identity, the sociocultural contexts of music teaching, and ethnography in musical communities.

Jo Saunders is responsible for the coordination of various strands of the research evaluation of the UK Government's National Singing Programme *Sing Up* (2007–2011). She has also supported colleagues on several other research and consultancy projects within the Department across the arts and humanities field. Jo read Music and Education (BA Hons, First class) at Homerton College, University of Cambridge before completing a PGCE in Music. She was awarded a studentship (1+3) by the ESRC to complete both her MPhil in Educational Research (Wolfson College, University of Cambridge) and PhD (Institute of Education, University of London). Her doctoral studies focused on the adolescent experience of the music classroom, including the formation and reformation of musical identities and engagement with the learning process.

Robert Stewart is Director of Music at Melbourne High School. Robert teaches voice at the Victorian College of the Arts and acts as a voice teacher and choral conductor at University High School; He is a past choral conductor at Monash University; soloist and professional singer with the Canadian Opera Company, Elmer Iseler Singers and St James Cathedral. He has performed with Jonathan Grieves-Smith, Sir Philip Ledger, Sir David Willcocks, Seiji Ozawa and, Doreen Rao.

Stephen Taberner was born in New Zealand, but moved to Sydney where a perfectly unorthodox life as jazz double bass player and computer programmer was hijacked by an extended encounter with world music choir "voices from the vacant lot". Before he knew it, he was a choirleader and then a singing songwriting double bass player. As a massed choir leader Stephen is best known for his work with the Choral Sea in Sydney (1996 and 1998), and the Millennium Chorus in Melbourne (2004–2006) and he is also notorious for his leadership of the Spooky Men's Chorale, which he formed in 2001. He currently directs the Spookies and community choir Yirriba as well as his work with the Millennium Chorus and an increasingly bewildering programme of singing or songwriting workshops throughout Australia.

Jenevora Williams has taught singing at The Royal College of Music Junior Department, Guildford School of Acting Conservatoire, many universities, and is Vocal Adviser and teacher-in-residence for the National Youth Choirs of Great Britain. After studying at Bristol University and the Guildhall School of Music and Drama, she had a 10-year performing career. This included singing frequently for Welsh National Opera with roles in Cosi Fan Tutte, The Magic Flute, Electra, Iphigenie and Idomeneo. As well as having a private teaching practice for students and professional singers, Jenevora has a PhD from the Institute of Education, London University, in the vocal health and development of boy choristers. She was the 2010 winner of the Van Lawrence Prize, awarded by the British Voice Association for her contribution to voice research. Current research projects are investigating aspects of teaching practice applicable to a variety of ages and musical styles. Jenevora is also writing a book on the subject of teaching singing to children and young adults.

Anthony Young is Head of Classroom and Choral activities at St. Laurence's College in South Brisbane. St. Laurence's boasts a choral program involving over 150 boys in 4 choirs with a further 450 students involved in classroom and instrumental music. He holds a Masters in Music Studies (choral conducting) together with an Australian Kodaly Certificate, an Arts degree in Literature and a Law Degree. He is an experienced choral conductor having studied with Dr. Eduard Bolcovak, Dr. John Nixon, and Dr. Rodney Eichenberger. At St. Laurence's he has enjoyed success in dealing with the male changing voice. He has studied the work of David Jorlett, James Jordan, Kenneth Phillips, Jerry Blackstone and Leon Thurmann amongst others. He is an experienced Music Educator having taught secondary music for almost 20 years in both state funded and private schools. He is presently undertaking doctoral research in Music Education at Queensland Conservatorium Griffith University.

Index

A
Abeles & Porter, 4–5, 96
Abeles, H., 5
AC/DC, 278, 289, 295
Adler, A., 3–10, 45–62, 82, 87, 342
Adolescence, 20–21, 23, 29, 55–56, 79, 85, 197–198, 274
Adolescent, 3, 6, 13–24, 55, 70, 80, 82, 84, 88, 90–91, 96, 113, 137, 142, 145, 152, 193–194, 198, 280, 316, 318–320, 337–338
Alternative rock, 259–269, 281–282
Ashley, M., 6–7, 111, 234–235, 242, 313, 315, 317, 321, 334
Australian National Male Voice, 314

B
Babies, 168, 170
Bannister, M., 9, 259–269
Barbershop, 8–9, 50, 57–59, 113, 201–214, 326, 328–330, 341–342, 348, 350
Barrett, M., 21, 33, 167
The Beatles, 262, 287, 290–291, 295
Beer, 72, 151, 157, 161
Bennett, A., 8–9, 287–294
Beynon, C., 48, 51, 53–54, 56
Big Bands, 312
Birralee Blokes, 70–73
Boy choristers, 28, 114, 126, 145–146, 216, 299–300, 304, 307–308
Boy's Music Ecosystem, 97, 102
Byrd, 3, 10, 124, 262

C
Cambiata, 16, 90, 145, 344
Canterbury, 28, 123
Cathedral, 3, 9, 17, 27–29, 38–41, 62, 111, 114–115, 123–146, 218–219, 299–300, 303, 305, 307, 314, 326, 332

Changing voices, 14–17, 19, 22, 24, 54, 73, 79–92, 318, 321–322, 344
Choir, 3, 7, 15–18, 28, 34, 38, 46–50, 53, 55–60, 70, 72–73, 79–91, 109–120, 125–127, 129, 133, 145, 152–154, 163, 190–191, 193, 196–198, 215–219, 222–229, 231, 235–242, 245–248, 259, 299–309, 311–319, 325–335
Choral directors, 6, 16–17, 55, 80, 83–84, 88, 90–91, 123, 126, 305, 329
Choral ensemble, 14–17, 49, 60, 79, 85, 89, 314
Choral teachers, 15, 19–21, 23, 79
Clift, S., 9, 117, 233–254
Connell, R., 228–229, 259, 272, 284
Conscientization, 83, 87
Cooksey, 6, 16–17, 110, 113, 143, 145, 314, 317–318, 321
CPME, *see* Critical Pedagogy for Music Education
Critical pedagogy for music education, 79, 82–83, 88–89, 91

D
Davidson, L., 33, 47–48, 50, 58, 110, 167, 169, 171, 224–225, 242–243
The Doors, 287, 291, 311
Drinking, 67, 72, 110, 119, 161, 217, 226–227, 272–273, 278–280
Dunedin Sound, 260–261, 263, 265–267
Durrant, C., 9, 47, 109–120, 233

E
Eisteddfod, 105, 225, 328
Elvis, 275–277, 291

363

F

Faulkner, R., 8–9, 47–48, 50, 58, 110, 215–229
Feminine, 5–7, 23, 29, 52, 80, 84, 87, 104, 119, 150–151, 154, 209–210, 242, 259, 265, 268, 272, 276, 337–338
Femininity, 4–5, 22, 67, 151, 210, 212–213, 223, 337
Fiji, 189–199
Fitzclarence, L., 7
Freer, 3, 7, 13–24, 111, 113, 314, 316
Freire, P., 82–83, 87
Frith, 262, 266, 277–278, 280, 283, 290, 292

G

Gackle, L., 6
Gates, J.T., 7, 18, 151–152
Gender, 3–8, 18, 22, 27–41, 49, 53–54, 60, 67, 80–84, 90, 95–96, 150, 155–157, 201–213, 215–217, 233–254, 260, 262–263, 265–266, 268, 282, 334, 337
Gender-incongruent, 4
Guitar, 5, 9, 95, 103, 173–175, 179, 182–183, 260–262, 264–265, 267–268, 278, 280, 287, 312, 319, 321

H

Hallam, S., 5
Harrison, S.D., 3–10, 48, 51–52, 54, 65–73, 79–80, 82, 87, 96, 149–161, 259–260, 313, 337–339, 342
Health, 71, 73, 117, 126, 128–131, 133–134, 146, 220, 233–238, 242–253, 303, 306, 338
Homophobia, 7, 67, 80
Homosexuality, 4, 151, 159
Howard, D.M., 28–29, 73, 128, 135, 142–143, 152, 234, 275
Humour, 72–73, 99, 226, 289, 316, 338–339, 343–344, 348–349, 352

I

Iceland, 9, 47, 49, 215–223, 225–227, 229
In-group, 81, 85, 88–89
Instrumental ensembles, 5, 331
Invented song-making, 168–169, 171–172

K

Kenway, 7
Kimmel, M.S., 216, 273, 281
Koza, J.E., 3, 7, 18, 80, 96, 151

L

Led Zeppelin, 278, 287–288
Leidertafel, 217
Liturgy, 123, 153–154, 300
Lynyrd Skynyrd, 278

M

Male Voice Festival in Cornwall, 8, 326, 334
Masculine, 3, 6–7, 23, 29, 48, 53–54, 67, 80–81, 85–86, 91, 150, 154, 156, 159, 161, 210, 215–229, 262, 267–268, 272–281
Masculinities, 8–9, 22–23, 71, 151, 158, 216, 228–229, 264, 273
Massed Singing, 69, 339–344
McKenzie, D., 14, 16
Middle school, 16, 22, 46, 51, 54, 79–91
Middle school choir directors, 84, 86
Middle school music teachers, 79
Miller, R., 313
Misogyny, 80, 281–282
Music Manifesto, 34
Music teachers, 14, 16, 22–23, 50, 52–53, 60, 69–70, 79–80, 106, 312, 337–339, 343

O

Opera, 29, 82, 90, 119, 124, 152, 279, 304, 306, 335, 341, 350
Out-group, 81, 85
Oxytocin, 234, 252–253

P

Performative, 81, 89, 91, 266
Performativity, 81–82, 88, 91, 229
Phallocentric, 268
Possible selves, 22, 87
Primary school, 27, 31, 34, 40, 67, 95, 114, 191–192, 194–197, 312–313, 315, 325, 334
Puberty, 6, 19, 55, 79, 126, 138, 145
Punk, 259–263, 280–281, 288, 293

R

Rebelliousness, 272, 283
Repertoire, 15, 17, 19–21, 24, 38, 47, 50, 54–60, 66, 70, 72–73, 83–84, 87, 90, 104, 112–114, 116, 150, 153, 161, 170, 179, 184, 190–196, 198, 217, 219–220, 222–223, 226–229, 233, 245, 253, 294, 311, 315–317, 320–321, 327, 329–333, 343, 348–349
Role models, 8, 99, 101, 281, 334
Rolling Stones, 277, 287
Rugby, 72, 120, 313–314, 325, 332, 335, 341

S

Schippers, 66, 282
Sea shanties, 90
Secondary school, 4, 48, 50–52, 55, 60, 67, 95, 100, 106, 112, 114, 193, 260, 302, 308, 311–322, 333–334
Self-identity, 79–82, 89
Self-image, 80
Sergeant, 29, 31, 290, 295
Sex, 4–9, 27–41, 55, 60, 68, 72, 84, 96, 127, 169, 222, 242, 245–246, 248–250, 252, 277–280, 302, 308, 311, 328
Sex-stereotyping, 4, 6
Sexuality, 4–5, 7, 9, 68, 80, 85, 116, 119, 154, 262, 275, 281
Singing pedagogy, 33, 39
Sing Up, 27, 34–41, 325–326, 329, 334–335
Sissy, 3–4, 7, 68
Social identity, 79, 81–82, 90, 198, 292
Social identity theory, 79, 81
Social justice, 61, 80
Spooky Men's Chorale, 9, 71–72, 347–352
Sport, 23, 34, 48, 53–54, 67–69, 80–81, 84–85, 89, 105, 111, 117–118, 120, 127, 133, 150–152, 157, 159, 161, 216, 221, 259, 263, 280, 306–307, 312–314, 317, 325, 332, 334–335, 341
Status Quo, 28, 149, 183, 272, 275–276, 278–280, 290–291, 295
Stereotypes, 67, 235, 262, 268, 313
Stereotyping, 4–7, 9
St. Olaf Choir, 15

T

Toronto, 46, 48–49, 54, 56–58, 62, 290

U

Uniforms, 73, 90–91

V

Vocal behaviours, 27, 29, 130, 167–168, 170, 172, 216
Vocal music, 4, 14–15, 45, 48, 50–51, 60, 350

W

Wales, 8, 72, 216, 225, 325, 328, 331
Welch, 3–10, 27–41, 111, 152, 167–168, 305, 318, 342
Wellbeing, 73, 233–254
Westminster Abbey, 9, 125, 299
Westminster Choir, 15, 318
Williams, J., 9, 86, 123–146, 216, 284, 307
Woodstock, 277, 287, 289, 294
Worship, 46, 49, 123, 149–161, 193–194, 309, 316

Y

Young, A., 56, 67–68, 311–322, 338